100 POWER TIPS FOR FPGA DESIGNERS

100 POWER TIPS FOR FPGA DESIGNERS

Evgeni Stavinov

Copyright

Copyright © 2011 by Evgeni Stavinov. All rights reserved.

No part of the material contained in this book, including all design, text, graphics, selection and arrangement of content and all other information may be reproduced or transmitted in any form or by any means, electronic or mechanical, without permission in writing from the author.

Any unauthorized use of the material in this book without the prior permission of Evgeni Stavinov may violate copyright, trademark and other applicable laws.

Third-Party Trademarks and Copyright

Spartan, Virtex, Xilinx ISE, Zynq are trademarks of Xilinx Corporation.
Incisive Palladium, NCSim are trademarks of Cadence Design Systems Inc.
Riviera, Riviera-PRO, Active-HDL and HES are trademarks of Aldec, Inc.
RocketDrive, RocketVision is a Trademark of GateRocket Corp.
Synplify, Synplify Pro, Identify are trademarks of Synopsys Corporation.
Stratix, Arria, and Cyclone are trademarks of Altera Corporation.
All other copyrights and trademarks are the property of their respective owner.

Limit of Liability/Disclaimer of Warranty

To the fullest extent permitted at law, the publisher and the author are providing this book and its contents on an "as is" basis and make no (and expressly disclaims all) representations or warranties of any kind with respect to this book or its contents including, without limitation, warranties of merchantability and fitness for a particular purpose. In addition, the publisher and the author do not represent or warrant that the information in this book accurate, complete or current.

Book Title: 100 Power Tips for FPGA Designers

ISBN: 978-1-461-18629-8

PREFACE

I've never thought of myself as a book writer. Over the course of my career I've written volumes of technical documentation, published several articles in technical magazines, and have done a lot of technical blogging. At some point I've accumulated a wealth of experience and knowledge in the area of FPGA design, and thought it was a good time to share it with a broader audience.

Writing a book takes time, commitment, and discipline. It also requires a very different skill set. Unfortunately, many engineers, including myself, are trained to use programming languages better than natural languages. Despite all that, writing a book is definitely an intellectually rewarding experience.

I would like to express my gratitude to all the people who have provided valuable ideas, reviewed technical contents, and edited the manuscript: my colleagues from SerialTek, former colleagues from Xilinx, technical bloggers, and many others.

ABOUT THE AUTHOR

Evgeni Stavinov is a longtime FPGA user with more than 10 years of diverse design experience. Before becoming a hardware architect at SerialTek LLC, he held different engineering positions at Xilinx, LeCroy and CATC. Evgeni holds MS and BS degrees in electrical engineering from University of Southern California and Technion - Israel Institute of Technology. Evgeni is a creator of OutputLogic.com, a portal that offers different online productivity tools.

TABLE OF CONTENTS

1	Introduction	1
2	FPGA Landscape	3
3	FPGA Applications	6
4	FPGA Architecture	9
5	FPGA Project Tasks	13
6	Overview Of FPGA Design Tools	20
7	Xilinx FPGA Build Process	24
8	Using Xilinx Tools In Command-line Mode	27
9	Xilinx Environment Variables	34
10	Xilinx ISE Tool Versioning	37
11	Lesser Known Xilinx Tools	38
12	Understanding Xilinx Tool Reports	40
13	Naming Conventions	43
14	Verilog Coding Style	51
15	Writing Synthesizable Code for FPGAs	59
16	Instantiation vs. Inference	68
17	Mixed Use of Verilog and VHDL	73
18	Verilog Versions: Verilog-95, Verilog-2001, and System Verilog	76
19	HDL Code Editors	84
20	FPGA Clocking Resources	87
21	Designing a Clocking Scheme	94
22	Clock Domain Crossing	99
23	Clock Synchronization Circuits	104
24	Using FIFOs	112
25	Counters	117

26	Signed Arithmetic	123
27	State machines	126
28	Using Xilinx DSP48 primitive	131
29	Reset Scheme	137
30	Designing Shift Registers	145
31	Interfacing to external devices	149
32	Using Look-up Tables and Carry Chains	154
33	Designing Pipelines	156
34	Using Embedded Memory	162
35	Understanding FPGA Bitstream Structure	171
36	FPGA Configuration	175
37	FPGA Reconfiguration	181
38	Estimating Design Size	185
39	Estimating Design Speed	192
40	Estimating FPGA Power Consumption	195
41	Pin Assignment	200
42	Thermal Analysis	204
43	FPGA Cost Estimate	209
44	GPGPU vs. FPGA	212
45	ASIC to FPGA Migration Tasks	214
46	Differences Between ASIC and FPGA Designs	218
47	Selecting ASIC Emulation or Prototyping Platform	221
48	Partitioning an ASIC Design into Multiple FPGAs	228
49	Porting Clocks	235
50	Porting Latches	238
51	Porting Combinatorial Circuits	241
52	Porting Non-synthesizable Circuits	244
53	Modeling Memories	249
54	Porting Tri-state Logic	252
55	Verification of a Ported Design	255

56	FPGA Design Verification	258
57	Simulation Types	262
58	Improving Simulation Performance	267
59	Simulation and Synthesis Results Mismatch	273
60	Simulator Selection	276
61	Overview of Commercial and Open-source Simulators	280
62	Designing Simulation Testbenches	282
63	Simulation Best Practices	285
64	Measuring Simulation Performance	293
65	Overview of FPGA-based Processors	296
66	Ethernet Cores	301
67	Designing Network Applications	305
68	IP Core Selection	310
69	IP Core Protection	315
70	IP Core Interfaces	318
71	Serial and Parallel CRC	322
72	Scramblers, PRBS, and MISR	332
73	Security Cores	336
74	Memory Controllers	339
75	USB Cores	346
76	PCI Express Cores	350
77	Miscellaneous IP Cores and Functional Blocks	354
78	Improving FPGA Build Time	356
79	Design Area Optimizations: Tool Options	361
80	Design Area Optimizations: Coding Style	366
81	Design Power Optimizations	372
82	Bringing-up an FPGA Design	375
83	PCB Instrumentation	379
84	Protocol Analyzers and Exercisers	383
85	Troubleshooting FPGA Configuration	385

86	Using ChipScope	390
87	Using FPGA Editor	396
88	Using Xilinx SystemMonitor	402
89	FPGA Failure Analysis	405
90	Timing Constraints	408
91	Performing Timing Analysis	411
92	Timing Closure Flows	417
93	Timing Closure: Tool Options	420
94	Timing Closure: Constraints and Coding Style	424
95	The Art of FPGA Floorplanning	428
96	Floorplanning Memories and FIFOs	439
97	Build Management and Continuous Integration	447
98	Verilog Processing and Build Flow Scripts	449
99	Report and Design Analysis Tools	450
100	Resources	452

Introduction	**Tips 1:5**
Efficient use of Xilinx FPGA design tools	**Tips 6:12**
Using Verilog HDL	**Tips 13:19**
Design, Synthesis, and Physical Implementation	**Tips 20:37**
FPGA selection	**Tips 38:44**
Migrating from ASIC to FPGA	**Tips 45:55**
Design Simulation and Verification	**Tips 56:64**
IP Cores and Functional Blocks	**Tips 65:77**
Design Optimizations	**Tips 78:81**
FPGA Design Bring-up and Debug	**Tips 82:89**
Floorplanning and Timing closure	**Tips 90:96**
Third party productivity tools	**Tips 97:99**
Resources	**Tip 100**

1
INTRODUCTION

Target audience

FPGA logic design has grown from being one of many hardware engineering skills a decade ago to a highly specialized field. Nowadays, FPGA logic design is a full time job. It requires a broad range of skills, such as a deep knowledge of FPGA design tools, the ability to understand FPGA architecture and sound digital logic design practices. It can take years of training and experience to master those skills in order to be able to design complex FPGA projects.

This book is intended for electrical engineers and students who want to improve their FPGA design skills. Both novice and seasoned logic and hardware engineers can find bits of useful information in this book. It is intended to augment, not replace, existing FPGA documentation, such as user manuals, datasheets, and user guides. It provides useful and practical design "tips and tricks," and little known facts that are hard to find elsewhere.

The book is intended to be very practical with a lot of illustrations, code examples and scripts. Rather than having a generic discussion applicable to all FPGA vendors, this edition of the book focuses on Xilinx FPGAs. Code examples are written in Verilog HDL. This will enable more concrete examples and in-depth discussions. Most of the examples are simple enough, and can be easily ported to other FPGA vendors and families, and VHDL language.

The book provides an extensive collection of useful online references.

It is assumed that the reader has some digital design background, and working knowledge of ASIC or FPGA logic design using Verilog HDL.

How to read this book

The book is organized as a collection of short articles, or Tips, on various aspects of FPGA design: synthesis, simulation, porting ASIC designs, floorplanning and timing closure, design methodologies, design optimizations, RTL coding, IP core selection, and many others.

This book is intended for both referencing and browsing. The Tips are organized by topic, such as "Efficient use of Xilinx FPGA design tools," but it is not arranged in a perfect order. There is little dependency between Tips. The reader is not expected to read the book from cover to cover. Instead, you can browse to the topic that interests you at any time.

This book is not a definitive guide into Verilog programming language, digital design or FPGA tools and architecture. Neither does it attempt to provide deep coverage of a wide range of topics in a limited space. Instead, it covers the important points, and provides references for further exploration of that topic. Some of the material in this book has appeared previously as more complete articles in technical magazines.

Software

The FPGA synthesis and simulation software used in this book is a free Web edition of Xilinx ISE package.

Companion web site

An accompanying web site for this book is:

http://outputlogic.com/100_fpga_power_tips

It provides most of the projects, source code, and scripts mentioned in the book. It also contains links to referenced materials, and errata.

2
FPGA LANDSCAPE

FPGA landscape is dominated by two main players: Xilinx and Altera. The two hold over 90% of the market share. Smaller FPGA vendors are Lattice Semiconductor and Actel, which provide more specialized FPGA features. All four are publicly traded companies.

Achronix and Tabula are new startup companies that offer unique FPGA features.

The following is a list of FPGA vendors mentioned above along with the key financial and product information. Financial information is provided courtesy of Yahoo! Finance, January 2011.

Xilinx Inc.

URL: http://www.xilinx.com
Market capitalization: $8.52B
Revenue (ttm): $2.31B
Number of full time employees: 2,948
Year founded: 1984
Headquarters: San Jose, California

Xilinx offers several FPGA families with a wide range of capabilities. Two newest families are Virtex-6 and Spartan-6.
Virtex-6 family offers the industry's highest performance and capacity. It's ideal for high speed, high density applications.
Spartan-6 provides a solution for cost-sensitive applications, where size, power, and cost are key considerations.

Altera Corporation

URL: http://www.altera.com
Market capitalization: $12.03B
Revenue (ttm): $1.76B
Number of employees: 2,551
Year founded: 1983
Headquarters: San Jose, California

Altera offers the following FPGA families: Stratix, Arria, and Cyclone.

Stratix-V is the latest addition to the Stratix family. It offers the highest performance and density.
Arria is a family of mid-range FPGAs targeting power sensitive and transceiver based applications.
Cyclone offers low-cost FPGAs for low-power cost-sensitive applications.

Actel/Microsemi Corporation

URL: http://www.actel.com

Market capitalization: $1.98B

Revenue (ttm): $518M

Number of employees: 2,250

Year founded: Actel was acquired by Microsemi Corp. in October 2010

Headquarters: Irvine, California

Actel FPGAs feature the lowest power usage and widest range of small packages.
Actel offers the following FPGA families:

- IGLOO, ProASIC3: low-power small footprint FPGAs
- SmartFusion: mixed-signal FPGA with integrated ARM processor
- RTAX/RTSX: high-reliability radiation-tolerant FPGA family

Lattice Semiconductor Corporation

URL: http://www.latticesemi.com

Market capitalization: $700M

Revenue (ttm): $280M

Number of employees: 708

Year founded: 1983

Headquarters: Hillsboro, Oregon

Lattice offers the following FPGA families:

- LatticeECP3: low power, SerDes-capable FPGAs
- LatticeECP2: low cost FPGAs
- LatticeSC: high-performance FPGAs
- MachX: non-volatile FPGAs with embedded Flash

Achronix Semiconductor

URL: http://www.achronix.com

Headquarters: Santa Clara, California

Achronix is a privately held company that builds the world's fastest FPGAs, providing 1.5 GHz throughput, which is a significant performance advantage over traditional FPGA technology.

Tabula

URL: http://www.tabula.com
Headquarters: Santa Clara, California

Tabula is a privately held company. It developed a unique FPGA technology, called Spacetime, which provides significantly higher logic, memory, and signal processing capabilities than traditional FPGAs.

3
FPGA APPLICATIONS

A few years ago, FPGAs were mainly used as "glue logic" devices between other electronic components, bus controllers, or simple protocol processors. This is not the case anymore. As FPGAs become larger and faster, the cost per logic gate drops. That enabled FPGA applications unthinkable before, possible. Modern FPGAs became viable ASIC replacement and are now found in consumer electronics devices. Although it's a common misconception that FPGAs are too expensive for high-volume products, this is not entirely true.

FPGAs became reliable enough to be used in mission critical applications, such as in space, military, automotive, and medical appliances. FPGAs are taking over as a platform of choice in the implementation of high-performance signal processing applications, replacing multiple dedicated DSP processors.

FPGA power consumption became low enough to be even used in battery-powered devices such as camcorders and cell phones.

FPGAs have a consistent track record of capacity growth, and they track Moore's law better than any other semiconductor device. As an example, XC2064 FPGA, introduced by Xilinx in 1985, had 1024 logic gates. The largest, Xilinx Virtex-7 XC7V2000T, has 15,636,480 gates, an increase of 10,000 times over the past 26 years. If the current trend of capacity and speed increase continues, FPGAs will essentially become highly integrated SoC platforms, which include multi-core processors, wide range of peripherals, and high capacity logic fabric, all in one chip.

Tighter integration of FPGA fabric and embedded processors will in turn raise the level of abstraction. It'll require less effort to develop a novel software application that includes an FPGA as one of its components. Instead of using multiple, off-the-shelf hardware components, such FPGA SoC can be fine-tuned to optimize the performance of a particular software application.

Another trend is migration of FPGA development tools to popular open-source frameworks. That will make the FPGA development more affordable and enhance interoperability among FPGA and other design tool vendors. Xilinx is already using an open-source Eclipse framework in its EDK.

There is a lot of interest in the industry and academy to raise the level of abstraction of the FPGA synthesis. Currently, most of the FPGA designs are hand-written in low-level hardware description languages (HDL). This approach delivers poor productivity, and there is a lot of customer demand for better tools that support high-level synthesis. There are several promising high-level synthesis tools and technologies, but this hasn't reached the mainstream yet. Two examples are Catapult-C Synthesis by Mentor Graphics, and AutoPilot by AutoESL Design Technologies (acquired by Xilinx in Jan. 2011).

Virtualization of tools, platforms, and hardware resources is on the cusp of wide acceptance. Virtualization allows better resource utilization by sharing. For example, pooling multiple development boards into a board farm, instead of assigning each board to a developer, will increase effective utilization of a board, and make the maintenance more efficient. Perhaps it's too early to tell, but virtualization has a potential to introduce new interesting and unexpected FPGA applications.

Virtualization is a key enabling technology for cloud computing environment. Cloud computing is defined as a model for enabling convenient, on-demand network access to a shared pool of configurable computing resources that can be rapidly provisioned and released with minimal management effort or service provider interaction. Cloud computing augments the power of virtualization by adding on-demand self service, scalability, and resource pooling. At the time of this book's writing, there are two companies that offer cloud-based FPGA development tool products: National Instruments, and Xuropa. An overview of typical FPGA applications by end market is shown in the following table.

Table 1: FPGA end markets and applications

End market	*Application*
Wireless communications	Cellular and WiMax base stations
Wireline communications	High speed switches and routers, DSL multiplexers
Telecom	Optical and radio transmission equipment, telephony switches, traffic managers, backplane transceivers
Consumer electronics	LCD TV, DVR, Set Top boxes, high end cameras
Video and image processing	Video surveillance systems, broadcast video, JPEG, MPEG decoders
Automotive	GPS systems, car infotainment systems, driver assistance systems: car parking assistance, car threat avoidance, back-up aid, adaptive cruise control, blind spot detection
Aerospace and Defense	Radar and sonar systems, satellite communications, radiation-tolerant space applications
ASIC prototyping	FPGA-based ASIC emulation and prototyping platforms
Embedded systems	System On Chip (SoC)
Test and Measurement	Logic Analyzers, Protocol Analyzers, Oscilloscopes
Storage	High-end controllers, servers

End market	Application
Data security	Data encryption: AES, 3DES algorithms, public key cryptography (RSA), Data integrity (SHA1, MD5)
Medical	Medical imaging
High performance and scientific computing	Acceleration of parallel algorithms, matrix multiplication, Black-Scholes algorithm for option pricing used in finance
Custom designs	Hardware accelerators that offload computing-intensive tasks from the embedded processors: checksum offload, encryption/decryption, parts of image and video processing algorithms, complex pattern matching

4
FPGA ARCHITECTURE

The key to successful design is a good understanding of the underlying FPGA architecture, capabilities, available resources, and just as important - the limitations. This Tip uses Xilinx Virtex-6 family as an example to provide a brief overview of the architecture of a modern FPGA.

The main architectural components, as illustrated in the following figure, are logic and IO blocks, interconnect matrices, clocking resources, embedded memories, routing, and configuration logic.

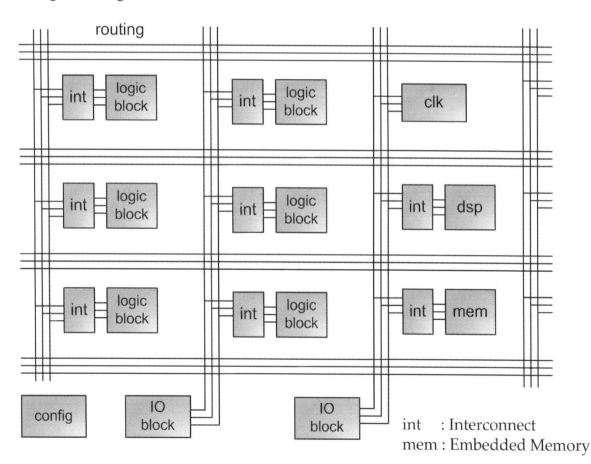

Figure 1: FPGA architecture

Many high-end FPGAs also include complex functional modules such as memory controllers, high speed serializer/deserializer transceivers, integrated PCI Express interface, and Ethernet MAC blocks.

The combination of FPGA logic and routing resources is frequently called FPGA fabric.

The term derives its name from its topological representation. As the routing between logic blocks and other resources is drawn out, the lines cross so densely that it resembles a fabric.

Logic blocks

Logic block is a generic term for a circuit that implements various logic functions. A logic block in Xilinx FPGAs is called Slice. A Slice in Virtex-6 FPGA contains four look-up tables (LUTs), eight registers, a carry chain, and multiplexers. The following figure shows main components of a Virtex-6 FPGA Slice.

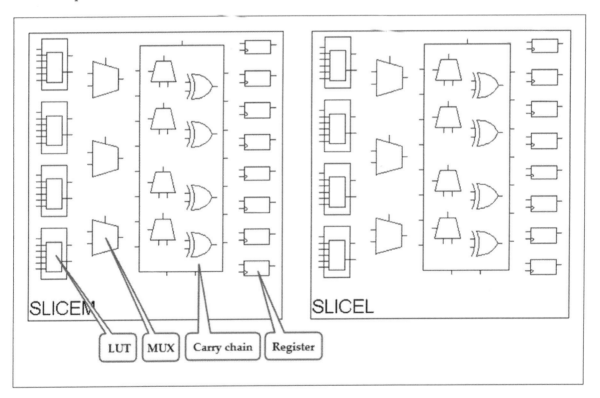

Figure 2: Xilinx Virtex-6 FPGA Slice structure

The connectivity between LUTs, registers, multiplexers, and a carry chain can be configured to form different logic circuits.

There are two different Slice types: SLICEM and SLICEL. A SLICEM has a multi-purpose LUT, which can also be configured as a Shift Register LUT (SRL), or a 64- or 32-bit read-only or random access memory.

Each Slice register can be configured as a latch.

Clocking resources

Each Virtex-6 FPGA provides several highly configurable mixed-mode clock managers (MMCMs), which are used for frequency synthesis and phase shifting.

Clocks to different synchronous elements across FPGA are distributed using dedicated low-skew and low-delay clock routing resources. Clock lines can be driven by global clock buffers, which allow glitchless clock multiplexing and the clock enable.

More detailed discussion of Xilinx FPGA clocking resources is provided in Tip #20.

Embedded memory

Xilinx FPGAs have two types of embedded memories: a dedicated Block RAM (BRAM) primitive, and a LUT configured as Distributed RAM

Virtex-6 BRAM can store 36K bits, and can be configured as a single- or dual-ported RAM. Other configuration options include data width of up to 36-bit, memory depth up to 32K entries, and error detection and correction.

Tip #34 describes different use cases of FPGA-embedded memory.

DSP

Virtex-6 FPGAs provide dedicated Digital Signal Processing (DSP) primitives to implement various functions used in DSP applications, such as multipliers, accumulators, and signed arithmetic operations. The main advantage of using DSP primitives instead of general-purpose LUTs and registers is high performance.

Tip #28 describes different use cases of DSP primitive.

Input/Output

Input/Output (IO) block enables different IO pin configurations: IO standards, single-ended or differential, slew rate and the output strength, pull-up or pull-down resistor, digitally controlled impedance (DCI). An IO in Virtex-6 can be delayed by up to 32 increments of 78 ps each by using an IODELAY primitive.

Serializer/Deserializer

Most of Virtex-6 FPGAs include dedicated transceiver blocks that implement Serializer/Deserializer (SerDes) circuits. Transceivers can operate at a data rate between 155 Mb/s and 11.18 Gb/s, depending on the configuration.

Routing resources

FPGA routing resources provide programmable connectivity between logic blocks, IOs, embedded memory, DSP, and other modules. Routing resources are arranged in a horizontal and vertical grid. A special interconnect module serves as a configurable switch box to connect logic blocks, IOs, DSP, and other module to horizontal and vertical routing. Unfortunately, Xilinx doesn't provide much documentation on performance characteristics, implementation details, and quantity of the routing resources. Some routing performance characteristics can be obtained by analyzing timing reports. And the FPGA Editor tool can be used to glean information about the routing quantity and structure.

FPGA configuration

The majority of modern FPGAs are SRAM-based, including Xilinx Spartan and Virtex families. On each FPGA power-up, or during a subsequent FPGA reconfiguration, a bitstream is read from the external non-volatile memory (NVM), processed by the configuration controller, and loaded to the internal configuration SRAM. Tips #35-37 describe the process of FPGA configuration and bitstream structure in more detail.

The following table summarizes this Tip by showing key features of the smallest, mid-range, and largest Xilinx Virtex-6 FPGA.

Table 1: Xilinx Virtex-6 FPGA key features

	XC6VLX75T	*XC6VLX240T*	*XC6VLX760*
Logic cells	74,496	241,152	758,784
Embedded memory (Kbyte)	832	2,328	4,275
DSP modules	288	768	864
User IOs	240	600	1200

5
FPGA PROJECT TASKS

Any new project that includes FPGAs has a typical list of tasks that a development team encounters during the project's lifetime, which range from the product's inception until a working FPGA design is ready to get out of the door. There are two types of tasks: project setup and design/development.

Project preparation and setup include project requirements, architecture documentation, FPGA selection, tools selection, and assembling a design team.

Design and development tasks include pin assignment, developing RTL, design simulation and verification, synthesis and physical implementation, floorplanning and timing closure, and board bring-up.

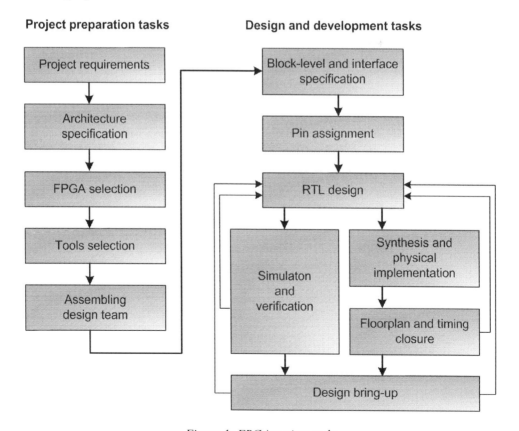

Figure 1: FPGA project tasks

Project preparation and setup tasks

Product and project requirements

It is hard to overestimate the importance of having properly documented product and project requirements. It puts all of the project/product stakeholders on the same page and eliminates ambiguity and second guessing later in the project life cycle. Having proper requirements documentation applies to commercial, research, and even student projects.

Typically, product requirements are driven by the sales and marketing team, and the transition to engineering project is handled by engineering managers and architects.

The level of detail varies. In a small startup it can be a document of a few pages, or even an email. For a large multi-FPGA product, such as an ASIC prototyping platform, military communication system, or high-end switch, the document is hundreds of pages long and written by several people.

Architecture specification

Architecture specification is based upon project specification. It is typically written by the most experienced engineer in a team, the system architect, who has broad experience in hardware, logic, and software design, is well-versed in writing specifications, and has good interpersonal skills. This engineer interacts closely with the sales and marketing team to clarify and adjust the requirements if needed.

Architecture specification addresses issues such as the technical feasibility of the project, top-level block diagram (which describes the partition between different components), main interfaces, and possible implementation options.

It is important to perform feasibility analysis at this stage to find that the project requirements are realistic and attainable and can meet performance, cost, size, and other goals.

An example of unrealistic requirement is a required processing speed of a deep-packet inspection engine that cannot be done in real time using the latest FPGAs. One solution is to plan using the next FPGA family that will be ready for production by the time the project enters the debug phase. Engineering samples might be used in the interim.

Software, hardware, and logic top-level block diagrams should include main interfaces. The interfaces have to be accurate, unambiguous, and interpreted the same way by all team members. The specification also includes overall partitioning into multiple FPGAs and interfaces between them.

Architecture specification is a living document that must be maintained and kept up-to-date. Engineering team members refer to the document to write more detailed block-level documents and to do design work. Sales and marketing teams use it to establish bill of material (BOM) and final product cost.

FPGA selection

FPGA selection process involves selecting FPGA vendor, family, capacity, and speed grade. It is not uncommon that a multi-FPGA project contains FPGAs from different vendors and families. It is typically not an issue to interface between heterogeneous FPGAs as soon as they meet project requirements.

Selecting FPGAs from different vendors complicates some of the project management tasks, such as having multiple tool flows and purchasing from different distributors. One of the reasons to select FPGAs from different vendors is that each vendor offers unique features. Examples are integrated memory controllers, SerDes that can operate at certain speed, logic capacity, or number of user IOs.

FPGA capacity estimate

FPGA capacity estimate, general guidelines and criteria for ASIC designs are discussed in more detail in Tip #38.

The most reliable way to do size estimate is to build a final RTL implementation. In some cases this is possible, such as in projects that require migration of an existing RTL base to the latest FPGA with improved characteristics. However, in most cases this is wishful thinking because most of the design is not yet written. The only remaining option is to estimate the size of each sub-module and add them up. It is possible that some of the modules are reused from the previous designs. Also, third party IP cores often include capacity utilization data. The rest of the modules can be prototyped.

A frequently made mistake is to determine only logic utilization in terms of slices, LUTs, and FFs. Other FPGA resources are overlooked, which can cause problems later on. Size estimate should include all FPGA resource types used in the design: embedded memories, DSP, IOs, clocks, PLL, and specialized cores such as PCI Express interface and Ethernet MAC.

FPGA speed analysis

Correct analysis of both FPGA fabric and IO speed is important for a couple of reasons. Maximum design speed affects selection of FPGA speed grade, which in turn affects the cost. Another reason is design feasibility.

A high speed network switch or a protocol processor can require running FPGA fabric at 300+ MHz frequencies, and is close to the limit of that FPGA family. Prototyping a small part of that design might meet timing. However, the complete design might not, because other factors, such as routing delays between modules, come into play. This is a common pitfall of using this method.

Another example is ASIC emulation/prototyping platform, which has different design characteristics. ASIC emulation designs are typically LUT-dominated, and run at low, sub 100MHz frequencies. However, if such a platform contains several FPGAs, the IO speed becomes the bottleneck that directly affects overall emulation frequency.

Higher design speed causes longer build times and more effort to achieve timing closure. Therefore, the goal is to use the lowest possible speed for the design. This will bring material and development costs down.

FPGA power analysis

An increasing number of FPGAs is used in power-sensitive applications. Power estimate can affect the FPGA selection, or even determine whether it's feasible to use an FPGA in a product at all.

An accurate power estimate requires a lot of design knowledge, including logic capacity, toggle rate, and exact I/O characteristics.

Tip #81 has a more detailed discussion on low-power optimization techniques.

Tools selection

Tools selection is largely determined by the FPGA vendor. There isn't much flexibility in choosing design tools; typically, there is a well-established vendor specific tool ecosystem. Some of the tools are described in Tip #6.

Assembling a design team

It is no longer practical for a single engineer to handle all project design tasks. Even a small FPGA design project requires a wide spectrum of expertise and experience levels from team members.

Some design tasks require a deep domain-level expertise, such as protocol or algorithm understanding. These tasks are carried out by engineers with advanced degrees in a particular field and little FPGA understanding. Other tasks require a lot of logic design experience to do efficient RTL implementation. Tool knowledge is required to do synthesis, floorplanning, and timing closure.

Another trend is workforce globalization. Members of the same team might reside in different locations around the globe. This adds a lot of communication overhead and makes collaboration and efficient project management more difficult.

Assembling a team and delegating the right tasks to each team member is essential for determining accurate and reliable project schedule.

FPGA design and development tasks

Detailed block-level and interface documentation

Detailed block-level and interface documentation is a task that is often done haphazardly, especially in small companies without well-established procedures.

Interface specification includes register description and access procedures between FPGA and software.

Block level specification describes interfaces, such as busses, between FPGAs and modules within an FPGA.

Pin assignment

FPGA pin assignment is a collaborative process of PCB and FPGA logic design teams to assign all top-level ports of a design to FPGA IOs. It usually involves several back-and-forth iterations between the two teams until both are satisfied with the results.

PCB designers are concerned with board routability, minimizing the number of board layers, signal integrity, the number of board components, bank assignment for power management scheme, and clocking.

FPGA logic designers are mainly concerned with IO layout and characteristics. IO layout affects floorplanning and timing closure. Certain IOs, such as high speed busses, have to be grouped together. Clocks have to be connected to clock-capable pins. Tristate and bidirectional pins have to be taken care of.

At the end of the pin assignment process the design has to pass all tool DRC checks, such as correct bank assignment rules and simultaneous switching output (SSO). It is difficult to observe all the individual rules. Using the Xilinx PinAhead tool is indispensable to streamline this task.

In most cases the logic designer will need to create a dummy design to prototype the right IO characteristics, because the real design is not available yet.

Pin assignment requires a significant amount of time and attention to detail. If not done correctly, it can cause a lot of problems at the later project stage. It might require board layout change and costly respin. The importance of this task is often underestimated, even by experienced designers.

RTL design

RTL design is the part of the project that usually consumes the most time and resources.

There are several sources that can cause RTL design change:

- Incorrect simulation
- Issues during synthesis and physical implementation
- Floorplanning and timing closure
- Problems during design bring-up

Simulation and verification

RTL code, whether it's Verilog or VHDL, is written for synthesis targeting a particular FPGA. It is not sufficient to pass all simulation test cases and assume that the code is ready. It is not, because the code might change as a result of various issues during synthesis, physical implementation, floorplanning, and timing closure stages.

This kind of problem often happens with inexperienced logic designers and incorrectly established design flows. Developers spend countless hours doing simulation of a module. When that module is put through the synthesis, numerous errors and warnings are uncovered, making all previous simulation results invalid.

A better design flow is to concurrently run newly developed RTL code through synthesis and simulation, and to fix all errors and critical warnings in the process. This step is expected to take several iterations.

Therefore, doing simulation and synthesis in parallel will lead to better designer time utilization and will improve the project's overall progress.

Synthesis and physical implementation

Synthesis and physical implementation are two separate steps during FPGA build. Synthesis can be done using Xilinx XST, as well as third party synthesis tools. Synthesis produces a design netlist. Physical implementation is done using Xilinx tools and produces a bitstream ready to be programmed into an FPGA.

In larger design teams, different team members might be involved in synthesis, physical implementation, and other build tasks, such as developing automation scripts.

Floorplanning and timing closure

Floorplanning and timing closure are the most unpredictable tasks in terms of correctly estimating completion time. Even the most experienced FPGA logic designers underestimate the amount of time and effort it takes to achieve timing closure. It might take dozens of iterations, and weeks of development time, to make floorplanning and RTL changes to close timing in a large design.

Design bring-up

Design bring-up on a hardware platform is the final stage before a design is ready for release.

Potential issues arise due to simulation and synthesis mismatch. This is discussed in Tip #59.

Post-mortem analysis

Many design teams perform a formal project post-mortem analysis upon project completion. It is used to identify root causes for different problems, such as missed deadlines or unforeseen technical issues. The goal of the post-mortem is to learn a lesson and design a plan to prevent such problems from occurring in the future.

6
OVERVIEW OF FPGA DESIGN TOOLS

Over the course of FPGA design cycle, engineers use variety of tools: simulation, synthesis, physical implementation, debug and verification, and many other. This Tip provides a brief overview of the most commonly used tools.

Simulators

Tool: ISIM
Company: Xilinx
http://www.xilinx.com/support/documentation/plugin_ism.pdf
Xilinx ISIM is an excellent choice for small to medium size FPGA designs. It's integrated with Xilinx ISE tools, and it is free.
The biggest ISIM disadvantage is that it doesn't scale well for larger designs. Comparing it to other commercial simulators, ISIM is much slower and requires more memory.
ISIM also offers a co-simulation option, which requires a separate license.

Tool: ModelSim PE, DE, SE
Company: Mentor Graphics
http://model.com
ModelSim simulator is the most popular choice for FPGA design simulation. It comes in three versions: PE, DE, and SE.

Tool: VCS
Company: Synopsys
http://www.synopsys.com/Tools/FunctionalVerification/Pages/VCS.aspx
VCS simulator is at the high end of the spectrum. It is the fastest, but the most expensive simulation tool. It is mainly used for doing functional simulation of ASIC designs, but is often used in large FPGA designs as well.

Tool: NCSim
Company: Cadence
http://www.cadence.com/products/ld/design_team_simulator/pages/default.aspx
NCSim is a core simulation engine, and part of Incisive suite of tools. It is intended for design and verification of ASICs and FPGAs.

Tool: Active-HDL, Riviera

Company: Aldec
http://www.aldec.com/Products/default.aspx
Active-HDL and Riviera are tools for FPGA and ASIC functional simulation and verification.

Tool: Icarus Verilog
http://bleyer.org/icarus
Icarus Verilog is an open source compiler implementation for Verilog HDL. Icarus is maintained by Stephen Williams and it is released under the GNU GPL license.

Tool: Verilator
http://www.veripool.org/wiki/verilator
Verilator is an open source Verilog HDL simulator written and maintained by Wilson Snyder. Its main feature is simulation speed.

Simulation tools are reviewed in more detail in Tip #61.

Synthesis tools

Synthesis tool is an application that synthesizes Hardware Description Language (HDL) designs to create a netlist. There are several synthesis tools for Xilinx FPGAs: Xilinx XST, Synopsys Synplify, Mentor Precision, and several others.
Xilinx XST produces a netlist in a proprietary NGC format, which contains both logical design data and constraints. Other synthesis tools produce a netlist in an industry standard EDIF format.

Tool: XST
Company: Xilinx
http://www.xilinx.com/itp/xilinx10/books/docs/xst/xst.pdf

Tool: Synplify Pro, Synplify Premier
Company: Synopsys
http://www.synopsys.com/tools/synplifypro.aspx

Tool: Precision RTL
Company: Mentor Graphics
http://www.mentor.com/products/fpga/synthesis/precision_rtl

Tool: zFAST
Company: EvE
http://www.eve-team.com/products/zfast.html

EvE zFAST is a synthesis tool dedicated for EvE ZeBu ASIC emulation platforms that use Xilinx FPGAs. The main feature of zFAST is the execution speed. For large ASIC designs it is an important requirement to be able to quickly produce a netlist.

Synopsys Synplify and Mentor Precision are synthesis tools used for general-purpose FPGA designs.

Providing a detailed comparison between synthesis tools is beyond the scope of this book. Each tool offers its unique advantages: faster execution speed, more compact netlist, better support for HDL language constructs, unique optimization features, modular design flows, and many others. It is recommended that you evaluate different synthesis tools before starting a new project.

Physical implementation tools

FPGA physical implementation tools are provided by the FPGA vendor itself. Xilinx FPGA physical implementation requires *ngdbuild, map, par,* and *bitgen* tools. Optional tools to perform different format conversions and report analysis are *trce, netgen, edif2ngd, xdl,* and many others. Those tools are integrated into ISE and PlanAhead GUI environment, and can also be accessed from the command line. The tools are installed in $XILINX/ISE/bin/{nt, nt64, lin, lin64} and $XILINX/common/bin/{nt, nt64, lin, lin64} directories. $XILINX is an environmental variable that points to the ISE installation directory.

Design debug and verification

Tool: RocketDrive, RocketVision
Company: GateRocket
http://www.gaterocket.com

GateRocket offers FPGA verification solutions. RocketDrive is a peripheral device that accelerates software-based HDL simulation. RocketVision is companion software package that provides advanced debugging capabilities.

Tool: Identify
Company: Synopsys
http://www.synopsys.com/iools/identify.aspx

The Identify RTL debugger allows users to instrument their RTL and debug implemented FPGA, still at the RTL level, on running hardware.

Tool: ChipScope
Company: Xilinx
http://www.xilinx.com/tools/cspro.htm

Lint tools

Lint tools perform automated pre-simulation and pre-synthesis RTL design rule checking and analysis. They help uncover complex and obscure problems that cannot be found by simulation and synthesis tools. Examples of design rules checked by lint tools are: clock domain crossing, combinatorial loops, module connectivity, coding style, implied latches, asynchronous resets, and many others.

Tool: nLint
Company: SpringSoft
http://www.springsoft.com
nLint is part of the Novas verification environment.

Tool: vlint
Company: Veritools
http://www.veritools.com
Basic and Advance Lint tools are integrated into Riviera-PRO tools from Aldec.
ModelSim simulator offers limited lint capability enabled by "-lint" command line option.

7
XILINX FPGA BUILD PROCESS

FPGA build process refers to a sequence of steps to build an FPGA design from a generic RTL design description to a bitstream. The exact build sequence will differ, depending on the tool used. However, any Xilinx FPGA build will contain eight fundamental steps: pre-build, synthesis, ngdbuild, map, place-and-route, static timing analysis, bitgen and post-build.

Ngdbuild, map, place-and-route, and bitgen steps are often referred as FPGA physical implementation, because they depend on the specific FPGA architecture. At the time of writing this book, there are no commercially available third party physical implementation tools for Xilinx FPGAs.

Xilinx provides two IDE tools to perform an FPGA build: ISE, and PlanAhead. There are several other third party IDE tools that can do FPGA builds: Synopsys Synplify, Aldec Riviera, and Mentor Graphics Precision.

The following figure illustrates Xilinx FPGA build flow.

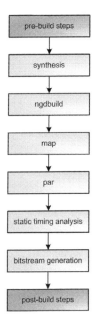

Figure 1: Xilinx FPGA build flow

Build preparation tasks

Build preparation tasks greatly depend on the complexity of the project and the build flow. The tasks might include the following:

- Getting the latest project and RTL file from a source control repository
- Assembling the project file list
- Setting environment variables for synthesis and physical implementation tools
- Acquiring tool licenses
- Incrementing build or revision number in the RTL code
- Replacing macros and defines in the RTL code

Synthesis

The simplest and most generic way to describe a synthesis is as a process of converting a design written in a Hardware Description Language (HDL) into a netlist. Xilinx Synthesis Technology (XST) synthesis tool produces a netlist in a proprietary NGC format, which contains both logical design data and constraints. Other synthesis tools produce a netlist in an industry standard EDIF format. Different synthesis tools are reviewed in Tip #6.

The following is an example of calling Xilinx XST:

```
$ xst -intstyle ise -ifn "/proj/crc.xst" -ofn "/proj/crc.syr"
```

XST contains over a hundred different options, not discussed in this Tip for brevity reasons. For the complete list of XST options refer to the Xilinx XST User Guide.

Netlist Translation

Xilinx NGDBUILD tool performs netlist translation into Xilinx Native Generic Database (NGD) file that contains a description of the design in terms of basic logic elements. Required NGDBUILD parameter is design name. Optional parameters are user-constraint files in UCF format, destination directory, FPGA part number, and several others.

The following is an example of calling NGDBUILD:

```
$ ngdbuild -dd _ngo -nt timestamp -uc /ucf/crc.ucf -p
xc6slx9-csg225-3 crc.ngc crc.ngd
```

MAP

Xilinx MAP tool performs mapping of a logical design into Xilinx FPGA. The output from MAP is a Native Circuit Description (NCD) file, which is a physical representation of the design mapped to the components of a specific Xilinx FPGA part. MAP has over thirty options described in the Command Line Tools User Guide. Some of the most frequently used are –p (part number), -ol (overall effort level), and -t (placer cost table). MAP has several options used during timing closure, area and performance optimizations, and discussed in more detail in other Tips.

The following is an example of calling MAP:

```
map -p xc6slx9-csg225-3 -w -ol high -t 1 -xt 0 -global_opt off -lc off -o crc_map.ncd crc.ngd crc.pcf
```

Place and Route (PAR)

A design place and route is performed using Xilinx PAR tool. PAR outputs an NCD file that contains complete place and route information about the design. Note that this is the same file type as produced by MAP. Some of the most frequently PAR options are –p (part number), -ol (overall effort level), and -t (placer cost table). Command Line Tools User Guide describes PAR options.

The following is an example of calling PAR:

```
par -w -ol high crc_map.ncd crc.ncd crc.pcf
```

Static Timing Analysis

Static timing analysis is performed using the Xilinx TRACE tool, described in Tip #91.

Bitstream generation

Bitgen is a Xilinx tool that creates a bitstream to be used for FPGA configuration. The following is a simplest example of calling Bitgen:

```
$ bitgen -f crc.ut crc.ncd
```

Bitgen has over a hundred command line options that perform various FPGA configurations, and is described in Command Line Tools User Guide.

Post-build tasks

After the FPGA bitstream is generated, the build flow might contain the following tasks:

- Parsing build reports to determine if the build is successful or not
- Copying and archiving bitstream and intermediate build files
- Sending email notifications to subscribed users

8

USING XILINX TOOLS IN COMMAND-LINE MODE

The majority of designers working with Xilinx FPGAs use ISE Project Navigator and PlanAhead software in graphical user interface mode. The GUI approach provides a pushbutton flow, which is convenient for small projects.

However, as FPGAs become larger, so do the designs built around them, and the design teams themselves. In many cases, GUI tools can become a limiting factor that hinders team productivity. GUI tools don't provide sufficient flexibility and control over the build process, and they don't allow easy integration with other tools. A good example is integration with popular build-management and continuous-integration solutions, such as TeamCity, Hudson CI and CruiseControl, which many design teams use ubiquitously for automated software builds.

Nor do GUI tools provide good support for a distributed computing environment. It can take several hours or even a day to build a large FPGA design. To improve the run-time, users do builds on dedicated servers, typically 64-bit multicore Linux machines that have a lot of memory, but in many cases, lack a GUI. Third-party job-scheduling solutions exist, such as Platform LSF, to provide flexible build scheduling, load balancing, and fine-grained control.

A less obvious reason eschewing GUI tools is memory and CPU resource utilization. ISE Project Navigator and PlanAhead are memory-hungry applications: each tool, for instance, uses more than 100 Mbytes of RAM. On a typical workstation that has 2-Gbytes memory, that's 5 percent--a substantial amount of a commodity that can be put to a better use.

Finally, many Xilinx users come to FPGAs with an ASIC design background. These engineers are accustomed to using command-line tool flows, and want to use similar flows in their FPGA design.

Those are some of the reasons why designers are looking to switch to command-line mode for some of the tasks in a design cycle.

Scripting Languages Choices

Xilinx command-line tools can run on both Windows and Linux operating systems, and can be invoked using a broad range of scripting languages, as shown in the following list. Aside from these choices, other scripts known to run Xilinx tools are Ruby and Python.

Perl

Perl is a popular scripting language used by a wide range of EDA and other tools. Xilinx ISE installation contains a customized Perl distribution. Users can enter Perl shell by running *xilperl* command:

```
$ xilperl -v # display Perl version
```

TCL

Tool Command Language (TCL) is a de facto standard scripting language of ASIC and FPGA design tools. TCL is very different syntactically from other scripting languages, and many developers find it difficult to get used to. This might be one of the reasons TCL is less popular than Perl.

TCL is good for what it's designed for—namely, writing tool command scripts. TCL is widely available, has excellent documentation and enjoys good community support.

Xilinx ISE installation comes with a customized TCL distribution. To start TCL shell use *xtclsh* command:

```
$ xtclsh -v # display TCL version
```

Unix bash and csh

There are several Linux and Unix shell flavors. The most popular are bash and csh.

Unlike other Unix/Linux shells, csh boasts a C-like scripting language. However, bash scripting language offers more features, such as shell functions, command-line editing, signal traps and process handling. Bash is a default shell in most modern Linux distributions, and is gradually replacing csh.

Windows batch and PowerShell

Windows users have two scripting-language choices: DOS command line and the more flexible PowerShell. An example of the XST invocation from DOS command line is:

```
>xst -intstyle ise -ifn "crc.xst" -ofn "crc.syr"
```

Build Flows

Xilinx provides several options to build a design using command-line tools. The four most popular options are direct invocation, xflow, xtclsh and PlanAhead.

The direct-invocation method calls tools in the following sequence: xst (or other synthesis tool), ngdbuild, map, place-and-route, trce (optional) and bitgen.

Designers can auto-generate the sequence script from the ISE Project Navigator.

The following script is an example of a direct-invocation build.

```
xst -intstyle ise -ifn "/proj/crc.xst" -ofn "/proj/crc.syr"
ngdbuild -intstyle ise -dd _ngo -nt timestamp -uc
/ucf/crc.ucf -p xc6slx9-csg225-3 crc.ngc crc.ngd
map -intstyle ise -p xc6slx9-csg225-3 -w -ol high -t 1 -xt 0
-global_opt off -lc off -o crc_map.ncd crc.ngd crc.pcf
par -w -intstyle ise -ol high crc_map.ncd crc.ncd crc.pcf
trce -intstyle ise -v 3 -s 3 -n 3 -fastpaths -xml crc.twx
crc.ncd -o crc.twr crc.pcf
bitgen -intstyle ise -f crc.ut crc.ncd
```

Using Xflow

Xilinx's XFLOW utility provides another way to build a design. It's more integrated than direct invocation, doesn't require as much tool knowledge, and is easier to use. For example, XFLOW does not require exit code checking to determine a pass/fail condition.

The XFLOW utility accepts a script that describes build options. Depending on those options, XFLOW can run synthesis, implementation, bitgen, or a combination of all three.

Synthesis only:

```
xflow -p xc6slx9-csg225-3 -synth synth.opt ../src/crc.v
```

Implementation:

```
xflow -p xc6slx9-csg225-3 -implement impl.opt../crc.ngc
```

Implementation and bitgen:

```
xflow -p xc6slx9-csg225-3 -implement impl.opt -config
bitgen.opt ../crc.ngc
```

Designers can generate the XFLOW script manually or by using one of the templates located in the ISE installation at the following location: *$XILINX\ISE_DS\ISE\xilinx\data*. Xilinx ISE software doesn't provide an option to auto-generate XFLOW scripts.

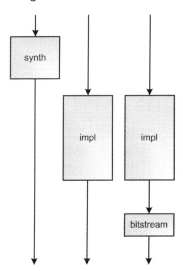

Figure 1: Xflow options

Using Xtclsh

Designs can also be built using TCL script invoked from the Xilinx *xtclsh*, as follows:

```
xtclsh crc.tcl rebuild_project
```

The TCL script can be written manually, and then passed as a parameter to *xtclsh*, or it can be auto-generated from the ISE ProjectNavigator.

Xtclsh is the only build flow that accepts the original ISE project in .xise format as an input. All other flows require projects and file lists, such as .xst and .prj, derived from the original .xise project.

Each of the xst, ngdbuild, map, place-and-route, trce and bitgen tool options has its TCL-equivalent property. For example, the xst command-line equivalent of the Boolean "Add I/O Buffers" is –iobuf, while –fsm_style is the command-line version of "FSM Style" (list).

Each tool is invoked using the TCL *"process run"* command, as shown in the following figure.

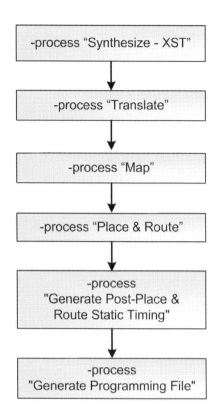

Figure 2: Xtclsh processes

Using PlanAhead

An increasing number of Xilinx users are migrating from ISE Project Navigator and adopting PlanAhead as a main design tool. PlanAhead offers more build-related features, such as scheduling multiple concurrent builds, along with more flexible build options and project manipulation.

PlanAhead uses TCL as its main scripting language. TCL closely follows Synopsys' SDC semantics for tool-specific commands.

PlanAhead has two command-line modes: interactive shell and batch mode. To enter an interactive shell, type the following command:

```
PlanAhead -mode tcl
```

To run the entire TCL script in batch mode, source the script as shown below:

```
PlanAhead -mode tcl -source <script_name.tcl>
```

The PlanAhead build flow (or run) consists of three steps: synthesis, implementation and bitstream generation, as illustrated in the following figure.

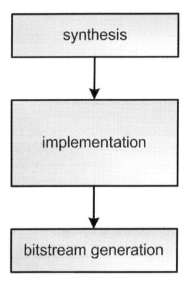

Figure 3: PlanAhead flow

The PlanAhead software maintains its log of the operations in the *PlanAhead.jou* file. The file is in TCL format, and located in *C:\Documents and Settings\<user name>\Application Data\HDI* on Windows, and *~/.HDI/* on Linux machines.

Users can run the build in GUI mode first, and then copy some of the log commands in their command-line build scripts.

Below is an example PlanAhead TCL script.

```
create_project pa_proj {crc_example/pa_proj} -part
xc6slx9csg225-3
set_property design_mode RTL [get_property srcset
[current_run]]
add_files -norecurse {crc_example/proj/.. /src/crc.v}
set_property library work [get_files -of_objects
[get_property srcset [current_run]] {src/crc.v}]
add_files -fileset [get_property constrset [current_run]] -
norecurse {ucf/crc.ucf}
set_property top crc [get_property srcset [current_run]]
set_property verilog_2001 true [get_property srcset
[current_run]]
launch_runs -runs synth_1 -jobs 1 -scripts_only -dir
{crc_example/pa_proj/pa_proj.runs}
launch_runs -runs synth_1 -jobs 1
launch_runs -runs impl_1 -jobs 1
set_property add_step Bitgen [get_runs impl_1]
launch_runs -runs impl_1 -jobs 1 -dir
{crc_example/pa_proj/pa_proj.runs}
```

In addition to providing standard TCL scripting capabilities, PlanAhead offers other powerful features. It allows query and manipulation of the design database, settings, and states, all from a TCL script. This simple script illustrates some of the advanced PlanAhead features that you can use in a command-line mode:

```
set my_port [get_ports rst]
report_property $my_port
get_property PULLUP $my_port
set_property PULLUP 1 $my_port
get_property PULLUP $my_port
```

The simple script adds a pull-up resistor to one of the design ports. The same operation can be done by changing UCF constraints and rebuilding the project, or using the FPGA Editor. But PlanAhead can do it with just three lines of code.

Many developers prefer using the *make* utility for doing FPGA builds. The two most important advantages of *make* are built-in checking of the return code and automatic dependency tracking. Any of the flows described above can work with *make*.

This Tip has discussed advantages of using Xilinx tools in command-line mode, explored several Xilinx build flows, and examined different scripting languages. The goal was not to identify the best build flow or a script language, but rather to discuss the available options and parse the unique advantages and drawbacks of each to help Xilinx FPGA designers make an informed decision.

Xilinx FPGA designers can base their selection process on a number of criteria, such as existing project settings, design team experience and familiarity with the tools and scripts, ease of use, flexibility, expected level of customization and integration with other tools, among others.

9
XILINX ENVIRONMENT VARIABLES

The very first task an FPGA designer encounters while working with command-line tools is setting up environment variables. The procedure varies depending on the Xilinx ISE version. In ISE versions before 12.x, all environment variables are set during the tool installation. Users can run command-line tools without any further action.

That changed in ISE 12.x. Users now need to set all the environment variables every time before running the tools. The main reason for the change is to allow multiple ISE versions installed on the same machine to coexist by limiting the scope of the environmental variables to the local shell or command-line terminal, depending on the operating system.

There are two ways of setting up environment variables in ISE 12.x. The simpler method is to call a script settings32.{bat,sh,csh} or settings64.{bat,sh,csh}, depending on the platform. The default location on Windows machines is *C:\Xilinx\12.1\ISE_DS*; on Linux, it's */opt/Xilinx/12.1/ISE_DS/*.

Linux bash example of calling the script is:

```
$ source /opt/Xilinx/12.1/ISE_DS/settings64.sh
```

The other option is to set the environment variables directly, as shown below.

Windows:

```
> set XILINX= C:\Xilinx\12.1\ISE_DS\ISE
> set XILINX_DSP=%XILINX%
> set PATH=%XILINX%\bin\nt;%XILINX%\lib\nt;%PATH%
```

UNIX/Linux bash:

```
$ export XILINX=/opt/Xilinx/12.1/ISE_DS/ISE
$ export XILINX_DSP=$XILINX
$ export PATH=${XILINX}/bin/lin64:${XILINX}/sysgen/util:${PATH}
```

UNIX/Linux csh:

```
% setenv XILINX   /opt/Xilinx/12.1/ISE_DS/ISE
% setenv XILINX_DSP $XILINX
% setenv PATH   ${XILINX}/bin/lin64:${XILINX}/sysgen/util:${PATH}
```

To test if the variable is set correctly on UNIX/Linux csh/bash:

```
% echo $XILINX
```

UNIX/Linux bash:

```
$ echo $XILINX
```

Windows:

```
> set XILINX
```

To disable the variable on UNIX/Linux csh:

```
% unsetenv XILINX
```

There are several other environment variables that affect Xilinx tools behavior. Some of them are shown in the following tables:

Name	XILINXD_LICENSE_FILE LM_LICENSE_FILE
Values	License file or license server in the format port@hostname
Details	Xilinx application licenses

Name	XIL_MAP_NODRC
Values	1
Details	Disable physical DRC errors. Applicable to MAP application.

Name	XIL_MAP_SKIP_LOGICAL_DRC
Values	1
Details	Disable logical DRC errors. Applicable to MAP application

Name	XIL_MAP_NO_DSP_AUTOREG
Values	1
Details	Disable the optimization where registers are pulled into DSP48 primitive. Applicable to MAP application

Name	XIL_PAR_DEBUG_IOCLKPLACER
Values	none
Details	In cases where clock design rules are violated, PAR aborts the execution with an error. To debug partially routed design and allow PAR to complete, set this environmental variable.

Name	XIL_PAR_NOIORGLLOCCLKSPL
Values	1
Details	Disable IO, regional and local clock placement. Applicable to PAR application.

Name	XIL_PAR_SKIPAUTOCLOCKPLACEMENT
Values	1
Details	Disable global clock placement. Applicable to PAR application.

Name	XIL_PROJNAV_PROCESSOR_AFFINITY_MASK
Values	Processor mask. For example, on a system with four processors setting 5 will enable processors 0 and 2, according to the OS allocation.
Details	On multi-processor machines, this environmental variable controls which processors are allowed to run.

Name	XIL_TIMING_HOLDCHECKING
Values	YES or NO
Details	Enable analysis of hold paths on FROM:TO constraints

Name	XIL_TIMING_ALLOW_IMPOSSIBLE
Values	1
Details	In case MAP application cannot meet a timing constraint, it aborts the execution. To allow MAP to bypass the error and complete, set this variable. The variable is intended to be used for mainly debug purposes during timing closure.

More detailed information about the above environmental variables can be found in answer records on Xilinx website and constraints documentation.

10
XILINX ISE TOOL VERSIONING

Xilinx ISE software is using two versioning systems: numeric and letter.

Numeric version is used for customer software releases. It uses <major version>.<minor version> format. For example: 10.1, 11.2, or 12.4.

Letter versioning is used internally at Xilinx. The format is <letter>.<build number>. For example: K.39 or M.57. The <letter> part corresponds to the <major version> of the numeric format. For example, K corresponds to 10, L to 11, and M to 12.

There isn't one to one correspondence between <minor version> and the <build number> parts of the numeric and letter formats. Xilinx does frequent tool builds internally, and when the software reaches production quality, it's released as a new <minor version>.

The software version is typically shown on top of each report. The following example is the top two lines on the XST report:

```
Release 12.1 - xst M.53d (nt)
Copyright (c) 1995-2010 Xilinx, Inc. All rights reserved.
```

Both numeric and letter software versions are typically shown in the "About" dialog.

11

LESSER KNOWN XILINX TOOLS

Xilinx ISE installation contains several lesser-known command-line tools that FPGA designers might find useful. ISE Project Navigator and PlanAhead invoke these tools behind the scenes as part of the build flow. The tools are either poorly documented or not documented at all, which limits their value to users.

The tools listed below are some of the most useful ones.

data2 mem: This utility, which is used to initialize the contents of a BRAM, doesn't require rerunning Xilinx implementation. The new BRAM data is inserted directly into a bitstream. Another data2mem usage is to split the initialization data of a large RAM consisting of several BRAM primitives into individual BRAMs.

fpga_edline: A command-line version of the FPGA Editor, fpga_edline can be useful for applying changes to the post-place-and-route .ngc file from a script as part of the build process. Some examples of use cases include adding ChipScope probes, minor routing changes, LUT or IOB property changes.

mem_edit: This is not a tool per se, but a script that opens Java applications. You can use it for simple memory content editing.

netgen: Here is a tool you can use in many situations. It gets a Xilinx design file in .ncd format as an input, and produces a Xilinx-independent netlist for use in simulation, equivalence checking and static timing analysis, depending on the command-line options.

ncgbuild: This is a tool that consolidates several design netlist files into one. It's mainly used for the convenience of working with a single design file rather than multiple designs and IP cores scattered around different directories.

obngc: This is a utility that obfuscates .ngc files in order to hide confidential design features and prevent design analysis and reverse-engineering. You can explore NGC files in FPGA Editor.

pin2ucf: You can use this utility to generate pin-locking constraints from NCD file in UCF format.

xdl: An essential tool for power users, Xdl has three fundamental modes: report device resource information, convert NCD to XDL and convert XDL to NCD. XDL is a text format that third-party tools can process. This is the only way to access post-place-and-route designs.

Example:
```
xdl -ncd2xdl <design_name>.ncd
```

xreport: This is a utility that lets you view build reports outside of the ISE Project Navigator software. It has table views of design summary, resource usage, hyperlinked warnings and errors, and message filtering.

xinfo: A utility that reports system information, xinfo also details installed Xilinx software and IP cores, licenses, ISE preferences, relevant environment variables and other useful information.

lmutil: A license management utility distributed by Macrovision Corporation, and used by Xilinx software. It is used to communicate with a license server to install, check-out, and poll for floating licenses. The following command is an example of polling for available ISE licenses on server with IP address 192.168.1.100:

```
$ lmutil lmdiag -c 2100@192.168.1.100 ISE
lmutil - Copyright (c) 1989-2006 Macrovision Corporation.
----------------------------------
License file: 2100@192.168.2.52
----------------------------------
"ISE" v2010.05, vendor: xilinxd
  License server: 192.168.1.100
  floating license no expiration date
  TS_OK: Checkout permitted when client is using terminal client
Feature:        ISE
Hostname:       shiitake
License path:   2100@192.168.1.100
```

reportgen: A utility that takes an NCD file as an input, and generates net delay, IO pin assignment, and clock region reports.

All the tools mentioned above are installed in $XILINX/ISE/bin/{nt, nt64, lin, lin64} and $XILINX/common/bin/{nt, nt64, lin, lin64} directories. $XILINX is an environmental variable that points to the ISE installation directory.

More inquisitive readers might want to further explore these directories to discover other interesting tools that can boost design productivity.

12

UNDERSTANDING XILINX TOOL REPORTS

FPGA synthesis and physical implementation tools produce a great number of reports that contain various bits of information on errors and warnings, logic utilization, design frequency, timing, clocking, etc. It requires a significant amount of experience with the design tools to efficiently navigate the reports and quickly find the required information. Xilinx and other FPGA design tools provide a GUI view of some of the most important and frequently used information in the reports, but this is not always sufficient.

Most of the reports have a consistent structure. They are organized into multiple sections, where each section contains a particular type of information. Examples of report sections are errors, warnings, IO properties, utilization by hierarchy.

The following list briefly describes most of the reports produced by Xilinx XST and physical implementation tools.

Report name: XST synthesis report
Tool: Xilinx XST
File Extension: .srp, .syr
A XST synthesis report contains information about synthesis options, HDL and low-level synthesis, design summary, and the estimates of logic utilization and performance.

Report name: translation report
Tool: NGDBUILD
File Extension: .bld
A translation report contains information about NDGBUILD run, including user-defined constraints, and partition implementation.

Report name: MAP report
Tool: MAP
File Extension: .mrp
This report contains information about the MAP run: design summary, removed logic, IO properties, logic utilization by hierarchy, and several other sections.
By default, a MAP report contains only basic information. Use -detail MAP option to enable the complete report.

Report name: physical synthesis report
Tool: MAP
File Extension: .psr

The physical synthesis report file contains information about MAP options responsible for different timing and area optimizations: global optimization (-global_opt), retiming (-retiming), equivalent register removal (-equivalent_register_removal), combinatorial logic optimization (-logic_opt), register duplication (-register_duplication), and power fine grain slice clock gating optimization (-power).

Report name: physical constraints report
Tool: MAP
File Extension: .pcf
A physical constraints report contains all physical constraints specified during design entry and added by the user.

Report name: place and route report
Tool: PAR
File Extension: .par
A place and route report contains different information about the PAR run: command line options, design utilization and performance summary, detailed clocking resources report, and partition implementation status.

Report name: IO pad report
Tool: PAR
File Extension: .pad
A pad report is a file that contains a list of all IO components used in the design, their associated FPGA pins, and characteristics, such as direction, IO standard, slew rate, and drive strength.

Report name: unrouted nets report
Tool: PAR
File Extension: .unroutes
This report contains a list of signals that could not be routed during Place and Route (PAR) stage. The presence of any signals in that report indicates a design error.

Report name: design rule check report
Tool: BITGEN
File Extension: .drc
The report contains various design rule checks (DRC) results performed by BITGEN. DCR can be disabled by specifying the –d (no DRC) BITGEN command line option.

Report name: bitstream generation report
Tool: BITGEN
File Extension: .bgn
This report contains information options used during the BITGEN, and the overall results.

Report name: timing report
Tool: Xilinx TRCE
File Extension: .twr, .twx

Report name: timing constraints interaction report

Tool: TRCE
File Extension: .tsi
Timing reports are described in greater detail in Tip #91
Many reports contain overlapping or complementary information. The following list organizes reports by types of information they provide.

Logic utilization

Logic utilization is reported in several reports during the FPGA build process.

Synthesis report (.syr, .srp) contains estimated utilization information, excluding IP cores that are added during translation stage, and before logic optimization performed during MAP.

MAP report (.mrp) provides post-placement logic utilization for the entire design, and the utilization break-down by individual module.

PAR report (.par) provides the most accurate post-routing logic utilization information.

Timing

Synthesis (.syr, .srp), and MAP (.mrp) reports contain estimated timing information performed at the logic level.

The complete timing information is generated after place and route stage. PAR report (.par) contains the overall timing score.

TRCE static timing analysis reports (.twr, .twx) contain detailed timing information organized by signals, endpoints, clock, or timing group.

IO information

MAP report (.mrp) provides post-placement information about the IO properties. The report doesn't contain any routing details.

PAD report (.pad) contains the complete post-routing IO information.

Clocking

Synthesis (.syr, .srp) report provides basic information about design clocks and the clock load (how many registers the clock is driving).

MAP (.mrp) report contains information about used clocking resources, such as MMCM, and global buffers. It also provides detailed information about control sets: the combination of clock, reset, clock enable, and logic load count.

PAR report (.par) provides detailed timing information about each clock in the design: skew, maximum delay, positive or negative slack, and summary of timing errors.

TRCE timing reports (.twr, .twx) contain the most complete and detailed timing information.

13
NAMING CONVENTIONS

With an increasing complexity of FPGA designs, design practices, methods, and processes are becoming increasingly important success factors. Good design practices have an enormous impact on an FPGA design's performance, logic utilization, more efficient use of FPGA resources, improved system reliability, team productivity, and faster time-to-market. Conversely, poor design practices can lead to higher development and system cost, lower performance, missed project schedules, and unreliable designs.

Tips #13-16 provide several rules and guidelines for Verilog naming conventions, coding style, and synthesis for an FPGA. The guiding principles are improving code readability and portability, facilitating code reuse, and consistency across different projects.

To be effective, rules and guidelines have to be formalized in a document, disseminated throughout design teams, and enforced by periodic code inspections and design reviews.

The scope of the documents may vary. In a small company it can contain a brief overview of acceptable naming conventions and coding styles. In a large, established company it can be an extensive set of documents covering different aspects of design practices, methods, and processes in great detail. In safety and mission-critical designs, such as military or medical applications, the emphasis is on following strict coding standards and processes that prevent a device failure from all possible sources. It is beneficial for the document to include checklists for signing off different stages of the design process: simulation, synthesis, physical implementation, and bring-up.

The goal of the document is twofold. One is establishing consistency and the same "look and feel" of the code written by different designers within a project or a company, regardless of their background and experience. The other is improved code readability and clarity, which helps reduce the number of defects or bugs.

The list of suggestions offered in Tips #13-16 is by far incomplete. Its main goal is to establish a basis for developing a more comprehensive set of rules and guidelines tailored for specific project or a team.

File header

It is hard to overestimate the importance of including a file header in every source code and script file. The header has to contain at least the proper copyright information and disclaimer. If desired, it can contain a brief description, name and e-mail of the design engineer, version, and a list of changes to that file. The most important reason for including the header is a legal one. A source code or a script file constitutes an intellectual property. The header establishes ownership and rights for that file, which can be used as evidence in a court of law during litigation, patent dispute, or copyright arbitration.

The following is an example of a file header.

```
/*----------------------------------------------------------
Copyright (C) 2011 OutputLogic.com
This source file may be used and distributed without
restriction provided that this copyright statement is not
removed from the file and that any derivative work contains
the original copyright notice and the associated disclaimer.
THIS SOURCE FILE IS PROVIDED "AS IS" AND WITHOUT ANY EXPRESS
OR IMPLIED WARRANTIES, INCLUDING, WITHOUT LIMITATION, THE
IMPLIED WARRANTIES OF MERCHANTIBILITY AND FITNESS FOR A
PARTICULAR PURPOSE.
Filename: top.v
Engineer: John Doe
Description: top-level module
----------------------------------------------------------*/
```

Verilog file organization

It is a good design practice to implement a single Verilog module in a file, as shown in the following code example.

```
// file: my_module.v
module my_module;
// module implementation...
endmodule // my_module
```

A module name should match the file name. Following this rule makes it easier to process and manage the projects. An exception might be a library file that contains multiple short modules.

File and directory names

Although it's legal to include spaces and other special characters in file and directory names in Linux and Windows operating systems, it is not a good design practice. Having spaces can cause obscure problems in tools and scripts. Linux command line utilities and shells were designed based on a premise that a space delimits a field value, rather than being an acceptable component of a file or directory name. So do tools that rely on those utilities and shells. Including quotes around the filename with spaces and special characters might not always work, for example when this filename is passed through multiple subshells and pipes.

As a rule, use only alphanumeric and underscore characters in file and directory names.

Try to give files and directories that are meaningful and unique names that may help describe their contents.

Uppercase vs. lowercase

Net, variable, module, instance, and other names in Verilog and SystemVerilog languages are case sensitive. Synthesis tools enforce that rule by default. However, there are several tool options that allow some flexibility. For example, XST provides -case option, which determines whether the names are written to the final netlist using all lower or all upper case letters, or if the case is maintained from the source. The synopsis of this option is:

```
xst run -case {upper | lower | maintain}
```

It is recommended that you name parameters, macros, constants, attributes, and enumerated type values in uppercase. Module, file, function, instance, and task names can be in lowercase. Don't use mixed case in names.

Comments

The liberal use of meaningful and non-obvious comments is encouraged in order to improve the code readability and help you to understand the design intent. Comment consistency is an important requirement, such as observing the maximum line size. Verilog allows single-line and multi-line comments.

```
reg my_reg; // this is a single-line comment
/*
    this is a multi-line comment
*/
```

There are comment styles, such as /** */, used by various tools to perform comment extraction to be used in documentation.

Using tabs for code indentation

Tabs are used for code indentation. However, tabs are not displayed in the same way on different computer systems. It is recommended that you configure a code editor to replace a tab character with whitespaces. It's customary to use four white characters to replace a single tab.

Newline characters

Code editors in Windows operating system use carriage return and line feed (CR/LF) character pair to indicate a newline. This is different than in Unix/Linux systems, which only use LF character. That difference will cause extraneous CR characters appear as ^M in files developed on Windows and viewed on Unix/Linux. Moreover, some tools and scripting languages might be sensitive to these extra characters, leading to incorrect results.

Some code editors provide an option of only using LF character for a newline. Also, there is a utility called dos2unix that can be used to remove extra CR characters.

Limit the line width

Standard column width for most terminals, editors, and printers is 80 characters. The motivation behind limiting the line width to 80 characters is to make the code more readable on different systems.

Identifiers

Two most popular HDL identifier coding styles are the following:

1. Mixed case, no underscores. Each word starts with an uppercase letter. Two or more consecutive uppercase letters are disallowed.

    ```
    reg MyReqister;
    wire MyNet;
    wire DataFromCPU; // incorrect: consecutive uppercase
    letters.
    ```

2. All lowercase, underscores between words.

    ```
    reg my_register;
    wire my_net;
    wire data_from_cpu;
    ```

The second coding style is more prevalent. Most of the tool and IP Core vendors, including Xilinx, have adopted this style. It is important to adopt and follow a single style that can be used by all developers and across different projects.

Escaped identifiers

Verilog standard provides a means of including any of the printable ASCII characters in an identifier. Such an identifier has to start with the backslash escape character (\) and end with space, tab, or newline character. The leading backslash and the terminating white space are not part of the identifier.

Escaped identifiers are used by automated code generators, ASIC netlisting, and other CAD tools that use special characters in identifiers. Escaped identifiers are extensively used in the code generated by various Xilinx cores. FPGA designers should avoid using escaped identifiers, because they make the code less readable, and that can cause it to be hard to find errors, such as mistyped trailing space.

The following is an example of a Xilinx shift register core that uses escaped identifiers. There is a terminating white space between the end of an identifier and a semicolon or a bracket.

```verilog
module shift_ram_coregen (input sclr,ce,clk,
          input [0 : 0] d,
          output [0 : 0] q);
  wire \BU2/sinit ;
  wire \BU2/sset ;
  wire \BU2/U0/i_bb_inst/Mshreg_f1.only_clb.srl_sig_62_1_9 ;
  wire \BU2/U0/i_bb_inst/Mshreg_f1.only_clb.srl_sig_62_0_8 ;
  wire \BU2/U0/i_bb_inst/N1 ;
  wire \BU2/U0/i_bb_inst/N0 ;
  wire \BU2/U0/i_bb_inst/f1.only_clb.srl_sig_62_5 ;
  wire NLW_VCC_P_UNCONNECTED;
  wire NLW_GND_G_UNCONNECTED;
  wire [0 : 0] d_2;
  wire [0 : 0] q_3;
  wire [3 : 0] \BU2/a ;

  assign d_2[0] = d[0], q[0] = q_3[0];
  VCC VCC_0 (.P(NLW_VCC_P_UNCONNECTED));
  GND GND_1 (.G(NLW_GND_G_UNCONNECTED));
  FDE #(.INIT ( 1'b0 ))
     \BU2/U0/i_bb_inst/f1.only_clb.srl_sig_62(
     .C(clk),
     .CE(ce),
     .D(\BU2/U0/i_bb_inst/Mshreg_f1.only_clb.srl_sig_62_1_9 ),
     .Q(\BU2/U0/i_bb_inst/f1.only_clb.srl_sig_62_5 ));
  SRLC32E #( .INIT ( 32'h00000000 ))
     \BU2/U0/i_bb_inst/Mshreg_f1.only_clb.srl_sig_62_1 (
     .CLK(clk),
     .D(\BU2/U0/i_bb_inst/Mshreg_f1.only_clb.srl_sig_62_0_8 ),
     .CE(ce),
     .Q(\BU2/U0/i_bb_inst/Mshreg_f1.only_clb.srl_sig_62_1_9 ),
     .Q31(),
     .A({\BU2/U0/i_bb_inst/N1 , \BU2/U0/i_bb_inst/N1 ,
\BU2/U0/i_bb_inst/N1 , \BU2/U0/i_bb_inst/N0 ,
\BU2/U0/i_bb_inst/N1 }));
  SRLC32E #(.INIT ( 32'h00000000 ))
     \BU2/U0/i_bb_inst/Mshreg_f1.only_clb.srl_sig_62_0(
     .CLK(clk),
     .D(d_2[0]),
     .CE(ce),
     .Q(),
     .Q31(\BU2/U0/i_bb_inst/Mshreg_f1.only_clb.srl_sig_62_0_8),
     .A({\BU2/U0/i_bb_inst/N1 , \BU2/U0/i_bb_inst/N1 ,
```

```
\BU2/U0/i_bb_inst/N1 , \BU2/U0/i_bb_inst/N1,
\BU2/U0/i_bb_inst/N1 }) );
   VCC \BU2/U0/i_bb_inst/XST_VCC( .P(\BU2/U0/i_bb_inst/N1 ));
   GND \BU2/U0/i_bb_inst/XST_GND( .G(\BU2/U0/i_bb_inst/N0 ));
   FDRE #( .INIT ( 1'b0 ))
   \BU2/U0/i_bb_inst/gen_output_regs.output_regs/fd/output_1(
      .C(clk),
      .CE(ce),
      .D(\BU2/U0/i_bb_inst/f1.only_clb.srl_sig_62_5),
      .R(sclr),
      .Q(q_3[0]));
endmodule
```

Name prefix

A meaningful name prefix can be used to categorize the net, register, instance, or other identifiers. For example, all the nets that originate from the memory controller can have "mem_" name prefix.

Name suffix

Name suffix can be used to provide additional information about the net, register, instance, or other identifiers.

For example, "_p" or "_n" suffix can indicate positive or negative polarity.

The following table provides a few examples of name suffixes.

Table 1: Examples of name suffixes

Suffix	Description
_p, _n	Positive or negative polarity
_ff, _q	An output of a register
_c	A signal driven by combinatorial gates
_cur	Current state
_next	Next state
_tb	Testbench

Clock names

Clock signal names can include frequency, and other characteristics, such as single-ended or differential clock, to make the name more descriptive. It is also customary to include "clk" as part of a clock name. The following are few examples of clock signal names.

```
wire clk50; // single-ended 50MHz clock
wire clk_200_p, clk_200_n; // 200MHz differential clock
wire clk_en; // clock enable
wire clk_333_mem; // 333MHz memory controller clock
```

Reset names

Reset names can include information about reset polarity (active high or low), synchronous or asynchronous, and global or local. The following are few examples of reset signal names.

```
reg reset, phy_reset; // active high reset
reg reset_n, reset_b;  // active low reset
reg rst_async; // asynchronous reset
```

Port names

Port names can end with a suffix that indicates port direction, as shown in the following examples.

```
input   [9:0]   addr_i;  // input
input   [31:0] DataI;   // input
output write_enable_o; // output
inout   [31:0] data_io; // bidirectional
inout   [31:0] ConfigB; // bidirectional
```

Module names

Module names have to be unique across the entire project, regardless of the hierarchy level the module is instantiated. Reserved Verilog or SystemVerilog keywords should not be used as module names.

Literals

Verilog provides a rich set of options to specify literals. Literals can be specified as a simple integer, for example 32, or as a based integer, for example 6'd32.

The syntax of specifying a based integer is:

    <size>'s<base><value>

<size> field specifies the total number of bits represented by the literal value. This field is optional. If not given, the default size is 32 bits

"s" field indicates a twos complement signed value. It is an optional field, and if not provided, the value is treated as an unsigned.

<base> field specifies whether the value is given as a binary, octal, decimal, or hex. If the base is not specified, a simple literal defaults to a decimal base.

<value> field specifies the literal integer value.

A simple literal integer defaults to a signed value. A based literal integer defaults to an unsigned value, unless explicitly specified as a signed using "s" field.

It is recommended that you describe literals using the base specification to avoid the possibility of introducing a mistake. For example, use 6'd32 instead of 32.

A common mistake is a mismatch of <size> and <value> of the same literal. For example, using 5'd32 will not cause any synthesis error, but results in truncation of the most-significant bit of value 32 (binary 'b100000), which will become 0.

If <size> is greater than <value>, <value> will be left-extended, as shown in the following examples.

```
wire [7:0] my_value;
assign my_value = 'b0; // left-extended to 8'h00
assign my_value = 'b1; // left-extended to 8'h01;
```

Verilog defines several rules for dealing with different literal sizes in assignment and other operators. A good overview of the rules and methods to avoid potential problems is described in the [1].

Resources

[1] "Standard Gotchas: Subtleties in the Verilog and SystemVerilog Standards That Every Engineer Should Know", by Stuart Sutherland. Published in the proceedings of SNUG Boston, 2006.
http://www.sutherland-hdl.com/papers/2007-SNUG-SanJose_gotcha_again_paper.pdf

14
VERILOG CODING STYLE

Using `include compiler directive

The file inclusion `include compiler directive" is used to insert the entire contents of a source file into another file during synthesis. It is typically used to include global project definitions, without requiring the repetition of the same code in multiple files. Another use case is inserting portions of a code into modules, as shown in the following example:

```
// file test_bench_top.v
// top-level simulation testbench
module test_bench_top;
    `include "test_case.v"
endmodule
// file test_case.v
initial begin
    //...
end
task my_task;
    //...
endtask
```

The syntax for `include compiler directive is defined as:

```
`include <filename>
```

<filename> can be the name of the file, and also contain an absolute or relative pathname:

```
`include "test_case.v"
`include "../../includes/test_case.v"
`include "/home/myprojects/test/includes/test_case.v"
```

It is recommended using only the filename in the `include, and not absolute or relative pathnames. That will make the code location-independent, and therefore more portable. Pathnames can be specified using synthesis or simulation tool options, such as XST –

`vlgincdir <directory_name>` (Verilog Include Directories), and ModelSim `+incdir+<directory_name>`.

Another recommendation is to keep included files simple and not to use nested `` `include `` directives.

Using `` `define `` compiler directive, `parameter`, and `localparam`

`` `define `` is a text macro substitution compiler directive. It is defined as:

`` `define <text macro> ``

`<text macro>` can include single- or multi-line text with an optional list of arguments.

`` `define `` has a global scope. Once a text macro name has been defined, it can be used anywhere in the project. Text macros are typically simple identifiers used to define state names, constants, or strings.

Text macro also can be defined as a synthesis or simulation tool option. For example, XST supports "`-define <text macro>`", and ModelSim has "`+define+<text macro>`" command line option.

The advantage of using command-line option is that, unlike using `` `define `` in a source code, it is independent on the compile order of the files.

`parameter` keyword defines a module-specific parameter, which has a scope of specific module instance. Parameter is used to provide different customizations to a module instance, for example, width of input or output ports. The following is an example of using `parameter` keyword.

```
    module adder #(parameter WIDTH = 8) (
      input [WIDTH-1:0] a,b, output [WIDTH-1:0] sum );

      assign sum = a + b;
    endmodule // adder

    // an instance of adder module
    adder # (16) adder1
    (.a(a[15:0]),.b(b[15:0]),.sum(sum[15:0]));
```

`localparam` keyword is similar to `parameter`. It is assigned a constant expression, and has a scope inside a specific module. It is defined as:

```
    localparam <identifier> = <value>;
```

It is recommended not to use `` `define `` and `parameter` for module-specific constants, such as state values, and use `localparam` instead.

Operand size mismatch

Verilog specification defines several rules to resolve cases where there is size mismatch between left and right-hand side of an assignment or an operator. The following are few examples.

```
reg [3:0] a;
reg [4:0] b;
reg c;
always @(posedge clk)
   if (a == b)   // a and b have a different size
       c <= 1'b1;

reg [3:0] a;
wire b;
wire [2:0] c;
wire [3:0] d;

a = b ? c : d;   // c and d have a different size
wire [9:0] a;
wire [5:0] b;
wire [1:0] c;
wire [7:0] d;
assign d = a | b | c;   // a,b,c,d have a different size
```

The rules that resolve the different cases of size differences can be complex and hard to follow. When two operands of different bit sizes are used, and one or both of the operands is unsigned, the smaller operand is extended with zeros on the most significant bit side to match the size of the larger operand. When the size of right-hand side is greater than the size on an assignment destination, the upper bits of right-hand side are truncated.

It is recommended to exactly match the bit size of the right and left side of operators and assignments to avoid automatic truncation or size extension by the synthesis tools.

A good overview of the rules and methods to avoid potential problems is described in [1].

Connecting ports in a module instance

Verilog defines two ways to connect ports in instantiated modules: by name and by port order. Using the ordered port connection method, the first element in the port list is connected to the first port declared in the module, the second to the second port, and so on. Connecting ports by name allows more flexibility. For example, an unconnected output port can be omitted. Although it requires larger amount of code than using "by order" method, it is more readable and less error-prone, especially for large modules with hundreds of ports. Port connectivity options are illustrated in the following example.

```verilog
// Lower level module
module low(output [1:0] out, input in1, in2);
    // ...
endmodule

// Higher-level module:
module high(output [5:0] out1, input [3:0] in1,in2);
    // connecting ports by order
    low low1(out1[1:0], in1[0], in2[0] )

    // connecting ports by order
    // error: in2 and in1 are swapped
    low low2(out1[3:2], in2[1], in1[1] )

    // connecting ports by name
    low low3(.out(out1[5:4]), .in1(in1[2]), .in2(in2[2]) )

    // connecting ports by name; an output is left unconnected
    low low4(.out(), .in1(in1[3]), .in2(in2[3]) )

endmodule
```

It is recommended to use "by name" port connection method in module instantiations.

Using variable part-select to define bit range

Variable or indexed part-select is defined by a starting point of its range, and a constant width that can either increase or decrease from the starting point. The following is an example of using variable part-select.

```verilog
wire [31:0] part_sel_in,
reg  [0:31] part_sel_out

assign part_sel_out[24 +:8]  = part_sel_in[7 -: 8];
assign part_sel_out[16 +:8]  = part_sel_in[15 -: 8];
assign part_sel_out[15 -:16] = part_sel_in[16 +: 16];
```

Using variable part-selects allows writing more compact and less error-prone code. In case of the above example, it prevents making a mistake in a bit range bounds.

```verilog
assign part_sel_out[24:31] = part_sel_in[7:0];
assign part_sel_out[16:24] = part_sel_in[15:8]; // error
assign part_sel_out[15:0]  = part_sel_in[16:31];
```

Using Verilog `for` statement

Verilog `for` statement can be used in many situations to implement shift registers, swapping bits, perform parity checks, and many other use cases. Using `for` statement for parallel CRC generation is discussed more in Tip #71.

The following is an example of using `for` statement in a loop.

```
module for_loop( output reg loop_out,
                 input [15:0] loop_in);
    integer iy;
    always @(*) begin
      for(iy=0;iy<16;iy=iy+1) begin
        loop_out = loop_out ^ loop_in[iy];
      end
    end
endmodule // for_loop
```

It is recommended to avoid using `for` statements for logic replication, and to restrict it only for simple repeat operations, such as swapping bits. Using it `for` statement in loops can create cascaded logic, which may result in sub-optimal logic utilization and timing performance.

Using functions

The following is a simple example of a Verilog function that performs XOR operation.

```
module function_example( input a,b, output func_out);
    function func_xor;
      input a, b;
      begin
        func_xor = a ^ b;
      end
    endfunction
    assign func_out = func_xor(a,b);
endmodule // function_example
```

It is recommended to use Verilog functions to implement combinatorial logic and other operations that don't require non-blocking assignments, such as synchronous logic. Using functions allows writing more compact and modular code. Verilog functions are supported by all synthesis tools.

Using `generate` blocks

`Generate` blocks were introduced in Verilog-2001 to enable easy instantiation of multiple instances of the same module, function, variables, nets, and continuous assignments. The following are two examples of using `generate`.

```verilog
// a conditional instantiation of modules
parameter COND1 = 1;

generate
if (COND1) begin : my_module1_inst
   my_module1 inst (.clk(clk), .di(di), .do(do));
end
else begin : my_module2_inst
   my_module2 inst (.clk(clk), .di(di), .do(do));
end
endgenerate

// using for loop in generate block
genvar ii;
generate
    for (ii = 0; ii < 32;  ii = ii+1) begin: for_loop
      my_module1 inst (.clk(clk), .di(di[ii]), do(do[ii]));
    end
end
endgenerate
```

Developing portable code

In the context of this book, code portability refers to the ability to synthesize an FPGA design with different synthesis tools, and targeting different FPGA families with minimum code modifications.

Even if code portability does not seem to be an important requirement in the beginning of the project, it's highly likely to have its benefits later on in the project's lifecycle. In the high-tech industry business, market requirements change rapidly. Because of this, large parts of the code will need to be reused in a completely different project, which utilizes different FPGA family or even a different vendor than was originally anticipated. It's almost impossible to predict how the code is going to be used over several years of its lifecycle. The code can be packaged as an IP core and licensed to various customers; the code be inherited by another company as the result of an acquisition; or the code may need to be migrated to a newer, more cost-effective FPGA family.

One recommendation for developing portable code is separating FPGA-specific components into separate files or libraries, and using generic wrappers. For example, Xilinx, Altera, and other FPGA vendors have different embedded memory primitives. However, components, such as RAMs, ROMs, and FIFOs, that take advantage of those memory primitives, have very similar interfaces. Not instantiating Xilinx BRAM directly in the code, but using a simple wrapper with generic address, data, and control signals will make the code much more portable.

Another method of improving portability is to develop generic RTL code instead of directly instantiating FPGA-specific components. Tradeoffs of inference vs. direct instantiation are discussed in Tip #16.

Synthesis tools support different subset of Verilog language. For example, XST doesn't support Verilog switch-level primitives such as `tranif`, while Synplify does. It is recommended to use language constructs supported by most of the synthesis tools.

Developing simple code

Always strive to develop a simple code. As in every programming language, Verilog allows writing elaborated statements, which are elegant from the functional standpoint, but unreadable. The following simple example illustrates this point.

```verilog
reg [5:0] sel;
reg [3:0] result1,result2,a,b;
always @(*) begin
    result1 = sel[0] ? a + b : sel[1] ? a - b :
              sel[2] ? a & b : sel[3] ? a ^ b :
              sel[4] ? ~a : ~ b;
    if(~|sel)
      result1 = 4'b0;
end // always
always @(*) begin
    casex(sel)
      6'bxxxxx1: result2 = a + b;
      6'bxxxx10: result2 = a - b;
      6'bxxx100: result2 = a & b;
      6'bxx1000: result2 = a ^+ b;
      6'bx10000: result2 = ~a;
      6'b100000: result2 = ~b;
      default:   result2 = 4'b0;
    endcase
end // always
```

The logic that implements `result1` and `result2` is functionally equivalent. However, using nested ternary operator and two assignment statements in `result1` is less transparent, and takes more mental effort to understand comparing to a more clear `case` statement of the `result2` logic.

Often, code clarity trumps implementation efficiency. The same piece of code is read by multiple developers over its lifetime. A more clearly-written code is easier to debug, and less prone to contain bugs in general.

Using Lint tools

Lint tools perform pre-simulation and pre-synthesis RTL design rule checking. They help uncover complex and obscure problems that cannot be found by simulation and synthesis tools. Examples of design rules checked by lint tools are clock domain crossing, combinatorial loops, module connectivity, coding style, implied latches, asynchronous resets, overlapping states, and many others. Tip #6 overviews some of the popular Lint tools.

Resources

[1] *"Standurd Gotchas: Subtleties in the Verilog and SystemVerilog Standards That Every Engineer Should Know",* by Stuart Sutherland. Published in the proceedings of SNUG Boston, 2006.

http://www.sutherland-hdl.com/papers/2007-SNUG-SanJose_gotcha_again_paper.pdf

15
WRITING SYNTHESIZABLE CODE FOR FPGAS

The Verilog language reference manual (LRM) provides a rich set of capabilities to describe hardware. However, only a subset of the language is synthesizable for FPGA. Even if a particular language structure is synthesizable, that doesn't guarantee that the code will pass physical implementation for a specific FPGA. Consider the following example.

```
reg [7:0] memory[1:2**22];
initial begin
    memory[1] = 8'h1;
    memory[2] = 8'h2;
end
```

The example will simulate correctly but will result in FPGA physical implementation failure. The code infers four megabytes of memory, which most modern FPGAs don't have. Also, synthesis tools will ignore `initial` block, which initializes the lowest two bytes of the memory.

This Tip provides several guidelines and recommendations to facilitate writing synthesizable code for FPGAs.

Follow synchronous design methodology

It is recommended that developers adhere to the principles of synchronous design for FPGAs, which include the following:

- Use synchronous design reset. This topic is discussed in more detail in Tip #29
- Avoid using latches; use synchronous registers whenever possible
- Avoid using gated, derived, or divided clocks
- Use clock enables instead of multiple clocks
- Implement proper synchronization of all asynchronous signals

Understand synthesis tool capabilities and limitations

A good knowledge of synthesis tool capabilities and limitations will improve FPGA design performance, logic utilization, and productivity of a designer. It is important to get familiar with the inference rules for a particular FPGA family, what language constructs a synthesis tool ignores or does not support, and the recommended coding style for registers, state machines, tri-states, and other constructs.

Ignored language constructs

Delay values and `timescale compiler directives are ignored by FPGA synthesis tools. Designers often use delay values to make it easier to analyze simulation waveforms, as shown in the following example.

```
`define DLY 1
always @(posedge clk) begin
     data_out <= #`DLY data_in;
end
```

Using such constructs is discouraged because of the potential synthesis and simulation mismatch. For example, if `DLY in the above example exceeds the clock period, the synthesized circuit will likely be functionally incorrect because it will not match simulation results.

Compiler directives such as `celldefine and `endcelldefine are ignored my most of the FPGA synthesis tools.

initial blocks are ignored by FPGA synthesis tools.

Synthesis tools provide various levels of support for Verilog gate-level primitives such as nmos, pmos, cmos, pullup, pulldown, tranif0, tranif1, tran, and others. For example, XST doesn't support Verilog tranif primitive, while Synplify does. Although Xilinx FPGA architecture doesn't have a direct equivalent for gate-level primitives, some synthesis tools convert them to a functionally-equivalent switch. The following is an example of an nmos conversion.

```
module nmos_switch (output out, input data, control);
    assign out = control ? data : 1'bz;
endmodule
```

Unsupported language constructs

User-defined primitives (UDP), repeat, wait, fork/join, deassign, event, force/release statements are not supported by synthesis tools.

Hierarchical references of registers and nets inside the modules are not supported.

```
module my_module1;
    assign my_net = top.my_module2.my_net;
endmodule
```

Level of support for case equality and inequality operators (=== and !==) depends on the synthesis tool. Some synthesis tools will produce an error when they encounter a case equality and inequality operator, while others will convert the operator to the logical equality one (== and !=).

2-state vs. 4-state values

4-state values ('0', '1', 'x', 'z') are inherently not synthesizable. FPGA architecture only supports 2-state values (logic '0' and '1'), and synthesis tools will apply different rules to optimize 'z' and 'x' values during the synthesis process. That will cause a mismatch between synthesis and simulation results (also see Tip #59) and other side effects. Only use 'z' values during the implementation of tri-stated IO buffers.

`translate_on`/`translate_off` compiler directives

`translate_off` and `translate_on` directives instruct synthesis tools to ignore portions of a Verilog code. These directives are typically used to exclude portions of a behavioral code in the models of IP cores. The following is an example of using these directives.

```
module bram_2k_9 ( input clka, input [0 : 0] wea,
    input [10 : 0] addra,
    output [8 : 0] douta,
    input [8 : 0] dina);

    // synthesis translate_off
    // ...
    // behavioral description of bram_2k_9

    // synthesis translate_on
endmodule   // bram_2k_9
```

`syn_keep`, `syn_preserve`, `syn_noprune` compiler directives

`syn_keep` directive prevents synthesis tools from removing a designated signal. It works on nets and combinatorial logic. This directive is typically used to disable unwanted optimizations and to keep manually created replications. The exact effect of `syn_keep` might be different between synthesis tools. For example, XST doesn't propagate the constraint to the synthesized netlist, which doesn't prevent optimization by the physical implementation tools.

`syn_preserve` prevents register optimization. XST also supports "Equivalent Register Removal" option, which is equivalent to `syn_preserve`.

`syn_noprune` ensures that if the outputs of an instantiated primitive are not used, the primitive is not optimized. XST also supports the "Optimize Instantiated Primitives" option, which is equivalent to `syn_noprune`.

`parallel_case, full_case` compiler directives

If the `full_case` directive is specified in a `case`, `casex`, or `casez` statement, it prevents synthesis tools from creating additional logic to cover conditions that are not described. Using a `full_case` directive can potentially result in more compact implementation.

`parallel_case` directive forces a case statement to be synthesized as a parallel multiplexer instead of the priority-encoded structure. Using `parallel_case` directives can potentially improve timing performance of a circuit.

The exact effect of `full_case` and `parallel_case` directives depends on the synthesis tool. Also, using those directives will also cause synthesis and simulation mismatch. For those reasons, using `full_case` and `parallel_case` directives in FPGA designs is not recommended. Instead, designers should change the implementation of a `case` statement to achieve the same effect. For example, removing overlapping `case` conditions will render a `parallel_case` directive unnecessary.

A more detailed discussion of using `full_case` and `parallel_case` directives is provided in [1].

`default_nettype compiler directive

Verilog-2001 standard defines a `` `default_nettype `` compiler directive. If that directive is assigned to "`none`", all 1-bit nets must be declared.

```
// no `default_nettype
wire sum; // declaration is not required
assign sum = a + b;
`default_nettype none
wire sum; // must be declared
assign sum = a + b;
```

`case, casez, casex` statements

Verilog defines `case`, `casez`, and `casex` statements. The `case` is a multi-way decision statement that tests whether an expression matches one of the case items. The following is an example of a `case` statement.

```verilog
reg [1:0] sel;
reg [2:0] result;
always @(*)
   case(sel)
     2'b00: result = 3'd0;
     2'b01: result = 3'd1;
     2'b10: result = 3'd2;
   endcase
```

Using case statements instead of a nested if-else will result in more readable code, better logic utilization, and the achieving of higher performance.

The casez and casex statements allow "don't care" conditions in the case item comparisons. casez treats 'z' values as don't-care, and the casex treats both 'z' and 'x' values as don't care. If any of the bits in the casez or casex expression is a don't-care value, then that bit position will be ignored. The following are examples of casez and casex.

```verilog
reg [1:0] sel;
reg [2:0] result;
// using casez
always @(*)
   casez(sel)
     2'b0?: result = 3'd0;
     2'b10: result = 3'd1;
     2'b11: result = 3'd2;
   endcase

// using casex
always @(*)
   casex(sel)
     2'b0x: result = 3'd0;
     2'b10: result = 3'd1;
     2'b11: result = 3'd2;
   endcase
```

The case expression can be a constant, as illustrated in the following example.

```verilog
reg [1:0] sel;
reg [2:0] result;
always @(*)
   case(1)
     ~sel[1]: result = 3'd0;
     sel[1] & ~sel[0]: result = 3'd1;
```

```
          sel[1] & sel[0]:   result = 3'd2;
       endcase
```

Using the don't-care condition in `casex` and `casez` items may easily lead to overlap or duplication of the case items. Also, using those statements will cause synthesis and simulation mismatch. The following is an example of a case statement with overlapping case items.

```
// casez statement contains overlapped case items
reg [1:0] sel;
reg [2:0] result;

always @(*)
   casez(sel)
     2'b0z: result = 3'd0;
     2'b10: result = 3'd2;
     2'b11: result = 3'd3;
     2'b01: result = 3'd1;   // overlap with 2'b0z
   endcase
```

Overlapping or duplication of the `case` items is permitted and in most cases will not trigger any simulation or synthesis warning. This is a dangerous and hard-to-debug condition. It is recommended that the developer avoids using `casex` and `casez` statements altogether.

Adding a default clause to `case` statements is a simple way to avoid the range of problems. There are two ways to achieve the same effect, shown in the following examples.

```
reg [1:0] sel;
reg [2:0] result;

// using default clause
always @(*)
   case(sel)
     2'b00: result = 3'd0;
     2'b01: result = 3'd1;
     2'b10: result = 3'd2;
     default: result = 3'd3;
   endcase

// assigning default value before case statement
always @(*)
   result = 3'd3;
   case(sel)
     2'b00: result = 3'd0;
     2'b01: result = 3'd1;
     2'b10: result = 3'd2;
   endcase
```

Mixing blocking and non-blocking assignments in `always` blocks

Verilog specifies two types of assignments that can appear in `always` blocks: blocking and non-blocking. Blocking and non-blocking assignments are used to describe combinatorial and sequential logic respectively. Blocking and non-blocking assignments should never be mixed in the same `always` block. Doing that can cause unpredictable synthesis and simulation results. In many cases synthesis tools will not produce any warning, but synthesized logic will be incorrect. The following two code examples illustrate mixed use of blocking and non-blocking assignments.

```
reg blocking, non_blocking;
always @(posedge clk) begin
   if(reset) begin
     blocking     =  0;
     non_blocking <= 0;
   end
   else begin
     blocking     = ^data;
     non_blocking <= |data;
   end
end

always @(*) begin
   blocking = ^data;
   non_blocking <= |data;
end
```

The correct way is to implement the above examples is as follows:

```
reg blocking, non_blocking;
always @(posedge clk) begin
   if(reset) begin
     non_blocking <= 0;
   end
   else begin
     non_blocking <= |data;
   end
end

always @(*) begin
   blocking = ^data;
end
```

Multiple blocking assignments

Blocking assignments in an `always` block are executed in order of their appearance. Although it's often convenient, it is recommended that the developer limits the use of multiple blocking assignments to modify the same variable inside an `always` block. The following two code examples show potential problems with using multiple blocking assignments.

```
reg signal_a, signal_b, signal_c, signal_d;
always (*) begin
   signal_a = signal_b & signal_c;
   // ...
   // additional code
   signal_d = signal_a & signal_e;
end
```

Accidentally changing the order of `signal_a` and `signal_d` assignments will break the functionality of a `signal_d`.

```
reg [15:0] signal_a, signal_b;
always (*) begin
   signal_a[15:12] = 4'b0;
   // ...
   // additional code
   signal_a = signal_b;
end
```

The last assignment to `signal_a` takes priority, and bits [15:12] of `signal_a` will never be reset.

Using named `always` blocks

The following is an example of a named `always` block.

```
reg reg_unnamed;
always @(posedge clk) begin : myname
   // only visible in the "myname" block
   reg reg_named;

   // post-synthesis name : myname.reg_named
   reg_named <= data_in;
   // post-synthesis name : reg_unnamed
   reg_unnamed <= ~reg_named;
end // always
```

Named blocks can be useful in several situations. Because the `always` block is uniquely identified, it is easier to find it in the simulation. Also, limiting the scope of the variables allows for the reuse of the same variable name.

Resources

[1] *"'full_case parallel_case', the Evil Twins of Verilog Synthesis"*, by Clifford Cummings. Published in the proceedings of SNUG Boston, 1999.

16

INSTANTIATION VS. INFERENCE

Instantiation and inference are two different methods of adding components to an FPGA design. Each method offers its advantages, but also has drawbacks.

Component instantiation directly references an FPGA library primitive or macro in HDL. The main advantage of the instantiation method is that it provides a complete control of all the component features, and FPGA resources it will use. Also, instantiation makes it simpler to floorplan the component. Instantiation has to be used for complex components that cannot be inferred. For example, it is not possible to infer Xilinx MMCM primitive, and the only way to use it is by direct instantiation. Xilinx CoreGen utility can be used to generate more complex components for instantiation, such as MMCM, DSP48, or FIFOs. Another reason for direct instantiation is when synthesis tool is unable to correctly infer the component.

Component inference refers to writing a generic RTL description of a logic circuit behavior that the synthesis tool automatically converts into FPGA-specific primitives. Inference results in more portable code that can be used to target different FPGA architectures. It also produces more compact and readable code. The main disadvantage of the inference method is that the inference rules vary between different synthesis tools, so that the same RTL may result in a synthesis error, or a functionally different circuit. Xilinx recommends using inference method whenever possible.

Inferring registers

All synthesis tools are capable to correctly infer registers for Xilinx FPGAs with rising or falling edge clock, clock enable, and synchronous or asynchronous reset. It is recommended to use a non-blocking assignment (<=) in Verilog `always` block for a register inference. The following are several Verilog examples of inferring registers.

```
module register_inference(input   clk,areset,sreset,
          input   [4:0] d_in,
          output reg [4:0] d_out);
   // positive edge clock, asynchronous active-high reset
   always @( posedge clk , posedge areset)
   if( areset )
     d_out[0] <= 1'b0;
   else
```

```verilog
      d_out[0] <= d_in[0];
   // negative edge clock, asynchronous active-low reset
   always @( negedge clk , negedge areset)
      if( ~areset )
         d_out[1] <= 1'b0;
      else
         d_out[1] <= d_in[1];
   // negative edge clock, no reset
   always @( negedge clk )
      d_out[2] <= d_in[2];

   // Positive edge clock, synchronous active-high reset.
   // The register is initialized with '1' upon reset.
   // The circuit is implemented using a register and a LUT.
   always @( posedge clk )
      if( sreset )
         d_out[3] <= 1'b1;
      else
         d_out[3] <= d_in[3];
// Positive edge clock, both synchronous and asynchronous resets
// Implemented using a register and additional logic
always @( posedge clk , posedge areset)
     if( sreset )
        d_out[4] <= 1'b1;
     else if( areset )
        d_out[4] <= 1'b0;
     else
        d_out[4] <= d_in[4];
endmodule // register_inference
```

Register initialization

There are several ways to perform register initialization, illustrated in the following examples.

```verilog
// Register initialization in initial block.
// That will work in simulation. However, initial block is ignored during synthesis

initial begin
    my_reg = 1'b0;
end

// Register initialization during declaration
reg my_reg = 1'b0;
```

```verilog
// Register initialization upon reset
always @( posedge clk , posedge reset)
   if( reset )
     my_reg <= 1'b0;
   else
     my_reg <= d_in;
```

Inferring memories

Xilinx FPGAs provide several types of embedded memories that can be inferred using various techniques. Tip #34 provides more detailed description of those techniques.

Inferring Shift Register LUT (SRL)

Xilinx FPGAs contain dedicated Shift Register LUT (SRL16 or SRL32) primitives to conveniently implement shift registers. SRL primitives are more limited than general-purpose shift registers. They don't have a reset, and only have access to serial out bit. The following is an example of inferring an SRL.

```verilog
wire srl1_out;
reg [7:0] srl1;

always @(posedge clk)
    srl1 <= srl_enable ? {srl1[6:0] , d_in[0]} : srl1;
assign srl1_out = srl1[7];
```

Inferring IO

If a port in a top-level module doesn't contain any constraints, it'll be implemented using an IO with default characteristics, which depend on the FPGA family. For Xilinx FPGAs, a synthesis tool will automatically infer IBUF, OBUF, OBUFDS, or another primitive that best describes the IO. Designers can specify port characteristics by using Verilog attributes or UCF constraints. However, Verilog attributes are specific to a synthesis tool, and UCF constraints are specific to FPGA family. The following are examples of Verilog attributes related to the IO.

Synopsys Synplify:

  xc_padtype, xc_pullup, xc_slow, xc_fast, xc_loc, syn_useioff.

Xilinx XST: (* IOSTANDARD = "iostandard_name" *)
       (* SLOW = "{TRUE|FALSE}" *)

Inferring IOB Registers

Every IO block in Xilinx FPGAs contains storage elements, referred to as IOB registers. The available options are input register, and output register for single or dual-data rate (DDR) outputs. Using IOB registers significantly decreases clock-to-input/output data time, which improves IO performance.

Placing a register in the IOB is not guaranteed, and it requires following a few rules. Register to be pushed into IOB, including output and tri-state enable, has to have a fanout of 1. Registers with a higher fanout have to be replicated. All registers that are packed into the same IOB must share the same clock and reset signal.
Designers can specify the following UCF constraint:

```
INST <register_instance_name> IOB = TRUE|FALSE;
```

The other way is to use a MAP "Pack I/O Registers into IOBs" property, which applies globally to all IOs. The command line MAP option is –pr {i|o|b}. "i" is only for input registers, "o" only for output registers, and "b" is for both input and output.
In most cases inferring DDR registers in the IOB requires an explicit instantiation of a primitive. However, the following example might work in a few cases.

```verilog
module ddr_iob( input clk,reset,
          input ddr_in, output  ddr_out);
reg q1, q2;
assign ddr_out = q1 & q2;
always @ (posedge clk, posedge reset)
   if (areset)
     q1 <=1'b0;
   else
     q1 <= ddr_in;
always @ (negedge clk, posedge reset)
   if (areset)
     q2 <=1'b0;
   else
     q2 <= ddr_in;
endmodule
```

Inferring latches

Latches are inferred from incomplete conditional expressions. For example, when *case* or *if* statements do not cover all possible input conditions, synthesis tool might infer a latch to hold the output if a new output value is not assigned. Xilinx XST will also produce a warning. Latch inference is shown in the following example.

```verilog
module latch( input  clk, input latch_en, latch_data,
          output reg latch_out);
```

```
    always @ (latch_en)
       if (latch_en)
          latch_out = latch_data;
endmodule // latch
```

In many cases latches are inferred unintentionally due to poor coding style practices. One way to avoid unintentional latches due to incomplete sensitivity list is to use Verilog-2001 implicit event expression list @(*) or @* in the *always* blocks. Also, always assign the default *case* or final *else* statement to a "don't care" or other default value.

In general, it is recommended to avoid using latches in FPGA designs. Tip #50 provides more information on problems related to using latches, and different methods of porting them.

Tri-stated buffers

The following is an example of how to infer a tri-stated output buffer in Xilinx FPGAs.

```
module tri_buffer( output tri_out, input tri_en, tri_in );
     assign tri_out = tri_en ? tri_in : 1'bz;
endmodule // tri_buffer
```

It is possible to use more complex expressions to infer tri-stated buffers. However, it's not recommended to mix tri-stated buffers with other logic, such as conditional `if` and `case` statements. The following is an example of not recommended way of inferring tri-stated buffers.

```
module tri_buffer2( output reg tri_out,
   input tri_en1, tri_en2, tri_in);
     always @ (*)
        if ( tri_en1 & tri_en2 )
           tri_out = 1'bz;
        else
           tri_out<=tri_in;
endmodule // tri_buffer2
```

Another recommendation is to include logic that infers tri-stated buffers at the design top-level.

Tip #54 provides more examples on using tri-stated buffers in FPGA designs.

Inferring complex arithmetic blocks

It is recommended not to attempt to infer complex arithmetic blocks, such as multipliers and dividers. That particular implementation might work, but it unlikely to be portable across different FPGA architectures and synthesis tools. Xilinx supports very configurable multiplier, divider, and other arithmetic cores that can be generated using CoreGen utility.

17
MIXED USE OF VERILOG AND VHDL

The need to use both Verilog and VHDL languages in the same design arises in several situations. A design team might decide for various reasons to switch to another language for the next project, while reusing some of the existing functional modules. Most often, it is the integration of a 3'rd party IP core written in a different language that results in a mixed language design. One example is Xilinx Microblaze processor, and most of its peripherals, which are written in VHDL, and need to be integrated into a Verilog project.

Xilinx XST synthesis tool and ISIM simulator provide full support of mixed Verilog/VHDL projects.

The following is a simple example that illustrates mixed use of Verilog and VHDL. The module `lfsr_counter` is written in VHDL, and instantiated in the module `top` written in Verilog. Verilog modules can also be instantiated in VHDL.

```verilog
// Verilog implementation of the top module
module top(input enable, rst, clk,
           output reg done_qo);
   always @(posedge clk, posedge rst)
     if(rst)
       done_qo <= 'b0;
     else
       done_qo <= lfsr_done;

   lfsr_counter lfsr_counter(
     enable , rst, clk, lfsr_done);
endmodule // top
```

```vhdl
-- VHDL implementation of the lfsr_counter
library ieee;
use ieee.std_logic_1164.all;
use ieee.std_logic_unsigned.all;

entity lfsr_counter is
   port (
     ce , rst, clk : in std_logic;
     lfsr_done : out std_logic);
end lfsr_counter;
```

```vhdl
architecture imp_lfsr_counter of lfsr_counter is
    signal lfsr: std_logic_vector (10 downto 0);
    signal d0, lfsr_equal: std_logic;
begin
    d0 <= lfsr(10) xnor lfsr(8) ;

    process(lfsr) begin
      if(lfsr = x"359") then
        lfsr_equal <= '1';
      else
        lfsr_equal <= '0';
      end if;
    end process;

    process (clk,rst) begin
      if (rst = '1') then
        lfsr <= b"00000000000";
        lfsr_done <= '0';
      elsif (clk'EVENT and clk = '1') then
        lfsr_done <= lfsr_equal;
        if (ce = '1') then
          if(lfsr_equal = '1') then
            lfsr <= b"00000000000";
          else
            lfsr <= lfsr(9 downto 0) & d0;
          end if;
        end if;
      end if;
    end process;
end architecture imp_lfsr_counter;
```

Source code and project files for this example can be found in the accompanied web site.

As long as all boundary rules are met, the process of mixing Verilog and VHDL modules is straightforward. Each synthesis tool might have slightly different rules and limitations. Xilinx XST user guide defines the following rules:

- Mixing of VHDL and Verilog is restricted to design unit (cell) instantiation only. A VHDL design can instantiate a Verilog module, and a Verilog design can instantiate a VHDL entity. Any other kind of mixing between VHDL and Verilog is not supported.

- In a VHDL design, a restricted subset of VHDL types, generics and ports is allowed on the boundary to a Verilog module. Similarly, in a Verilog design, a restricted subset of Verilog types, parameters and ports is allowed on the boundary to a VHDL entity or configuration.

- Configuration specification, direct instantiation and component configurations are not supported for a Verilog module instantiation in VHDL.
- VHDL and Verilog libraries are logically unified
- To instantiate a VHDL entity in the Verilog module, declare a module name with the same as name as the VHDL entity that you want to instantiate, and perform a normal Verilog instantiation. The name is case sensitive.
- To instantiate a Verilog module in a VHDL design, declare a VHDL component with the same name as the Verilog module to be instantiated, and instantiate the Verilog component as if you were instantiating a VHDL component.

Note that simulating mixed language designs with commercial simulators might require separate license.

18

VERILOG VERSIONS: VERILOG-95, VERILOG-2001, AND SYSTEM VERILOG

Verilog started out as a proprietary hardware modeling language in 1984 and enjoyed considerable success. In 1990, Cadence Design Systems transferred the language into the public domain as part of the efforts to compete with VHDL. In 1995, Verilog became an IEEE standard 1364-1995, commonly known as Verilog-95.

Verilog-95 had been evolving, and in -2001 IEEE released another standard, 1364-2001, also known as Verilog-2001. It contained a lot of extensions that cover the shortcomings of the original standard, and introduced several new language features. In 2005 IEEE published a 1364-2005 standard, known as Verilog 2005. It included several specification corrections and clarifications, and a few new language features.

IEEE published several SystemVerilog standards. The latest one is 1800-2009, which was published in 2009. SystemVerilog is a superset of Verilog, and contains features intended for better support of design verification, improving simulation performance, and making the language more powerful and easy to use.

Verilog-2001 is a predominant Verilog version used by the majority of FPGA designers, and supported by all synthesis and simulation tools.

Verilog-2001

Xilinx XST and other FPGA synthesis tools have an option to enable or disable Verilog-2001 constructs. In XST it's done by using *-verilog2001* command line option. In Synplify, use "*set_option -vlog_std v2001*" command.

The following is a brief overview of some of the most important differences between Verilog-95 and Verilog-2001.

Verilog-2001 added explicit support for two's complement signed arithmetic. In Verilog-95 developers needed to hand-code signed operations by using bit-level manipulations. The same function under Verilog-2001 can be described by using built-in operators and keywords.

Auto-extending 'bz and 'bx assignments. In Verilog-95 the following code
```
wire [63:0] mydata = 'bz;
```

will assign the value of z to mydata[31:0], and zero to mydata[63:32].

Verilog-2001 will extend 'bz and 'bx assignments to the full width of the variable.

A generate construct allows Verilog-2001 to control instance and statement instantiation using if/else/case control. Using generate construct, developers can easily instantiate an array of instances with correct connectivity. The following are several examples of using generate construct.

```
// An array of instances
module adder_array(input [63:0] a,b, output [63:0] sum);
generate
genvar ix;
   for (ix=0; ix<=7; ix=ix+1) begin : adder_array
      adder add (a[8*ix+7 -: 8],
         b[8*ix+7 -: 8],
         sum[8*ix+7 -: 8]);
   end
endgenerate
endmodule // adder_array

module adder(input [7:0] a,b, output [7:0] sum );
   assign sum = a + b;
endmodule // adder

// If...else statements
module adder_array(input [63:0] a,b, output [63:0] sum);
parameter WIDTH = 4;
generate
if (WIDTH < 64) begin : adder_gen2
   assign sum[63 -: (64-WIDTH)] = 'b0;

   adder # (WIDTH) adder1 (a[WIDTH-1 -: WIDTH],
      b[WIDTH-1 -: WIDTH],sum[WIDTH-1 -: WIDTH]);
end
else begin : adder_default
   adder # (64) adder1 (a, b, sum);
end
endgenerate
endmodule // adder_array

// case statement
module adder_array(input [63:0] a,b, output [63:0] sum);
generate
case (WIDTH)
   1: begin : case1
      assign sum[63 -: 63] = 'b0;
```

```
      adder #(WIDTH) adder1 (a[0], b[0], sum[0]);
    end
    default: begin : def
      adder # (64) adder1 (a, b, sum);
    end
endcase
endgenerate
endmodule // adder_array
```

Verilog-2001 adds support for multi-dimensional arrays. Synthesis tools place several restrictions on synthesis of multi-dimensional arrays. For example, XST supports arrays of up to two dimensions. It doesn't allow selecting more than one element of an array at one time. Multi-dimensional arrays cannot be passed to tasks or functions.

The following code example describes an array of 256 x 16 wire elements, 4-bit wide each:

```
wire [3:0] multi_dim_array [0:255][0:15];
```

More concise port declaration.

```
// Verilog-95
module adder(a,b,sum);
    input [7:0] a,b;
    output [7:0] sum;
assign sum = a + b;
endmodule // adder


// Verilog-2001
module adder(input [7:0] a,b, output [7:0] sum );
    assign sum = a + b;
endmodule // adder
```

Verilog-2001 adds support for exponential or power operator "**". It's convenient in many cases, for example, for determining memory depth calculations. Synthesis tools support exponential with several restrictions. XST requires that both operands are constants, with the second one is non-negative. The values x and z are not allowed. If the first operand is 2, the second can be variable.

The following are code examples of using the exponent.

```
localparam BASE = 3,
           EXP = 4;
assign exp_out2 = BASE**EXP;
// this code is synthesized as a shift register
assign exp_out1 = 2**exp_in;
```

Comma-separated and combinational sensitivity list.

```
// Verilog-95
always @(a or b);
    sum = a + b;
// Verilog-2001
always @(a,b);
    sum = a + b;
always @(*);
    sum = a + b;
```

Required net declarations.

Verilog-95 requires that all 1-bit nets, that are not ports, and are driven by a continuous assignment, must be declared. That requirement is removed in Verilog-2001. Instead, the Verilog-2001 standard adds a new `default_nettype` compiler directive. If that directive is assigned to "none," all 1-bit nets must be declared.

```
// Verilog-95
wire sum;
assign sum = a + b;
// Verilog-2001
wire sum; // not required
assign sum = a + b;
`default_nettype none
wire sum; // must be declared
assign sum = a + b;
```

SystemVerilog

SystemVerilog standard is designed to be a unified hardware design, specification, and verification language. It's a large standard that consists of several parts: design specification methods, embedded assertion language, functional coverage, object oriented programming, and constraints. The main goal of the SystemVerilog is to create a unified design and verification environment by taking the best features and building on the strengths of Verilog, VHDL, and hardware verification languages. SystemVerilog enables a major leap in productivity by combining a diverse set of tools and methods into one, removing fragmentation of a system design between software and hardware engineers, and sharing the results.

SystemVerilog contains several extensions to the existing Verilog specifications that are designed to reduce the number of lines of code, encourage design reuse, and improve simulation performance. SystemVerilog is also fully backwards compatible with previous Verilog versions.

SystemVerilog is supported by most of the commercial simulators: ModelSim, VCS, NCSim, and others. Synthesizable portion of the SystemVerilog standard is supported by

Synplify and Precision synthesis tools. At the time of writing of this book, Xilinx XST doesn't provide any SystemVerilog support.

Design synthesis and verification environments are often written using both SystemVerilog and Verilog languages. One approach used in large designs is illustrated in the following figure.

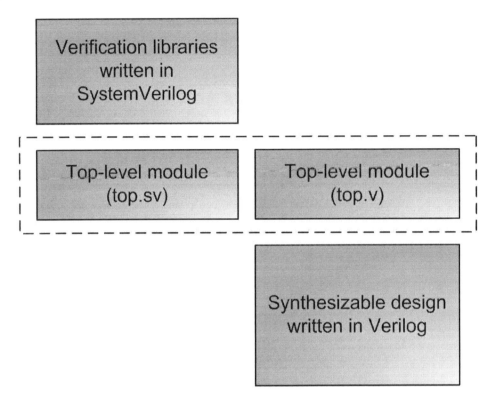

Figure 1: Mixed use of Verilog and SystemVerilog

The top-level module is implemented in both Verilog and SystemVerilog. That makes it compatible with all FPGA synthesis tools that don't support SystemVerilog. The design can be readily integrated with the verification libraries written in SystemVerilog.

The following is a brief overview of some of the features unique to SystemVerilog.

Data types

SystemVerilog defines the following new data types:

Table 1: SystemVerilog data types

Data type	*Description*
int	32-bit signed integer, 2-state

shortint	16-bit signed integer, 2-state
longint	64-bit signed integer, 2-state
bit	User defined vector size, 2-state
byte	8-bit signed integer, 2-state
logic	User defined vector size, 2-state

2-state data types accept 0 and 1 values.

4-state data types accept 0,1, z, and x values.

SystemVerilog provides the ability to create a custom grouping of signals and variables, similar to C programming language. It defines the following features to support grouping: Typedefs, Enumerated types, Structures, Unions, and Static casting.

Below are several examples of SystemVerilog data types.

```
bit x;
enum {STATE1, STATE2, STATE3} state;
typedef enum { red=0,green,yellow } Colors;
integer a,b;
a = green*3 // 3 is assigned to a
b = yellow + green; // 3 is assigned to b
struct {
   bit [31:0] characteristic;
   bit [31:0] mantissa;
     } float_num;
float_num.characteristic = 32'h1234_5678;
float_num.mantissa = 32'h0000_0010;
typedef union{
   int u1;
   shortint u2;
} my_union;
```

SystemVerilog provides strongly typed capabilities to avoid multiple interpretations and race conditions that plague Verilog designs.

Port connectivity

SystemVerilog provides ".name" and implicit ".*" methods to describe port connectivity. That allows significant code compaction.

```
// Verilog
adder add (a,b,sum);

// SystemVerilog
adder add (.a,.b,.sum);
```

```
adder add (.*);
```

Interfaces and Modports

The `interface` and `modport` SystemVerilog constructs enable encapsulation of port lists and interconnect between module instances. The following is a simple example:

```
// Define the interface
interface adder_if;
    logic [7:0] a, b;
    logic [7:0] sum;
endinterface: adder_if

module top;
    // Instantiate the interface
    adder_if adder_if1();
    adder_if adder_if2();

    // Connect the interface to the module instance
    adder add1 (adder_if1);
    adder add2 (adder_if2);
endmodule
module adder(adder_if if);
    // access the interface
    assign if.sum = if.a + if.b;
endmodule // adder
```

Object Oriented Programming (OOP)

SystemVerilog enables better support for Object Oriented Programming (OOP). OOP raises the level of abstraction by building data structures with self-contained functionality that allows data encapsulation, hiding implementation details, and enhances the re-usability of the code.

The following table shows SystemVerilog constructs and structures that enable OOP.

Table 2: SystemVerilog OOP structure

	Verilog	*SystemVerilog*
Block definition	Module	Module, class
Block instance	Instance	Object
Block name	Instance name	Object handle
Data types	Registers and wires	Variables
Functionality	Tasks, functions, always block, initial block	Tasks, functions

Constraints, Coverage, and Randomization

SystemVerilog provides extensive support for coverage-driven verification, directed and constrained random testbench development.

Assertions

Assertions augment functional coverage by providing multiple observation points within the design. Usually, both RTL designers and verification engineers instrument the design with assertions. Assertions can be placed both inside the RTL code, which makes updates and management easier, or outside, to keep synthesizable and behavioral parts of the code separate. SystemVerilog provides assertion specification that is used in verification environments of many ASIC designs. SystemVerilog assertions can be applied to the following elements of a design: variable declarations, conditional statements, internal interfaces, and state machines.

Assertions are supported by several commercial simulators, for example ModeSim and VCS.

A small subset of the SystemVerilog assertions specification allows synthesizable assertions. Unfortunately, only a handful of FPGA design tools support synthesizable assertions. One of them is Synopsys Identify Pro that has assertion synthesis and debug capabilities.

19
HDL CODE EDITORS

Source code editors have features specifically designed to speed up, simplify, and automate creation, browsing, and searching of the source code. Choosing the right source code editor can make a significant impact on personal productivity. Important features of a code editor are: syntax highlighting, auto complete, bracket matching, and management of large projects. Other useful features include: interfacing with different tools such as source control, build manager, or script interpreters, cross platform support, and customizations. Because Verilog and VHDL are not as widely used as programming and scripting languages such as C, Java, and Perl, not all source code editors support them.

The choice of a code editor is mainly driven by personal preferences, availability of specific features or lack of thereof, and operating system support. The following is a brief overview and basic comparison of some of the popular code editors that support Verilog and VHDL languages.

Vi/Vim

URL: http://vim.sourceforge.net
OS: Unix/Linux, Windows, Mac
License: open source

Vi is a lightweight command-line based editor. Vim is an extended version of Vi, and stands for "Vi Improved." Vi/Vim is designed to perform all editing functions without using a mouse or menus, which allows for very fast code editing. Some Vim versions, for example gVim, have basic GUI support.

Vi/Vim macros and plug-ins enable a high level of customization. There are several Vim macros for Verilog and VHDL syntax highlighting.

Emacs/XEmacs

URL: http://www.gnu.org/software/emacs

http://www.veripool.org/wiki/verilog-mode
OS: Unix/Linux, Windows, Mac
License: open source

Emacs is another venerable code editor that has been in use for over three decades. Both Emacs and Vi editors are undisputed leaders in terms of adoption by ASIC and FPGA developers on Linux platforms.

XEmacs is a version of Emacs that offers a GUI toolbar, and other features.

Both Emacs and Vi were originally developed for Unix, and later ported for Windows and Mac operating systems.

A popular Verilog mode for Emacs is available on Veripool.org. It provides context-sensitive highlighting, auto indenting, and macro expansion capabilities. It supports all Verilog and SystemVerilog versions. It is written and actively maintained by Michael McNamara and Wilson Snyder.

UltraEdit

URL: http://www.ultraedit.com
OS: Windows, Linux, Mac
License: commercial
Vendor: IDM Computer Solutions, Inc

UltraEdit is a popular and highly acclaimed text editor. Its main features include: macros, tag lists, syntax highlighting, and autocomplete files for different programming languages, including Verilog and VHDL, project management, regular expressions for search-and-replace, remote editing of files via FTP, integrated scripting language, file encryption/decryption, and many more.

Crimson Editor

URL: http://www.crimsoneditor.com
OS: Windows
License: open source (GPL)

Crimson Editor is a source code editor for Windows. It features a small installation size, fast loading time, and syntax highlighting for many programming languages, including Verilog and VHDL.

Notepad++

URL: http://notepad-plus-plus.org
License: open source (GPL)
OS: Windows

Notepad++ is a popular code editor that supports Verilog and VHDL syntax highlighting. It is written in C++, and designed for high execution speed.

IDE Code Editors

Most of the IDE tools used during FPGA design have an integrated code editor. Examples are Xilinx ISE, Mentor ModelSim, and Synopsys Synplify. Integrated code editors offer unique features such as hyperlinking, and excellent project management capabilities.

20
FPGA CLOCKING RESOURCES

This Tip uses Xilinx Virtex-6 as an example to overview different types of FPGA clocking resources: dedicated clock routing, clock buffers, and clock managers.

FPGAs provide dedicated low-skew routing resources for clocks. A skew is defined as the difference in arrival times of a clock edge to synchronous logic elements connected to it. Not only can a skew impact the achievable clock speed of a circuit but, in the worst case, it can cause incorrect operation of the circuit. Low-skew clock routing can also be used for non-clock signals, such as reset or high-fanout controls.

Xilinx FPGA die is divided into several clock regions as is illustrated in the following figure.

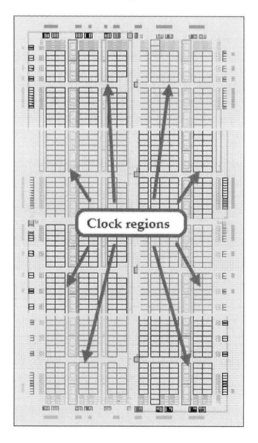

Figure 1: Eight clock regions

Virtex-6 FPGAs have between six to 18 clock regions, depending on the device.

There are three types of clocks: global, which can drive synchronous logic on the entire die; regional, which can drive logic in specific and adjacent regions; and IO, which can serve the logic specific to that IO.

Tradeoffs for selecting clock type are performance and availability. IO clocks are the fastest, but have a very limited amount of logic they can drive. Global clocks are easier to use, because they can reach the entire die. However, there are more regional clocks than global clocks.

Clock buffers

Xilinx provides several clock buffer primitives to support different clock types, listed in the following table:

Table 1: Clock buffers for different clock types

Buffer type	*Primitive*
Single-ended input buffer	IBUFG, BUFGP*
Differential input buffer	IBUFDS, IBUFGDS, IBUFGDS_DIFF_OUT
Global buffer	BUFG, BUFGP*, BUFGCE, BUFGMUX, BUFGCTRL
Regional buffer	BUFR, BUFH, BUFHCE
Local clock buffer	BUFIO

*BUFGP includes both IBUFG and BUFG

Synthesis tools will automatically infer BUFG or BUFGP primitive for simple clocks, as illustrated in the following example.

```
module clock_buffer_inference(input clk, reset,
        input data_in,
        output reg data_out);
always @(posedge clk, posedge reset)
   if (reset)
     data_out <= 0;
   else
     data_out <= data_in;
endmodule // clock_buffer_inference
```

Design summary of XST synthesis report indicates that BUFGP clock buffer was used.

```
=============================
* Design Summary
=============================
```

```
Top Level Output File Name : clock_buffer_inference.ngc
Primitive and Black Box Usage:
------------------------------
# FlipFlops/Latches       : 1
#      FDC                : 1
# Clock Buffers           : 1
#      BUFGP              : 1
# IO Buffers              : 3
#      IBUF               : 2
#      OBUF               : 1
```

It is possible to disable automatic insertion of a global buffer. XST provides "Add I/O Buffers (-iobuf)" option to enable or disable automatic global buffer insertion.

Regional and local clocks, differential clocks, and circuits with clock-enable signal require explicit instantiation of appropriate clock buffer primitives.

Mixed-mode Clock Manager

Mixed-mode Clock Manager (MMCM) is a clock management primitive in Xilinx Virtex-6 devices. Its main functions are support for clock network deskew, frequency synthesis, phase shifting, and jitter reduction. MMCM leverages features from PLL and Digital Clock Manager (DCM) primitives in previous Xilinx FPGA families. The following figure shows a detailed MMCM block diagram.

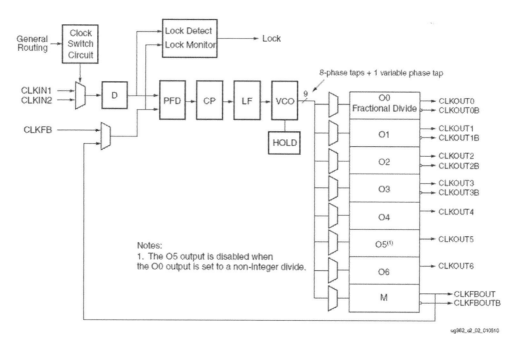

Figure 2: MMCM block diagram (Source: Xilinx User Guide 362)

At the heart of the MMCM is a voltage-controlled oscillator (VCO) with a frequency ranging between 400 MHz and 1600 MHz. VCO is connected to programmable frequency dividers and eight equally-spaced output phases (0°, 45°, 90°, 135°, 180°, 225°, 270°, and 315°). MMCM also supports dynamic, fine-grained phase shifting.

The MMCM can also serve as a frequency synthesizer for a wide range of frequencies and clock duty cycles.

The following is an example of using MMCM.

```verilog
module clock_mmcm(input clk, reset,
          input data_in,
          output reg data_out);
   wire clk_i,locked,clkfb;
   clk_mmcm mmcm(
     .CLK_IN1             (clk),
     .CLKFB_IN            (clkfb),
     .CLK_OUT1            (clk_i),
     .CLKFB_OUT           (clkfb),
     .RESET               (reset),
     .LOCKED              (locked));
always @(posedge clk_i, posedge locked)
if (locked)
   data_out <= 0;
else
   data_out <= data_in;
endmodule // clock_mmcm
```

Design summary of XST synthesis report shows that the circuit used MMCM, IBUFG, and BUFG clocking resources.

```
============================
*   Design Summary
============================
Top Level Output File Name          : clock_mmcm.ngc
Primitive and Black Box Usage:
--------------------------
# FlipFlops/Latches        : 1
#       FDC                : 1
# Clock Buffers            : 1
#       BUFG               : 1
# IO Buffers               : 4
#       IBUF               : 2
#       IBUFG              : 1
#       OBUF               : 1
# Others                   : 1
#       MMCM_ADV           : 1
```

MMCM is a highly configurable primitive. Instead of manual instantiation of MMCM, it is recommended to use Clock Wizard in Xilinx CoreGen tool to create a customized clock manager instance. Clock Wizard provides an easy-to-use interface to configure attributes, and include all the necessary clock buffers, which ensures correct use of the MMCM primitive.

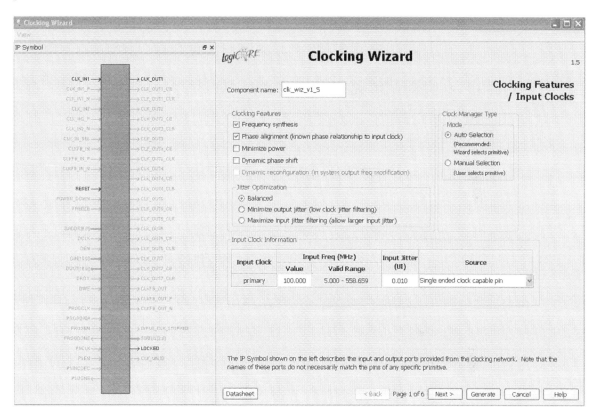

Figure 3: Xilinx CoreGen Clocking Wizard

Digital Clock Manager

Digital Clock Manager (DCM) is a clock management primitive used in Spartan-6, Virtex-5, and earlier Xilinx FPGA families. Its main functions are eliminating clock insertion delay, frequency synthesis, and phase shift. DCM has a very different design than MMCM or PLL. DCM block diagram is shown in the following figure.

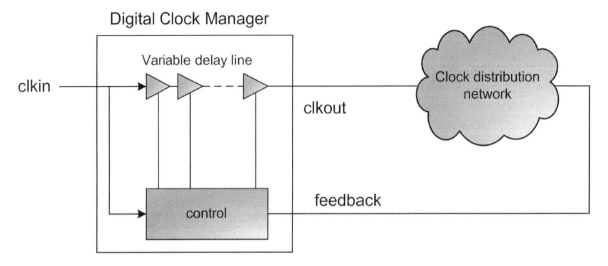

Figure 4: DCM block diagram

The control module inside the DCM compares the phases of the input clock and the feedback from the clock distribution network to estimate the delay. Then, the control module adjusts the delay between the input and output clocks using a variable delay line to achieve phase alignment.

Delay removal is shown in a timing report as a negative delay from the output to input clock of a DCM, as is illustrated in the following figure.

```
Maximum Data Path at Slow Process Corner: clk to data_out
  Location              Delay type        Delay(ns)  Physical Resource
                                                     Logical Resource(s)
  -----------------------------------------------------------------------
  L4.I                  Tiopi                0.904   clk
                                                     clk
                                                     dcm/clkin1_buf
                                                     ProtoCompl.IMUX.1
  BUFIO2_X0Y23.I        net (fanout=1)       0.426   dcm/clkin1
  BUFIO2_X0Y23.DIVCLK   Tbufcko_DIVCLK       0.170   SP6_BUFIO_INSERT_ML_BUFIO2_0
                                                     SP6_BUFIO_INSERT_ML_BUFIO2_0
  DCM_X0Y2.CLKIN        net (fanout=1)       0.638   dcm/dcm_sp_inst_ML_NEW_DIVCLK
  DCM_X0Y2.CLK0         Tdmcko_CLK          -1.199   dcm/dcm_sp_inst
                                                     dcm/dcm_sp_inst
  BUFGMUX_X2Y3.I0       net (fanout=2)       0.652   clkfb
  BUFGMUX_X2Y3.O        Tgi0o                0.209   dcm/clkout1_buf
                                                     dcm/clkout1_buf
  OLOGIC_X13Y2.CLK0     net (fanout=1)       1.436   clk_i
  -----------------------------------------------------------------------
  Total                                      3.436ns (0.084ns logic, 3.352ns route)
```

negative delay

Figure 5: DCM negative delay

Clock multiplexing

Xilinx provides a BUFGMUX primitive that can multiplex between two global clock sources. It also ensures a glitch-free operation when the input clock selection is changed.

Resources

[1] Xilinx Virtex-6 FPGA Clocking Resources, User Guide UG362
http://www.xilinx.com/support/documentation/user_guides/ug362.pdf

21
DESIGNING A CLOCKING SCHEME

Designing a clocking scheme in complex FPGA designs is a challenging task that requires a good knowledge of clocking resources supported by the target FPGA and their limitations, an understanding of the tradeoffs between different design techniques, and the following of good design practices. An incorrectly designed or suboptimal clocking scheme can lead to poor design performance in the best case, or random and hard-to-find failures in the worst.

Examples of the FPGA clocking resources knowledge include the amount of different resources in a target FPGA, clock types (such as regional and global), frequency limitations and jitter characteristics of different clock managers, and the maximum number of clocks that can be used in a single clock region.

This Tip discusses options to implement different parts of the clocking scheme and provides an overview of some of the recommended design practices.

Using dedicated clocking resources

An internally generated clock is an output of a combinatorial logic or a register, as shown in the following figure.

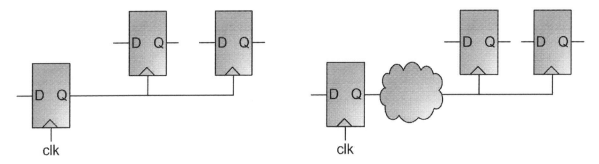

Figure 1: internally generated clocks

A clock generated by a combinatorial logic might have glitches, which can be falsely interpreted as a valid clock edge, and cause a functional problem in a design. Therefore, never use an output of combinatorial logic as a clock.

Internally generated clocks use general routing resources and, therefore, have longer delays compared with the dedicated clock routing. The consequence is additional clock skew, which makes the process of meeting timing more difficult. That becomes even more important if a lot of logic is using that internal clock.

As a general rule, avoid using internally generated clocks and use dedicated clocking resources whenever possible.

An overview of dedicated clocking resources provided by Xilinx FPGAs is provided in Tip #20.

Using a single clock edge

With the exception of few special circuits, such as capturing double data rate (DDR) data, always use an either positive or negative clock edge for registering data. One problem with using both edges is the duty cycle of the clock, which might not always be 50%.

Using differential clocks

It is recommended to use differential clocks for high frequencies. As a rule of thumb, high frequency is generally considered to be above 100MHz. The main advantage of differential clocks over single-ended counterparts is common-mode noise rejection, which provides better noise immunity. Differential clocks with PECL, LVPECL, and LVDS signal levels are popular choices to clock high-speed logic.

Xilinx FPGAs provide several dedicated primitives to use for differential clocking: IBUFDS, IBUFGDS, IBUFGDS_DIFF_OUT, OBUFDS, OBUFTDS, and others.

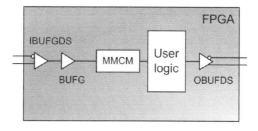

Figure 2: Using dedicated clocking resources

Using gated clocks

Clock gating is a technique that disables clock inputs to registers and other synchronous elements in the design using control signal. Clock gating is very effective in reducing power consumption and widely used in ASIC designs. However, using gated clocks in FPGA designs is discouraged. Tip #49 provides more information and examples on gated clocks and discusses some of the conversion techniques.

Using clock signal as a control, reset, or data input

It is not recommended to use clock signal as control, reset, or data input to general-purpose logic. The following are Verilog examples of such circuits.

```verilog
module clock_schemes(input clk1,clk2,clk3,clk4,clk5,
          input data_in,
 output reg data_out1,data_out2,data_out3,data_out4,data_out5,
data_out6);
  wire data_from_clock, reset_from_clock, control_from_clock;
  // Clock used as data input
  assign data_from_clock = clk1;
  always @(posedge clk1)
    data_out1 <= ~data_out1;

  always @(posedge clk2)
    data_out2 <= ~data_out2 & data_from_clock;
  // Clock used as reset input
  assign reset_from_clock = clk3;
  always @(posedge clk3)
    data_out3 <= ~data_out2;

  always @(posedge clk4, posedge reset_from_clock)
    if (reset_from_clock)
      data_out4 <= 0;
    else
      data_out4 <= data_in;

  // Clock is used as control
  assign control_from_clock = clk5;
  always @(posedge clk5)
    data_out5 <= ~data_out5;

  always @(*)
    data_out6 = control_from_clock ? data_in : data_out6;
endmodule // clock_schemes
```

Source synchronous clocks

Many external devices interfacing with FPGA use a source synchronous clock along with the data. If the interface is running at high speed, it might require the calibration of the clock edge to capture data at the center of the data window. To implement dynamic calibration, Xilinx MMCM primitive provides a dynamic reconfiguration port (DRP), which allows programmatic phase shifting of the clock. The following figure illustrates that the output clock from the MMCM is shifted such that the rising edge of the clock samples the data in the middle of the window.

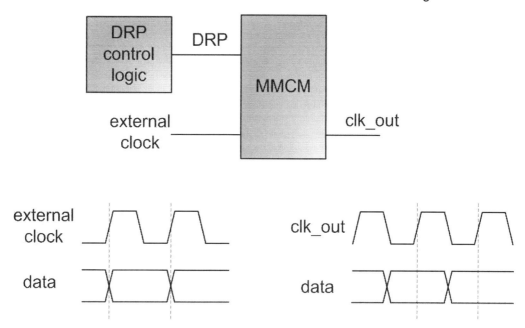

Figure 3: Using phase shifting of the clock

Clock multiplexing

Multiplexing clocks from several sources is required in designs that operate the same logic from different clock sources. One example is Ethernet MAC, which uses 2.5MHz, 25MHz, or 125MHz clocks depending on the negotiated speed of 10Mbs, 100Mbs, or 1Gbs, respectively. Another example is a power-on built-in self test (BIST) circuit, which uses a clock different from the one used during a normal operation.

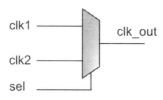

Figure 4: Clock multiplexing

It is recommended to use a dedicated clocking resource to implement clock multiplexing, to ensure that input and output clocks are using dedicated clock lines instead of general purpose logic. The input clock frequencies could be unrelated to each other. Using combinatorial logic to implement a multiplexor can generate a glitch on the clock line at the time of the switch. A glitch on the clock line is hazardous to the whole system because it could be interpreted as a valid clock edge by some registers but be missed by others.

Xilinx provides a BUFGMUX primitive that can multiplex between two global clock sources. It also ensures a glitch-free operation when the input clock selection is changed. Clock multiplexing requires careful timing constraints of all paths from an input to an output clock of the multiplexer.

Detecting clock absence

One method of detecting clock absence is to use an oversampling technique by another higher speed clock. The disadvantage of this method is the availability of another clock. An alternative method is to use the `locked` output from Xilinx MMCM primitive, as shown in the following figure.

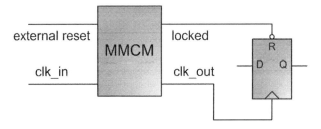

Figure 5: Using locked output to detect clock absence

22

CLOCK DOMAIN CROSSING

Most FPGA designs utilize more than one clock. An example of a multi-clock design is illustrated in the following figure.

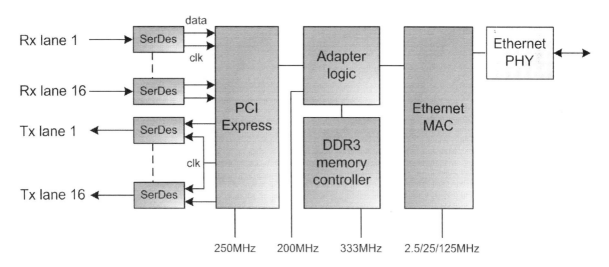

Figure 1: An example of a multi-clock design

The design implements a PCI Express to Ethernet adapter and is shown to illustrate the potential complexity of a clocking scheme. It has a 16-lane PCI Express, tri-mode Ethernet, DDR3 memory controller, and the bridge logic. 16 Serializer/Deserializer (SerDes) modules embedded in FPGA are used to receive PCI Express data, one for each lane. Each SerDes outputs a recovered clock synchronized to the data. A shared clock is used for all PCI Express transmit lanes. Tri-mode Ethernet MAC requires 2.5MHz, 25 MHz, and 125MHz clocks to operate at 10Mbs, 100Mbs, or 1Gbs speed, respectively.

The memory controller uses a 333MHz clock, and the bridge logic utilizes a 200MHz clock. In total, there are 23 clocks in the design. Each clock domain crossing – from PCI Express to bridge, bridge to Ethernet, and bridge to memory controller – requires using a different technique to ensure reliable operation of the design.

Metastability

Metastability is the main design problem to be considered for implementing data transmission between different clock domains.

Metastability is defined as a transitory state of a register which is neither logic '0' nor logic '1'. A register might enter a metastable state if the setup and hold timing requirements are not met. In a metastable state a register is set to an intermediate voltage level, which is neither a "zero" nor a "one" logic state. Small voltage and temperature perturbations can return the register to a valid state. The transition time and resulting logic level are indeterminate. In some cases, the register output can oscillate between the two valid states. Metastability conditions arise in designs with multiple clocks, or asynchronous inputs, and result in data corruption.

The following are some of the circuit examples that can cause metastability.

Example 1

A state machine may enter an illegal state if some of the inputs to the next state logic are driven by a register in a different clock domain. This is illustrated in the following figure.

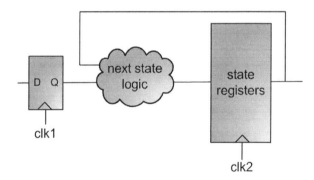

Figure 2: State machine enters an incorrect state

The exact problem that may occur due to metastability depends on the state machine implementation. If the state machine is implemented as one-hot – that is, there is exactly one register for each state – then the state machine may transition to a valid, but incorrect, state.

Example 2

An input data to a Xilinx BRAM primitive and the BRAM itself are in different clock domains.

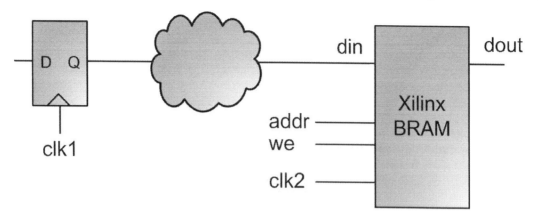

Figure 3: BRAM and its inputs are in different clock domains

If the input data violates the setup of hold requirements of a BRAM, that may result in data corruption. The same applies to other BRAM inputs, such as address and write enable.

Example 3

The output of a register in one clock domain is used as a synchronous reset to a register in another clock domain. The data output of the right register, shown in the figure below, can be corrupted.

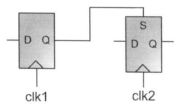

Figure 4: Metastability due to synchronous reset

Example 4

Data coherency problem may occur when a data bus is sampled by registers in different clock domains. This case is illustrated in the following figure.

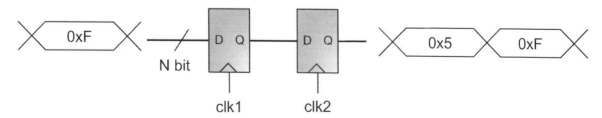

Figure 5: Data coherency

There is no guarantee that all the data outputs will be valid in the same clock. It might take several clocks for all the bits to settle.

Calculating Mean Time Between Failure (MTBF)

Using metastable signals can cause intermittent logic errors. Mean time between failure, or MTBF, is a metric that provides an estimate of the average time interval between two successive failures of a specific synchronous element. Synchronization circuits, such as using the two registers described in Tip #23, help increase the MTBF and reduce the probability of en error to practical levels, but they do not completely eliminate it.

There are several practical methods for measuring the metastability capture window described in the literature. The one applicable to Xilinx FPGA is Xilinx Application Note XAPP094 [1].

However, MTBF can be only determined using statistical methods. A commonly used MTBF equation is:

$$MTBF = \frac{exp(T * \tau)}{f1 * f2 * To}$$

f_1 and f_2 are the frequencies of two clock domains.
The product $T*\tau$ in the exponent describes the speed with which the metastable condition is resolved.
T_o is the duration of a critical time window during which the synchronous element is likely to become metastable.
T_o, T, and τ are circuit specific.
As an example, for f_1=1MHz, f_2=1KHz, T_0=30ps, $T*\tau = 10$,
MTBF = exp(10)/(1MHz * 1KHz * 30ps) = 734,216 sec = 204 hours.

Clock Domain Crossing (CDC) analysis

In complex multi-clock designs, the task of correctly detecting and verifying all clock domain crossing is not simple. Design problems due to CDC are typically not detected in a functional simulation. Unfortunately, there are only a few adequate tools from the functionality and cost perspective that perform automatic identification and verification of the CDC schemes used in FPGA designs.

Mentor Graphics Questa software provides a comprehensive CDC verification solution, including RTL analysis, identification of all clocks and clock domain crossings, and generation of assertions and metastability models.

The Xilinx XST synthesis tool provides a `-cross_clock_analysis` option to perform inter-clock domain analysis during timing optimization.

Resources

[1] Metastable Recovery in Virtex-II FPGAs, Xilinx Application Note XAPP094
http://www.xilinx.com/support/documentation/application_notes/xapp094.pdf

23

CLOCK SYNCHRONIZATION CIRCUITS

Synchronization circuit captures an asynchronous input signal and produces an output, which is synchronized to a clock edge. Synchronization circuits are used to implement the proper clock domain crossing of a signal, and prevent setup and hold time violation. The choice of a circuit depends on different data and clock characteristics: the number of signals that cross the clock domains, how those signals are used – as a control or data, and the frequency relationship of the clocks. The following diagram shows an example of a system where a single-clock pulse in 250MHz clock domain needs to be transferred to a slower 100MHz domain.

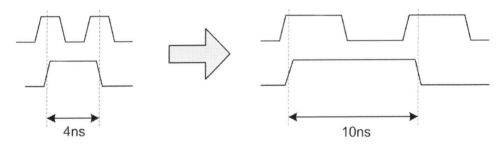

Figure 1: Clock domain crossing of a single-clock pulse

Synchronization using two registers

One approach to solving a metastability problem on individual signals is based on simple synchronizer comprising three registers, shown in the following figure.

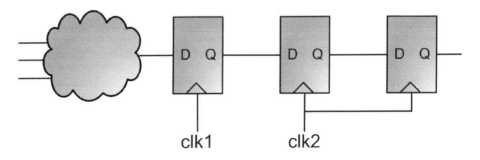

Figure 2: A simple synchronizer using two registers

The following is the implementation example.

```verilog
module synchronizer(input clk1,clk2,
      input reset,
      input data_in,
      output reg data_out);
   reg data_in_q, data_out_q;
   always @(posedge clk1, posedge reset)
     if(reset)
       data_in_q <= 1'b0;
     else
       data_in_q <= data_in;
   always @(posedge clk2, posedge reset)
     if(reset) begin
        data_out_q <= 1'b0;
        data_out   <= 1'b0;
   end
   else begin
        data_out_q <= data_in_q;
        data_out   <= data_out_q;
   end
endmodule // synchronizer
```

It is important to add proper timing constraints to cover all the paths between two clock domains. In the above example the only path is `data_in_q`.

The following is the example of timing constraints in Xilinx UCF format.

```
# clk1 period constraint
NET "clk1" TNM_NET = clk1;
TIMESPEC TS_clk1 = PERIOD "clk1" 5 ns HIGH 50%;

# clk2 period constraint
NET "clk2" TNM_NET = clk2;
TIMESPEC TS_clk2 = PERIOD "clk2" 4.1 ns HIGH 50%;

# constrain the paths between clk1 and clk2 domains
TIMESPEC "TS_CDC_1" = FROM "clk1" TO "clk2" 5ns;

# another way to constrain the path between clk1 and clk2
# TIMESPEC "TS_CDC_1"  = FROM "clk1" TO "clk2"  TIG;
```

The following is the section from the timing analysis report, which covers `TS_CDC_1` constraint.

==

```
Timing constraint: TS_CDC_1 = MAXDELAY FROM TIMEGRP "clk1" TO
TIMEGRP "clk2" 5ns;

 1 path analyzed, 1 endpoint analyzed, 0 failing endpoints
 0 timing errors detected. (0 setup errors, 0 hold errors)
 Maximum delay is   3.094ns.
--------------------------------------------------
Slack (setup paths):  1.906ns (requirement - (data path -
clock path skew + uncertainty))
    Source:                data_in_q (FF)
    Destination:           data_out_q (FF)
    Requirement:           5.000ns
    Data Path Delay:       2.248ns (Levels of Logic = 0)
    Clock Path Skew:       -0.811ns (2.532 - 3.343)
    Source Clock:          clk1_BUFGP rising
    Destination Clock:     clk2_BUFGP rising
    Clock Uncertainty:     0.035ns

Maximum Data Path at Slow Process Corner: data_in_q to
data_out_q
Location          Delay type       Delay(ns)    Logical Resource(s)
-------------------------------------------------
ILOGIC_X0Y7.Q4   Tickq              1.220        data_in_q
                                                 data_in_q
SLICE_X1Y7.AX    net (fanout=1) 0.914            data_in_q
SLICE_X1Y7.CLK   Tdick              0.114        data_out_q
-------------------------------------------------
Total 2.248ns (1.334ns logic, 0.914ns route)
      (59.3% logic, 40.7% route)
-------------------------------------------------
Hold Paths: TS_CDC_1 = MAXDELAY FROM TIMEGRP "clk1" TO
TIMEGRP "clk2" 5 ns;
-------------------------------------------------
Slack (hold path):  1.227ns (requirement - (clock path skew +
uncertainty - data path))
  Source:                  data_in_q (FF)
  Destination:             data_out_q (FF)
  Requirement:             0.000ns
  Data Path Delay:         1.162ns (Levels of Logic = 0)
  Positive Clock Path Skew: -0.100ns (0.986 - 1.086)
  Source Clock:            clk1_BUFGP rising
  Destination Clock:       clk2_BUFGP rising
  Clock Uncertainty:       0.035ns

Minimum Data Path at Fast Process Corner: data_in_q to
data_out_q
```

```
Location         Delay type        Delay(ns)    Logical Resource(s)
--------------------------------------------------------------
ILOGIC_X0Y7.Q4   Tickq              0.656       data_in_q
                                                data_in_q
SLICE_X1Y7.AX    net (fanout=1)     0.447       data_in_q
SLICE_X1Y7.CLK   Tckdi(-Th)        -0.059       data_out_q
--------------------------------------------------------------
Total            1.162ns (0.715ns logic, 0.447ns route)
                 (61.5% logic, 38.5% route)
--------------------------------------------------------------
```

The figure below illustrates an incorrect way to implement the synchronizer.

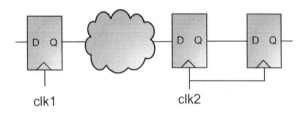

Figure 3: Incorrect synchronizer implementation

The problem with this implementation is combinational logic between adjacent registers in different clock domains. If combinational logic is located before the first synchronizing register, it becomes sensitive to glitches produced by the combinational logic. That increases the probability of propagating and invalid data across the synchronizer.

Using this synchronization circuit requires caution if it's used to synchronize busses. The problem is that the circuit cannot guarantee that all the outputs will be valid in the same clock. It might take several clocks for all the bits to settle.

This synchronizer will not work correctly if the frequency of clk1 is faster than clk2, such as in the example shown in the beginning of this Tip. If duration of the valid data is short, and it's sampled with a slower clock, the data can be missed. It should only be used when the input changes are slow relatively to the capturing `clk2`.

Synchronization using edge detection

The following figure shows a circuit that implements a synchronizer using edge detection technique.

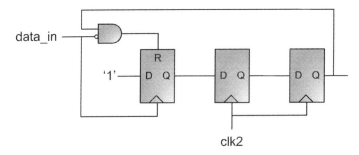

Figure 4: Synchronization using edge detection

The Verilog implementation of the circuit is given below.

```verilog
module edge_detector(  input clk2,reset,
          input data_in,
          output reg data_out);
   reg data_in_q, data_out_q;
   wire reset_in;
   assign reset_in = (~data_in & data_out) | reset;
   always @(posedge data_in, posedge reset_in)
     if(reset_in)
       data_in_q <= 1'b0;
     else
       data_in_q <= 1'b1;
   always @(posedge clk2, posedge reset)
     if(reset) begin
       data_out_q  <= 1'b0;
       data_out    <= 1'b0;
     end
     else begin
       data_out_q <= data_in_q;
       data_out   <= data_out_q;
     end
endmodule // edge_detector
```

The principle of the operation of the circuit is illustrated in the following waveform.

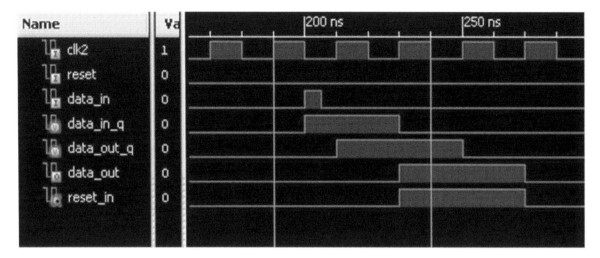

Figure 5: Edge synchronization waveform

The input data is used as a clock to the leftmost register. That allows it to capture pulses that are shorter than the `clk2` period. When the input data is deasserted, and the pulse propagated to the rightmost register, the leftmost register is cleared.

The disadvantage of this circuit is that is uses data signal as a clock.

Synchronization using an asynchronous FIFO

Using asynchronous FIFO is a robust approach to synchronize data busses. This method is easy to use, and works reliably for any data and clock frequencies.

The disadvantage is significant amount of logic and embedded memory resources required to implement a FIFO. In Xilinx FPGAs the smallest FIFO implemented with distributed memory is 16 entries. Another disadvantage is the latency added by the FIFO.

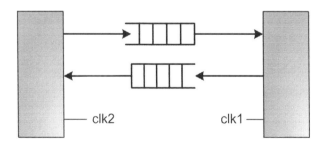

Figure 6: Using asynchronous FIFO for synchronization

Synchronization using Grey code

Grey code is a data encoding technique where only one bit at most changes every clock. Grey code can be used for data bus synchronization. This method is widely used for implementing counters, empty, full, and other control signals in asynchronous FIFOs, which cross FIFO read/write clock domains.

Synchronization using handshake

Handshake synchronizers rely on request-acknowledgement protocols to ensure delivery of the data. The following figure shows a top-level block diagram of a handshake synchronizer.

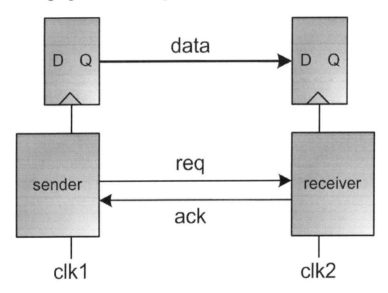

Figure 7: Handshake synchronizer

A request is sent from the source clock domain. The destination domain receives the request, performs its synchronization, captures the data, and sends back an acknowledgement. The source domain receives the acknowledge, and can prepare to send the next data. The advantage of the handshake synchronizer is that it doesn't require synchronizing the data, which can save a lot of logic resources. The disadvantage is the latency incurred during exchanging request/acknowledge for each data transfer.

Synchronization using asynchronous oversampling

Synchronization technique using asynchronous oversampling is described in [1]. The technique uses multiple phases of a mixed mode clock manager (MMCM) in Virtex-6 FPGAs to oversample the input data, and performing subsequent edge detection.

Resources

[1] Virtex-6 FPGA LVDS 4X Asynchronous Oversampling at 1.25 Gb/s, Xilinx Application Note XAPP881
http://www.xilinx.com/support/documentation/application_notes/xapp881_V6_4X_Asynch_OverSampling.pdf

[2] Clifford Cummings, *"Synthesis and Scripting Techniques for Designing Multi-Asynchronous Clock Designs"*, SNUG-2001, San Jost
http://www.sunburst-design.com/papers/CummingsSNUG2001SJ_AsyncClk.pdf

24
USING FIFOS

FIFO stands for first-in first-out. It's a very configurable component, and finds many uses in FPGA designs. Some usage examples are clock domain crossing, data buffering, bus width conversion, interfacing between producer/consumer modules.

The following figure shows an example of using FIFOs in a PCI Express to Ethernet adapter. The FIFOs perform data buffering between modules with different clock frequency and datapath width.

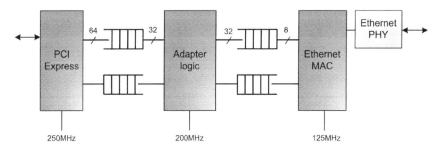

Figure 1: FIFO usage example

FIFO architecture

The following figure shows a simplified architecture of a FIFO.

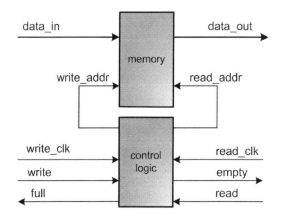

Figure 2: FIFO architecture

A FIFO has two main components: memory to store the data, and control logic. Control logic is responsible for maintaining address read and address write pointers to the memory, and updating status flags. There are several other status flags that can be exposed to the user: almost full, almost empty, FIFO data counter, read underflow, write overflow, and others.

A FIFO can be synchronous or asynchronous. Synchronous FIFO has the same read and write clocks. In asynchronous FIFO, read and write clocks are independent. Designing a reliable and high-performing asynchronous FIFO presents unique challenges. Memory module has to be dual-ported, and support concurrent read and write from two clock domains. Control logic has to implement proper clock domain crossing from the write pointer logic to empty flag and from the read pointer logic to full flag.

Several commercial solutions of clock domain crossing in FIFO control logic are using a Gray counter. An important property of a Gray counter is one bit change for every transition. Using the value of such a counter in unrelated clock domain for comparison is not going to generate a glitch.

FIFO configuration options

FPGA designers have several options of implementing a FIFO circuit. Xilinx provides several highly configurable FIFO cores. A custom FIFO can also be designed using embedded FPGA memory and logic.

Xilinx FIFO cores provide the following configuration options:

- FIFO depth: between 16 and 4 million entries.
- FIFO data width: from 1 to 1024 bit.
- Read to write port aspect ratio: from 1:8 to 8:1.
- One or separate FIFO read and write clock domains.
- Memory type: Block RAM, distributed RAM, built-in FIFO, shift register.
- Error checking (ECC)
- Data prefetch (first word fall-through).
- Status flags: full, empty, almost_full, almost_empty, read and write data count, overflow and underflow error.

Design challenges in using FIFOs

The following is a list of common challenges FPGA designers face when using FIFOs.

- Designers must take special precautions when using asynchronous FIFOs.
- Asynchronous FIFOs may operate in two unrelated read and write clock domains.

- Control and status signals are synchronous to either read or write clocks.

For example, full, almost full, write count, and write signals are synchronous to the write clock; empty, almost empty, read count, and read signals are synchronous to read clock. Xilinx also recommends not relying on cycle accuracy of the status flags in asynchronous FIFOs. It is possible to have inconsistent cycle time behavior in different chips, due to process, voltage, and temperature variation. This can lead to arcane problems that are difficult to debug.

A frequent logic error is FIFO overflow and underflow. A FIFO overflow occurs when there is a write when the FIFO is already full. An underflow is a read from an empty FIFO. Overflow and underflow conditions are relatively simple to monitor. A designer can implement a circuit that latches an error bit when write and full, or read and empty flags are asserted in the same clock. Some Xilinx FIFO configurations provide overflow and underflow error flags. Designs can be set up to trigger on the FIFO access error bits by the integrated logic analyzer (ILA), and read the waveform by the ChipScope software.

Designers should take into account the FIFO read latency. Usually, the data is available on the next clock cycle after an FIFO read. If FIFO data outputs are registered, the latency is two clocks. Some Xilinx FIFO configurations provide prefetch option, which is also called first word fall-through, where read data is available on the same clock cycle as the read strobe. The data is prefetched on the FIFO read side as soon as it's written to an empty FIFO.

FIFOs have an option to use synchronous or asynchronous reset. Logic driving a synchronous reset should be in the same clock domain.

Calculating FIFO depth

One of the FIFO usage models is buffering the data between producer and consumer, as shown in the following figure.

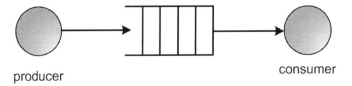

Figure 3: FIFO producer-consumer model

The overall producer data rate should not exceed the consumer rate of processing the data. A FIFO is not designed to overcome the rate difference. No matter how deep the FIFO is, it is going to eventually overflow if the producer's data rate is consistently higher than consumer's. An FIFO is intended to overcome temporary producer-consumer rate differences by buffering the excess data.

To accurately calculate the minimum required FIFO depth, designers need to have a good knowledge of the producer and consumer data characteristics such as arrival and departure rate, and burst duration. Underestimating FIFO depth will lead to the user having to exert significant effort to debugging and understanding the root cause of the problem, and consequent redesign. FPGA logic resources are expensive; therefore it is also important not to overestimate the FIFO depth.

Queuing theory defines theoretical models for various producer and consumer traffic characteristics. However, in most cases the models are too restrictive, and aren't applicable to the real-world situations.

Other analysis methods include computer simulations of the traffic conditions, or finding the FIFO size empirically by prototyping a similar system.

Designers can also use the following two simplified models: constant pace burst calculation, and variable pace length.

Constant pace burst calculation model

Let's denote $P(t)$ the rate of data production, and $C(t)$ the rate of data processing or consumption. This model assumes that P and C are constant for the time T – the duration of a burst. By the end of a burst, $P*T$ data units were written to a FIFO, and $C*T$ were read. The number of remaining data units is $L = T*(P-C)$. L is the maximum size of the FIFO. This is a very simplistic model that assumes constant rate of data production and consumption. It also can't handle the situation when the next burst starts before all the data from the previous burst has being read.

The following example illustrates how to use this model.

1500 Byte Ethernet packets arrive every 50us and are written into an 8-bit FIFO. The arrival rate is 1Gbit/sec. The FIFO read rate is 100Mreads/sec.
$P(t) = (1Gbit/sec)/8bit = 125Mwrites/sec$
$C(t) = 100Mreads/sec$
$T = 1500Byte/(1Gbit/sec) = 12us$
$L = T*(P-C) = 12*(125-100) = 300$

The FIFO has to be 300 entries deep to sustain the traffic. Intuitive interpretation of the results is as follows:

If the processing rate was close to zero, the entire packet will have to be stored in the FIFO, which will require 1,500 entries. If the processing rate is faster than the arrival rate, the FIFO depths will need to be 0. The closer the processing rate is to the arrival rate, the smaller the FIFO needs to be.

Variable pace length model

When the data arrival and processing rates are not constant, the previous model can be modified as follows:

$$L[Tx] = \int_{t1}^{Tx} [P(t) - C(t)]dt$$

$$L = max\ \{L[Tx]\}$$

t1 is burst start time, and *L[Tx]* is the FIFO length at any given time during the burst. *L[Tx]* will vary during the burst because of the changing arrival and processing rates. To find the maximum FIFO length, use the maximum value of the *L[Tx]*.

The constant pace burst calculation model is a special case of the variable pace length model when the arrival and processing rates are constant.

25

COUNTERS

Counters are used in virtually every FPGA design for different purposes: timers, utility counters, or even state machines. There are several different counter types: the most basic binary counter, prescaler, Johnson, LFSR, and others. Counters can count in the up or down direction, have a load input to start with predefined value, have synchronous or asynchronous reset, stop when reaching certain threshold or free-running, and many other configurations. Understanding the tradeoffs between different counter types and configurations and choosing the right one for a particular design can save a lot of logic resources, and improve performance.

Binary counter

Binary counter is the simplest and the most flexible counter type. It allows sequential count up or down, from 0 to 2^N -1, where N is the number of bits. The main disadvantage of a binary counter is significant amount of combinatorial feedback logic.

The following is an example implementation of a 32-bit binary counter.

```
module counter_binary(input clk,
          input reset,
          input counter_binary_en,
          output reg [31:0] counter_binary,
          output reg  counter_binary_match);
  always @(posedge clk)
    if(reset) begin
      counter_binary       <= 'b0;
      counter_binary_match <= 1'b0;
    end
    else begin
      counter_binary       <= counter_binary_en
        ? counter_binary + 1'b1
        : counter_binary;
      counter_binary_match <=
        counter_binary == `MATCH_PATTERN;
    end
```

```
endmodule // counter_binary
```

Johnson counter

The Johnson counter can be used to generate counters in which only one output changes on each clock cycle. The Johnson counter is made of a simple shift register with an inverted feedback. Johnson counters have 2N states, where N is the number of registers, compared to 2^N states for a binary counter. These counters are sometimes called "walking ring" counters, and are found in specialized applications, such as decade counters, or for generating a clock-like pattern with many different phases.

The following figure shows an example of a 3-bit Johnson counter.

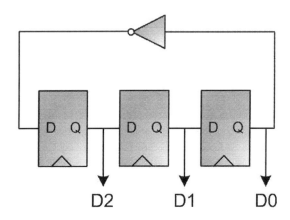

Figure 1: Johnson counter

The following is an example implementation of a 32-bit Johnson counter.

```
module counter_johnson(input clk,
          input reset,
          input counter_johnson_en,
          output reg [31:0] counter_johnson_q,
          output reg counter_johnson_match);
  always @(posedge clk, posedge reset)
    if(reset) begin
      counter_johnson_q     <= 'b0;
      counter_johnson_match <= 1'b0;
    end
    else begin
      counter_johnson_q     <= counter_johnson_en
        ? {counter_johnson_q[30:0], ~counter_johnson_q[31]}
        : counter_johnson_q;
      counter_johnson_match <=
        counter_johnson_q == `MATCH_PATTERN;
```

```
      end
endmodule // counter_binary
```

LFSR counter

Linear Feedback Shift Register (LFSR) is a shift register whose input is a linear function. Some of the outputs are combined using an XOR operation, and form a feedback. The LFSR operation is deterministic, and produces a repeating sequence of known values. LFSR counters are based on the LFSR registers. The main feature of LFSR counters is speed. The main disadvantage is that the output counting sequence is not incremental, like in a binary counter.

The following is an example implementation of a 32-bit LFSR counter that matches 32'h81234567 value. The code is generated using online LFSR generation tool offered by OutputLogic.com.

```
module lfsr_counter(
          input clk,
          input reset,
          input ce,
          output reg lfsr_done);

  reg [31:0] lfsr;
  wire d0,lfsr_equal;

  xnor(d0,lfsr[31],lfsr[21],lfsr[1],lfsr[0]);
  assign lfsr_equal = (lfsr == 32'h1565249);

  always @(posedge clk,posedge reset) begin
    if(reset) begin
      lfsr <= 32'h0;
      lfsr_done <= 0;
    end
    else begin
      if(ce)
        lfsr <= lfsr_equal ? 32'h0 : {lfsr[30:0],d0};
        lfsr_done <= lfsr_equal;
    end
  end
endmodule
```

Prescaler counter

The prescaler counter can be used to implement a faster binary counter by cascading smaller-size counters. Each cascade acts as a clock divider by downscaling the high-frequency clock. The main advantage is lower logic utilization. The disadvantage is less flexibility: such a counter has lower count granularity, and cannot count any value.

The following figure shows an example of a two-stage prescaler counter.

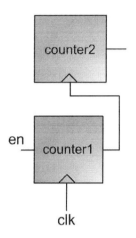

Figure 2: Prescaler counter

The following is an example implementation of a 32-bit prescaler counter. It consists of two cascaded 16-bit binary counters.

```
module counter_prescaler(input clk,
         input reset,
         input counter_prescale_en,
         output [15:0]  counter_prescale,
         output reg counter_prescale_match);
  reg [15:0] counter_prescale_low,counter_prescale;
  always @(posedge clk)
    if(reset) begin
      counter_prescale_low <= 'b0;
    end
    else begin
      counter_prescale_low <= counter_prescale_en
        ? counter_prescale_low + 1'b1
        : counter_prescale_low;
    end
  always @(posedge counter_prescale_low[15], posedge reset)
    if(reset) begin
      counter_prescale       <= 'b0;
      counter_prescale_match <= 1'b0;
    end
    else begin
      counter_prescale       <= counter_prescale + 1'b1;
      counter_prescale_match <=
        counter_prescale == `MATCH_PATTERN_PRESCALE;
```

```
     end
endmodule // counter_prescaler
```

Performance and logic utilization comparison

The following table summarizes performance and logic utilization of several 32- and 64-bit counter types. The first two are standard 32- and 64-bit binary counters. The next two counters are Xilinx counter cores generated using CoreGen application. Counter number five from the top is a 32-bit binary counter implemented using Xilinx DSP48 primitive. Prescaler, LFSR and Johnson are 32-bit counters.

All the counters were built for Xilinx Spartan-6 LX45 FPGA with -3 speed grade.

Table 1: performance and logic utilization of different counters

Counter	*Registers*	*LUTs*	*Slices*	*Max frequency, MHz*
Binary 32 bit	33	8	13	364
Binary 64 bit	65	12	19	310
Binary 32 bit using Xilinx core	33	8	14	257
Binary 64 bit using Xilinx core	65	12	20	216
Xilinx DSP48 32 bit	0	6	2	345
Prescaler 32 bit	33	5	10	440
LFSR 32 bit	33	15	9	303
Johnson 32 bit	33	8	9	375

In order to understand performance differences between different counters, it is useful to compare the number of logic levels, logic and routing delays of the worst path, and maximum fanout. The following table shows the information that was extracted from the project timing report.

Table 2: logic and routing delays of different counters

Counter	*Levels of logic*	*Logic delay, ns*	*Route delay, ns*	*Max fanout*
Binary 32 bit	3	1.1	1.6	3
Binary 64 bit	3	1.0	2.15	3
Binary 32 bit using Xilinx core	5	2.0	2.1	2

Counter	Levels of logic	Logic delay, ns	Route delay, ns	Max fanout
Binary 64 bit using Xilinx core	11	2.6	3.2	2
Xilinx DSP48 32 bit	N/A	N/A	N/A	N/A
Prescaler 32 bit	4	1.45	0.4	1
LFSR 32 bit	3	1.3	2.0	8
Johnson 32 bit	3	1.1	1.5	3

All the counters have expected register utilization: 32 or 64 bit data and one bit match.

The number of LUTs of and LFSR counter is higher than expected because this particular implementation uses additional LUTs as a pattern match.

A DSP48 counter utilizes 6 LUTs because of some logic external to DSP48 primitive.

For small and medium size counters, the slice utilization difference for the same counter width is not significant.

Among 32-bit counters, prescaler counter has the highest performance and the one generated by Xilinx CoreGen is the lowest. This is consistent with the logic level number and logic delay results.

The above performance and logic utilization results are only shown as an example, and should be interpreted judiciously. The results will vary significantly for different FPGA families, speed grades, tool options, and counter configuration.

All the source code, project files and the reports are available on the accompanying website.

26
SIGNED ARITHMETIC

Signed arithmetic is widely used in digital signal processing (DSP), image and video processing algorithms, communications, and many other FPGA designs. The first Verilog-95 standard didn't provide a good support for two's complement signed arithmetic. Developers needed to hand-code signed operations by using bit-level manipulations. That changed in Verilog-2001, which added explicit support for signed arithmetic, such as special keywords and built-in signed operators. To enable Verilog-2001, use `-verilog2001` command line option in XST, and "*set_option -vlog_std v2001*" command in Synplify.

Verilog support for signed expressions

Verilog standard defines `signed`, `unsigned` reserved words, and `$signed`, `$unsigned` system tasks.

The `signed` reserved word declares register and net data types as signed. It can also be placed on module port declarations. When either the date type or the port is declared signed, the other inherits the property of the signed data type or port.

The `unsigned` reserved word declares a register and net data types to be unsigned.

`$signed` and `$unsigned` system tasks perform type cast from signed to unsigned and vice versa.

The following code provides an example of using signed/unsigned reserved words and system tasks.

```
integer val1; // 32-bit signed, 2's complement
reg [31:0] val2; // 32-bit unsigned
wire signed [15:0] val3; // 16-bit signed
wire unsigned [15:0] val4; // unsigned keyword is optional
assign val4 = $unsigned(val3); //type-cast to unsigned
assign val3 = $signed(val4);   //type-cast to signed
reg[5:0] val5 = 6'shA; // sign specifier before the base,
                       // sign extended to binary 111010
```

Signed shift operators

There are two types of shift operators: logical, denoted as << and >>, and signed or arithmetic, denoted as <<< and >>>.

Both logical and signed left shift operators, << and <<<, shift the left operand to the left by the number of bit positions given by the right operand. The rightmost bit positions will be filled with zeroes.

The logical right shift operator, >>, shifts its left operand to the right by the number of bit positions given by the right operand. It will fill the vacated bit positions with zeros.

If the result type is unsigned, the signed right shift operator, >>>, will fill the vacated bit positions with zeroes. If the result is signed, the operator will perform sign extension of the leftmost, or sign, bit. The following examples illustrate different shift operators:

```
reg [7:0]         init1 = 8'h1;
reg signed [7:0]  init2 = 8'h80;

reg [7:0]         shift1, shift2;
reg signed[7:0]   shift3, shift4;

initial shift1 = init1 << 2;    // result is 8'h04
initial shift2 = init1 <<< 2;   // result is 8'h04
initial shift3 = init2 >> 2;    // result is 8'h02
initial shift4 = init2 >>> 2;   // result is 8'h0E
```

Arithmetic operations

Arithmetic operations are based on the data type of the operands. If all operands are signed, the result is calculated using signed arithmetic. If either operand is unsigned, the arithmetic is unsigned.

```
wire signed [15:0] x, y;
wire signed [16:0] sum_signed;
wire [16:0] sum_unsigned;

assign sum_signed = x + y; // 2's complement addition
assign sum_unsigned = $unsigned(x) + y; // unsigned addition
```

Absolute value

The following is an example of calculating an absolute value of a signed number.

```
reg signed [11:0] val = 12'h801; // -2047 in signed decimal
wire signed [11:0] abs_val;
assign abs_val = val[11] ? ~val + 1'b1 : val;
```

```
        // If the sign bit is set, perform 2's complement
        // The result is 12'h7FF or 2047 in signed decimal
```

Arithmetic negation

Verilog supports arithmetic negation operator, as shown in the following example:

```
assign b = invert ? -a : a;
```

Synthesis tools usually implement this code by subtracting *a* from zero, and adding a multiplexor to select either positive or negative value.

There are several caveats that FPGA designers should be aware of when working with the signed arithmetic. Circuits that implement using signed arithmetic might have logic utilization differences that can be compared to the unsigned implementation. Logic utilization may increase or decrease, depending on the circuit.

There might be a mismatch between simulation and synthesis results. Performing post-synthesis gate level simulation can help you to be more confident that the logic was implemented correctly.

Because FPGA synthesis tools provide different level of support for signed arithmetic, the portability of the code might become an issue. Designers should always consult synthesis tool user guide for support of signed arithmetic constructs.

27
STATE MACHINES

A Finite State Machine (FSM), or simply a state machine, is defined as a model composed of a finite number of states, transitions between those states, and actions. State machines are widely used in FPGA designs to implement control logic, packet parsers, algorithms, and for many other purposes. State machines can differ in complexity from a simple two-state structure to implement a control circuit, to a very complex structure with over a hundred states to implement a communication protocol.

The following figure shows a block diagram of a Mealy state machine, whose outputs are determined by both current state and the value of its inputs.

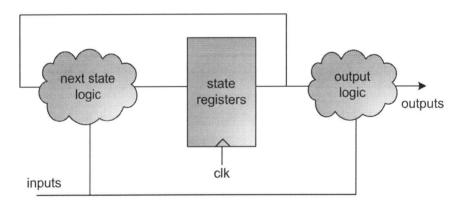

Figure 1: Mealy state machine

State machine coding techniques

Synthesis tools automatically infer state machine tools if the RTL follows the following coding guidelines (for Verilog HDL):

- State registers must be initialized using synchronous or asynchronous reset, or with register power-up value.

- State register type can be an integer or a set of parameters.

- Next-state equations can be described in a sequential or a separate combinatorial *always* block.

The following is an example of a state machine implementation with four states. It uses separate combinatorial *always* block for the next state logic. The circuit implemented in the example doesn't serve any practical purpose. The goal is to illustrate different state machine coding techniques and to show how synthesis tools implement them.

```verilog
module state_machines( input clk,
          input reset,
          input [3:0] state_inputs,
          output reg [3:0] state_outputs);
  localparam STATE_INIT   = 3'd0,
    STATE_ONE     = 3'd1,
    STATE_TWO     = 3'd2,
    STATE_THREE   = 3'd3;
  reg [2:0] state_cur,
            state_next;
  always @(posedge clk) begin
    if(reset) begin
      state_cur     <= STATE_INIT;
      state_outputs <= 4'b0;
    end
    else begin
      state_cur          <= state_next;
      state_outputs[0] <= state_cur == STATE_INIT;
      state_outputs[1] <= state_cur == STATE_ONE;
      state_outputs[2] <= state_cur == STATE_TWO;
      state_outputs[3] <= state_cur == STATE_THREE;
    end
  end
  always @(*) begin
    state_next = state_cur;
    case(state_cur)
      STATE_INIT:  if(state_inputs[0]) state_next = STATE_ONE;
      STATE_ONE:   if(state_inputs[1]) state_next = STATE_TWO;
      STATE_TWO:   if(state_inputs[2]) state_next = STATE_THREE;
      STATE_THREE: if(state_inputs[3]) state_next = STATE_INIT;
    endcase
  end
endmodule // state_machines
```

XST produces the following synthesis log:

====================================
* HDL Synthesis

```
========================================
Synthesizing Unit <state_machines>
  Found 4-bit register for signal <state_outputs>.
  Found 3-bit register for signal <state_cur>.
  Found finite state machine <FSM_0> for signal <state_cur>.
-----------------------------------------
 | States            | 4
 | Transitions       | 8
 | Inputs            | 4
 | Outputs           | 4
 | Clock             | clk (rising_edge)
 | Reset             | reset (positive)
 | Reset type        | synchronous
 | Reset State       | 000
 | Encoding          | auto
 | Implementation    | LUT
-----------------------------------------
Summary:
Inferred 4 D-type flip-flop(s).
Inferred 1 Finite State Machine(s).
========================================
HDL Synthesis Report
Macro Statistics
# Registers                           : 1
  4-bit register                      : 1
# FSMs                         : 1
========================================
Low Level Synthesis
========================================
Analyzing FSM <MFsm> for best encoding.
Optimizing FSM <state_cur> on signal <state_cur[1:2]> with
gray encoding.
------------------
State | Encoding
------------------
000   | 00
001   | 01
010   | 11
011   | 10
------------------
```

The above log shows that XST recognized four states in the state machine and changed the original state encoding to gray.

State machine synthesis options

The following is the list of XST synthesis options related to the state machine implementation.

FSM Encoding Algorithm (-fsm_encoding switch).

Auto: This is the default setting. XST will select the best encoding algorithm for each FSM. In the above example, XST has chosen gray.

One-hot: One register is associated with each state.

Gray: Encoding that guarantees only one bit change between two consecutive states.

Compact: Minimizes the number of bits in the state register.

Other encoding options are Johnson, Sequential, Speed1, and user-specific.

Other FPGA synthesis tools, such as Synopsys Synplify, provide similar FSM encoding options. However, the rules for automatic state extraction and optimization are different and, in most cases, proprietary.

RAM-Based FSM

XST provides an option to implement state machines using Block RAM resources. That is controlled by an -fsm_style switch. If XST cannot implement a state machine with BRAM, it issues a warning and implements it with LUTs. One case when a state machine cannot be implemented with BRAM is when it has an asynchronous reset.

The advantage of this option is more compact implementation of large state machines. A BRAM can be easily configured with any initial state values and can accommodate hundreds of states.

The following figure shows an implementation of a state machine with 256 states, 3-bit state inputs, and 10-bit outputs.

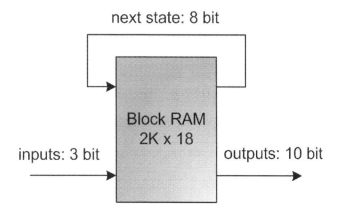

Figure 2: BRAM-based state machine

Safe FSM implementation

A state machine may enter an invalid state for various reasons. It can happen, for example, if state inputs and state registers are in different clock domains. If the state inputs aren't properly synchronized, state registers can enter a metastable state. When the state registers exit the metastable state, they can hold any value, including the one that is not part of the state machine's defined set of states.

In that event, the state machine will permanently stay in that state and will not react to state inputs. Other catalysts for entering an invalid state are single event upset (SEU) errors, which can occur in radioactive environments. They are caused by either a high-energy neutron or an alpha particle striking sections of the FPGA silicon that contain configuration data.

XST provides an option to recover from an invalid state by adding additional logic. That is controlled by the `-safe_implementation` switch. FPGA designers can implement other mechanisms to detect or correct an entry to an invalid state.

Safe FSM implementation is used in mission-critical systems, such as aerospace, medical, or automotive, where an FPGA must function in a harsh operating environment, gracefully recover from any error it encounters, and continue working.

In other cases, such as during the debug phase, designers do want the state machine to stay in an illegal state in order to be able to more easily find the root cause of the problem.

28

USING XILINX DSP48 PRIMITIVE

Xilinx DSP48 primitive is usually associated with digital signal processing applications. For example, high-definition video processing applications take advantage of the fixed precision multiplication. Floating-point processing is used in military radars. DSP48 primitives are cascaded to implement complex multiplications used in Fast Fourier Transforms (FFTs). Another commonly used function that takes advantage of DSP48 is the Finite Impulse Response Filter (FIR).

However, DSP48 primitive is highly configurable and can be used in a wide range of other applications, not only DSP-related ones. That has a benefit of saving a significant amount of FPGA logic resources.

DSP48 primitive is part of all Xilinx Virtex and Spartan FPGA families. The primitive has a different name and offers a slightly different feature set in each family. It's called DSP48E1 in Virtex-6, DSP48E in Virtex-5, DSP48A1 in Spartan-6, and DSP48A in Spartan-3.

DSP48 primitive supports a plethora of application and use cases. Some of them are adders and subtractors, multipliers and dividers, counters and timers, Single Instruction Multiple Data (SIMD) operations, pattern matching, and barrel shift registers. It supports signed and two's complement arithmetic and up to 48-bit operands. If needed, multiple DSP48 modules can be cascaded. DSP48 can operate at a speed of up to 600MHz in Virtex-6 and 390MHz in Spartan-6 FPGAs.

The following figure shows the block diagram of Virtex-6 DSP48E1 primitive.

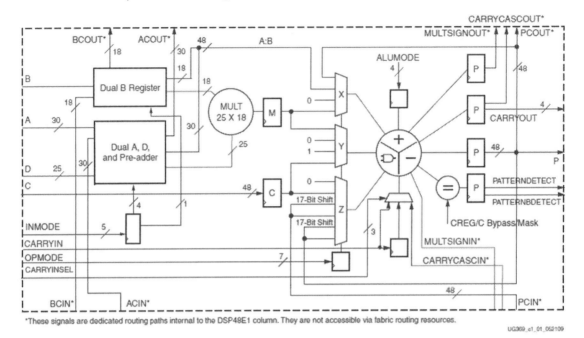

Figure 1: DSP48 block diagram (source: Virtex-6 FPGA DSP48E1 Slice, User Guide 369)

DSP48 consists of three main components: 25x18 bit multiplier, logic unit that performs three-input arithmetic and logic operations, input and output registers.

Implementation options

There are three main methods of using DSP48 primitives in the design.

A DSP48 primitive can be instantiated directly. This method enables a low-level access to all DSP48 features.

Xilinx CoreGen utility can be used to generate an IP core that takes advantage of the DSP48. The advantage of this method is that it is user-friendly and produces logic that is optimized for speed or area.

The most portable method is to infer DSP48 primitive by using certain coding styles and synthesis tool options. XST synthesis tool can automatically implement adders, subtractors, multipliers, and accumulators using DSP48. XST provides the following synthesis options that control the usage of DSP48 primitives.

Use DSP block (-use_dsp48 switch)

Auto: XST examines the benefits of placing each macro in DSP48 primitive, and then determines the most efficient implementation. Auto is the default setting.
Yes: XST places all macros in the DSP48 blocks whenever possible.
No: XST uses FPGA logic resources.

DSP Utilization Ratio (-dsp_utilization_ratio switch)

This option provides control over how XST takes advantage of available DSP48 resources. By default, XST attempts to use all available DSP48 resources.

The following are Verilog examples of a multiplier and an adder. They illustrate a coding style necessary to infer DSP48 primitive during the synthesis. The examples are built for Xilinx Spartan-6 LX45 FPGA with -3 speed grade and are available at the accompanying website.

Multipliers

The following is an example implementation of an 8-bit signed multiplier.

```
module mult(input clk,
          input reset,
          input signed [7:0] a ,b,
          output reg signed [15:0] c);
  always @(posedge clk)
    if(reset)
      c <= 'b0;
    else
      c <= a * b;
endmodule // mult
```

XST synthesis produces the following report:

```
=========================================
* HDL Synthesis
=========================================
Synthesizing Unit <mult>.
    Found 16-bit register for signal <c>.
    Found 8x8-bit multiplier for signal <a[7]_b[7]_OUT>
    Summary:
      inferred   1 Multiplier(s).
      inferred   16 D-type flip-flop(s).
Unit <mult> synthesized.

=================================================================
*          Advanced HDL
=================================================================
Synthesizing (advanced) Unit <mult>.
Found pipelined multiplier on signal <a[7]_b[7]_OUT>:1
pipeline level(s) found in a register connected to the
multiplier macro output. Pushing register(s) into the
multiplier macro.
```

```
INFO:Xst:2385 - HDL ADVISOR - You can improve the performance
of the multiplier Mmult_a[7]_b[7]_OUT by adding 1 register
level(s).
Unit <mult> synthesized (advanced).
=================================================================
Advanced HDL Synthesis Report

Macro Statistics
# Multipliers                                           : 1
8x8-bit registered multiplier                           : 1
=================================================================
```

The synthesis report indicates that XST correctly inferred 8x8 bit multiplier as a multiplier macro and also pushed the 16-bit output register inside the macro.

Another multiplier type is multiplication by a constant. It can also be implemented by inferring a DSP48 primitive. An alternative implementation of multiplication by a constant is using an addition operation on a shifted multiplicand value. For instance, multiplication by 100 can be implemented as:

```
// c=a*100
assign c = a<<6 + a<<5 + a<<2;
```

Adder

The following is an example implementation of a 48-bit adder with a registered output.

```
module adder_sync_reset(input clk, reset,
           input [47:0] a,b,
           output reg [47:0] c);

  always @(posedge clk)
    if(reset)
      c <= 'b0;
    else
      c <= a + b;
endmodule // adder_sync_reset
=================================================================
*HDL Synthesis
=================================================================
Synthesizing Unit <adder_sync_reset>.
    Found 48-bit register for signal <c>.
    Found 48-bit adder for signal <a[47]_b[47]_OUT>
    Summary:
      inferred   1 Adder/Subtractor(s).
      inferred  48 D-type flip-flop(s).
```

```
Unit <adder_sync_reset> synthesized.
=============================================================
Advanced HDL Synthesis Report

Synthesizing (advanced) Unit <adder_sync_reset>.
Found registered addsub on signal <a[47]_b[47]_OUT>:
1 register level(s) found in a register connected to the addsub
macro output. Pushing register(s) into the addsub macro.
Unit <adder_sync_reset> synthesized (advanced).
=============================================================
```

As in the previous example, the synthesis report indicates that XST correctly inferred 48-bit adder as a macro and also pushed the 48-bit output register inside the macro.

The following example shows the same implementation of a 48-bit adder with a registered output, but the register is reset asynchronously.

```
module adder_async_reset( input clk, reset,
         input [47:0] a,b,
         output reg [47:0] c);
  always @(posedge clk, posedge reset)
    if(reset)
      c <= 'b0;
    else
      c <= a + b;
endmodule // adder_async_reset
```

XST still correctly infers a 48-bit counter macro. However, it doesn't push the output register inside the macro.

Double data rate technique

Typical FPGA designs run at much lower speeds than DSP48 primitive can support. In some cases designers can take advantage of the full computing performance of DSP48 by running the data through the primitive at the double data rate speed. An example use case is two low-speed video or protocol data streams that require the same processing.

The following figure illustrates the technique.

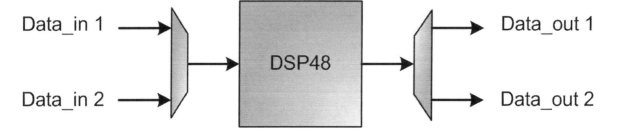

Figure 2: Processing the data at double data rate

Two datastreams are multiplexed into a single stream at twice the rate. The resulting datastream is processed by the DSP48 primitive and then demultiplexed back to two separate processed streams. For this technique to work, the data rate has to be at least twice as slow at the maximum supported rate of the DSP48. For example, if a DSP48 primitive can operate at 600MHz, the input data rate cannot exceed 300MHz.

There are several challenges that designers need to consider before using this technique. The amount of logic required to do multiplexing and demultiplexing of the datastreams can be substantial. Two datastreams have to have the same number of register delays. Single and double data rate clock domains have to be phase-aligned. And, finally, multiplexing and demultiplexing logic has to be placed in close proximity to the DSP48 primitive because it might operate at a very high frequency.

29
RESET SCHEME

The choice of a reset scheme has a profound effect on the performance, logic utilization, reliability, and robustness of the design. Different reset schemes have been discussed at length in magazines, white papers, online forums, and other technical publications. Reset scheme design is often a topic of heated debates among team members. Despite all that, there is no definitive answer on which reset scheme should be used in a given FPGA design.

Designing a good reset scheme that meets all the product requirements is a complex task. Factors that affect the decision making include previous experience of the designers, taking advantage of a working reset scheme from another similar design, using a third party IP core, and others.

In general, FPGA designers have the following options to choose from: asynchronous reset, synchronous reset, no reset, or a hybrid scheme that includes a combination of reset types. This Tip analyzes advantages and drawbacks of different reset schemes in order to enable FPGA designers to make the best decision applicable to a particular design.

Asynchronous reset

Asynchronous reset is defined as an input signal to a register or another synchronous element, which, when asserted, performs a reset of that element independent of the clock. Xilinx FPGA registers have the following configuration options: active high or low reset, and set or clear state upon reset assertion.

The following Verilog code is an example of implementing a register with an asynchronous reset.

```verilog
reg [7:0] my_register;
always @(posedge clk, posedge rst) begin
  if(rst)
    my_register <= 8'h0;
  else
    my_register <= data_in;
end
```

Disadvantages of using asynchronous reset

Using asynchronous reset can cause intermittent design problems that are hard to troubleshoot. The following example illustrates the problem caused by delayed reset release. The circuit is a two-bit shift register. Upon reset, the left register is cleared and the right one is set.

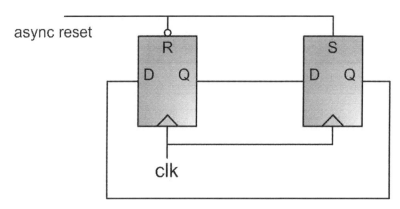

Figure 1: Shift register with asynchronous reset

After the reset is released, the contents of the right and left registers are toggled every rising clock edge. The following is a code example and a simulation waveform of the circuit.

```
reg shift0, shift1;
always @( posedge clk , posedge reset)
  if( reset ) begin
     shift0 <= 1'b0;
     shift1 <= 1'b1;
  end
  else begin
     {shift1,shift0} <= #1 {shift0,shift1};
end
```

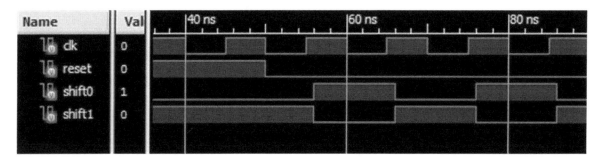

Figure 2: shift0 and shift1 toggle every clock

Because of the routing delays on the reset net, the reset of the left and right registers are not released at the same time. The functional problem with the circuit occurs when the reset of the left register is released before rising the edge of the clock, whereas the right register still stays at reset. The following simulation waveform illustrates the problem.

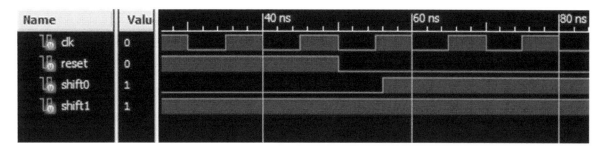

Figure 3: shift0 and shift1 are stuck at logic '1'

When the reset to the right register is finally released, both registers contain logic value of '1'.

The above example is not a hypothetical scenario. That can happen to state machines and other control logic in a real FPGA design with high logic utilization, and a high-fanout reset net. The reset release might not be seen at the same time by all state machine registers due to large delays. That can cause incorrect register initialization, and the state machine entering an invalid state. The problem debug is exacerbated by the fact that it is not reproducible in simulation, and it occurs intermittently in different FPGA builds.

The following figure illustrates another problem with using an asynchronous reset. It shows a circuit that consists of two registers. The data output of the left register is used as an input to a combinatorial logic "cloud". The output of the "cloud" is driving an asynchronous reset of the right register.

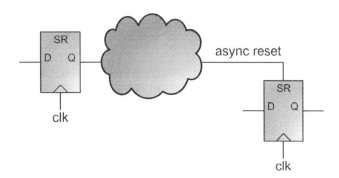

Figure 4: Asynchronous reset is driven by a combinatorial logic

One problem with this circuit is that there is a glitch on the asynchronous reset signal, which can be interpreted as a valid reset. Another problem is that if the asynchronous reset signal is not covered by the timing constraint, the right register might not be reset at the right time with respect to the clock, and as a consequence would be set to incorrect value.

By default, asynchronous reset nets are not included in the static timing analysis. Designers need to properly constrain all asynchronous reset nets, which is a more complex procedure than constraining synchronous elements.

Using asynchronous reset may result in sub-optimal logic utilization. Asynchronous resets prevent synthesis tools from performing certain logic optimizations, such as taking advantage of internal registers of DSP48 primitive (discussed in more detail in Tip #28). Several non-obvious logic optimization cases related to Control Sets when using synchronous resets are discussed in [2] and [3].

As shown in the first example, asynchronous reset nets rely on the propagation delays within an FPGA. As a consequence, the design might behave differently for slightly different supply voltages or temperature conditions. That will also cause design portability issues to different FPGA families and speed grades.

Advantages of using asynchronous reset

Despite the numerous problems listed above, using asynchronous reset offers several advantages. Asynchronous reset doesn't require a clock to always be active. If a clock originates from an external device, and that device has periods with an anticipated loss of clock, for example during a power-saving mode, than synchronous reset cannot be used. Another advantage is faster physical implementation of a design. Asynchronous reset nets usually have more relaxed timing constraints comparing to the synchronous reset. It takes place and route tools less effort and time to meet those constraints. In large FPGA designs that utilize tens of thousands of registers and take several hours to build, any reduction in build time is a significant advantage.

The following figure shows an example of a simple circuit to generate an asynchronous reset.

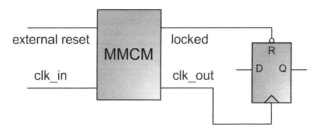

Figure 5: Using Xilinx MMCM locked output as a reset

The circuit uses inverted `locked` output of Virtex-6 MMCM primitive as a reset.

Synchronous reset

Synchronous reset is defined as an input signal to a register or another synchronous element, which, when asserted, performs a reset of that element. As the name suggests, synchronous reset takes place on the active edge of the clock. Xilinx FPGA registers with synchronous reset have the same configuration options as the ones with asynchronous reset. Moreover, the same hardware primitive can be configured as a register with either synchronous or asynchronous reset. The following is a Verilog example of implementing a register with a synchronous reset.

```
reg [7:0] my_register;
always @(posedge clk) begin
  if(rst)
    my_register <= 8'h0;
  else
    my_register <= data_in;
end
```

Xilinx recommends using synchronous reset scheme whenever possible. It adheres to synchronous design practices and avoids many problems discussed in the "Asynchronous reset" section.

As soon as the timing constraints are met, the design behavior is consistent for different voltages, temperature conditions, and process variations across different FPGA chips. That also makes the design more portable. Synchronous resets ensure that the reset can only occur at an active clock edge. Therefore, the clock works as a filter for small glitches on reset nets. Using synchronous reset is advantageous from the design logic utilization perspective. At the register level there is no difference in utilization: the same hardware primitive can be configured as a register with either synchronous or asynchronous reset. However, using synchronous reset helps synthesis and physical implementation tools perform different area optimizations.

No reset

Implementing synchronous logic without reset is yet another option that FPGA designers have at their disposal. The following is an example of implementing a register without a reset.

```
reg [7:0] my_register;
always @(posedge clk) begin
  my_register <= data_in;
end
```

By default, the register is initialized with '0' on FPGA power-up. Designers can initialize the register with any value during its declaration, as shown in the following example.

```
reg [7:0] my_register = 8'h55;
```

Implementing synchronous logic without reset offers some advantages. Reset nets, especially in large designs, consume a large amount of FPGA routing resources. Not using tens of thousands of reset signals helps improve design performance and decrease build time. Not using reset also enables replacing registers with dedicated FPGA primitives, such as Xilinx Shift Register LUTs (SRL), which can significantly lower overall logic utilization.

The disadvantage of not using reset is a less flexible design, which can only be initialized on FPGA power-up.

Hybrid reset scheme

In practice, reset scheme of a large FPGA design often contains a mix of reset types: synchronous, asynchronous, and no reset at all. The following figure depicts an example of such a hybrid reset scheme.

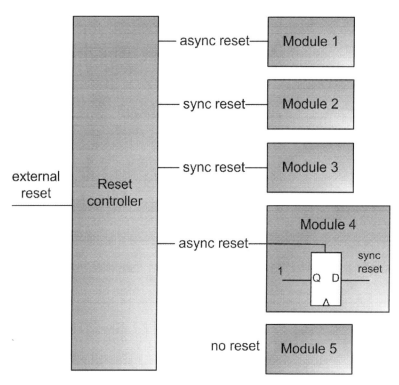

Figure 6: An example of a hybrid reset scheme

Modules 2 and 3 have synchronous reset in different clock domains. Module 1 uses asynchronous reset. Module 5 has no reset. Module 4 converts an asynchronous reset to synchronous internally.

An external asynchronous FPGA reset is connected to the Reset Controller. The Controller performs external reset synchronization, and sequences resets to Modules1-4 upon external reset release. Designing a robust reset synchronization circuit has unique challenges and pitfalls, which are discussed in [4].

The following figure is the FPGA die view of a hybrid reset scheme. Reset Controller is floor planned close to the center of the chip. The external reset input is coming from one of the IO pins. From the Reset Controller resets are distributed to different modules across the chip.

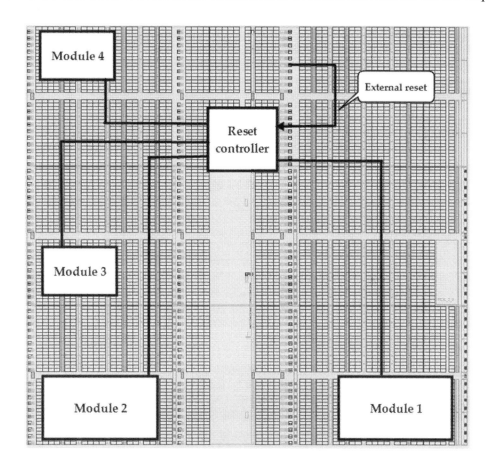

Figure 7: FPGA die view of a reset scheme

There are at least a couple of reasons for using a hybrid reset scheme. Large FPGA designs contain several IP cores and functional components with mixed reset schemes, which are often inflexible and cannot be changed.

A more subtle reason is related to the routing delays. A delay between two modules can exceed one or more clock periods. As an example, a routing delay across the mid-size Virtex-6 FPGA die is over 10ns. If the clock period is 3ns, it takes more than three clocks to cross the die. The consequence is that it's not feasible to design a pure synchronous reset scheme in a large FPGA.

Designs without external reset

Often a design doesn't have an external reset. One way to generate an explicit reset signal is to use a dedicated STARTUP_VIRTEX6 primitive, which Xilinx provides for Virtex-6 FPGAs. Designers can take advantage of the End Of Sequence (EOS) output of the STARTUP_VIRTEX6 primitive, which indicates the end of FPGA configuration. EOS signal is asynchronous, and will require a proper synchronization circuit to provide a clean synchronous reset.

However, this approach is not portable. For example, Xilinx Spartan FPGAs don't have an equivalent primitive.

Synthesis tool options

Synthesis tools provide several command-line options and attributes to control design reset.

XST has Asynchronous to Synchronous option (command line `-async_to_sync`), which treats all asynchronous reset signals as synchronous. It the option is enabled, it applies to all inferred sequential elements. The option will cause the mismatch between the original RTL and the post-synthesis netlist, and has to be used with caution.

"Use Synchronous Set" (`use_sync_set`) and "Use Synchronous Reset" (`use_sync_reset`) attributes control the use of dedicated synchronous set or reset inputs of a register. Those attributes have `auto`, `yes`, and `no` options. When the `no` option is specified, XST avoids using dedicated set or reset. In the `auto` mode, which is a default, XST attempts to estimate whether using dedicated synchronous set or reset will produce better results based on various metrics.

"Use Synchronous Set/Reset" attributes are applicable to the entire design or a particular instance.

Resources

[1] Ken Chapman, "*Get Smart About Reset: Think Local, Not Global*", Xilinx White Paper WP272.
http://www.xilinx.com/support/documentation/white_papers/wp272.pdf

[2] Ken Chapman, "*Get your Priorities Right – Make your Design Up to 50% Smaller*", Xilinx White Paper WP275.
http://www.xilinx.com/support/documentation/white_papers/wp275.pdf

[3] Philippe Garrault, "*HDL Coding Practices to Accelerate Design Performance*", Xilinx Xcell Journal Issue 55.
http://www.xilinx.com/publications/archives/xcell/Xcell55.pdf

[4] Clifford E. Cummings, "*Get Asynchronous & Synchronous Reset Design Techniques - Part Deux*", SNUG 2003, Boston.
http://www.sunburst-design.com/papers/CummingsSNUG2003Boston_Resets.pdf

30

DESIGNING SHIFT REGISTERS

Shift registers find many uses in FPGA designs. Some of the shift register applications are converters between serial and parallel interfaces, logic delay circuits, pulse extenders, barrel shifters, and waveform generators. Linear Feedback Shift Register (LFSR) is a special type of shift register, whose input bit is a linear function of its previous state. LFSR is used in pseudo-random number generators, fast counters, Cyclic Redundancy Checkers (CRC), and many other applications.

Shift registers can have the following configuration options: shift register length, left or right data shift, clock enable, shift data multiple bits (barrel shifter), synchronous or asynchronous reset.

There are four main methods to implement shift registers in Xilinx FPGAs using flip-flops, SRLs, BRAMs, and DSP48 primitives. Each method offers advantages and drawbacks in terms of speed, logic utilization, and functionality.

Shift register implementation using flip flops

The following is a Verilog example of a shift register with clock enable, synchronous reset, one bit width, and 64-bit depth.

```
module shift_flops(input clk,reset,enable,
                   input shift_din,
                   output shift_dout );
  localparam SHIFT_REG_SIZE = 64;
  reg [SHIFT_REG_SIZE-1:0] shift_reg;
  assign shift_dout = shift_reg[SHIFT_REG_SIZE-1];
  always @(posedge clk)
    if(reset) begin
      shift_reg  <= 'b0;
    end
    else begin
      shift_reg  <= enable
        ?{shift_reg[SHIFT_REG_SIZE-2:0] , shift_din}
        :shift_reg;
    end
```

```
endmodule // shift_flops
```
An alternative implementation of the same shift register using Verilog `for` loop.
```
always @(posedge clk)
  if(reset) begin
    shift_reg   <= 'b0;
  end
    else begin
      for(ix=1; ix < SHIFT_REG_SIZE; ix = ix + 1)
        shift_reg[ix]   <= enable
          ? shift_reg[ix-1]
          : shift_reg[ix];
      shift_reg[0]   <= enable ? shift_din : shift_reg[0];
    end
```

Shift register implementation using SRL

Xilinx provides a RAM-based shift register IP core. It generates fast, compact FIFO-style shift registers using SRL primitives. User options allow creating either fixed-length or variable-length shift registers, specify width and depth, clock enable, and initialization.

The disadvantage of the SRL-based shift register is that it supports only left shift operation, and no reset. This is due to limitations of the SRL primitive.

Shift register implementation using Block RAMs

The following figure shows an example of a shift register implementation using a dual port BRAM.

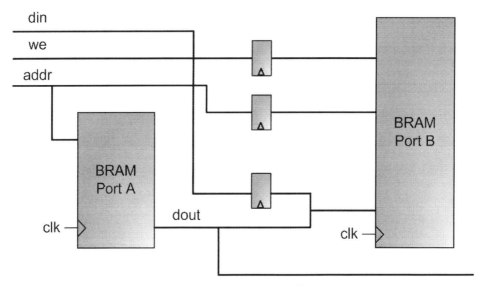

Figure 1: Shift Register Using Dual Port BRAM

The shift operation is performed by doing read from port A of the BRAM, concatenating delayed *din* with the data output from the port A, and writing the result to port B. The BRAM is configured in the write-first mode. That is, if both read and write operations to the same address are performed in the same clock, the write operation takes priority.

Another implementation option is a FIFO style, where each BRAM address contains a shift register value. This approach allows building very deep shift registers.

The shift register can operate at the full BRAM clock rate, which depends on the FPGA family and speed grade.

Shift register implementation using DSP48 primitive

Barrel shifter can be implemented using one or two DSP48 primitives. This implementation option is discussed in Tip #28.

Shift register synthesis options

XST provides Shift Register Extraction option to enable or disable shift register macro inference using SRL primitives.
-shreg_extract XST switch controls enabling shift register extraction for the entire project. Local control over shift register extraction can be achieved by placing `shreg_extract` attribute immediately before the module or signal declaration, as shown in the following Verilog example.

```
(* shreg_extract = "{yes | no}" *)
    reg [15:0] my_shift_register;
```

For the complete description of shift register implementation options and coding styles refer to the XST user guide documentation.

Logic utilization and performance results

The following table summarizes logic utilization and performance results for a 64-bit deep 1 bit data shift register using implementations discussed above.

All the shift registers were built for Xilinx Spartan-6 LX45 FPGA with 3-speed grade.

Table 1: Shift registers utilization and performance results

	Max freq	*Slices*	*LUTs*	*Regs*	*DSP48*	*BRAMs*
Flip flops	440	9	0	64	0	0
SRL	490	2	2	2	0	0
BRAM	275	1	0	2	0	1

	Max freq	*Slices*	*LUTs*	*Regs*	*DSP48*	*BRAMs*
DSP48	333	0	0	0	2	0

Shift register implementation using SRL has the highest performance. It is also more compact compared to the flip flop implementation.

The above performance and logic utilization results are only shown as an example, and should be interpreted judiciously. The results will vary significantly for different FPGA families, speed grades, tool options, and counter configuration.

All the source code, project files and the reports are available on the accompanying website.

31

INTERFACING TO EXTERNAL DEVICES

FPGA designers have a plethora of options for designing an interface between FPGA and external devices. They can choose different bus type, electrical properties and speed.

Busses taxonomy

A bus is a design component used to connect two or more modules or devices. The following figure shows taxonomy of different busses.

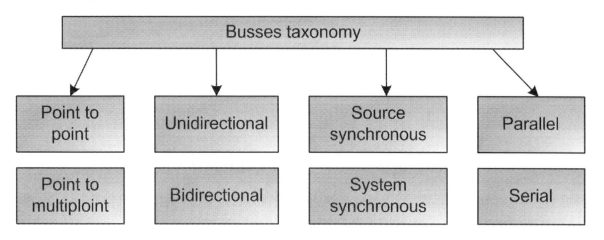

Figure 1: Busses Taxonomy

Point-to-point: a bus is connected to only two modules or devices. The advantage of a point-to-point bus is better signal integrity.

Point-to-multipoint: a bus is connected to more than two modules or devices. The advantage of a point-to-multipoint bus is lower pin count and simpler board design due to lower number of traces.

Unidirectional: the bus is driven by a single device or module connected to a bus. The advantage of a unidirectional bus is simpler implementation, and simpler termination scheme at the board level.

Bidirectional: the bus can be driven by any device or module connected to a bus. The advantage is lower pin count due to sharing of the same bus signals.

Source synchronous clock: is a technique of sourcing the clock along with the data on a bus. One advantage of this method is that it simplifies the clocking scheme of the system, and decouples bus driver from the recipients. This clocking scheme is used in several high-speed interfaces, for example SPI or PCI Express. The clock signal can be separate, or embedded into the data, and recovered on the receive side.

System synchronous clock: devices and modules connected to a bus are using a single clock. Unlike source synchronous method, system synchronous clocking scheme doesn't require a separate clock domain at the receiving device.

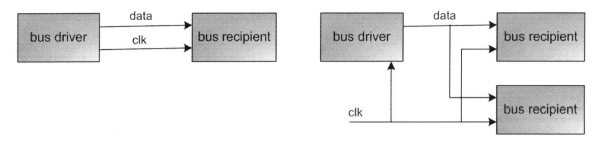

Figure 2: Source (on the left) and system (on the right) synchronous clocking scheme

Parallel busses

Parallel busses are typically used in low or medium frequency busses. There is no clear definition of what constitutes low or medium frequency, but the rule of thumb is below 100MHz is the low frequency, and between 100MHz and 300MHz is medium frequency.

Xilinx provides several primitives that can be used for designing parallel busses.

IDDR: a dedicated register that converts input dual data rate (DDR) data into a single data rate (SDR) output used in FPGA fabric.

ODDR: a dedicated register that converts input SDR data into a DDR external output.

IODELAY: design element used to provide a fixed or adjustable delay to the input data, and fixed delay to the output data. IODELAY is mainly used for data alignment of incoming and outgoing data.

IDELAYCTRL: used in conjunction with IODELAY for controlling the delay logic. One of the IDELAYCTRL inputs is a reference clock, which must be 200MHz to guarantee the tap delay accuracy in the IODELAY.

Adjusting input and output delays are required for calibrating a parallel bus operating at high frequencies. The adjustment process is dynamic and is performed after the board power up and periodically during the operation. There are several reasons for performing dynamic bus calibration. For instance, temperature and voltage fluctuations affect signal delay. In addition, trace delays on the PCB and inside the FPGA vary due to differences in manufacturing process. Because of the variable delays on different signals, parallel bus data may become skewed.

Serial busses

Parallel busses don't scale well to higher operating frequencies and bus width. Designing a parallel bus at high frequency is challenging because of the skew between multiple data signals, tight timing budget, and more complex board layout that requires to performing length-match of all bus signals. To overcome these challenges, many systems and several well-known communication protocols have migrated from a parallel to a serial interface. Two examples of this are Serial ATA, which is a serial version of the ATA or Parallel ATA, and PCI Express, which is the next generation of parallel PCI.

Another advantage of serial busses is a lower pin count. A disadvantage of a serial bus is that it has a more demanding PCB design. High speed serial links typically runs at multi-gigabit speed. As a result, they generate a lot more electromagnetic interference (EMI) and consume more power.

An external serial data stream is typically converted to the parallel data inside the FPGA. The module that does that is called SerDes (Serializer / Deserializer). A serializer takes in parallel data and converts it to a serial output at much higher rate. Conversely, a deserializer converts a high-speed serial input to a parallel output. Disadvantages of using SerDes are additional communication latency due to the extra steps required to perform serialization and deserialization; more complex initialization and periodic link training; and larger logic size.

The following figure shows a full duplex serial bus implemented as two SerDes modules.

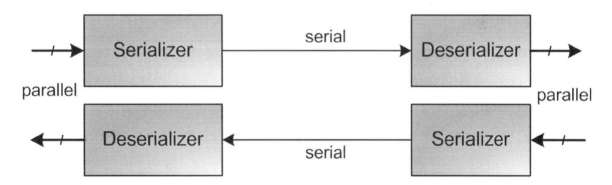

Figure 3: Full duplex serializer/deserializer

Xilinx provides several primitives that can be used for designing a serial bus.

ISERDES: a dedicated serial to parallel data converter to facilitate high-speed source synchronous data capturing. It has SDR and DDR data options and 2-to 6-bit data width.

GTP/GTX: an embedded transceiver module in some of the Virtex and Spartan FPGAs. It is a complex module, highly configurable, and tightly integrated with the FPGA logic resources. The following figure shows a block diagram of Virtex-6 GTX transceiver.

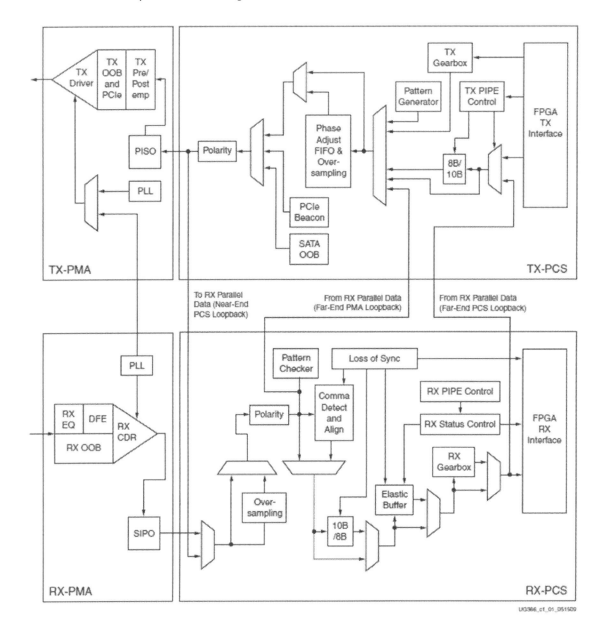

Figure 4: Transceiver block diagram (source: Virtex-6 FPGA GTX Transceivers, UG366)

Aurora

Aurora is a very efficient low-latency point-to-point serial protocol that utilizes GTP transceivers. It was designed to hide the interface details and overhead of the GTP. Xilinx provides an IP core with a user-friendly interface that implements Aurora protocol. Among the features that the core provides are different number of GTP channels, simplex and duplex operations, flow control, configurable line rate and user clock frequency.

The following figure illustrates point to point communication using Aurora core.

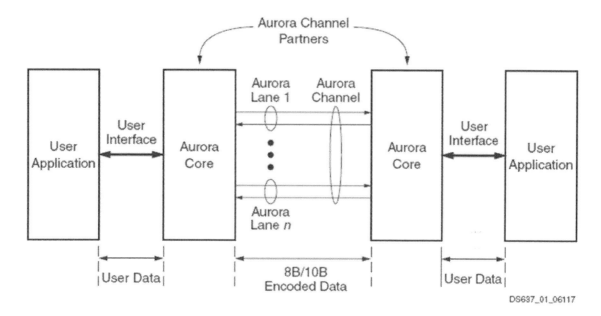

Figure 5: Using Aurora core (Source: Xilinx Aurora User Guide)

32

USING LOOK-UP TABLES AND CARRY CHAINS

Look-up tables and carry chains are combinatorial elements of a slice. In most cases, synthesis tools infer look-up tables and carry chains automatically from an HDL description. Sometimes designers want to use them explicitly to achieve higher performance. Another use is to gain low-level access for implementing custom circuits, for example priority trees, adders, or comparators, which contain carry chain structures and look-up tables.

Xilinx provides CARRY4 primitive to instantiate a carry chain structure, shown in the following figure.

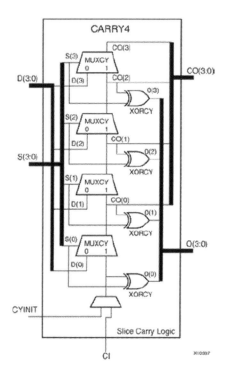

Figure 1: Carry chain logic (Source: Xilinx Virtex-6 Libraries Guide)

MUXCY and XORCY primitives that are part of the carry chain structure can also be instantiated directly.

Xilinx provides a variety of primitives for instantiating look-up tables. Some of the Virtex-6 family look-up tables are LUT5, LUT6, and LUT2. A detailed description of the look-up and carry chain primitives can be found in Xilinx Library Guide documentation for a specific FPGA family.

The following is a simple example of using three look-up tables to implement a 12-bit OR function.

```
// High-level Verilog implementation
assign user_out = |user_in[11:0];
// Implementation using explicit look-up tables instantiation
wire out, out1_14;
LUT6 #(
    .INIT ( 64'hFFFFFFFFFFFFFFFE ))
  out1 (
    .I0(user_in[3]),
    .I1(user_in[2]),
    .I2(user_in[5]),
    .I3(user_in[4]),
    .I4(user_in[7]),
    .I5(user_in[6]),
    .O(out));
  LUT6 #(
    .INIT ( 64'hFFFFFFFFFFFFFFFE ))
  out2 (
    .I0(user_in[9]),
    .I1(user_in[8]),
    .I2(user_in[11]),
    .I3(user_in[10]),
    .I4(user_in[1]),
    .I5(user_in[0]),
    .O(out1_14));
  LUT2 #(
    .INIT ( 4'hE ))
    out3 (
      .I0(out),
      .I1(out1_14),
      .O(user_out));
```

The INIT parameter to LUT2 and LUT6 primitives defines look-up table's logical function. It's calculated by assigning a 1 to corresponding INIT bit value when the associated inputs are applied. For example, the INIT value of 64'hFFFFFFFFFFFFFFFE in the above example indicates that the output of *out1* LUT6 instance is 0 for an all-zero input combination and 1 otherwise.

33
DESIGNING PIPELINES

Pipelines are used extensively in protocol and packet processing, DSP, image and video algorithms, CPU instruction pipelines, encryption/decryption, and many other designs.

Pipelining is defined as a process of splitting a logic function into multiple stages, such that each stage executes a small part of the function. The first pipeline stage can start processing a new input while the rest of the pipeline is still working on the previous input. This enables higher throughput and performance. However, pipelining also adds additional latency and logic overhead.

Latency, throughput, and the initiation interval are used to describe pipeline performance. Latency is defined as the number of clock cycles from the first valid input till the corresponding result available on the output of the pipeline. The initiation interval is the minimum number of clock cycles that must elapse between two consecutive valid inputs. Throughput is a measure of how often the pipeline produces the valid output.

To achieve the optimal performance of a pipeline, the amount of combinatorial logic between registered stages has to be balanced.

FPGA implementation of high performance pipelines presents unique challenges, and requires a good understanding of FPGA architecture, synthesis and physical implementation tool options in order to meet logic utilization and performance goals. A pipeline can be a complex logic structure that includes various synchronous components, such as DSPs, BRAMs, and Shift Register LUTs (SRLs). The pipeline can split into to several branches and merge back. It might include clock enable connected to every synchronous element to stall the pipeline when the input data is not available.

The following two figures show examples of complex pipelines. The first one implements a 32-bit AES encryption round. It includes registers, BRAMs, DSP, and four synchronized 8-bit dapathaths with feedback. The second one is the alpha-blending of two data streams.

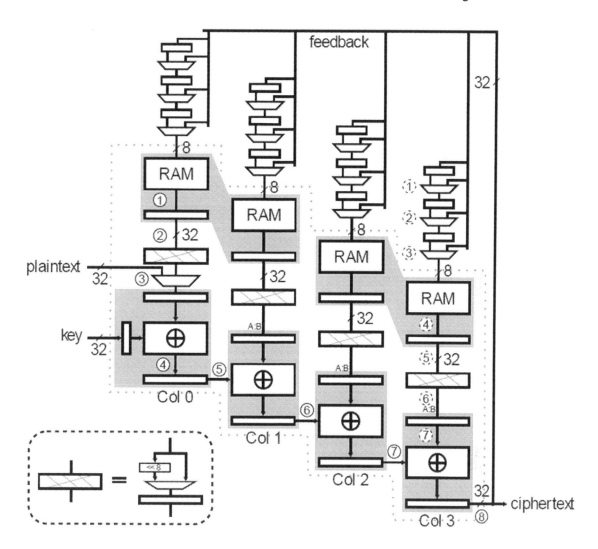

Figure 1: AES round (courtesy of Saar Drimer, PhD dissertation, 9/2009, University of Cambridge)

158   *100 Power Tips for FPGA designers*

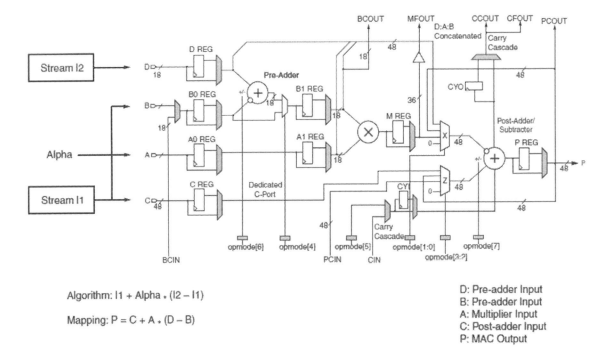

Figure 2: Alpha-blending pipeline (Source: Xilinx White Paper WP387)

Pipeline data width can vary from 1 to 256 bits, or even more than that. For example, the main datapath of a PCI Express Gen2 16-lane protocol processing engine can be 256 bit wide, and run at 250 MHz in order to process data at the bus speed. If the depth of such a pipeline is 8 stages, then the number of the pipeline registers is at least 256x8=2048. The pipeline also has to have clock enable signal connected to each synchronous element to stall when the data is not available. Therefore, the fanout of the clock enable signal in such a pipeline is 2048. Such a high fanout causes large routing delays, and decreased performance.

The following example of a simple pipeline is used to illustrate this problem.

```
module pipeline(input clk, reset, enable,
            input [127:0] data_in,
            output reg [127:0] data_out);
  reg [127:0] data_in_q,data_in_dq, data_in_2dq, data_in_3dq;
  always @(posedge clk)
    if(reset) begin
      data_in_q    <= 'b0;
      data_in_dq   <= 'b0;
      data_in_2dq  <= 'b0;
      data_in_3dq  <= 'b0;
      data_out     <= 'b0;
```

```
      end
    else begin
      data_in_q     <= enable ? data_in     : data_in_q;
      data_in_dq    <= enable ? data_in_q   : data_in_dq;
      data_in_2dq   <= enable ? data_in_dq  : data_in_2dq;
      data_in_3dq   <= enable ? data_in_2dq : data_in_3dq;
      data_out      <= enable ? data_in_3dq : data_out;
    end
endmodule // pipeline
```

The following figure shows a Xilinx FPGA Editor view of a high fanout `enable` net.

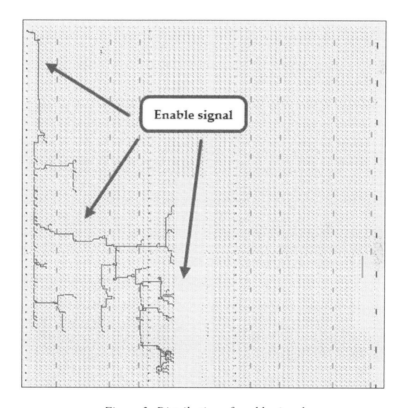

Figure 3: Distribution of enable signal

Executing FPGA Editor `delay` command on the `enable` net produces the following results (only part of the log is shown):

```
delay
Building the delay mediator...
Net "enable":
    driver - comp.pin "enable.I", site.pin "H21.I"
    1.987ns - comp.pin "data_out_212.CE", site.pin
"SLICE_X0Y72.CE"
```

```
        1.893ns - comp.pin "data_out_30.CE", site.pin
"SLICE_X0Y74.CE"
        1.799ns - comp.pin "data_out_211.CE", site.pin
"SLICE_X0Y76.CE"
        1.425ns - comp.pin "data_out_17.CE", site.pin
"SLICE_X1Y52.CE"
        1.799ns - comp.pin "data_out_26.CE", site.pin
"SLICE_X5Y82.CE"
        2.625ns - comp.pin "data_out_35.CE", site.pin
"SLICE_X7Y67.CE"
        5.815ns - comp.pin "data_out_751.CE", site.pin
"SLICE_X40Y31.CE"
        5.900ns - comp.pin "data_out_7111.CE", site.pin
"SLICE_X40Y32.CE"
        5.688ns - comp.pin "data_out_691.CE", site.pin
"SLICE_X40Y33.CE"
        5.697ns - comp.pin "data_out_891.CE", site.pin
"SLICE_X40Y34.CE"
        5.078ns - comp.pin "data_out_491.CE", site.pin
"SLICE_X40Y42.CE"
        4.996ns - comp.pin "data_out_851.CE", site.pin
"SLICE_X40Y50.CE"
        5.790ns - comp.pin "data_out_75.CE", site.pin
"SLICE_X42Y31.CE"
        4.594ns - comp.pin "data_out_412.CE", site.pin
"SLICE_X43Y57.CE"
```

The delay of the `enable` net from source to destination registers ranges between 1.276ns to 5.9ns.

There are several approaches to reduce the maximum delay. One option is to use dedicated low-skew routes. However, FPGAs have limited amount of dedicated routes, which are also used by the global clocks. Another method is to manually replicate the logic that drives clock enable in order to reduce the fanout. That can be also achieved by limiting the maximum fanout of a net. Xilinx XST provides -max_fanout global synthesis option, which sets the fanout limit on nets. If the limit is exceeded, the logic gates are replicated. Floorplanning can be used to constrain the area of the pipeline logic, which also reduces routing delays. Finally, the entire pipeline can be redesigned such that it doesn't require a global `enable` signal.

Limiting maximum fanout of the above example to 20 results in significant improvement, as shown in the following FPGA Editor log (only part of the log is shown):

```
delay
Net "enable_IBUF_33":
```

```
    1.038ns - comp.pin "enable_IBUF_13.D6", site.pin
"SLICE_X33Y58.D1"
    0.934ns - comp.pin "enable_IBUF_11.A6", site.pin
"SLICE_X34Y58.A3"
    0.581ns - comp.pin "enable_IBUF_9.A6", site.pin
"SLICE_X34Y65.A4"
    0.930ns - comp.pin "enable_IBUF_12.A6", site.pin
"SLICE_X35Y58.A3"
    0.722ns - comp.pin "enable_IBUF_10.C6", site.pin
"SLICE_X35Y65.C2"
    0.380ns - comp.pin "enable_IBUF_8.A6", site.pin
"SLICE_X40Y64.A3"
    driver  - comp.pin "enable_IBUF_7.C", site.pin
"SLICE_X40Y65.C"
    0.291ns - comp.pin "enable_IBUF_7.D6", site.pin
"SLICE_X40Y65.D3"
Net "enable_IBUF_8":
    0.453ns - comp.pin "data_out_851.CE", site.pin
"SLICE_X36Y62.CE"
    0.288ns - comp.pin "data_out_701.CE", site.pin
"SLICE_X36Y64.CE"
    0.468ns - comp.pin "data_out_8111.CE", site.pin
"SLICE_X36Y67.CE"
    0.365ns - comp.pin "data_out_881.CE", site.pin
"SLICE_X40Y60.CE"
    driver  - comp.pin "enable_IBUF_8.A", site.pin
"SLICE_X40Y64.A"
    0.965ns - comp.pin "data_out_791.CE", site.pin
"SLICE_X40Y78.CE"
    1.251ns - comp.pin "data_out_751.CE", site.pin
"SLICE_X40Y85.CE"
```

Now, the maximum delay of the `enable` net is 1.251ns.

Another consideration is the efficient packing of pipelined designs into Slices. A Xilinx Virtex-6 Slice contains eight registers and four LUTs. In a register-dominated pipeline, in which the number of LUTs and registers is not balanced, Slice LUTs can be wasted. XST provides the `-reduce_control_set` option, which reduces the number of control sets and improves logic packing into Slices during MAP.

Retiming is a register-balancing technique that can be used for improving the timing performance of a pipeline. Retiming moves registers across combinatorial logic, but does not change the number of registers in a cycle or path from a primary input to a primary output of the pipeline. In Xilinx, build flow retiming is controlled by `-retiming` MAP option.

34
USING EMBEDDED MEMORY

Xilinx FPGAs have two types of embedded memories: a dedicated Block RAM (BRAM) primitive, and a LUT configured as Distributed RAM. Each memory type can be further configured as a single- and dual-ported RAM or ROM.

The following figure shows the embedded memory taxonomy in Xilinx FPGAs.

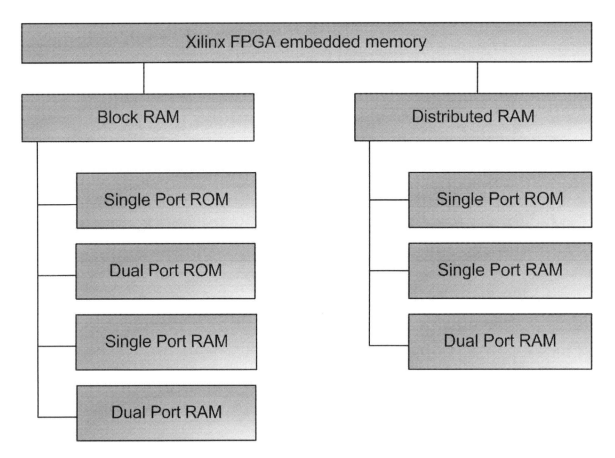

Figure 1: Xilinx FPGA embedded memory taxonomy

Block RAM

The following figure shows the IO ports of a Virtex-6 BRAM primitive.

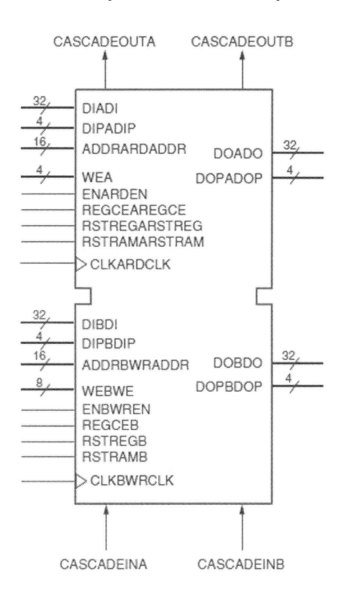

Figure 2: BRAM primitive (source: Xilinx User Guide UG363)

A BRAM in Virtex-6 FPGAs can store 36K bits, and can be configured as a single- or dual-ported RAM. Other configuration options include data width from 1 to 36 bit, memory depth up to 32K entries, enabling or disabling of data error detection and correction, register outputs, and cascading of multiple BRAM primitives.

There are three ways to incorporate a BRAM in the design. A BRAM can be directly instantiated using one of the primitives such as RAMB36E1 or RAMB18E1. This method enables low-level access to all BRAM features. The Xilinx CoreGen tool can be used to generate a customizable core, such as a FIFO, which includes BRAMs.

BRAMs can be inferred if the RTL follows the coding style defined by a synthesis tool. The main advantage of the inference method is code portability. The following is an example of a simple single-port RAM, which infers a BRAM during synthesis.

```verilog
module bram_inference(input clk,
                      input [15:0]       mem_din,
                      input [9:0]        mem_addr,
                      input              mem_we,
                      output reg [15:0]  mem_dout);

  reg [15:0] ram [1:1024];
  always @(posedge clk) begin
    if(mem_we)
      ram[mem_addr] <= mem_din;
    mem_dout <= ram[mem_addr];
  end
endmodule // bram_inference
```

Synthesizing this example with XST produces the following log.

```
=================================================================
*   HDL Synthesis
=================================================================
Synthesizing Unit <bram_inference>.
Found 1024x16-bit single-port RAM <Mram_ram> for signal <ram>.
    Found 16-bit register for signal <mem_dout>.
    Summary:
      inferred   1 RAM(s).
      inferred  16 D-type flip-flop(s).
Unit <bram_inference> synthesized.
=================================================================
*   Advanced HDL Synthesis
=================================================================
Synthesizing (advanced) Unit <bram_inference>.
INFO:Xst:3040 - The RAM <Mram_ram> will be implemented as a
BLOCK RAM, absorbing the following register(s): <mem_dout>
    -----------------------------------------------
    | ram_type           | Block
    -----------------------------------------------
    | Port A
```

```
        |       aspect ratio    | 1024-word x 16-bit
        |       mode            | read-first
        |       clkA            | connected to signal <clk>
        |       weA             | connected to signal <mem_we>
        |       addrA           | connected to signal <mem_addr>
        |       diA             | connected to signal <mem_din>
        |       doA             | connected to signal <mem_dout>
        | optimization          | speed
        ---------------------------------------------------------
Unit <bram_inference> synthesized (advanced).
=========================================================
Advanced HDL Synthesis Report
Macro Statistics
# RAMs                                                  : 1
 1024x16-bit single-port block RAM                      : 1
=========================================================
```

The log indicates that XST inferred one BRAM, and also absorbed a 16-bit `mem_dout` register.

The inference rules and limitations are specific to a synthesis tool. For example, XST cannot infer dual-ported BRAMs with different port widths, read and write capability on both ports, or different clocks on each port.

BRAM initialization

It is often required to preload BRAM with predefined contents after FPGA configuration is complete. Designers have several options to perform BRAM initialization. If a memory is generated using CoreGen tool, BRAM contents can be initialized from a special memory coefficient (COE) file passed to C_INIT_FILE_NAME parameter. The following is an example of a COE file.

```
; 32-byte memory initialization
memory_initialization_radix = 16;
memory_initialization_vector =
6c600000,
6c800001,
6ca00002,
b8000006,
6c600007
```

If a BRAM is instantiated directly using RAMB36E1 or RAMB18E1 primitives, the contents can be initialized using INIT_A and INIT_B attributes directly in the code. The following is partial code to instantiate a `RAMB36E1` primitive.

```
RAMB36E1 #(
```

```
    .INIT_00(256'h1234),
    .INIT_01(256'h5678),
    .READ_WIDTH_A(18),
    .READ_WIDTH_B(9),
    //...other attributes
)
RAMB36E1_instance (
    .WEA(WEA),
    .WEBWE(WEBWE)
    //...other ports
);
```

The disadvantage of both methods is that it requires re-synthesis of the design after changing BRAM initialization values.

Xilinx FPGA Editor allows making modifications to BRAM contents. The following figure illustrates using FPGA Editor to perform BRAM initialization.

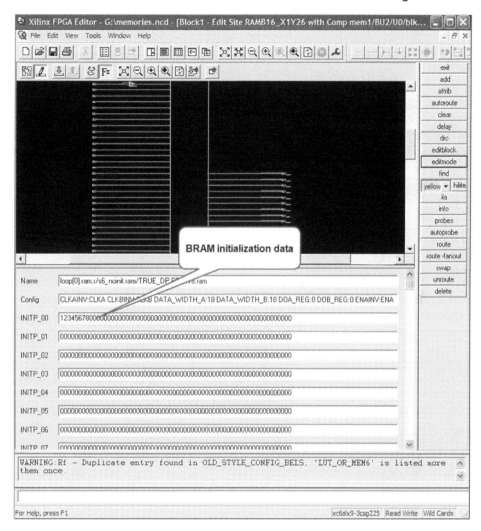

Figure 3: BRAM initialization using FPGA Editor

There are 128 INIT_A/B parameters 256 bit each, which cover the entire contents of a BRAM. Using FPGA Editor is convenient for making small BRAM modifications. It doesn't require performing re-synthesis or full physical implementation, only bitstream generation using Xilinx *bitgen* tool. The disadvantage of this method is the need to know physical locations of a BRAM module, which can change between builds.

The last method to do BRAM initialization is using Xilinx *data2mem* utility.

BRAM design challenges

There are several pitfalls and design challenges FPGA developers might encounter while using BRAMs.

All BRAM inputs, including reset, address, and data, are synchronous to the clock of the corresponding port. Not observing setup and hold timing requirements on the inputs will result in data corruption or other functional problems.

Asserting BRAM reset will cause the reset of flags and output registers. However, it has no impact on internal memory contents.

BRAM primitive has relatively slow clock-to-data time on the output data port. It ranges from 1.6ns to 3.73ns in Virtex-6 FPGAs depending on the speed grade and configuration. One implication of this is the inability to connect complex combinatorial logic to the data output in high speed designs. Enabling BRAM output register will reduce clock-to-data time to the value ranging between 0.6ns and 0.94ns, depending on the speed grade and configuration. The disadvantage of using an output register is increased read latency.

A BRAM has a minimum read latency of one clock. Designers have an option of using Distributed RAM in asynchronous read mode, which has no read latency.

Using BRAM in a dual-ported mode might result in data corruption in case of colliding writes from both ports.

Using BRAM primitives in high speed designs requires careful floorplanning, because routing delays to and from a BRAM might consume significant part of the timing budget. Distributed RAM, which is implemented using generic logic resources, doesn't have this problem.

Distributed RAM

Distributed RAMs are implemented used general purposed logic resources. Similarly to BRAM, there are three ways to incorporate a Distributed RAM in the design: directly instantiation of one of the Distributed RAM primitives, using CoreGen tool to generate a customizable core, and inferring in the RTL.

The following code example of a ROM, which infers Distributed RAM during synthesis.

```
module rom_inference(input clk,
                     input [2:0] mem_addr,
                     output reg [15:0] mem_dout);
  reg [15:0] rom [1:8];
  always @(posedge clk) begin
    mem_dout <= rom[mem_addr];
  end
endmodule // rom_inference
```

Synthesizing this example with XST produces the following log.

```
=========================================================
*       HDL Synthesis
=========================================================
```

```
Synthesizing Unit <rom_inference>.
Found 8x16-bit single-port Read Only RAM <Mram_rom> for
signal <rom>.
Found 16-bit register for signal <mem_dout>.
Summary:
  inferred   1 RAM(s).
  inferred  16 D-type flip-flop(s).
=========================================================
HDL Synthesis Report
Macro Statistics
# RAMs                                                 : 1
 8x16-bit single-port Read Only RAM                    : 1
# Registers                                            : 1
 16-bit register                                       : 1
=========================================================

*   Advanced HDL Synthesis
=========================================================
INFO:Xst:3048 - The small RAM <Mram_rom> will be implemented
on LUTs in order to maximize performance and save block RAM
resources. If you want to force its implementation on block,
use option/constraint ram_style.
        -------------------------------------------------
        | ram_type              | Distributed
        -------------------------------------------------
        | Port A
        |    aspect ratio       | 8-word x 16-bit
        |    weA                | connected to signal <GND>
        |    addrA              | connected to signal <mem_addr>
        |    diA                | connected to signal <GND>
        |    doA                | connected to internal node
        -------------------------------------------------
Unit <rom_inference> synthesized (advanced).
=========================================================
Advanced HDL Synthesis Report
Macro Statistics
# RAMs                                                 : 1
 8x16-bit single-port distributed Read Only RAM        : 1
# Registers                                            : 16
 Flip-Flops                                            : 16
=========================================================
```

Both BRAM and Distributed RAM require synchronous data write. However, unlike BRAM, Distributed RAM has an asynchronous read mode with zero latency. Distributed RAMs are typically used for small RAMs and ROMs.

Resources

[1] Virtex-6 FPGA Memory Resources, Xilinx User Guide UG363
http://www.xilinx.com/support/documentation/user_guides/ug363.pdf

[2] Xilinx Block Memory Generator
http://www.xilinx.com/products/ipcenter/Block_Memory_Generator.htm

[3] Xilinx Distributed Memory Generator
http://www.xilinx.com/support/documentation/ip_documentation/dist_mem_gen_ds322.pdf

35

UNDERSTANDING FPGA BITSTREAM STRUCTURE

Bitstream is a commonly used term to describe a file that contains the full internal configuration state of an FPGA, including routing, logic resources, and IO settings. The majority of modern FPGAs are SRAM-based, including Xilinx Spartan and Virtex families. On each FPGA power-up, or during subsequent FPGA reconfiguration, a bitstream is read from the external non-volatile memory such as flash, processed by the FPGA configuration controller, and loaded to the internal configuration SRAM.

There are several situations when designers need to have a good understanding of internal structure of the FPGA bitstream. Some examples are low-level bitstream customizations that cannot be performed using parameters to the FPGA physical implementation tools, implementing complex configuration fallback schemes, creating short command sequences for partial FPGA reconfiguration via internal configuration port (ICAP), reading configuration status, and others. Unfortunately, reverse engineering and tampering with the bitstream to illegally obtain proprietary design information belongs to the list of use cases.

Bitstream format

Xilinx FPGA bitstream structure is shown in the following figure.

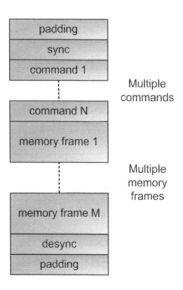

Figure 1: Xilinx FPGA bitstream structure

The bitstream consists of the following components: padding, synchronization word, commands for accessing configuration registers, memory frames, and desynchronization word.

Padding

Padding data is a sequence of all zeros or all ones and is ignored by the FPGA configuration controller. Padding data is required for separating bitstreams in non-volatile memory. It is convenient to use all ones for padding, because this is the state of flash memories after performing an erase operation.

Synchronization word

Synchronization word is a special value (0xAA995566) that tells the FPGA configuration controller to start processing subsequent bitstream data.

Desynchronization word

Desynchronization word indicates to the FPGA configuration controller the end of the bitstream. After desynchronization, all bitstream data is ignored until the next synchronization word is encountered.

Commands

Commands are used to perform read and write access to FPGA configuration controller registers. Some of the commands that are present in every bitstream are IDCODE, which uniquely identifies the FPGA device the bitstream belongs to, Frame Address Register (FAR) and Frame Data Register (FDRI), and No Operation (NOOP) that is ignored.

Memory frames

Memory frame is a basic configuration unit in Xilinx FPGAs. A frame has a fixed size, which varies in different FPGA families. In Virtex-6 devices a frame has 2592 bits. Every Virtex-6 device has a different number of frames ranging from 7491 in the smallest LX75T to 55548 in the largest LX550T. A frame is used for independent configuration of several slices, IOs, BRAMs, and other FPGA components. Each frame has an address, which corresponds to a location in the FPGA configuration space. To configure a frame, bitstream uses a sequence of FAR and FDRI commands.

The Virtex-6 FPGA Configuration User Guide [1] contains sufficient documentation on a bitstream structure and commands to access registers in the FPGA configuration controller. However, the detailed documentation of memory frames is unavailable not only for Xilinx FPGAs but also for FPGAs from other vendors.

Xilinx bitgen utility

Bitgen is a Xilinx utility that takes a post place-and-route file in Native Circuit Description (NCD) format and creates a bitstream to be used for FPGA configuration. Bitgen is a highly configurable tool with more than 100 command-line options that are described in the Command Line Tools User Guide [2]. Some of the options are bitstream output format, enabling compression for reducing the bitstream size and FPGA configuration speed, using CRC to ensure data integrity, encrypting the bitstream, and many others.

Example

The following is an example of a short bitstream used for a difference-based partial reconfiguration. It is parsed by a script that annotates bitstream commands with a user friendly description. The script is written in Perl and is available on the accompanying website.

```
FFFFFFFF    Padding
FFFFFFFF    Padding
000000BB    Bus Width
11220044    8/16/32 BusWidth
FFFFFFFF    Padding
FFFFFFFF    Padding
AA995566    SYNC command
20000000    NO OP
30008001    write 1 word to CMD
00000007    RCRC command
20000000    NO OP
20000000    NO OP
30018001    write 1 word to ID
04250093    IDCODE
30008001    write 1 word to CMD
00000000    NULL command
30002001    write 1 word to FAR
00000000    FAR [Block 0 Top Row 0 Col 0 Minor 0]
30008001    write 1 word to CMD
00000001    WCFG command
20000000    NO OP
30002001    write 1 word to FAR
0000951A    FAR [Block 0 Top Row 1 Col 42 Minor 26]
20000000    NO OP
30004195    write 405 words to FDRI
    data words  0...404
30002001 write 1 word to FAR
001014A8 FAR [Block 0 Bot Row 0 Col 41 Minor 40]
20000000 NO OP
```

```
300040F3 write 243 words to FDRI
    data words 0...242
3000C001 write 1 word to MASK
00001000 MASK
30030001 write 1 word to CTL1
00000000 CTL1
30008001 write 1 word to CMD
00000003 LFRM command
20000000 NO OP
20000000 NO OP
20000000 NO OP
30002001 write 1 word to FAR
00EF8000 FAR [Block 7 Top Row 31 Col 0 Minor 0]
30000001 write 1 word to CRC
1C06EA42 CRC
30008001 write 1 word to CMD
0000000D DESYNCH command
20000000 NO OP
```

Examination of the bitstream reveals synchronization and desynchronization commands, IDCODE that belongs to Virtex-6 LX240T FPGA, and two frames of 405 and 243 words each.

Resources

[1] Virtex-6 FPGA Configuration User Guide UG360
http://www.xilinx.com/support/documentation/user_guides/ug360.pdf

[2] Xilinx Command Line Tools User Guide
http://www.xilinx.com/support/documentation/sw_manuals/xilinx12_2/devref.pdf

36
FPGA CONFIGURATION

The configuration of all modern FPGAs falls into two categories: SRAM-based, which uses an external memory to program a configuration SRAM inside the FPGA, and non-volatile FPGAs, which can be configured only once.

Lattice and Actel FPGAs use a non-volatile configuration technology called Antifuse. The main advantages of a non-volatile FPGA configuration are simpler system design that doesn't require external memory and configuration controller, lower power consumption, lower cost, and faster FPGA configuration time. The biggest disadvantage is fixed configuration.

Most modern FPGAs are SRAM-based, including the Xilinx Spartan and Virtex families. On each FPGA power-up, or during subsequent FPGA reconfiguration, a bitstream is read from the external non-volatile memory, processed by the configuration controller, and loaded to the internal configuration SRAM. The configuration SRAM holds all the design information to configure logic, IO, embedded memories, routing, clocking, transceivers, and other FPGA primitives.

The following figure shows Xilinx Virtex-6 configuration architecture.

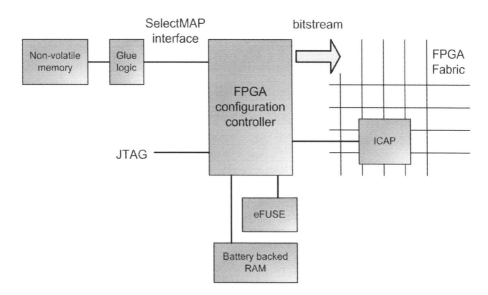

Figure 1: Xilinx Virtex-6 configuration architecture

The configuration is performed by the configuration controller inside the FPGA. The bitstream is stored in external non-volatile memory, such as flash. The external memory is connected to the configuration controller using the SelectMAP interface, which is Xilinx-specific. Additional glue logic might be required to bridge the SelectMAP and external memory interfaces. In addition, a bitstream can be loaded into the configuration controller via JTAG or ICAP. Bitstreams can be optionally encrypted to provide higher security. Internal Battery Backed RAM (BBR) and eFuse hold an encryption key required for bitstream decryption.

Each bit of the FPGA configuration memory, also called configuration memory cell, is initialized with the corresponding bit in the bitstream. The output of each memory cell is connected to a configurable functional block, such as LUT, register, BRAM, IO, routing, and others. The following figure shows a configuration memory cell connected to a multiplexer to set a specific routing path between components in the FPGA fabric. The logic state of zero or one is set during the FPGA configuration stage.

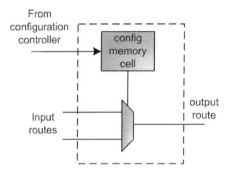

Figure 2: FPGA routing configuration

Xilinx FPGA configuration modes

There are several FPGA configuration modes that address different usage modes. The following figure shows taxonomy of Xilinx FPGA configuration modes.

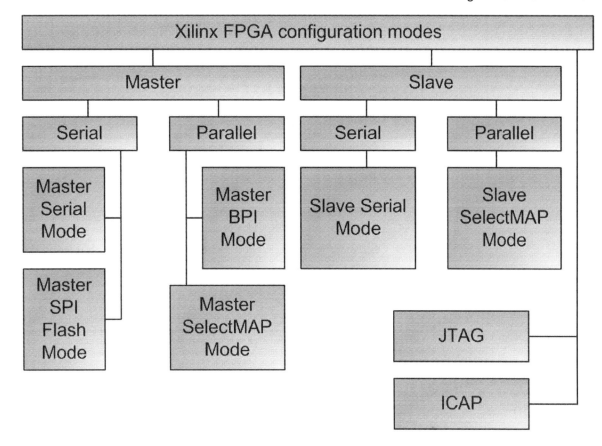

Figure 3: Taxonomy of FPGA configuration modes

Configuration modes are divided into two categories: master and slave. In master configuration modes, an FPGA controls configuration process. In slave modes, FPGA configuration is controlled by an external device, such as a microcontroller, CPLD, or another FPGA. In addition, there are two special configuration modes using JTAG and Internal Configuration Access Port (ICAP). There are four data width sizes to support different external memories: 32-bit, 16-bit, 8-bit, and 1-bit (serial).

The following is a brief overview of configuration modes.

JTAG

JTAG interface is mainly used during the debug. A special adapter is connected to dedicated FPGA pins to interface with Xilinx ChipScope and iMPACT software applications.

ICAP

A dedicated ICAP primitive interfaces with the user logic to perform configuration from within the FPGA fabric.

Master Serial Mode

In Master Serial Mode the FPGA is controlling the Xilinx Platform Flash to provide the configuration data. Xilinx Platform Flash is a special non-volatile flash memory designed to interface with Xilinx FPGAs directly using the SelectMAP interface.

Master SPI Flash Mode

In Master SPI Flash Mode, the FPGA is controlling serial SPI Flash to provide the configuration data.

Master SelectMAP Mode

In Master SelectMAP Mode, the FPGA is controlling Xilinx Platform Flash to provide 8- or 16-bit wide configuration data.

Master BPI Mode

In Master BPI Mode, the FPGA is controlling a parallel NOR Flash to provide 8- or 16-bit wide configuration data.

Slave Serial and SelectMAP Mode

In Slave Serial Mode, an external device, such as a microcontroller, CPLD, or another FPGA, controls the FPGA configuration process.

Designing FPGA configuration scheme

There are several design considerations for selecting the most appropriate FPGA configuration scheme for a particular design. The main selection criteria are:

- Choosing whether the configuration process is controlled by an external device (slave modes), or by FPGA itself (master modes). Master modes are the simplest from a system complexity standpoint but may not be suitable for all designs. The slave mode interface can be as simple as connecting the serial interface directly to the processor's IO pins and toggling them to read the bitstream data into the configuration controller.

- Choosing the type of external non-volatile memory and its size for storing one or several FPGA bitstreams. Although the cost of an external memory is relatively low compared with the cost of an FPGA, it still is not negligible. Designers can choose among SPI flash, parallel NOR flash, or Xilinx Platform Flash. In some designs an FPGA can be configured directly from the Host using an external processor connected to an FPGA configuration controller using one of the slave modes.

- The choice of the data width – serial, 8-bit, 16-bit, or 32-bit – affects the configuration speed and the available number of FPGA IOs for the design.
- Field upgradability of the configuration bitstream can be an important requirement. The configuration scheme has to support cases in which the bitstream is getting corrupted while being programmed into a non-volatile memory.
- Xilinx FPGAs provides an option to encrypt a bitstream in cases in which higher design security is required. Decryption keys can be stored either in internal BBR or eFuse. BBR storage is volatile and requires an external battery. The advantage of using BBR is the relative ease of reprogramming the keys when compared with a non-volatile eFuse.

Calculating configuration time

In many applications FPGA configuration time is critical, and it is important to accurately estimate the time during configuration scheme selection. The configuration time depends on the bitstream size, clock frequency, and the data width of the configuration interface, and is defined by the following formula:

```
Config time = bitstream size * clock frequency * data width.
```

The following table provides the expected configuration times for the smallest and largest Xilinx Virtex-6 FPGAs using a 50MHz clock over different data widths of the configuration interface.

Table 1: FPGA configuration time

Virtex-6 FPGA	Bitstream size	Config time over Serial interface	Config time over 8-bit interface	Config time over 32-bit interface
LX75T	26,239,328	525ms	66ms	16.4ms
HX565T	160,655,264	3.2sec	402ms	100.4ms

Xilinx configuration-related primitives

The following table provides a list of configuration-related primitives supported by Xilinx Virtex-6 FPGAs.

Table 2: Xilinx Virtex-6 configuration-related primitives

Primitive	Description
USR_ACCESS_VIRTEX6	Enables access to a 32-bit configuration register within configuration logic

Primitive	Description
ICAP_VIRTEX6	Enables access to all configuration controller functions within FPGA fabric
CAPTURE_VIRTEX6	Enables readback register capture control
FRAME_ECC_VIRTEX6	Enables error detection and correction of configuration frames
EFUSE_USR	Provides internal access to 32-bit non-volatile fuses specific to the design
DNA_PORT	Provides access to a Device DNA port, which holds a unique device ID

Resources:

[1] Configuration for Xilinx Virtex-6 FPGA
http://www.xilinx.com/products/design_resources/config_sol/v6/config_v6.htm

37
FPGA RECONFIGURATION

The term reconfiguration refers to reprogramming an FPGA after it is already configured. There are two types of FPGA reconfiguration: full and partial. Full reconfiguration reprograms the entire FPGA, whereas partial reconfiguration replaces certain parts of the design while the rest of the design remains operational. Partial reconfiguration is not considered a special case of full reconfiguration, because both are fundamentally the same. Performing a partial FPGA reconfiguration is done using the same methods as full configuration: JTAG, ICAP, or SelectMAP interface, which is described in Tip #37. The bitstream structure is the same for both full and partial reconfiguration methods.

FPGA reconfiguration offers several benefits. It allows for the sharing of the same FPGA fabric across multiple designs. That in turn reduces FPGA size, cost, and system complexity. Full and partial reconfiguration opens the possibility for many innovative FPGA applications that would be cost prohibitive to implement otherwise. Some of the application examples that take advantage of the FPGA reconfiguration are DSP, audio, or video processors that change the processing algorithm based on the user input, communication controllers with integrated deep packet inspection engine, which switch a packet processor based on the protocol, and many others.

There is a lot of industry and academic research on the subject of FPGA reconfiguration, which produces a constant stream of interesting application notes, research papers, and dissertations.

Although partial reconfiguration is not a new functionality, it has not yet reached the mainstream. Design and implementation flows, tool support, and even the nomenclature are constantly evolving to become more user friendly. The ultimate goal is to provide a simple and transparent design flow to FPGA developers without requiring them to have detailed knowledge of configuration logic and bitstream structure.

Partial reconfiguration is a complex functionality riddled with multiple challenges during design implementation, tool flow, and the reconfiguration procedure itself. One challenge is to complete a smooth handoff during FPGA configuration change without disrupting the operation of the remaining design, or compromising its integrity. The FPGA fabric and IOs cannot be kept at reset, which is the case during full reconfiguration. Another challenge is preventing the static part of the design from entering an invalid state while the dynamic part is being changed. Designers must properly define and constrain interfaces between static and dynamic parts so that FPGA physical implementation tools place logic and use exactly the same routing resources for both.

There are three partial reconfiguration flows that can be used for Xilinx FPGAs: difference-based, partition based, and using dynamic reconfiguration port.

Difference-based partial reconfiguration

Difference-based partial reconfiguration [2] is most suitable for making small design changes to LUT equations, IO characteristics, and BRAM contents. The following is a simple difference-based partial reconfiguration code and flow example. It can run on a Xilinx ML605 Virtex-6 development board.

```
// original module: turn on LED when both buttons are pressed
module top(input btn0,btn1,output led);
    assign led = btn0 & btn1;
endmodule // top

// partial reconfiguration module: turn on LED when either
button is pressed
module top_pr(input btn0,btn1, output led);
    assign led = btn0 | btn1;
endmodule // top_pr

# Constraints file: the same for both designs
NET "btn0" LOC = "A18"  ;
NET "btn1" LOC = "H17"  ;
NET "led"  LOC = "AD21" ;

# LUT that implements LED function is locked into specific
slice.
# For the original design LUT function is btn0 & btn1
# For the partial reconfig design LUT function is btn0 | btn1
INST "led" AREA_GROUP = "led";
AREA_GROUP "led" RANGE = SLICE_X65Y168:SLICE_X65Y168;

# bitgen command to generate a partial reconfiguration bitstream
# ActiveReconfig and Persist options prevent global reset
# during configuration change
$ bitgen -g ActiveReconfig:Yes -g Persist:Yes -r top_orig.bit
top_pr.ncd top_pr.bit
```

`top_orig.bit` : the bitstream of the original design

`top_pr.ncd` : the post place-and-route output of the partial reconfiguration design

`top_pr.bit` : the resulting partial reconfiguration bitstream

The difference-based partial reconfiguration flow of the above example consists of the following steps:

(1) Build `top` module. The result is `top_orig.bit` bitstream file

(2) Build `top_pr` module. The result is `top_pr.ncd` post place-and-route file

(3) Use `top_orig.bit` bitstream and `top_pr.ncd` to generate a bitstream that contains the difference in the LED LUT equation between the two designs.

Partition-based partial reconfiguration

Unlike the difference-based variation, partition-based partial reconfiguration flow supports reconfiguring large parts of the FPGA design. At the time of writing this book, it is supported by the PlanAhead tool for the Xilinx Virtex-6 family only (Spartan-6 FPGAs are not supported). PlanAhead provides an integrated environment to configure, implement, and manage partial reconfiguration projects using partitions. A very brief overview of the design and implementation flow is as follows:

- The FPGA developer designates parts of the design to be reconfigured.
- A region that contains necessary logic, embedded memory, IO, and other resources is allocated on FPGA die.
- The developer defines all possible design variants to occupy that region.
- The PlanAhead tool manages all the details of building such as design, including managing multiple netlists, static, and reconfigurable parts on the design, performing DRC, and producing appropriate bitstreams.

Xilinx application note XAPP883 [3] provides an example of using partial reconfiguration to enable fast configuration of an embedded PCI Express interface block.

Dynamic Reconfiguration

Another method of changing settings in Xilinx GTX transceivers, Mixed Mode Clock Manager (MMCM), and SystemMonitor primitives is by using the dynamic reconfiguration port (DRP). DRP provides a simple interface to the user logic and doesn't require detailed knowledge of configuration registers and the bitstream structure. As an example, DRP allows dynamic change of output clock frequency, phase shift, and duty cycle of MMCM [4].

Resources

[1] Xilinx FPGA partial reconfiguration portal
http://www.xilinx.com/tools/partial-reconfiguration.htm

[2] Difference-Based Partial Reconfiguration, Xilinx Application Note XAPP290
http://www.xilinx.com/support/documentation/application_notes/xapp290.pdf

[3] PCI Express Partial Reconfiguration, Application Note XAPP883
http://www.xilinx.com/support/documentation/application_notes/xapp883_Fast_Config_PCIe.pdf

[4] MMCM Dynamic Reconfiguration, Xilinx Application Note XAPP878
http://www.xilinx.com/support/documentation/application_notes/xapp878.pdf

38
ESTIMATING DESIGN SIZE

There are several situations which call for an estimate of the amount of required FPGA resources needed. Estimating is one of the tasks to perform when starting a new FPGA-based project. Migration of an existing design to a new platform that uses a different FPGA family requires knowledge of whether the design is going to fit. Estimating the capacity of an ASIC design in terms of different FPGA resources is needed for porting the ASIC design to an FPGA-based prototyping platform.

Accurately estimating design size is important for several reasons. Firstly, it affects the selection of FPGA family and size. Use of a larger than necessary FPGA device increases the complexity and size of the PCB, power consumption, and the overall system cost. Overestimating the required capacity of an FPGA-based prototyping platform for ASIC designs affects the platform selection, and makes it more expensive. On the other hand, underestimating the design size may lead to significant project delays due to the PCB redesign needed to accommodate a larger FPGA.

There is no well-defined methodology to estimate FPGA design size that can apply to all cases and situations. Estimating the amount of FPGA resources of an existing design targeting a different FPGA family is easier than estimating for a new design, whose size is unknown. Methodologies like using the size of existing functional components and IP cores, and doing extrapolation can be employed for a new design. Using an open-source IP core with similar features can be helpful. Additionally, an analytical approach of estimating the size of individual state machines and pipeline stages can be applied as well, albeit experimental results usually produce far more accurate estimates and instill a higher confidence level.

An FPGA has different resources: LUTs and registers, DSP blocks, IO, clocking, routing, and specialized blocks such as PCI Express interface, Ethernet MAC, and transceivers. It is a common mistake to only estimate logic resources, which are LUTs and registers. For many designs, such as those using embedded processors, it is also important to estimate embedded memory. However, porting an ASIC design to FPGA requires estimating the amount of required clocking resources. Estimating each FPGA resource – logic, memory, clocking, and others – is a different task, which requires a different approach.

To help with these tasks, Xilinx PlanAhead has an option to estimate logic and memory resources without requiring design synthesis and physical implementation. Synopsys Certify can perform area estimates for different design blocks.

Estimating logic resources

The very first task to complete when estimating FPGA logic resources – LUTs and registers – is to decide which metrics to use. Designers have several options to choose from: logic cells, LUTs, registers, or ASIC gates. Performing an estimate using more than one metrics (for example: slices and LUTs) will produce more accurate results. The following table shows the logic capacity of the smallest and largest Xilinx Virtex-6 FPGAs expressed using different metrics.

Table 1: Xilinx Virtex-6 FPGA logic resources

	Virtex-6 LX75T (smallest)	*Virtex-6 LX760 (largest)*
Logic Cells	74,496	758,784
Slices	11,640	118,560
LUTs	46,560	474,240
Registers	93,120	948,480
ASIC gates*	1,117,440	11,381,760

* 1 Logic cell is approximately 15 ASIC gates

Using LUTs

LUT metrics are often used for estimating ASIC design size targeting FPGA. One reason for this is that ASIC designs ported to FPGA are usually LUT-dominated, meaning the ratio of registers to LUTs is heavily biased towards LUTs.

Note that earlier Xilinx FPGA families, such as Virtex-4 and Spartan-3, have 4-input LUTs, whereas Virtex-5, Virtex-6, and Spartan-6 have 6-input LUTs.

Using registers

In some cases, it is convenient to use registers as a metric. They are easier to count when performing size estimates for register-dominated designs, such as the ones that are heavily pipelined or contain large state machines.

Using logic cells

FPGA capacity is often measured in terms of logic cells. A logic cell is an equivalent of a four-input LUT and a register. The ratio between the number of logic cells and six-input LUTs is 1.6 to 1. Logic cells provide a convenient metrics that normalize the differences between FPGAs of the same family. The logic cell metric is a Xilinx specific, and should not be used to compare different FPGA families. The number of logic cells in Xilinx FPGA is reflected in the device name. For example, Virtex-6 LX75T FPGA contains 74,496 logic cells.

Using slices

Many FPGA IP vendors provide the size of the IP cores in slices. A Xilinx Virtex-6 slice contains four LUTs and eight registers. Other FPGA families contain different numbers. For example, a slice in Xilinx Virtex-4 FGPA contains two LUT and two registers. Xilinx Virtex-5 contains four LUTs and four registers. For that reason, using slices to compare logic utilization of different FPGA families will produce inaccurate results.

Slices can provide a more realistic and accurate estimate than LUTs and registers, because they take into account packing efficiency, as described below.

Slice packing efficiency

Packing efficiency is calculated as the ratio of used LUTs or registers to their total number in all occupied slices.

Xilinx memory controller (MIG) design is used as an example to illustrate slice packing efficiency. The following table shows slice, LUT, and register utilization of the memory controller after floorplanning and physical implementation are done for Virtex-6 LX75T FPGA.

Table 2: Slice packing efficiency of LUTs and registers

	Used in the design	*Total in occupied slices*	*Packing efficiency, %*
Slices	978		
LUTs	2,579	978*4=3,912 (*)	66
Registers	2,343	978*8=7,824 (**)	30

* There are 4 LUTs in one Xilinx Virtex-6 slice
** There are 8 registers in one Xilinx Virtex-6 slice

Note that even though the number of LUTs and registers are balanced in this particular design, the slice packing efficiency is relatively low. Using registers as a metric for the size estimate of this design would be very inaccurate, and require adding a 70% margin.

Using ASIC gates

The capacity of an ASIC design is typically measured in terms of 2-input logic gates. This is a convenient metric to use when estimating the capacity of the FPGA-based prototyping platform, because it allows comparing the capacities of different FPGA families and vendors. However, because this metric is normalized to 2-input gates, it doesn't always provide an accurate measure of the ASIC design size. Xilinx provides the following formula to conversion ASIC gates to Virtex-6 logic cells:

```
1 logic cell = 15 ASIC gates
```

Using this conversion, a 100-million gate ASIC design will require the equivalent of 6.7 million logic cells, or nine Virtex-6 LX760 FPGAs.

Estimating memory resources

In is important to estimate the amount of embedded FPGA memory required by the design. Many designs, such embedded processors, use large amounts of FPGA memory to store data. The following table shows the amount of memory available in the smallest and largest Xilinx Virtex-6 FPGAs.

Table 3: Xilinx Virtex-6 FPGA memory resources

	Virtex-6 LX75T (smallest)	*Virtex-6 LX550T (largest)*
Block RAM	702 KByte	3,240 KByte
Distributed memory	130.6 KByte	1,035 KByte

Also, an additional memory required for debug instrumentation, such as adding ChipScope Integrated Logic Analyzer (ILA), should be taken into consideration.

Estimating clocking resources

An FPGA has limited amount of clocking resources: clock managers, global buffers, clock multiplexors, and dedicated clock routes. Even if the FPGA has sufficient logic and memory resources to accommodate a particular design, that might not be the case with the clocking resources. ASIC designs are known for having complex clock trees and wide use of gated clocks, which can be difficult to map into available FPGA clocking resources. The following table shows different available clocking resources in the smallest and largest Xilinx Virtex-6 FPGAs.

Table 4: Xilinx Virtex-6 FPGA clocking resources

Clocking resource	*Virtex-6 LX75T (smallest)*	*Virtex-6 LX550T (largest)*
Mixed Mode Clock Manager (MMCM)	6	18
Global clock routes	32	32
Regional clock routes	36	108

Estimating routing resources

Various blocks inside the FPGA are connected using routing resources. Designers have little control of how the routing resources are used. FPGA place-and-route tools use them "behind the scenes" to implement design connectivity in the most optimized way. However, it is impractical to quantify the amount of routing resources required for a particular design. Neither do FPGA vendors provide sufficient documentation on performance characteristics, implementation details, and quantity of the routing resources. Some routing performance characteristics can be obtained by analyzing timing reports. In addition, Xilinx FPGA Editor can be used to glean information about the routing structure.

The following figure shows Xilinx FPGA interconnect between slices and global routing as seen in the FPGA Editor.

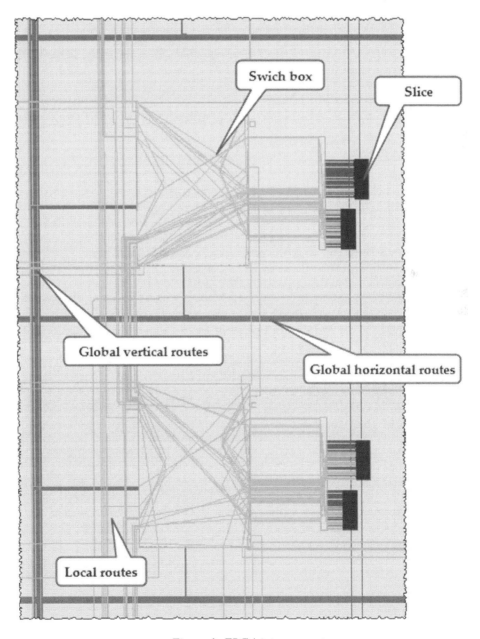

Figure 1: FPGA interconnect

The figure shows slices connected to the adjacent interconnect switch boxes using local routes. Switch boxes connect between each other using both local and global vertical and horizontal routes. A grid-like FPGA routing structure is shown in the following figure.

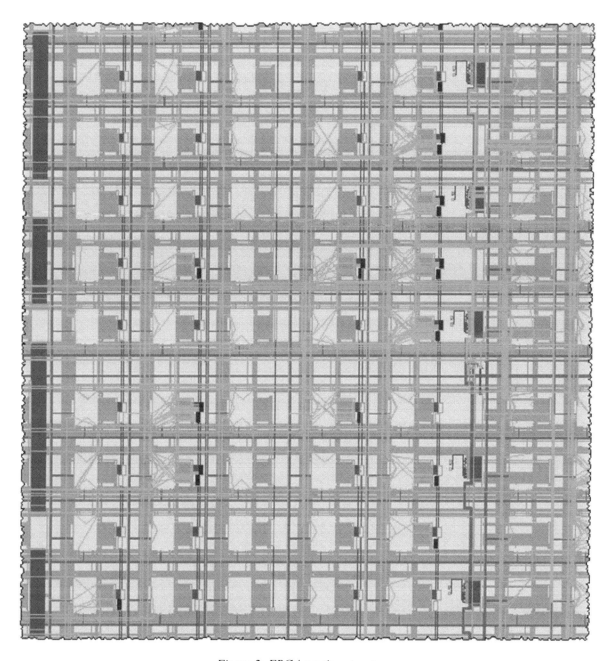

Figure 2: FPGA routing structure

Some FPGA designs make use of a lot of routing resources, which can cause the router tool to fail. A good example of such a design is a Graphics Processing Unit (GPU) ASIC ported to an FPGA-based prototyping platform. It consists of a large number of processors interconnected in a mesh structure.

Solutions to alleviate routing problems include performing logic replication in order to reduce the fanout, and changing the design floorplan. Some of these measures can significantly increase the logic utilization. PlanAhead can be used to visualize routing congestion in different areas of FPGA.

Estimating the overhead

It is important to account for the overhead and leave sufficient margin during the estimate of different FPGA resources. There are different overhead sources outlined below.

Using different synthesis and physical implementation tool options can result in significant variation of the logic and memory utilization. This is discussed in more detail in Tip #79. It is recommended to build the design using different tool options in order to establish a utilization range.

FPGA synthesis tools can produce different utilization results. It is recommended to use the same synthesis tool for both resource estimate and the actual design.

FPGA slice utilization should not exceed 75%. That number can be lower in order to provide enough space to accommodate additional design features.

Adding debug instrumentation, such as ChipScope ILA core, to the design may require a lot of memory resources.

Logic utilization may increase during the timing closure as a result of logic replication and other code changes.

39

ESTIMATING DESIGN SPEED

Correctly estimating design speed affects FPGA speed grade selection, consumed power, and the system cost. Overestimating the speed unnecessarily increases power consumption, takes more effort to meet timing requirements, and increases the cost. Conversely, underestimating the speed may result in increased area utilization due to logic changes, or even require a redesign of the PCB to accommodate a higher performing FPGA from a different family.

The term `speed grade` indicates the maximum frequency and other performance ratings of a particular FPGA for a given family. Xilinx Virtex-6 FPGAs have three speed grades: -1 (slowest), -2, and -3 (fastest).

The following table provides performance characteristics of Xilinx Virtex-6 FPGA for different speed grades. The numbers indicate maximum performance.

Table 1: Performance of Xilinx Virtex-6 FPGA for different speed grades

	-3 (fastest)	-2	-1
Register clock-to-output delay, ns	0.29	0.33	0.39
Block RAM frequency, MHz	450-600	400-540	325-450
IO double data rate, Gbit/sec	1.4	1.3	1.25
IO single data rate, Mbit/sec	710	710	650
GTX/GTH transceivers, GHz	6.6/11.182	6.6/11.182	5.0/10.32

In practice, it is difficult to achieve maximum performance of logic and BRAM resources, because of the additional routing and logic delays.

There is no a single approach to estimate the design speed. In many designs, the speed requirement is driven by the external communication interface. For example, using PCI Express Gen2, 4-lane configuration will require running the user logic interfacing with the PCI Express at 250MHz. Gigabit Ethernet MAC providing an 8-bit interface to the user logic has to operate at 125MHz. In other designs the speed requirements are more flexible. FPGA implementations of a video processing algorithm can double the datapath width to lower the design speed. There is usually no hard requirement on the performance of an ASIC design running on an FPGA-based prototyping platform. In most cases the prototyped design runs at a fraction of the speed of the ASIC. It is beneficial to strive to improve the performance because it will decrease the validation time.

Design area and performance goals are usually interrelated. Often, measures taken to improve design area lead to decreased performance. This factor has to be taken into account when performing design speed estimates. Also, using different synthesis and physical implementation tool options can result in significant variation of the design performance. It is recommended to build the design using different tool options in order to establish an achievable performance range. It is up to the designer to decide what margin is sufficient.

It is important not to rely on the design performance results provided by the synthesis tool. Those are estimates, which can be very different from those done by a timing analyzer after the place-and-route.

The speed of an ASIC design ported to a multi-FPGA prototyping platform is dictated not only by the critical paths within an FPGA, but also by the communication speed between the FPGAs. The inter-FPGA communication speed can often become the performance bottleneck. Because FPGAs have a limited amount of user IOs, the interfaces between FPGAs are frequently implemented by multiplexing the signals, and using high-speed serializer/deserializer (SerDes) transceivers. The multiplexing ratio dictates the overall frequency.

The following example examines a simple case of determining the system performance. An ASIC design consists of a CPU connected to a peripheral controller via a 64-bit bus. The design is partitioned into two FPGAs using a SerDes.

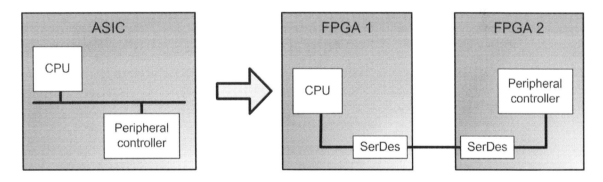

Figure 1: Partitioning an ASIC design into two FPGAs

Scenario 1

The SerDes is implemented using four Xilinx GTX transceivers. The transceivers are full-duplex, and running at speed of 5Gbit/sec. The transceivers use 8b/10b error correction scheme for the data, which adds 20% overhead.

The system performance is calculated as follow:

```
f = 5 Gbit/sec * 4 channels * 0.8 / 64 bit = 256 Mhz
```

Scenario 2

The SerDes is implemented using 16 differential pairs of regular FPGA IO pins. The IOs are double data rate (DDR), and running at speed of 320MHz. 8b/10b error correction scheme is used for the data.

The system performance is calculated as follows:

```
f = 320 MHz * 16 data bits * 2 (DDR) * 0.8 / 64 bit = 128 Mhz
```

This is, in fact, considered a very high system performance for the prototyping platform. Real designs require a lot more signals to be transferred between FPGAs. Also, prototyping platforms are more complex with more FPGAs and communication channels between them. These factors significantly increase the multiplexing ratio, and lower the maximum performance. ASIC designs running on FPGA-based prototyping platforms typically achieve speeds of 10-100MHz.

40
ESTIMATING FPGA POWER CONSUMPTION

Xilinx provides three main tools to perform FPGA power consumption estimate and analysis: PlanAhead Power Estimator, XPower Estimator (XPE), and XPower Analyzer (XPA). This Tip provides a brief overview of those tools. Several power optimization techniques are discussed in Tip #81.

PlanAhead Power Estimator

PlanAhead provides a tool to perform early power estimation based on the design resources. The power estimator uses RTL and signal toggle rates as input, and produces total and quiescent power estimates broken down by clocks, IOs, logic, and BRAM. It also provides Credibility Level metrics that can be High, Medium, or Low.

Figure 1: PlanAhead Power Estimator results

XPower Estimator Spreadsheet

XPower Estimator Spreadsheet (XPE) is an easy-to-use Microsoft Excel spreadsheet that allows experimentation with different design options to perform power estimates. Design parameters, such as clocks, IOs, logic and memory resources, and toggle rates can be either entered directly or imported from the existing MAP report. The following figure shows the XPE summary page, which provides the estimate of the total on-chip power broken down by dynamic and quiescent components, and junction temperature.

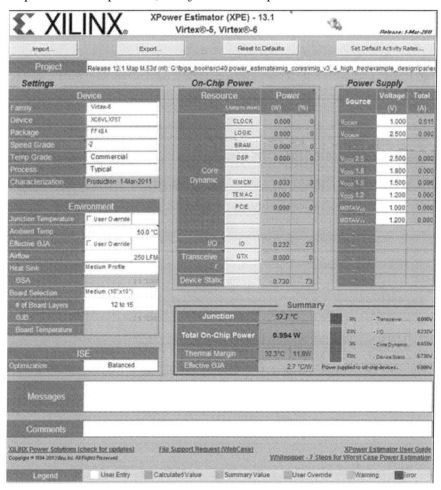

Figure 2: XPE summary page example

XPower Analyzer

Xilinx XPower Analyzer (XPA) is a utility that estimates power after the design implementation. XPA utilizes more design data, such as precise IO characteristics and toggle rates, and therefore is more accurate than XPE spreadsheet and PlanAhead Power Estimator.

The following is a command-line example of using XPower:

```
$ xpwr example.ncd example.pcf -v -o example.pwr -wx example.xpa
```

The required parameter is the NCD file produced by MAP or PAR. Optional files are PCF, produced by MAP, VCD, which includes signal activity rates, or XPA – power report settings file in XML format.

XPower produces power report in text format. It contains several sections: project settings, power consumption and thermal summaries, detailed power information broken down by clocks, logic, IO pins, and signals. It also provides a summary of dynamic and quiescent power, and power supply currents broken down by supply source.

Example

To showcase the XPower Analyzer and PlanAhead Power Estimator capabilities, Xilinx memory controller core (MIG) has been used as an example design. The core provides a balanced mix of features to demonstrate different components of the FPGA power consumption: high IO toggle rates, substantial logic utilization and the number of used IOs, and fast clock.

The core was built for Virtex-6 LX75T- FF484 FPGA with -2 speed grade. The following table provides main characteristics of the design relevant to the power consumption.

Table 1: Design characteristics

Frequency, MHz	*Memory technology*	*Slice utilization*	*Number of IOs*
533	DDR3	1495	44

The following table shows the activity rates used for the power estimate.

The activity rates are default. Users can provide more accurate activity rate information by performing functional simulation and passing the resulting NCD file as a parameter to the XPower tool.

Table 2: Design activity rates

Default Activity Rates (%)	
FF Toggle Rate	12.5
IO Toggle Rate	12.5
IO Enable Rate	100
BRAM Write Rate	50.0
BRAM Enable Rate	25.0
DSP Toggle Rate	12.5

The following table contains the on-chip power summary produced by XPA and broken down by individual resources.

Table 3: XPA on-chip power summary by resources

Resource	Power (mW)	Used	Available
Clocks	99	6	-
Logic	20.2	2579	46560
Signals	27.5	3788	-
IOs	421	40	240
MMCM	115	1	6
Quiescent	729	-	-
Total	1,412	-	-

It is interesting to note that the IO's power is a significant contributor to the overall power consumption. That is the consequence of using internal IO terminations by the memory controller design. Another interesting result is almost even quiescent and dynamic power consumption. Dynamic power in the table above is the sum of clocks, logic, signals, IOs, and MMCM components.

The following table contains the power summary of the same design produced by the PlanAhead Power Estimator.

Table 4: PlanAhead Power Estimator summary by resources

Resource	Power (mW)	Credibility Level
Clocks	279	High
Clock Manager	134	-
Logic	57	High
Block RAM	60	-
IOs	1,339	Medium
Quiescent	760	-
Total	2,629	High

PlanAhead Power Estimator and XPA results are close for quiescent power estimates. However, there is a significant difference between IO and total power estimates. One reason for that discrepancy is that physical constraints, such as IO characteristics, are taken into consideration in the XPA estimates.

Power usage numbers are very specific to FPGA device and design, and might differ by as much as an order of magnitude between smallest designs running on power-efficient Spartan-6 and the largest Virtex-6 FPGAs. The goal of this example is to show the capabilities of the tool, and illustrate what information it provides, rather than serve as a reference.

The example design and complete power reports used in this Tip are available on the accompanying website.

Resources

[1] Xilinx Power Solutions
http://xilinx.com/power
This is the most comprehensive website related to Xilinx FPGA power estimate and analysis.

[2] Seven Steps to an Accurate Power Estimation using XPE, Xilinx White Paper WP353
http://www.xilinx.com/support/documentation/white_papers/wp353.pdf

[3] XPower User Guide, Xilinx User Guide UG440
http://www.xilinx.com/support/documentation/user_guides/ug440.pdf

41
PIN ASSIGNMENT

FPGA pin assignment is a collaborative process of PCB and FPGA logic design teams to assign all top-level ports of a design to FPGA IOs. At the end of the process PCB components are placed and routed, and the board passes SPICE and other simulations. FPGA design can be synthesized and implemented, and it passes DRC. Pin assignment completion is achieved as a result of series of trade-offs between PCB and FPGA logic design teams.

The following figure illustrates the pin assignment process.

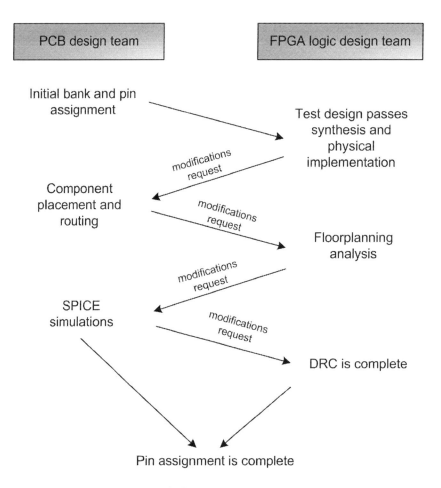

Figure 1: Pin assignment process

PCB design team usually initiates the pin assignment process. There are more pinout-related constraints associated with the board design comparing to FPGA logic design: board size, FPGA banking rules, power and clocking scheme, decoupling capacitors, terminations, signal integrity considerations, and many others. FPGA design team faces different sets of constraints: connecting clocks to the clock-capable IOs, assignment of pins in such a way that the design can meet timing, among others.

After electronic component selection and their initial placement, PCB designers perform initial pin assignment and pass it to the FPGA logic design team.

FPGA design team uses the pinout for synthesis and physical implementation. Typically, a complete RTL is not available that early in the design cycle. One approach is to create a test design that represents the final one in terms of pin characteristics: all pins have the same direction, are single-ended or differential, and include the same clocks. The test design should also include special signals, such as high-speed SerDes transceiver inputs/outputs. All IP cores with complex IO scheme, such as memory controller, PCI Express interface, Ethernet MAC, should be part of the test design.

Successfully passing physical implementation will prove feasibility of the pin assignment, and uncover a lot of other problems.

Unfortunately it's a common mistake not to pay proper attention to this step, or even skipping it completely. Tight project deadlines, false sense of confidence, and other factors cause even the most experienced designers to ignore this step and move on. The consequences of this are extra cost due to board redesign, and lost time.

FPGA design team then passes all pin change requests and other recommendations back to the PCB design team.

PCB design team incorporates the changes, and continues with the component place and route, and board-level SPICE simulations. FPGA design team performs floorplanning analysis, and Design Rules Check (DRC). Floorplanning analysis is especially important for the high-speed design, where timing closure is difficult to achieve. Checks might include making sure that all the IOs belonging to the same bus or module are grouped together.

After exchanging several pinout modification requests, both PCB and FPGA design teams converge to an acceptable pin assignment and are ready to sign off.

The main challenge of the pin assignment process is that it occurs very early in the product design process. At that time, FPGA logic design is in the very early stages, or might not have even started yet. PCB designers have yet to finalize all the electronic component selection, board size, and the number of board layers.

Another challenge that can affect pin assignment is the need to define clocking scheme and speed of all interfaces. That leaves designers with fewer options for future changes. For example, the decision of running a bus at Single Data Rate (SDR), instead of Double Data Rate (DDR) because of the FPGA IO speed limitation, will require twice as many pins.

It's a good idea not to use all the available pins in the FPGA, but leave some room for future product enhancements or potential changes of the peripheral components. One good example is the USB 2.0 PHY interface. USB 2.0 PHY chips have two interfaces with very different pin count: USB Transceiver Macrocell Interface (UTMI) and USB Low Pin Interface (ULPI). If the existing PHY chip with ULPI interface becomes obsolete, or requires replacement for any other reason to UTMI chip, that will create a problem.

Xilinx offers PlanAhead tool that helps designers improve pin assignment process. The following figure shows device and package views of a Spartan-6 LX25T FPGA.

The left side shows the device, or die, view, as seen by the FPGA logic designers. The right size is a package view as seen by the PCB designers.

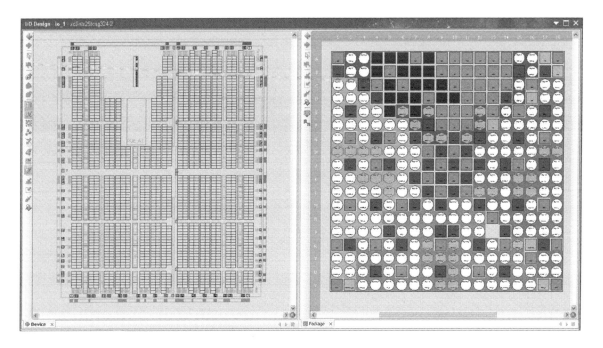

Figure 2: PlanAhead device and package views

Design Rules Check (DRC)

Design Rules Check is an essential step during the pin assignment. Pin assignment cannot be completed before a design passes all the design rules.

The following are some of the design rules that need to be checked:

IO port and clock logic rules: clocks are connected to the clock-capable IO, differential signals use correct polarity.

FPGA banking rules: IO standards legality and consistency, special power pins are correctly connected.

Simultaneously Switching Noise (SSN) rules: SSN is defined as the voltage fluctuation caused by the simultaneous switching of groups of IO signals. SSN causes dynamic voltage drop on power supply lines, which can affect performance of the output drivers and can lead to excessive jitter on critically timed signals. Xilinx PlanAhead includes SSN predictor tool to calculate estimated noise margin.

Performing manual DRC is impractical due to the complexity of design rules. Xilinx PlanAhead can perform DRC automatically.

42
THERMAL ANALYSIS

Performing an accurate thermal analysis is important for several reasons. It affects the mechanical design of a printed circuit board (PCB) and the enclosure. The analysis results dictate whether it is required to use heat sinks, fans, and other solutions to improve heat dissipation. In addition, using fans complicates mechanical design because they require taking measures to reduce the noise.

The goal is to design a system such that the junction temperature is kept within safe limits. Not doing so will dramatically decrease FPGA reliability, longevity, and in some cases, functionality. Thermal analysis has to cover all operating conditions of the FPGA: from a controlled lab environment with near constant temperature, to a space or other extreme hot/cold environment. Power analysis, discussed in Tip #40, is tightly intertwined with the thermal analysis.

The following figure shows mechanical components that affect thermal performance of the FPGA: top and bottom heat sinks, thermal pad and vias. Other factors that affect thermal performance are size and quality of direct thermal attachment pad, usage of thermal grease, amount of air flow, PCB area, and the number of copper layers.

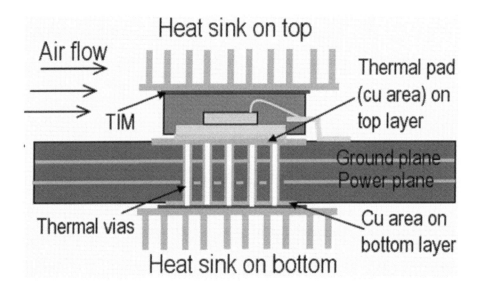

Figure 1: Thermal management (source: National Semiconductors Application Note 2026)

Modeling for thermal analysis

The following equation defines the relationship between ambient temperature, junction temperature, power dissipation, and junction-ambient thermal resistance:

$$T_J = (\Theta_{JA} \cdot P_D) + T_A$$

T_J is a junction temperature. It is defined as the highest temperature of the actual semiconductor in an electronic device, and is usually specified in the device datasheet. For Virtex-6 devices, the maximum junction temperature T_J is +125°C. The nominal junction temperature is +85°C, and used for static timing analysis and power consumption calculations. DC and Switching Characteristics datasheet defines operating range, minimum, maximum, and nominal junction temperatures for different Xilinx FPGA families.

T_A is an ambient temperature and P_D is a power dissipation. Θ_{JA} is a junction-ambient thermal resistance, representing the ability of the material to conduct heat, and measured in units of °C/W.

The following figure shows a model frequently used for thermal analysis.

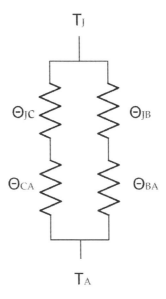

Figure 2: Thermal model

Θ_{JC} is a junction-case thermal resistance specific for a device. For Virtex-6 FPGA packages Θ_{JC} is typically less than 0.20°C/W.

Θ_{CA} is a case-ambient thermal resistance. It is calculated by adding all thermal resistance components on top of the device case: heatsinks, fans, thermal grease and other materials, and the airflow contribution.

There are two heat dissipation paths: junction-case-ambient, and junction-PCB-ambient. Because the two paths are in parallel, the overall Θ_{JA} can be expressed as:

$$\Theta_{JA} = (\Theta_{JCA} \cdot \Theta_{JBA}) / (\Theta_{JCA} + \Theta_{JBA})$$

Θ_{JCA} component is the thermal resistance through the package top surface to ambient, and equals to

$$\Theta_{JCA} = \Theta_{JC} + \Theta_{CA}.$$

Θ_{JBA} component is the thermal resistance through the PCB to ambient, and equals to

$$\Theta_{JBA} = \Theta_{JB} + \Theta_{BA}.$$

The model takes into account the PCB thermal resistance. For a small PCB with low number of layers, the model is reduced to Θ_{JCA}, because the board thermal resistance component Θ_{JBA} is large, and doesn't have significant contribution to the overall thermal resistance. The larger the PCB and the more layers, the smaller the Θ_{JBA} component is. The following table illustrates the impact of the PCB size and the number of layers on the thermal performance.

Table 1: Impact of the PCB on Θ_{JA} (source: Xilinx User Guide UG365)

Xilinx 35 x 35mm FF1148		θ_{JA} (°C/W) for Different Board Sizes		
		4 x 4 in	10 x 10 in	20 x 20 in
Layer Count of Mounted Board	4	9.1 [1]	8.3	--
	8	8.0	5.5	4.9
	12	7.5	4.7	4.4
	16	7.2	4.5	4.2
	24	--	4.3	4.0

It is important to select the correct model for a thermal analysis. For example, not taking a PCB component into consideration may result in a very inaccurate estimate, as shown in the above table.

Thermal Management Options

Bare package

A bare package or a passive heatsink is recommended for low-end FPGAs with small packages, 1-6W power dissipation, and moderate air flow.

Passive heatsink

The purpose of a heatsink is to conduct heat away from a device. A heatsink is made of high thermal conductivity material, usually aluminum or copper. Increasing the surface area of a heatsink, for example fins, facilitates heat removal. An interface between a heatsink and a device, for example using thermal grease, applying strong contact pressure, and surface characteristics, are important for good thermal transfer.

Using a passive heatsink is recommended for mid-range FPGAs with 4-10W power dissipation in a system with good air flow.

Active heatsink

Using the combination of a heatsink and a fan is recommended for high-end FPGAs with large packages and 8-25W power dissipation.

Example

Find the maximum allowed power dissipation of a device given junction and ambient temperatures:

$T_J = +85°C$
$T_A = +55°C$
The device is Virtex-6 with $\Theta_{JC} = 0.20°C/W$.
Thermal resistance of a heatsink and fan is $\Theta_{CA} = 1.80°C/W$.
$\Theta_{JB} = 0.40°C/W$, and $\Theta_{BA} = 2.60°C/W$.

To find the maximum allowed power dissipation a PD requires solving the following equations:

$T_J = (\Theta_{JA} \cdot P_D) + T_A$
$\Theta_{JA} = (\Theta_{JCA} \cdot \Theta_{JBA}) / (\Theta_{JCA} + \Theta_{JBA})$
$\Theta_{JCA} = \Theta_{JC} + \Theta_{CA} = 0.2 + 1.8 = 2.0 \ °C/W$
$\Theta_{JBA} = \Theta_{JB} + \Theta_{BA} = 0.4 + 2.6 = 3.0 \ °C/W$
$\Theta_{JA} = (2.0 \cdot 3.0) / (2.0 + 3.0) = 1.2 \ °C/W$
$P_D = (T_J - T_A) / \Theta_{JA} = (85 - 55) / 1.2 = 25 \ W$

Therefore, for a given junction and ambient temperatures, and thermal resistances, the power dissipation of the FPGA should not exceed 25 Watt.

Resources

[1] Xilinx XPower Estimator (XPE) tool for performing thermal and power analysis
http://www.xilinx.com/products/design_resources/power_central

[2] Considerations for heatsink selection, Xilinx White Paper WP258
www.xilinx.com/support/documentation/white_papers/wp258.pdf

[3] Virtex-6 Packaging and Pinout Specifications, Xilinx User Guide UG365
www.xilinx.com/support/documentation/user_guides/ug365.pdf

[4] National Semiconductor Application Note 2026
www.national.com/an/AN/AN-2026.pdf

43
FPGA COST ESTIMATE

In many designs FPGA is the most expensive electronic component. High and medium capacity FPGAs can cost from several hundred to several thousand dollars. Therefore, minimizing FPGA cost is important and can significantly affect the total cost of the product.

Accurate FPGA cost estimation is not a simple task, and it depends on many factors. Technical characteristics that affect the FPGA cost are:

- FPGA family: lower cost Spartan-3, Spartan-6 to higher performance Virtex-5, Virtex-6
- Capacity: from 3,840 logic cells (smallest Spartan-6) to 758,784 logic cells (largest Virtex-6)
- Speed grade: -L1 (low power), -2, -3, -4 (fastest)
- Temperature range: Commercial (Tj = 0°C to +85°C), Industrial (Tj = –40°C to +100°C)
- Package type: smallest TQG144 to largest FF1924

Purchase quantity also has significant impact on the cost. Smaller quantities cost more per unit. The final cost also depends on the negotiation results with the FPGA distributor.

Also, as one FPGA family is getting older and needs replacement, the older FPGAs are getting more expensive, which makes the newer FPGA family more attractive in terms of cost. FPGA prices skyrocket as the family approaches the end of production date. Those are general pricing principles applicable to the entire electronic chip industry.

To make FPGA comparison data more meaningful, designers frequently use additional metrics, such as cost per logic cell and cost per user IO.

The goal of the FPGA cost estimate process is to take into consideration the above factors to find a sweet spot that meets the functional requirements of the engineering team as well as the cost requirements of the marketing and sales team.

The following tables show sample Xilinx FPGA prices.

Table 1: Lowest capacity Xilinx Virtex-6 LX75T prices (source: FindChips.com, February 2011)

Number user IOs	Capacity, logic cells	Speed grade	Cost, $	Cost per logic cell, cents	Cost per user IO, $
240	74,496	-1	625	0.8	2.6
240	74,496	-2	771	1.0	3.2
240	74,496	-3	1093	1.5	4.6
360	74,496	-1	718	1.0	2.0
360	74,496	-2	899	1.2	2.5
360	74,496	-3	1258	1.7	3.5

Table 2: Highest capacity Xilinx Virtex-6 LX760 prices (source: FindChips.com, February 2011)

Number user IOs	Capacity, logic cells	Speed grade	Cost, $	Cost per logic cell, cents	Cost per user IO, $
1200	758,784	-1	15,622	2.1	13.0
1200	758,784	-L1	19,528	2.6	16.3
1200	758,784	-2	20,714	2.7	17.3

Table 3: Lowest capacity Xilinx Spartan-6 LX4 prices (source: FindChips.com, February 2011)

Number user IOs	Capacity, logic cells	Speed grade	Cost, $	Cost per logic cell, cents	Cost per user IO, $
106	3,840	-L1	12	0.313	0.113
106	3,840	-2	10.4	0.271	0.098
106	3,840	-3	11.4	0.297	0.108
132	3,840	-L1	13	0.339	0.098
132	3,840	-2	11.4	0.297	0.086
132	3,840	-3	12.4	0.323	0.094

The prices are provided for illustration purpose only. The final price depends on the quantity and distributor, and is subject to significant change in time. However, a simple analysis of the price relationships between different families, capacities, speed grades, and user IOs yields some important results.

Price increase with capacity is non-linear, as indicated in the cost per logic cell ratio. It increases from 0.8 cents/logic cell for the smallest, Virtex-6 LX75, to 2.7 cents/logic cell for the largest, Virtex-6 LX760.

There is a non-linear cost increase for an FPGA with the same capacity and the number of user IOs and a faster speed grade. The exception is a low power -L1 speed grade, which is actually more expensive.

Cost per user IO decreases for an FPGA with the same capacity and speed grade.

The cost of a high-capacity FPGA is higher than the total cost of multiple smaller FPGAs with equivalent capacity. For example, it requires 10 Virtex-6 LX75 to reach the equivalent capacity of a single Virtex-6 LX760. However, the cost of 10 Virtex-6 LX75 is $6,250, less than half as much as a single Virtex-6 LX760, which costs $15,622. The rule of thumb is that low- and medium-capacity FPGAs are more price efficient than high-capacity ones using cost per logic cell and cost per user IO metrics.

44
GPGPU VS. FPGA

When starting a new design, system architects often ask themselves if they have to use an FPGA, or if there are alternatives, such as a General Purpose Graphics Processing Unit (General Purpose GPU, or GPGPU).

GPGPU has been gaining momentum and has been used in a variety of applications from solving partial differential equations in the finance industry, to accelerating Matlab simulations and high-resolution medical imaging. nVidia CUDA Zone, a web portal for GPGPU developers on the nVidia CUDA GPGPU platform, lists over 1,500 different applications. GPGPU-based applications became so widespread that Amazon Web Services (AWS) started supporting GPGPU as a cloud computing resource.

There is no clear answer as to when GPGPU can replace an FPGA, and vice versa. That question is application dependent. Typically, GPGPU is used to accelerate certain classes of compute-intensive software applications. The only interface current GPU cards provide for the Host connectivity is PCI Express. GPU has a limited amount of on-chip and on-board memory. FPGA, on the other hand, can be used in a broader range of applications, not just for software acceleration. FPGAs have customizable IOs, so it can interface with virtually any device. The disadvantage of FPGAs is cost.

System architects might want to consider criteria such as interface, speed, latency, and cost in order to make an informed decision of whether to use FPGA or GPGPU in their next design.

Interface

All modern GPU cards use PCI Express protocol as the interface to the Host. At the time of writing of this book, the fastest configuration is PCI Express Gen2 x16, which can deliver up to 6.4 GB/sec of useful payload. Even if it's sufficient for all video applications and most GPGPU acceleration applications, it still might not be enough for some. One example is multi-link network processing applications that are traditionally implemented using high-end FGPAs.

Another FPGA advantage is that it has highly configurable and flexible interfaces—hundreds of general-purpose IOs, high-speed embedded SerDes modules—that can be customized for different needs.

Throughput

Throughput, or speed, is highly dependent on the application. The main strength of both FPGA and GPGPU is their high level of parallelism. GPGPU excels in Single Instruction Multiple Data (SIMD) applications, such as DSP, image, and video processing. The performance degrades in applications that have more complex control flow and require larger memory, such as compilers. FPGA achieves peak performance if an application doesn't require external memory access, and uses only logic resources and embedded memory.

Latency

FPGA designs can have very low and consistent latency and are well-suited for real-time systems, which require a response time of 1ms or less. Some examples are TCP/IP checksum offload on high speed links (1GbE, 10GbE, or higher), fast encryption/decryption, or hard real-time weapons systems.

GPGPU can have much higher latency due to the architectural limitations. There are several factors that contribute to relatively high and inconsistent GPGPU latency. One is PCI Express interface between a GPU card and the Host, which is used in all modern GPU cards. Another is memory access latency both on the Host side and on the GPU card.

Cost

It is a common misconception that FPGA logic resources are much more expensive than those of GPGPUs. Indeed, high-end, high-capacity FPGAs are very expensive and can cost several thousand dollars (see Tip #43 for an FPGA cost analysis). However, there are several factors that determine the overall cost of the system. Application development time is a significant cost factor that is often overlooked. Developing an efficient application for a modern GPU is a complex task and requires specialized skills and experience. Also, it's not simple to find an experienced developer in both FPGA and GPGPU who can bridge the gap between the two.

It is difficult to perform a meaningful cost and performance comparison between FPGA and GPGPU in general terms. The best and the most accurate way to compare the cost and performance is by prototyping. The basis can be an existing software application that runs on a GPGPU, and needs to be ported to FPGA. Tips #38 to #43 discuss different aspects of FPGA selection and process and can be helpful here. Conversely, an existing FPGA design can be ported to a GPGPU.

Resources

[1] GPGPU portal
http://gpgpu.org/about

[2] nVidia CUDA
http://www.nvidia.com/object/cuda_home_new.html

45
ASIC TO FPGA MIGRATION TASKS

The most common reason for migrating an ASIC design to FPGA is the prototyping of the ASIC design on an FPGA-based platform during its development. This is the focus of the discussion in Tips #45-55. Those Tips are the most useful for system engineers and architects who evaluate different commercial emulation solutions and custom-built alternatives, for logic designers tasked with porting an ASIC design to an FPGA-based prototyping platform, and for verification engineers who need to adapt existing testbenches to a new environment.

Implementing an FPGA-based prototype of an ASIC design requires overcoming a variety of development challenges, such as creating an optimal partition of the original design, meeting speed and capacity goals, porting RTL without compromising functionality, and making sure that ported design is functionally equivalent to the original.

There is no existing methodology, sometimes called Design-for-Prototyping, to migrate from an ASIC to FPGA that is applicable to every design. However, the overall flow and migration tasks remain the same: capacity and speed estimate, selection of emulation or prototyping platform, design partition, RTL modifications, synthesis and physical implementation, and, finally, verification of the ported design. This process is shown in the following figure.

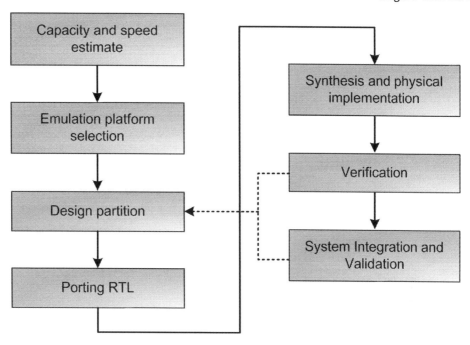

Figure 1: ASIC to FPGA migration tasks

The overall objective of the migration process is to modify the original RTL as little as possible so as to avoid introducing new bugs or increasing coverage holes.

Capacity estimate

Accurate capacity estimate of an ASIC design is important for several reasons. It directly affects selection of the emulation or prototyping platform, the architecture of the partitioned design, and cost. Underestimating the capacity will result in an inability to emulate the entire design. Incurring unnecessary costs is the result of overestimating capacity.

Different approaches to performing ASIC design capacity estimates are discussed in Tip #38.

Speed estimate

An accurate speed estimate affects the usage model of the emulation or prototyping platform. In most cases it is unrealistic to expect the ported FPGA-based design to run at the same speed as the ASIC design. FPGAs are inherently slower than ASICs, and there is an additional communication delay between FPGAs that constitute the emulation or prototyping platform. If the platform runs less than an order of magnitude slower than the original design—for example, at half or quarter speed—then most of the verification tasks can be performed on such a platform. It the speed is ten to one hundred times slower, some of the verification tasks will not be performed.

A good example is a system on chip (SoC) with multi-core processors. It typically takes up to five minutes to boot an embedded operating system on such an SoC. If the emulation platform speed is ten times slower, the boot time increases tenfold to an hour. Such a system can still be used for some of the verification tasks that require a running operating system. However, if the emulation speed is one hundred times slower and it takes half a day to boot an operating system, such a platform becomes completely unusable for many of the embedded software verification tasks.

Speed estimate is discussed in Tip #39.

Selecting emulation or prototyping platform

Selecting emulation or prototyping platforms can be a long and complex process, which includes evaluating existing platforms, making sure that all the requirements and goals such as emulation capacity, speed, cost, coverage, and tool support are met.

Platform selection process is discussed in Tip #47.

Partitioning of an ASIC design into multiple FPGAs

A typical ASIC design is too large to fit into a single FPGA and needs to be partitioned to run on a multi-FPGA platform. Design partition is the process of assigning parts of the ASIC design to individual FPGAs. Partition process might be a complex optimization task that includes meeting a platform's cost, speed, and capacity goals, while ensuring proper connectivity between FPGAs and reasonable complexity of the partition process. Some of the design partition approaches are discussed in Tip #48.

Porting RTL

Developers need to overcome numerous challenges when porting an ASIC design RTL to FPGA. Clock trees of an ASIC design need to be ported to specific clocking resources of individual FPGAs and distributed across different FPGAs on an emulation platform.

ASIC design RTL might contain several design elements, such as transistors, transmission gates, bidirectional signals, and non-digital circuits that have no direct equivalent in FPGA architecture and need to be modeled.

Most of ASIC designs include intellectual property (IP) cores. The IP cores can range from relatively simple functional blocks from the Synopsys DesignWare library (which can be easily replaced with FPGA equivalents) to complex memory controllers, bus-connection subsystems such as PCI Express or USB, and CPU cores. Xilinx and other FPGA vendors provide many, but certainly not all, possible replaceable IP cores.

Tips #49-54 discuss porting of clocks, latches, memories, tri-state logic, combinatorial and non-synthesizable circuits in more detail.

Synthesis and physical implementation

The next step after porting the RTL is to perform design synthesis and physical implementation. The tasks included in this step are resolving ASIC and FPGA synthesis tool differences; specifying timing, area, and IO design constraints; choosing proper synthesis and physical implementation tool options; and, finally, performing timing closure of the design.

Although modern FPGA tools and design flows resemble the ones used in ASIC design, there are still several fundamental differences that developers need to address. ASIC synthesis tools, such as Synopsys Design Compiler, support a wider range of Verilog constructs and are less restrictive in general, compared with the FPGA synthesis tools. FPGA and ASIC tools might support different synthesis directives and options related to design optimization. ASIC tools are capable of handling much larger and more complex designs with denser routing and more logic levels. FPGA physical implementation tools might fail to build some designs due to placement or routing failure. In those cases, designers might need to make additional RTL changes, or repartition the design.

Ported design verification

Ported design verification is the remaining task in the migration process. Its goal is to make sure that the ported design is functionally equivalent to the original one and still complies with the specification. Verification tasks include software functional simulation, performing emulation or prototyping on a hardware platform, and equivalence checking. This step is described in Tip #55.

System integration and validation

Silicon validation and system integration are tasks performed after the chip is taped out. The main focus is on-board and system-level tasks to ensure that the chip is functioning correctly and can properly integrate into the system. The chip is plugged into a specially designed board. Next, a tester applies stimulus to chip's inputs and captures the outputs. Then, the outputs are compared to the expected values, and the pass/fail result is produced. The process is typically automated and performed concurrently on multiple boards operating at different conditions. There are many ways to generate the stimulus and compare the expected values, such as predefined sets of test vectors, self-generated pseudo-random patterns using Multiple Input Shift Register (MISR) signatures, and others. If one of the test sequences fails, the same sequence is run on the emulation platform in order to determine the root cause of the problem.

46

DIFFERENCES BETWEEN ASIC AND FPGA DESIGNS

ASIC designs are different from the FPGA counterparts in several fundamental ways described below.

Programmability and customization

FPGAs are programmable devices by design that allow a high level of customization. A new design can be implemented and run on an FPGA in a matter of minutes or hours. In contrast, implementing a new ASIC or a full-custom design is very expensive, and takes months to create a new set of masks and fabricate a new silicon.

Design cycle time

A design cycle of an FPGA-based design can take as little as a week. A full design cycle of an ASIC or a full-custom design can easily take a year. The verification of an ASIC design is much longer and more complex that FPGA, and involves more engineering resources.

Cost

FPGAs have much higher cost than the equivalent ASIC. The cost difference can be compared using different metrics: per device, per equivalent capacity unit (typically ASIC gate), or cost per pin.

Design size

ASIC designs have a higher gate density, measured in transistors per silicon area. It also takes more transistors in FPGA to implement the same logic function as in ASIC because that logic is programmable and includes configuration capabilities and more routing. ASIC designs, measured in ASIC gates, can be one or two orders of magnitude larger than FPGA designs. Intel processors, nVidia GPUs, or Freescale SoC reached the size of hundreds of millions of ASIC gates, whereas the largest FPGA is less than ten million gates.

Power

FPGAs have a higher power consumption than ASICs. Advances in the CMOS process to reduce transistor size, and improvements in synthesis and physical implementation tools related to power optimizations techniques enabled FPGAs to be used in power-sensitive applications. Still, there is a significant power consumption gap between FPGAs and ASICs.

Performance

ASIC designs are faster. FPGA designs can typically run up to 400MHz. The peak performance of the fastest Xilinx-6 DSP48 embedded primitive is 600MHz. At the time of writing this book many multi-core processor SoCs exceeded 1GHz barrier, and the fastest Intel processor now runs at 3.2 GHz speed. Several conducted studies conclude that the performance difference is five times higher in favor of the ASIC compared to the frequency of the same FPGA design with the same fabrication process.

The main reason for such a big difference in performance is a different FPGA design architecture that includes configurable logic blocks, IO blocks which provide off-chip interface and routing that makes the connections between the logic and IO blocks.

Logic

FPGAs contain configurable logic blocks to implement the functionality of a circuit. In Xilinx FPGAs a logic block is called Slice, which contains several look-up tables (LUTs), registers, a carry chain, and some other logic depending on the FPGA family and slice type. This is fundamentally different than an ASIC standard cell, which is a non-configurable group of transistors that enables an abstract logic representation using a hardware description language (HDL).

The number of tional logic levels between registers in FPGA designs is several times lower than in ASIC designs. For example, in an FPGA design running at 300 MHz and using the fastest device, the number of logic levels typically doesn't exceed 5. An equivalent ASIC circuit can have tens of logic levels.

Because of such a big difference in the number of logic levels, the overall logic composition of an ASIC design is different from the FPGA. A typical ASIC design ported to FPGA is LUT-dominant. That is, it contains much more LUTs than registers. That causes inefficient use of FPGA logic resources and suboptimal packing of LUT and registers into slices.

Routing

Routing refers to the interconnect between logic blocks and IO. An FPGA routing has two fundamental differences from ASIC. First, there is a fixed amount of FPGA routing resources, arranged as a horizontal and vertical grid. That routing layout makes the average connection length between two logic blocks longer, compared to a custom ASIC routing. Longer FPGA routes require additional buffers to overcome signal degradation. The second difference is that FPGA routing is programmable, which is the feature which enables FPGA configurability.

Clocking

Clock tree structure is custom-build for each ASIC design. FPGAs already include built-in clock management primitives that perform frequency synthesis and phase-locked loop (PLL), and dedicated low-skew clock routing resources. ASIC designs are using a clock gating technique to save more power than FPGA designs.

Design flow

There are many similarities between ASIC and FPGA design processes. Both include RTL synthesis, place and route, and timing closure steps. FPGA tools are sophisticated enough to support hierarchical design flow, low-level control over logic floorplanning, timing analysis, and support for script-based build flows.

However, there are a few fundamental differences between ASIC and FPGA design flow. FPGA flows don't require clock tree synthesis and scan chain insertion, because they are already part of the FPGA. Floorplanning FPGA design, and performing place and route are done by an FPGA design engineer, whereas those tasks might be performed at the ASIC foundry. Testing and verification of an ASIC design is an important part of the design process. Such tasks as a built-in self test (BIST), and automatic test pattern generation (ATPG) are non-existent in FPGA design process, because FPGA silicon has already been tested during manufacture.

Resources

[1] Ian Kuon and Jonathan Rose, *"Quantifying and Exploring the Gap Between FPGAs and ASICs"*, Springer, 2009, ISBN: 978-1-4419-0738-7

[2] Ian Kuon and Jonathan Rose, *"Measuring the Gap Between FPGAs and ASICs"*, IEEE Transactions on Computer-Aided Design of Integrated Circuits and Systems (TCAD), Vol. 26, No. 2, pp 203-215, Feb. 2007

47

SELECTING ASIC EMULATION OR PROTOTYPING PLATFORM

Verification of today's multi-million gate ASIC designs requires speed that in most cases cannot be provided using software-based simulation. ASIC emulation or prototyping on an FPGA-based platform is a cost-effective option available to design and verification engineers. It can speed up your software-based simulation exponentially, which will improve coverage and decrease the overall time-to-market availability of the product. Another role of prototyping is to provide a pre-silicon platform for early system integration of the design for firmware and applications software.

Selecting an emulation or prototyping platform that is capable of accelerating ASIC design verification is a complex process that can take you a long time before you make the final decision. The process includes a thorough evaluation of existing platforms and making sure that all of the technical and budgetary requirements like emulation capacity, speed, cost, coverage, and tool support are met. One of the platform evaluation goals is to uncover any hidden issues and perform a feasibility analysis. FPGA-based platforms are more restrictive than the ones based on custom processors. Some ASIC designs might have a fundamental problem of being partitioned, synthesized, or implemented for a specific FPGA-based platform.

Nomenclature

There is no consistent terminology that defines the different kinds of hardware acceleration platforms. Terms like emulation, prototyping, co-emulation, co-simulation, and in-circuit emulation are often used interchangeably, and the difference is not always clear.

There are several differences between emulation and prototyping platforms. Emulation platforms provide better debuggin capabilities close to the ones available in software simulators. That allows you to use emulation platforms in a wider range of project phases: from the block-level simulation to full-chip ICE (In-Circuit Emulation) and debug. Emulation platforms offer a more integrated solution such as a push-button build and debug flows, and more sophisticated software tools. Prototyping platforms lack good debug visibility, and are typically used during pre-silicon system integration and software debug. A prototyping platform might be a simple bare bones board with rudimentary software tools. The performance, or the emulation speed, of a prototyping platform is better: tens of MHz comparing to a few MHz in the emulation platform. Emulation platforms are usually more expensive than prototyping platforms.

Another class of acceleration platforms is simulation accelerators, or co-simulators. As the name suggests, co-simulators assist software simulators by running a portion of the design at a higher speed on a dedicated hardware platform. Typically, that part is synthesizable. The behavioral testbench is running on a host and communicates with the hardware platform using proprietary protocol over JTAG, Ethernet, PCI Express, or other high speed links. Xilinx ISIM simulator supports a co-simulation mode where part of the design runs on an FPGA.

Co-emulation is a more recent addition to the list of hardware acceleration tools. The primary distinction from a co-simulation is that the communications to the hardware platform is raised to the transaction level rather than being at the implementation level. In-circuit emulation (ICE) is not a platform, but instead is a method explaining how the hardware acceleration platform is used.

Architecture

Hardware acceleration platforms are designed using two main architectures based on FPGAs, or custom processors. FPGA-based platforms are usually cheaper, have faster emulation speed, and typically are used for ASIC prototyping. Emulation platforms are designed using hundreds, or even thousands of custom processors. They offer full design visibility, have higher capacity, and faster compile times.

Cost

Emulation platforms are usually more expensive than prototyping counterparts, and can easily reach several million dollars for the highest capacity configurations. Usually, the cost of a commercial hardware acceleration platform is proportional to its capacity. Additional components that add to the cost of ownership include maintenance cost, the cost of verification libraries, transaction models, tool add-ons, and device emulators.

Typically, platform vendors provide a lease option. Because the emulation or prototyping platform is required only for a relatively short period of time, typically a few months till the design tape-out, it is more cost effective to lease it rather than buy.

Frequently used metrics to compare different platforms in terms of their cost are cost-per-gate, and cost-per-emulation-cycle.

Capacity

The capacity of an ASIC emulation or prototyping platform is typically measured in terms of equivalent 2-input ASIC gates. Using these metrics allows the comparison of the capacity of very different platform architectures. Capacity can range from several million ASIC gates to over a billion for high-end emulation platforms. Different approaches to perform ASIC design capacity estimate are discussed in Tip #38.

On-chip memory

Many ASIC designs require a significant amount of on-chip memory for embedded processors, system caches, FIFOs, packet buffering, and other applications. Emulation and prototyping platforms provide a wide range of memory capacities from Megabyte to a Terabyte.

Emulation Speed

Different approaches to perform emulation speed estimates are discussed in Tip #39.

Partition

A typical ASIC design is too large to fit into a single FPGA, and needs to be partitioned to run on a multi-FPGA platform. The partition process might be a complex optimization task that includes meeting platform's cost, speed, and capacity goals, while ensuring proper connectivity between FPGAs, and reasonable complexity of the partition process. Different partitioning options are discussed in Tip #48.

Software tools

Hardware acceleration platform vendors provide very different software tools, ranging from automated partitioning software, to IDE, optimized synthesis tool, and debugger. Good software tools are the key to improving verification productivity.

Custom platforms

Intel Atom prototyping platform

One of the designs prototyped on a custom Xilinx FPGA-based platform is the Intel Atom processor. The following picture shows the prototyping platform.

*Figure 1: Intel Atom emulation platform (source: **"Intel Atom processor core made FPGA-synthesizable"**, Microarchitecture Research Lab, Intel corporation)*

This platform is not available for general use, and is shown as an example of a custom platform.

Build vs. Buy

Modern high-end FPGAs certainly make the task of designing a custom hardware acceleration platform realistic. Several high-end FPGAs have enough capacity, user IOs, and embedded memory to emulate small to medium-size ASIC designs.

Building a custom FPGA-based hardware acceleration platform can offer a significantly higher emulation speed approaching the maximum speed that an FPGA supports. In some cases running the emulation at 200-300MHz is a realistic expectation.

A custom-built platform can have features or capabilities that commercial platforms don't provide. For example, a custom-built platform can have a very high amount of external memory, a particular communication interface such as 10 Gigabit Ethernet, or a specific connectivity between FPGAs.

The main disadvantage of building a custom platform is significant design and bring-up time and effort. A hardware acceleration platform has a very short life cycle, from a few months to a year. By using an off-the-shelf platform, engineering teams can focus on ASIC design verification, rather than on building a short-lived platform.

Also, there is no definitive answer as to which approach is cheaper. There are several factors that affect the cost: the complexity of the custom-build platform, engineering effort, and the number of units to be manufactured.

Third party ASIC emulation and prototyping platforms

The following is a list of major ASIC emulation and prototyping platforms and tools.

Platform: Incisive Palladium

Company: Cadence

http://www.cadence.com/products/sd/palladium_series/pages/default.aspx

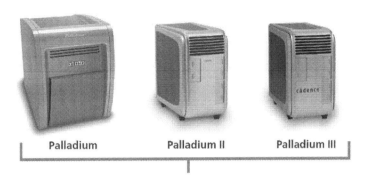

Figure 2: Palladium systems (source: Cadence Palladium datasheet)

Cadence Incisive Palladium Enterprise Simulator is a high-performance emulation platform. It is based on multiple custom processor-based compute engines designed for running verification applications. Palladium provides easy-to-use compiler optimized for fast runtime, and a broad ecosystem of verification libraries, software tools, and hardware add-ons to support emulation and system level hardware/software co-verification. Key features of the platform are (source: Cadence Palladium datasheet):

- Capacity: up to 2 Billion gates
- Dedicated user memory: up to 1 Terabyte
- IO pins: up to 60 thousand
- Emulation speed: up to 4 MHz
- Compile time: 10-30MGate/hour on a single workstation
- Transaction and assertion-based accelerations
- SpeedBridge adapters for connecting a wide range of peripheral devices using PCI Express, Ethernet, USB, AXI, and many other protocols.

Palladium is considered the market leader in providing hardware acceleration solutions for ASIC design verification.

Platform: Veloce

Company: Mentor Graphics

http://www.mentor.com/products/fv/emulation-systems/veloce

The Veloce product family is a high performance simulation acceleration and pre-silicon, emulation solution. It is based on multiple custom-designed processors. Veloce product line offers five scalable verification platforms with capacities from 8 million gates up to 512 million gates

Platform: ZeBu-Server

Company: EvE

http://www.eve-team.com

ZeBu-Server is an FPGA-based system emulation platform with capacity of up to 1 Billion gates and emulation speed of up to 30MHz. ZeBu-Server primarily aims at large-scale, multi-core chip and system emulation applications. ZeBu-Server is the highest performance emulator on the market. It uses Xilinx Virtex-5 LX330 FPGAs.

Products: RocketDrive, RocketVision

Company: GateRocket

http://www.gaterocket.com

GateRocket offers RocketDrive, a small FPGA-based peripheral, which acts as accelerator for the HDL simulator, and RocketVision, a companion software debugging option.

Platform: HES

Company: Aldec

http://www.aldec.com

Aldec Hardware Emulation System (HES) allows using off-the-shelve prototyping FPGA boards for simulation acceleration and emulation. The strength of the tool is in automated design compilation, standard testing interface, and integration with leading hardware/software debugging tools such as Synopsys Certify.

Company: Dini Group

http://www.dinigroup.com/new/index.php

Dini Group offers high-capacity FPGA boards for ASIC prototyping and emulation systems. The following figure shows an FPGA-based prototyping platform from Dini Group using 16 Xilinx Virtex-5 FPGAs.

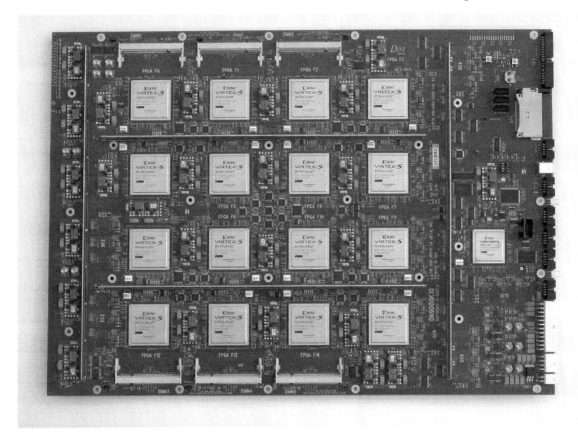

Figure 3: FPGA-based prototyping platform (courtesy of Dini Group)

48

PARTITIONING AN ASIC DESIGN INTO MULTIPLE FPGAS

A typical ASIC design is too large to fit into a single FPGA and needs to be partitioned to run on a multi-FPGA platform. Design partition is a process of assigning parts of the ASIC design to individual FPGAs. Partition process might be a complex optimization task that includes meeting platform's cost, speed, and capacity goals while ensuring proper connectivity between FPGAs and reasonable complexity of the partition process. There are several commercial partition tools that employ proprietary algorithms to perform partitioning of a complex ASIC design into multiple FPGAs. Designers can develop custom scripts that perform partition for simpler ASIC designs with clearly defined module boundaries.

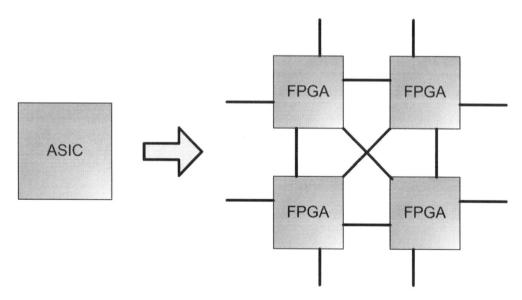

Figure 1: Partitioning an ASIC design into multiple FPGAs

The process of choosing and implementing a design partition includes several steps: requirements definition, feasibility analysis, identifying partition points, selecting FPGAs, defining interfaces between FPGAs, designing clocking and reset schemes, selecting partition tool, and defining partition flow. After the partition is done, designers might want to perform different optimizations.

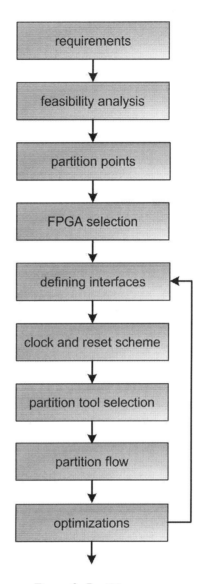

Figure 2: Partition process

Requirements

Requirements can be divided into two groups: soft and hard. Hard requirements are inflexible and must be met. Cost, platform capacity, the amount of on-board memory, the minimum number of user IOs, and specific peripheral devices (such as USB, PCI Express, and Ethernet) are hard requirements. Emulation speed and target FPGA utilization are soft requirements because they can be changed without significant impact on the platform functionality.

Feasibility analysis

The goal of the feasibility analysis is to determine whether the partition is required and, if it is, whether the design can be partitioned to fit into a specific FPGA-based prototyping platform. Even small ASIC designs that can fit into a single FPGA based on the capacity estimate might require partition if that FPGA has insufficient embedded memory, DSP, user IO, or clocking resources. At this point it is important to get a ballpark estimate of the number of required FPGAs, their capacity, and the interconnected structure. Another area of concern is whether there are hidden issues with synthesis and physical implementation flow: Partitioned design is too complex to be built, logic utilization of some of the FPGAs is too high, logic multiplexing ratio on the FPGA-to-FPGA interfaces exceeds the synthesis tool limit, routing is too congested and causes place-and-route tool errors, and other issues.

Identifying partition points

Most of the ASIC designs are modular and lend themselves to straightforward partitioning into multiple FPGAs. Examples are SoC with multi-core CPU subsystems, caches, memory controllers, and other peripherals, interconnected by busses with a low signal count. Other designs, such as graphics processors (GPU) with a more complex mesh interconnect structure between modules, might require automated partitioning tools to find the optimal partition points.

FPGA selection

FPGA selection includes choosing the minimum number of FPGAs required for partition, their capacity, and speed. The hardware platform doesn't have to consist of homogeneous FPGAs or be symmetrically interconnected. It can contain FPGAs with different capacities, from different families and even different vendors, as long as the partitioned design meets all the requirements.

The following picture shows a block diagram of a simple 2-FPGA prototyping board from Dini Group with asymmetric connectivity.

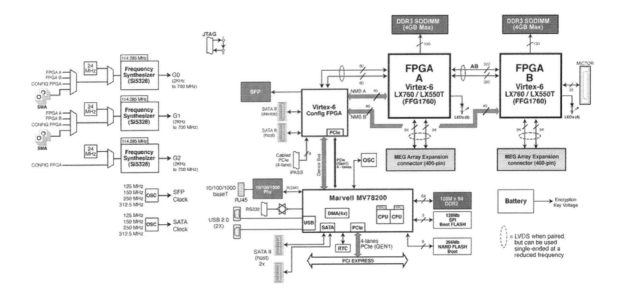

Figure 3: FPGA-based prototyping board (courtesy: Dini Group)

Interfaces

When a design is partitioned to multiple FPGAs, the total number of IOs needed for the entire design increases. This is known as Rent's rule and is expressed as:

$$T = t \cdot g^p$$

Where T is the total number of pins, g is the design size, p is "Rent's exponent" between 0.5 and 0.8, and t is a constant.

The implication of this rule is that the number of IOs in the partitioned design does not decrease as fast the size of partitioned modules. Splitting the original ASIC design into multiple FPGAs will require more pins than in the original design.

In general, a higher number of external pins available for signal interfaces between FPGAs allows for a lower multiplexing ration of the signals, which directly affects the overall emulation speed. This point is discussed in Tip #39.

Clocking scheme

The clock distribution scheme in a multi-FPGA system can be complex. One of the main challenges is tackling the clock skew. The overall clock skew becomes the combination of skews on the board and inside the FPGAs. When a clock is generated inside one FPGA and distributed to the others, the board skew component for each receiving FPGA has to be balanced. If not, it will cause hold-time violations. There are several clock distributions schemes to combat this issue. One is a loop-back clock structure, in which the clock-generation FPGA also receives the same clock. Another technique is replication of the clocking network to eliminate or avoid the board skew component.

The following figure illustrates the clock loop-back technique. An external clock enters FPGA 1, goes through a PLL, and is distributed to FPGAs 2 and 3 and back to FPGA 1. An important requirement is that the returning clock signal has the same delay to each of the FPGAs.

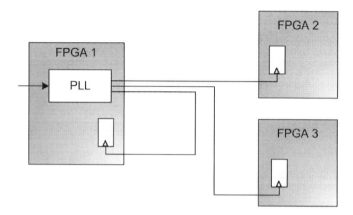

Figure 4: Clock loop-back technique

In large, multi-clock designs, several different clock distribution schemes may co-exist on the same prototyping board. For such designs, performing a manual partition that completes all necessary clock conversions is impractical. This is a task for partition tools that can do it automatically.

Reset scheme

One requirement for designing a reset scheme is that the logic in all FPGAs on the prototyping board comes out of reset at the same time. That imposes some limitations on reset line delays and the choice of a synchronous or asynchronous reset scheme.

Selecting partitioning tool

Partition options can be categorized into three main groups: manual partition, automatic partition, and semi-automatic partition that includes some manual changes.

Manual partition can be relatively simple to perform on a small modular design. It allows for the highest level of customization that automatic partition tools lack. Another reason is the high cost of partition tools. However, the cost of using the manual partitioning approach includes the cost of writing and maintaining the conversion scripts, performing verification of the partitioned design, and might exceed the cost of partition tools.

Partition can be performed at the RTL or post-synthesis netlist level, typically in Electronic Design Interchange Format (EDIF). One advantage of performing partition at the netlist level is that it's easier to perform accurate area estimates. Another advantage is that it's easier for an automated tool to find an optimal partition when working with a single flat netlist database. However, most of the custom-developed scripts perform partition at the RTL level.

Automatic partitioning tools typically offer the following features:

- Perform coarse area estimation for a specific prototyping board.
- Perform feasibility analysis on a prototyping board without pin assignments and undefined connectivity between FPGAs.
- Including both pin and area requirements as part of the process of finding the optimized partition.
- Can perform partition at either RTL or post-synthesis netlist levels.
- Support for multiple third-party and custom prototyping board.

Even with using partition tools, it's difficult to achieve a full automation of the partition process. Every ASIC design has some unique features that require manual intervention. Also, partition tools might not perform some parts of the design optimization. In practice, the partition flow will start with some manual modifications using scripts and be completed by the automated tool.

Partition flows

There are two main partition flows: top-down and bottom-up.

In the top-down flow, the entire design is synthesized into a single flat netlist, usually in EDIF format, and then the netlist is partitioned using an automated tool. Some advantages of the top-down approach include a more compact netlist because the synthesis tool performs cross-module optimization on the entire design. A partitioning algorithm could be applied to the entire design with different constraints, resulting in a more optimal partition. The timing analysis can also be more accurate and cause higher performance.

In the bottom-up flow, the entire design is first partitioned into modules, such that each module fits into a single FPGA. Then each module is synthesized. Among the advantages of the bottom-up approach is that it can be more suitable for manual partition flow. Also, the runtime for very large designs can be faster than with the top-down approach because of the smaller netlist database.

Algorithms

Most of the partitioning algorithms used in commercial software tools are either patented or constitute company trade secret. An efficient partitioning algorithm is a significant competitive advantage of the product. It can result in faster build time, better performance, or lower logic utilization.

Many algorithms use an approach called simulated annealing to find the optimal partition. The algorithm represents a flattened design netlist as a graph. Then, the search space for finding the optimal solution is limited by applying constraints, such as speed and capacity goals, the number of IOs, and other metrics. The end result of the algorithm is the optimal cut in the graph, which represent the partition.

Optimizations

After successful partition, designers might want to perform different optimizations to improve emulation speed, decrease FPGA utilization by rebalancing the logic, or increase the speed of partition, synthesis, and physical implementation flow. Logic replication achieves good results for improving routability or design speed.

Frequently, decreasing the overall design build time is more important than performing other optimizations because it allows new designs to build quicker after making modifications, which speeds up the verification process.

Partitioning tools

Tool: Certify
Company: Synopsys
http://www.synopsys.com/Systems/FPGABasedPrototyping/Pages/Certify.aspx
Synopsys Certify is considered the best tool to perform ASIC design partitioning into multiple FPGAs. The tool can perform both automatic and manual partitions. It can resolve the board routability issues for custom and off-the-shelf prototyping boards. It reads-in the netlist of the target board and applies a routing algorithm to map the connections between partitions onto wires on the board.

Tool: ACE Compiler
Company: Auspy Development Inc.
http://www.auspy.com
The Auspy Custom Emulator (ACE) Compiler tool performs a multiple-FPGA design partition and integrates with commercial and custom prototyping platforms. The tool allows multi-language design import and full bottom-up synthesis for accurate gate-level estimation.

Many vendors of FPGA-based prototyping platforms also provide design partition tools specific for their platforms. One example is the EvE ZeBu-Server.

49

PORTING CLOCKS

Clocking implementation is fundamentally different between ASIC and FPGA designs. ASIC designs require manual clock tree synthesis, balancing clock delays, and other tasks. On the other hand, FPGAs have built-in clocking resources: PLLs, frequency synthesizers, phase shifters, and dedicated low-skew clock routing networks. ASIC designers have more freedom to implement fully custom clock networks. A predefined clock tree structure in FPGA makes the design much simpler. However, that becomes a disadvantage when porting an ASIC design to FPGA.

Clock trees of an ASIC design need to be ported to the quivalent clocking resources of individual FPGAs, and distributed across different FPGAs on the emulation platform.

An FGPA has a limited amount of clocking resources. For example, the largest Xilinx Virtex-6 LX760 FPGA has 18 Mixed Mode Clock Manager (MMCM) blocks. It's sufficient for most of the FPGA designs. However, that might not be enough for ASIC designs with a large number of custom clock trees. Another FPGA limitation is the limited number of global clocks that can enter one clock region.

Clock gating

ASIC designs are optimized for low power, and make extensive use of a clock gating technique for power optimization. The following figure shows an example of a gated clock, where the clock inputs of two registers are connected to a combinatorial logic.

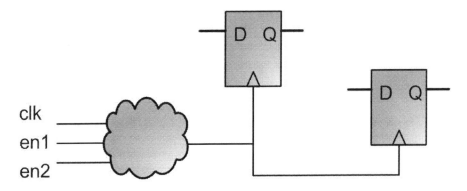

Figure 1: Gated clock

Under certain logic conditions based on `en1` and `en2` inputs, the clock coming to the registers is turned off, effectively both disabling the register, and conserving power.

Clock gating can lead to suboptimal performance results in FPGAs. The reason is that FPGAs are using dedicated high-speed and low-skew routing resources for clock nets. When the clock of a sequential element is gated, it is taken off the dedicated high-speed clock routes, and connected to a general-purpose routing instead. The resulting implementation introduces clock skew, and leads to poor performance and potential setup and hold-time violations. It is recommended that one performs conversion of all gated clocks to their functionally equivalent implementation.

Converting gated clocks

Gated clock conversion is a process of modifying the logic so that the clock inputs of the registers are connected directly to dedicated clock routes instead of combinatorial or sequential logic outputs.

One way to perform a gated clock conversion is to insert a multiplexer in front of the data input, and then connect the clock net directly to the clock input. The following figure shows the resulting circuit.

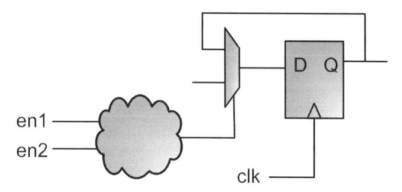

Figure 2: Converted gated clock using feedback and multiplexor

Another gated clock conversion method takes advantage of the enable input of the register, as shown in the following figure.

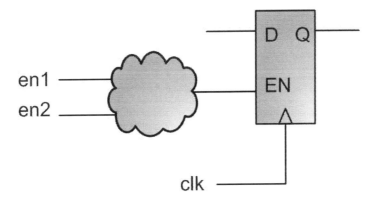

Figure 3: Converted gated clock using enable input

Tool options for automatic gated clock conversion

Some synthesis tools, such as Synopsys Synplify Pro and Synplify Premier, perform automatic gated clock conversion. To perform the conversion, Synopsys Synplify Pro and Synplify Premier require certain design conditions to be met: the gated clock logic must be combinatorial, clock signal has to be constrained, and the synchronous primitive driven by a gated clock must not be a black box.

Gated clocking schemes provided in the above examples are simple. In real designs, the gated clocking logic is more complex, and can drive not only registers, but memories, DSP blocks, and other primitives. A synthesis tool might not be able to perform automatic gated clock conversion in all cases.

Clock enables

Unlike gated clocks, ASIC designs that contain the logic with clock enables in the majority of cases do not require special porting techniques. FPGA synchronous primitives – registers, Block RAMs, DSP48 – already have dedicated clock enable input, which is automatically used by synthesis tools.

Porting clock management primitives

In most cases ASIC clock management modules, such as PLLs, can be directly ported into FPGA counterparts with a minor interface adaptation. Xilinx FPGAs provide a variety of configurable clock management modules such as DCM, PLL, and MMCM, clock buffers, clock multiplexors, and other clock-related resources. A more detailed discussion on Xilinx FPGA clocking resources is provided in Tip #20.

50
PORTING LATCHES

Latches are used for different purposes in ASIC designs. Time borrowing is one of the latch usage models. That technique allows significant performance improvement in heavily pipelined designs and is briefly described below. Another motivation to use latches is that they use much less area. A register uses twice as many transistors as a latch. A common master-slave register implementation used in ASIC designs consists of two cascaded latches.

The figure below illustrates time borrowing technique. The technique takes advantage of latches that replace registers along the critical timing paths. They take up a portion of a clock period from adjacent registers and, by doing so, effectively increase the clock period. The theory behind the time borrowing technique is discussed in several papers, some of which are mentioned in [1]

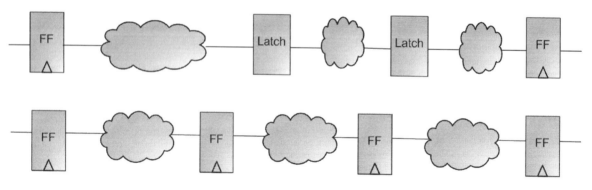

Figure 1: Time borrowing using latches

Both latches and registers are implemented using the same Xilinx FPGA hardware primitive. That hardware primitive shares the same input and output data, reset, and enable signals, and can be configured as a register with an edge-sensitive clock or as a latch with a transparent gate enable. Therefore, unlike ASIC implementation, latches use the same area in FPGA and offer no advantage.

Even though both latches and registers are storage elements, they are fundamentally different. A latch is level-sensitive and transparent whenever the gate enable input is active. I.e., as long is the gate enable is active, there is a direct path between data input and output. The data is stored in latch when the gate enable becomes inactive. On the other hand, a register is an edge-sensitive element. The data is stored in a register either on the rising or falling edge of the clock.

Using transparent latches in FPGA designs is not desirable for several reasons. When a latch is in the transparent state, glitches on the data input can pass to the output. Static timing analysis (STA) of a design with only synchronous registers is much simple than the one with transparent latches because the STA tool only needs to consider either the falling or rising edge of the clock. On the contrary, the STA of a design with latches needs to account for both the rising and falling edge of a gate enable and its duration for each latch. That makes latches subject to duty cycle jitter, as their behavior depends on the arrival times of both the rising and falling edge of a gate enable. Designs with edge-sensitive registers only need to consider the arrival time of one clock edge and are therefore immune to the duty cycle jitter. The STA of latch-based pipeline designs with transparent latches is even more challenging due to the characteristics of the time borrowing. A delay in one pipeline stage depends on the delays in all previous pipeline stages. Such high dependency across pipeline stages makes it very difficult to take into account all the factors that affect static timing analysis. The timing analysis complexity of such a design grows non-linearly with the number of pipeline stages.

Because of the above reasons, latch-based designs require more careful and elaborated timing constraints to ensure correct operation. Designers that perform synthesis and physical implementation of a latch-based design need to have a deep understanding of the full design intent and multiple timing relationships in order to add proper timing constraints.

It is recommended to convert all transparent latches in the ASIC design to equivalent logic circuits using edge-sensitive registers. There isn't a universal conversion methodology applicable to all possible latch coding styles.

Most synthesis tools infer latches from incomplete conditional expressions, such as an `if` statement without a corresponding `else`, as shown in the following examples.

```
// no reset
always @(*)
  if(enable)
    d_out[0] <= d_in[0];

// a latch with asynchronous reset
always @(*)
  if(reset)
    d_out[1] = 1'b0;
  else if(enable)
    d_out[1] = d_in[1];

// a latch with asynchronous set
always @(*)
  if(set)
    d_out[2] = 1'b1;
```

```verilog
  else if(enable)
    d_out[2] = d_in[2];
```

Xilinx XST produces the following log whenever it recognizes a latch.
```
Synthesizing Unit <latches>.
WARNING:Xst:737 - Found 1-bit latch for signal <d_out<2>>.
WARNING:Xst:737 - Found 1-bit latch for signal <d_out<0>>.
WARNING:Xst:737 - Found 1-bit latch for signal <d_out<1>>.
Latches may be generated from incomplete case or if
statements. We do not recommend the use of latches in
FPGA/CPLD designs, as they may lead to timing problems.
Summary:
  inferred   3 Latch(s).
=======================================
HDL Synthesis Report

Macro Statistics
# Latches                                      : 3
1-bit latch                                    : 3
```

The conversion should be performed using recommended register coding style, which to some extent depends on a synthesis tool. A simple method is to convert gate enable input of a latch into a clock:

```verilog
// a register with synchronous reset and positive edge clock
wire clk = enable;

always @(posedge clk)
  if(reset)
    d_out[1] <= 1'b0;
  else
    d_out[1] <= d_in[1];
```

The implementation variants of the above example can be a positive or negative edge clock (Xilinx FPGAs don't support dual-edge registers), synchronous or asynchronous reset, and register set or clear upon reset assertion.

Resources

[1] *Statistical Timing Analysis for Latch-based Pipeline Designs.* M. C. Chao, L. Wang, K. Cheng, S., and Kundu. s.l.: IEEE/ACM, 2004. Proceedings of the 2004 IEEE/ACM international Conference on Computer-Aided Design.

51

PORTING COMBINATORIAL CIRCUITS

A combinatorial circuit is defined as logic that doesn't contain synchronous components, such as registers. This Tip discusses different challenges encountered during porting ASIC combinatorial circuits to FPGA.

Self-timed circuits

A good example of a self-timed circuit is the Synchronous RAM array controller. Memory read or write functions trigger a sequence of micro-transactions within a controller to access asynchronous RAM array: address decoding, precharge, accessing a memory cell, data demultiplexing, and other operations. What appears to the user as a single-clock SRAM read is actually a self-timed sequence of events.

Self-timed circuits rely on precise routing and logic delays that are impossible or very difficult to replicate in FPGA architecture. One method of porting a self-timed circuit is to add an artificial high-frequency clock that runs at the speed of the fastest micro-transaction and synchronizes the logic to that clock. If it proves too difficult to implement or it introduces too many logic modifications, the entire circuit can be rewritten as a synthesizable model.

Latches and Flip-flops

Gate-level implementation of latches and flip-flops in most cases can be modeled as an FPGA register or latch. There are several types of flip-flops and latches that cannot be directly ported to FPGA and require custom implementation. Examples are flip-flops with both synchronous and asynchronous resets, set and clear, scan chain, double-edge clock, and several others.

Combinatorial loops

ASIC designs contain many circuits with combinatorial loops: gate-level implementation of latches and flip-flops, keepers, and many others.

The following figure provides some examples of circuits with combinatorial loops. The left circuit is a keeper built using two invertors connected back to back. This circuit is used in ASIC designs as a storage element, or a bus keeper (or also called bus-hold), which keeps the logic value on a bus in the absence of active drivers. The example in the middle is an SR latch. The example on the right is a register reset fed back from the logic driven by the register output.

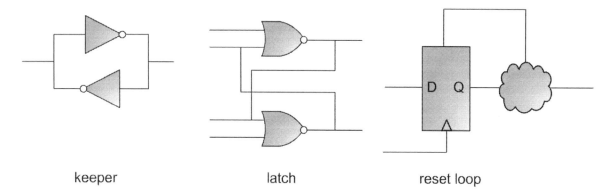

keeper   latch   reset loop

Figure 1: Example of circuits with combinatorial loops

The following is the Verilog code for the examples. The entire project can be downloaded from the book's website.

```verilog
module combinatorial_loop_examples(
                                  input clk,
                                  input latch_s,latch_r,
                                  output latch_q,latch_q_b,
                                  inout keeper0, keeper1,
                                  input  reset_loop_i,
                                  output reg reset_loop_o);
  // latch
  nor nor1(latch_q,   latch_s,latch_q_b);
  nor nor2(latch_q_b, latch_r,latch_q);

  // keeper
  nor not1(keeper0, keeper1);
  not not2(keeper1, keeper0);

  // reset loop
  wire reset_loop_i_b = ~reset_loop_o & reset_loop_i;

  always @(posedge clk, posedge reset_loop_i_b)
    if(reset_loop_i_b)
      reset_loop_o <= 'b0;
    else
      reset_loop_o <= reset_loop_i;
endmodule
```

Circuits that contain combinatorial loops can be synthesized for FPGA, but in most cases they will not function correctly. Combinatorial loop behavior depends on propagation delays through the logic in the loop and are therefore unpredictable.

The Xilinx XST synthesis tool will usually produce a combinatorial loop warning for simple (but not all) cases. Some loops might not synthesize at all by causing an infinite computation cycle that synthesis tools cannot handle.

For the above examples, XST produces warnings only for keeper and latch but not for the reset loop example. The Xilinx timing analyzer will also produce a warning that it cannot analyze some of the paths due to combinatorial loops.

The above examples are simple. In large real life designs, combinatorial loops can span multiple logic levels and might be very difficult to detect by simple code inspection or a simulation.

Software tools for commercial emulation platforms such as Cadence Palladium, Mentor Veloce, and EvE ZeBu employ various loop-breaking algorithms. The underlying idea behind the loop-breaking algorithms is to insert a synchronous element in the correct place in the loop without changing the circuit functionality. The inserted synchronous element can be clocked at the same or at a faster clock frequency, also known as oversampling technique.

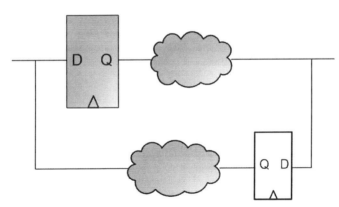

Figure 2: A register is inserted to break the combinatorial loop

Detecting and resolving combinatorial loops manually is especially challenging. It requires very good familiarity with design intent, circuit functionality, and implementation details. Typically, circuit porting to emulation platform is performed by a team of system or verification engineers and not by the original IC designers.

There are simple measures that designers can take to eliminate some of the combinatorial loops. They can remodel flip flops and latches by directly using an FPGA register and latch primitives. Many ASIC designs contain scan chains or other test logic that is not required in the emulated design. By tying off those circuits a lot of combinatorial loops are eliminated.

52

PORTING NON-SYNTHESIZABLE CIRCUITS

ASIC designs contain many circuits that are either not synthesizable at all or synthesized incorrectly for FPGAs. Some circuits cannot be synthesized due to the fundamental limitation of FPGA architecture. Examples include circuits that contain absolute delays, transistors and other switch-level primitives, 4-state Verilog values, signal strength, resistors, and capacitors.

FPGA synthesis tools provide different levels of Verilog language support. Xilinx XST is most strict in terms of what Verilog constructs can be synthesized. Synopsys Synplify provides a wider range of synthesizable Verilog constructs. Dedicated synthesis tools for ASIC emulation platforms, such as EvE ZeBu, provide the best Verilog language support.

The synthesizable subset of the Verilog language is usually well documented, and can be found in the synthesis tool user guide.

The rest of the Tip describes approaches and provides examples of porting different types of non-synthesizable circuits.

Absolute delays

Absolute delays are used to accurately model delays across delay lines and logic gates. Absolute delays are widely used in self-timed and asynchronous circuits. Delays can be implemented as a trace of specific length, or a chain of gates.

The following are Verilog delay examples using inertial delays, transport delays, and chains of *not* gates.

```
always @(*)
   #25 net_delayed = net_source;
not #(10) n1 (not_1, not_in);
not #(10) n2 (not_2, not_1);
not #(10) n3 (not_out, not_2);
always @(posedge clk)
    reg_out <= #5 reg_in;
```

Absolute delays don't have an equivalent representation in the existing FPGA architectures. Most of the FPGA synthesis tools will produce a warning and ignore the delay.

There isn't a good method of porting absolute delays without a major redesign of the circuit. One modeling approach is to convert an asynchronous circuit with a delay to a synchronous circuit by adding a high-speed oversampling clock.

Drive strength

Drive strength values are used in many ASIC circuits. Examples include RAM array controllers, power supply circuits, pull-up and pull-down resistors, IO circuits, and many others.

Verilog language defines the following signal strengths levels for each of the 0 and 1 logic level: *supply, strong, pull, weak,* and *highz*.

The following is an example of a one-bit storage unit that uses drive strength. The circuit is modeled as two back-to-back inverters and an access pass gate. Inverters are using *pull0* and *pull1* strength. When the pass gate is enabled, a signal with a *strong0* or *strong1* drive level overrides the *pull0* or *pull1* strength of the inverters.

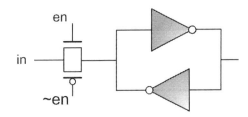

Figure 1: Bit storage circuit using drive strength

The Verilog model:
```
not (pull1,pull0) n1 (val_b, val);
not (pull1,pull0) n2 (val, val_b);
nmos n3 (in, val, en);
pmos n4 (in, val, ~en);
```

Drive strength doesn't have an equivalent representation in the existing FPGA architectures. Most of the FPGA synthesis tools will produce a warning and ignore the drive strength.

There isn't a good method of porting drive strength without a major redesign of the circuit. One modeling approach is to convert a single-bit net with assigned drive strength to a multi-bit bus. Each bus value is associated with a unique drive strength.

Logic strength

In addition to the drive strength, Verilog language provides four logic strength values that a signal can accept: 0, 1, z, and x. Most synthesis tools support only logic 0 and 1 values of the signals. Values of z and x are either ignored or produce a synthesis error.

In the technical literature, the logic strength range of a signal is often referred to as 4-state for 1,0,z, and x values, and 2-state for 1 and 0 values.

Many ASIC circuits are modeled using 4-state logic strength. A good example are tri-stated circuits, which use 0,1 to model logic levels and z to model a tri-state state. x is used to represent an unknown value. For example, after power-on a signal can be assigned x until the circuit comes out of reset and the signal is properly initialized. An unknown value x is very important for ASIC design verification, because it allows easy detection of error conditions.

Designers want to preserve the same 4-state behavior in the FPGA emulation model, which only supports 2-state. There isn't a generic solution that applies to all cases. One approach is to represent a 4-state logic strength using a two-bit bus.

Modeling 4-state values also includes porting all 4-state specific Verilog operators. Verilog has special equality and inequality operators that apply to 4-state signals: === and !==. Arithmetic, conditional, and relational operators produce different results if applied on 4-state and 2-state values.

The following table shows the results of evaluating 2-state and 4-state equality expressions.

Table 1: Evaluating equality expressions

{a,b}	a == b	a === b
00	1	1
01, 10	0	0
11	1	1
0x, x0	x	0
1x, x1	x	0
xx	x	1

Synthesis tools have different levels of support for 4-state logic and operators. For example, Xilinx XST will produce an error after encountering a === operator. Other synthesis tools will produce a warning and replace a 4-state === operator with a 2-state == equivalent.

Porting transistor-based circuits

ASIC designs frequently use custom-build circuits that contain CMOS switch-level primitives. Such circuits often achieve better performance and the most compact area utilization.

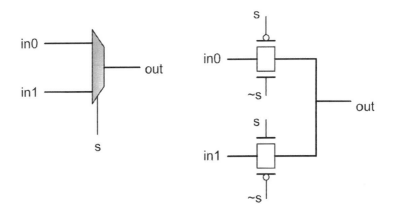

Figure 2: Two-to-one multiplexor implementation using pass gates

Xilinx XST doesn't support `cmos`, `pmos`, `nmos`, `tran`, `tranif0`, `tranif1` and other Verilog switch-level primitives. Synopsys Synplify provides limited synthesis support of `tran`, `tranif0`, and `tranif1` pass gates.

One way to port transistor-based circuits is to model them as a simple switch statement. The following are Verilog implementations of the two-to-one multiplexor using RTL model and with pass gates.

```
module mux2x1(input mux_in0, mux_in1, mux_sel,
              output mux_out_rtl,mux_out_passgate,
       mux_out_remodeled);
  assign mux_out_rtl = mux_sel ? mux_in1 : mux_in0;

  // non-synthesizable passgate implementation
  nmos p0 (mux_out_passgate,mux_in0, ~mux_sel);
  pmos p1 (mux_out_passgate,mux_in0, mux_sel);

  nmos p2 (mux_out_passgate,mux_in1, mux_sel);
  pmos p3 (mux_out_passgate,mux_in1, ~mux_sel);

  // implementation using remodelled transistors
  nmos_model p4 (mux_out_remodeled,mux_in0, ~mux_sel);
  pmos_model p5 (mux_out_remodeled,mux_in0, mux_sel);

  nmos_model p6 (mux_out_remodeled,mux_in1, mux_sel);
  pmos_model p7 (mux_out_remodeled,mux_in1, ~mux_sel);
endmodule // mux2x1

module nmos_model(output out,input in,ctrl);
   assign out = ctrl ? in : 1'bz;
endmodule

module pmos_model(output out,input in,ctrl);
```

```
    assign out = ~ctrl ? in : 1'bz;
endmodule
```

A two-to-one multiplexor is just a simple example of a transistor-based circuit. ASIC designs implement much more complex circuits using switch-level primitives: custom 256-1 multiplexors, latches and half-latches, flip-flops, custom state machines, memory arrays, and many others. A general approach to porting such circuits is to "divide and conquer." First, try to remodel individual switch elements. If that doesn't help solving all synthesis and physical implementation issues, remodel larger blocks.

Behavioral models

Non-digital components of an ASIC design, such as delay lines and transistors, are typically modeled using a behavioral subset of Verilog.

Behavioral models present a unique challenge. They are designed to represent circuit behavior and not to reflect internal design structure. Behavioral models are used in many cases; for example, by an IP core vendor, which delivers a netlist. A model might be as complex as necessary to represent the core but too complex for converting to a synthesizable design.

Small circuits are modeled using Verilog User Defined Primitives (UDP). UDP is non-synthesizable with most of the synthesis tools.

53

MODELING MEMORIES

Memories are part of virtually every ASIC design. There are different types of memories: asynchronous RAM, synchronous RAM (SRAM), pipelined Zero Bus Turnaround (ZBT), Double Data Rate (DDR) DRAMs, Read Only Memory (ROM), and the list can go on. Memory sizes vary from a few-byte scratchpad, to several hundred kilobyte processor cache. Memory data widths vary from a single bit to 256-bit and even wider.

Typically, ASIC designs contain either on-chip SRAM, or a memory controller to interface with the external DDR DRAM. Xilinx provides memory controller (MIG) core with a full source code access that can be customized to model the one used in ASIC design.

In most cases asynchronous RAMs and SRAMs are foundry-specific and need to be converted to an FPGA-friendly functionally-equivalent Verilog model. Xilinx XST and other FPGA synthesis tools are capable of correctly infer and synthesize SRAMs that directly map into Xilinx BRAM or distributed RAM memory primitives.

In some cases, designers might need to modify the logic surrounding the memory in addition to modeling the memory itself. One example is asynchronous RAM. Xilinx embedded memories are synchronous, and have access latency of one or more clocks. Another example is write-enable for each of the data bits. Xilinx BRAM primitive has only byte-write enable. ASIC designs might use multi-port memories. An FPGA has a limited amount of embedded memory that might not be sufficient for some of the designs, such as large processor cashes. An ASIC memory might contain special features, such as error repair, redundancy, or built-in self test that don't have Xilinx equivalent.

Xilinx embedded memories have three access modes – read-first, write-first, and no-change – that can model most of the ASIC SRAM memories.

Tip #34 provides more details on Xilinx embedded memory features, and the rules on how to correctly infer BRAM or distributed RAM in HDL code.

There is a well-known technique to model bit-write enable using Xilinx BRAM. The technique takes advantage of a dual-port BRAM to perform read-modify-write operation in a single clock cycle. The following figure illustrates how it's done.

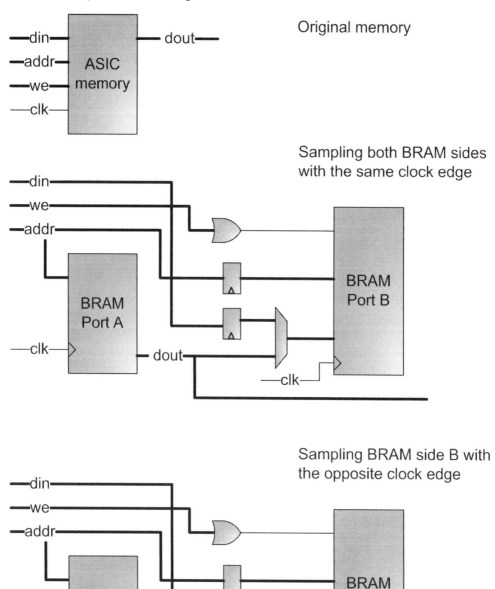

Figure 1: Implementing bit-write enable using BRAM

The dual-port BRAM can pipeline the write operation and achieve a throughput of one read-modify-write operation per clock cycle. To do so, the designer uses Port A as the read port, Port B as the write port, and uses one common clock for both ports. The read address is routed to Port A. A copy of the read address is delayed by one clock and routed to Port B. The data from Port A is multiplexed with the input data and write-enable bus, and used as the data input to Port B.

A similar solution is to implement read-modify-write operation on rising and falling edge of the clock. Rising clock edge is fed to Port A and delay registers. Port B is clocked by the falling clock edge.

The disadvantage of this method is the extra logic required to delay address and data busses, and multiplex the data input to Port B.

A simple design accompanied with the book provides an example of those two methods.

Xilinx BRAM and distributed memory primitives can be used to model a ROM. Methods of preloading ROM with a custom pattern are described in Tip #34. Small size ROMs can be modeled directly in the RTL using Verilog *case* statement.

Large ASIC SRAM and ROM memories can be modeled using off-the-shelf components. However, the disadvantage is decreased design performance and additional design complexity due to the need to interface with additional on-board chips.

54

PORTING TRI-STATE LOGIC

Tri-state logic is used extensively in ASIC designs to implement bidirectional busses. Xilinx FPGA architecture doesn't support internal bidirectional signals. It only supports tri-stated output for the external IOs. However, in many cases XST and other Xilinx FPGA synthesis tools will correctly synthesize the original RTL by performing conversion of the tri-stated signals into combinatorial logic.

The following is a Verilog example that models a tri-stated output buffer.

```
assign tri_out = out_en ? data_out : 1'bz;
```

XST infers the tri-stated output buffer as OBUFT primitive.

```
OBUFT tri_out_OBUFT (
     .I(data_out),
     .T(out_en),
     .O(tri_out));
```

The XST synthesis report contains the following log:

```
=========================================================
*       HDL Synthesis
=========================================================
Synthesizing Unit <tristates>.
    Found 1-bit tristate buffer for signal <tri_out>
    Summary:
       inferred   1 Tristate(s).
=========================================================
HDL Synthesis Report
Macro Statistics
  # Tristates                                  : 1
   1-bit tristate buffer                       : 1
=========================================================
```

The following is Verilog example of an internal signal driven by two tri-state buffers.

```
module tristates( input clk,reset,
                  input [1:0] d1_in,
                  input d1_en,
```

```
                        input [1:0] d2_in,
                        input d2_en,
                        output reg dout);
  tri tri_internal;
  assign tri_internal = d1_en ? |d1_in : 1'bz;
  assign tri_internal = d2_en ? ^d2_in : 1'bz;
  always @(posedge clk, posedge reset) begin
    if(reset)
        dout <= 0;
    else
        dout <= tri_internal;
  end
endmodule // Tristates
```

XST synthesizes the following circuit, which includes a register and a look-up table:

```
      wire tri_internal;
      FDC dout (
            .C(clk),
            .CLR(reset),
            .D(tri_internal),
            .Q(dout));
      LUT6 #( .INIT ( 64'hFF7DFF7DFF7D287D ))
            tri_internalLogicTrst1 (
        .I0(d2_en),
        .I1(d2_in[0]),
        .I2(d2_in[1]),
        .I3(d1_en),
        .I4(d1_in[0]),
        .I5(d1_in[1]),
        .O(tri_internal));
```

The XST synthesis report contains the following log:

```
=============================================
* HDL Synthesis
=============================================
Synthesizing Unit <tristates>.
    Found 1-bit register for signal <dout>.
    Found 1-bit tristate buffer for signal <tri_internal>
    Summary:
        inferred   1 D-type flip-flop(s).
        inferred   2 Tristate(s).
Unit <tristates> synthesized.
```

```
=============================================
HDL Synthesis Report
Macro Statistics
# Registers                                  : 1
   1-bit register                            : 1
# Tristates                                  : 2
   1-bit tristate buffer                     : 2
# Xors                                       : 1
   1-bit xor2                                : 1
=============================================
*    Low Level Synthesis
=============================================
```
WARNING:Xst:2039 - Unit tristates: 1 multi-source signal is replaced by logic (pull-up yes): tri_internal.

XST has a *TRISTATE2LOGIC* constraint that enables or disables conversion of the tri-stated signals into logic. XST cannot perform the conversion if the tri-stated signal is connected to a black box or to a top-level output.

The Synopsys Synplify synthesis tool provides another option related to tri-stated signals, called "Push Tristates." When that option is enabled, the tool pushes tri-stated signals through multiplexors, latches, registers, and buffers, and propagates the high-impedance state. The advantage of pushing tri-stated signals to the periphery is improved timing results. The following figure shows a circuit before and after applying "Push Tristates."

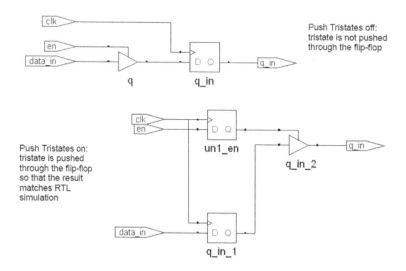

Figure 1: Synplify "Push Tristates" option (source: Synopsys Synplify User Guide)

When a synthesis tool cannot resolve a tri-stated signal, the designer has no choice but to manually change the circuit to the equivalent one without a tri-state.

55
VERIFICATION OF A PORTED DESIGN

After completing all the ASIC migration tasks that require modifications of the original design – partitioning into multiple FPGAs, porting RTL, synthesis and physical implementation - the remaining task is to make sure that the ported design is functionally equivalent to the original one. This is the task of verification, which is intended to test that the design still functions according to the specifications.

A straightforward approach to verify ported design is to subject it to the same array of functional simulation and other tests as the original ASIC design.

The following figure illustrates the process.

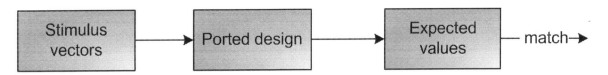

Figure 1: Replacing original ASIC design with the ported one

Simulation stimulus vectors are applied to the ported design instead of the original, and the same expected values are checked. Simulation runtime is expected to be similar to the original ASIC design, even though the ported design did undergo several transformations. This is the disadvantage of this method, because simulation runtime is significant, and can take several days for large ASIC designs.

Another approach shown in the figure below is a side-by-side simulation of the original ASIC and ported designs. The same stimulus vectors are fed into inputs of both designs. Instead of using the module that checks expected values, the outputs of the ported design are compared with the ones from the ASIC. The prerequisite is that the ASIC design is already verified, and produces correct outputs. This approach works well on small designs. It doesn't scale to larger designs in terms of simulation speed, because the size of the ported design is much higher that the module that performs expected value checking.

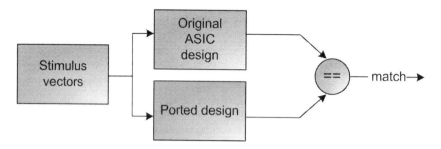

Figure 2: Comparing the results from original and ported designs

If the simulation testbench is synthesizable, the entire system that includes the ported design, synthesizable testbench, stimulus vector generator, and expected values checker, can be run on the emulation or prototyping platform. That approach, also illustrated in the following figure, is much faster than a software-based functional simulation.

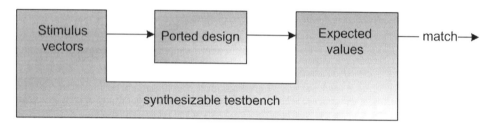

Figure 3: Performing tests on an emulation or prototyping platform

The disadvantage of this method is that it requires rebuilding the system for every code change in order to run it on the emulation or prototyping platform. That can take minutes or several hours, depending on the nature of the change.

Equivalence checking

Equivalence checking is the process of comparing an original, or "golden," design with the modified one in order to determine that both are functionally equivalent and the modified design still complies with the original specification. The following figure depicts a simplified equivalence checking setup.

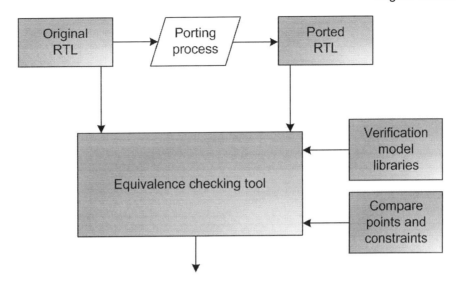

Figure 4: Equivalence checking process

The original ASIC design, the ported design, verification model libraries, compare points, and other constraints are inputs to the third party equivalence checking tool. Compare points describe the primary inputs and outputs, registers and latches, black boxes, and other design components. Constraints include design clock information. Equivalence checking tools typically require synthesizable RTL. Alternatively, the tools can work with a synthesized gate level netlist.

The main advantage of using equivalence checking is that it is faster than functional simulation. However, equivalence checking does not replace functional simulation. Instead, it serves as another method during the design verification process to improve coverage, and increase your confidence level that the ported design functions according to the specification.

There are several commercial equivalence checking tools, such as Cadence Conformal Logic Equivalence Checker (LEC), Mentor Graphics FormalPro, and Synopsys Formality. Each one provides a unique set of features, which might or might not be applicable to a particular design flow used in porting an ASIC design to FPGA.

Using synthesizable assertions

An assertion-based methodology is widely used during the verification process. Assertions augment the functional coverage by providing multiple observation points within the design. Usually, both RTL designers and verification engineers instrument the design with assertions. Assertions can be placed both inside the RTL code, which makes updates and management easier, or outside, to keep synthesizable and behavioral parts of the code separate. SystemVerilog provides assertion specification, a small subset of which is synthesizable assertions. Only a handful of FPGA design tools support synthesizable assertions. One of them is Synopsys Identify Pro that has assertion synthesis and debug capabilities.

56

FPGA DESIGN VERIFICATION

Verification is the process of comparing a design's behavior against the designer's intent. Verification of an ASIC design is a broad and complex subject. There are many tools that perform formal and functional verification of an ASIC design. Various verification techniques are topic of academic and industrial research.

However, FPGA verification is still an emerging field. FPGA verification flows and methodologies are not as structured and defined as ASIC. Often FPGA design teams don't have a verification plan at all. Design verification is performed by doing haphazard and disorganized functional simulations without any clear goals.

The gap between ASIC and FPGA verification methodologies is caused by a few reasons.

The cost of an error in FPGA design is not as steep as in ASIC. Frequently, fixing an FPGA bug only requires a new build and reconfiguring the FPGA. "Trial and error" debug methodology lends itself well to being used in small FPGA designs. Unfortunately, that so-called methodology is also the result of a faster time-to-market requirement, at the expense of product quality. By contrast, ASIC teams spend up to 80% of the overall design time on verification.

ASIC design teams are larger than FPGA ones and therefore have more engineering resources to perform more stringent and thorough verification. Also, ASIC projects have bigger budgets and so can afford to buy or license more tools.

Verification is more rigorous in mission-critical FPGA designs, such as medical or military applications, but still it lags behind the ASIC.

Verification process is usually metric-driven, which enables measuring the progress, and being able to determine when the design is ready. Coverage is used as a metric for evaluating the verification progress, and directing verification efforts by identifying tested and untested portions of the design. It is defined as the percentage of verification objectives that have been met.

There are two main types of coverage metrics: (i) those that can be automatically extracted from the design code, such as code coverage; and (ii) those that are user-specified in order to tie the verification environment to the design intent or functionality. The latter is also known as functional coverage. The following figure shows an example of a FPGA system verification flow.

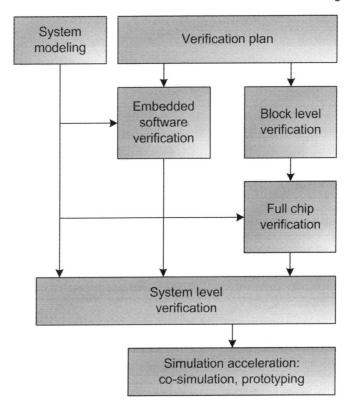

Figure 1: System verification flow plan

A large design can contain several FPGAs and embedded software. Verification of such a design is a system-level effort. The flow plan starts with the System Verification Plan, which defines the scope of work, specifies tasks, selects the tools, and establishes the verification coverage metrics. In parallel, the verification team develops different device and system-level models.

Verification of a digital logic is broken into block-level verification that focuses on simulating individual functional blocks. Next, verification is performed at the full-chip level for individual FPGAs. Finally, there is a system-level verification that combines all FPGAs, embedded software, and system and device models.

System-level verification can be followed by different acceleration methods, such as co-simulation, or system prototyping. By using dedicated prototyping boards and tools, the team can perform system-level verification using real peripheral devices instead of models.

The above flow is very generic, but it can still be applied to different designs: from a small single FPGA board and a single developer, to a board with 10+ FPGAs, embedded software running operating system, and a large cross-functional design team.

Functional Coverage

SystemVerilog provides extensive support for coverage-driven verification. It enables monitoring the coverage of variables and expressions, automatic and user-defined coverage bins with sets of values, transitions, or cross products, filtering conditions at multiple levels, events and sequences to automatically trigger coverage sampling, directives to activate, query, control, and regulate coverage. SystemVerilog includes functional coverage directly in the language by specifying a `covergroup` construct. A `covergroup` specification can include several components that encapsulate the coverage model: a clocking event, a set of coverage points, cross coverage between the coverage points, and various coverage options and arguments. The `covergroup` construct is a user-defined type. It is defined once and can be used in different contexts.

The following example defines coverage group `cover_group1` with three coverage points associated with a pixel position and color. The values of the variable position and color are sampled at the positive edge of signal `clk`.

```
enum { red, green, blue } color;
logic [1023:0] offset_x, offset_y;

covergroup cover_group1 @(posedge clk);
    c: coverpoint color;
    x: coverpoint offset_x;
    y: coverpoint offset_y;
endgroup
```

Code Coverage

Unlike functional coverage, code coverage provides no feedback on the code functional correctness. It provides a measure of completeness of testing and is complementary to functional coverage. Code coverage information is generated by a verification tool from design RTL or gate-level source. There are several types of code coverage described in the following table.

Table 1: Code Coverage Types

Code coverage type	Description
Statement coverage	Counts the execution of each statement on a line
Branch coverage	Counts the execution of each conditional "if/then/else" and "case" statement
Condition coverage	Analyzes the decision made in "if" and ternary statements
Expression coverage	Analyzes the expressions on the right hand side of assignment statements

Toggle coverage	Counts each time an object or a variable transitions from one state to another
State machine coverage	Counts the states, transitions, and paths within a state machine

Randomization

Stimulus randomization is an important verification technique. Its formal name is Constrained Random Testing Verification. This methodology allows you to achieve better results by focusing on corner cases when exhaustive coverage is not possible.

The following is an example of a simple 32-bit adder.

```
module adder(input [31:0] a,b,
             output [31:0] sum,
             input clk,reset);
always @(posedge clk)
  if(reset)
    sum <= 'b0;
  else
    sum = a + b;
endmodule // adder
```

Assuming the clock period is 100MHz, it'd take several thousand years to exhaustively simulate the adder:

```
Time = 2^32+32 * 10ns / 31.56 ms/year = 5845 years
```

In most of the real-world FPGA designs, exhaustive coverage is unachievable. The best known verification approach that produces a good level of confidence is constraint-driven verification. One type of constraint-driven verification is directed method, where a set of known stimulus test vectors is applied to the DUT. Randomization of stimulus data can be more effective method.

There is a broad range of randomization techniques and tools available to verification engineers including broadly and narrowly constrained randomization, different random variable distributions, and others.

Verilog language defines `$random(seed)` system task to do randomization. SystemVerilog provides much richer set of features to perform randomization.

Every SystemVerilog class object has a built-in `randomize()` method. It supports two types of random properties: `rand` and `randc`. `rand` can repeat values without exhausting all of them. `randc` is exhausting all values before repeating any. Randomization is controlled using a `constraint` block. Constraint values can be weighted to follow a specific random distribution.

57
SIMULATION TYPES

Designers can perform different simulation types during FPGA development cycle: RTL, functional, gate-level, and timing.

RTL simulation is performed using the original Verilog or VHDL code.

Functional simulation, also known as post-synthesis simulation, is performed using a functional RTL model of the gate level netlist produced by a synthesis tool. Functional gate level RTL models contain simulation models of the FPGA-specific primitives, such as LUTs and registers. The reason for calling it a functional simulation is that it doesn't contain any technology-specific timing, placement, or routing information about the design.

Gate-level timing simulation is performed on the design after the place and route stage. This is the most accurate simulation type, since it contains all the placement, routing and timing delay information.

RTL simulation is much faster than functional and gate-level timing simulation, because the simulation database is the smallest, and doesn't contain placement, routing, and timing information of the final FPGA design. This is one reason why RTL simulation is performed the most often. In FPGA design flow, functional and gate-level timing simulation is typically performed when designers suspect that there might be a mismatch between RTL and functional or gate-level timing simulation results, which can lead to an incorrect design. The mismatch can be caused for several reasons discussed in more detail in Tip #59.

Note that the nomenclature of simulation types is not consistent. The same name, for instance "gate-level simulation", can have slightly different meaning in simulation flows of different FPGA vendors. The situation is even more confusing in ASIC simulation flows, which have many more different simulation types, such as transistor-level, and dynamic simulation.

The following figure shows simulation types designers can perform during Xilinx FPGA synthesis and physical implementation process.

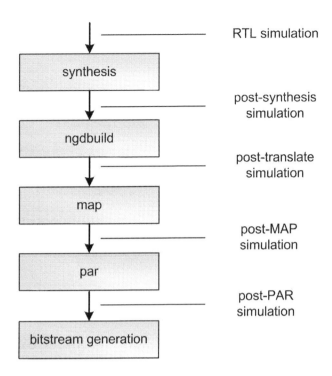

Figure 1: Simulation types

Xilinx FPGA designers can perform simulation after each level of design transformation from the original RTL to the bitstream.

The following example is a 12-bit OR gate implemented in Verilog.

```
module sim_types(input [11:0] user_in, output user_out);
  assign user_out = |user_in;
endmodule
```

XST post-synthesis simulation model is implemented using LUT6 and LUT2 primitives, which are parts of Xilinx UNISIMS RTL simulation library.

```
wire out, out1_14;

LUT6 #( .INIT ( 64'hFFFFFFFFFFFFFFFE ))
  out1 (
    .I0(user_in[3]),
    .I1(user_in[2]),
    .I2(user_in[5]),
    .I3(user_in[4]),
    .I4(user_in[7]),
    .I5(user_in[6]),
    .O(out));
```

```verilog
LUT6 #( .INIT ( 64'hFFFFFFFFFFFFFFFE ))
  out2 (
    .I0(user_in[9]),
    .I1(user_in[8]),
    .I2(user_in[11]),
    .I3(user_in[10]),
    .I4(user_in[1]),
    .I5(user_in[0]),
    .O(out1_14));

LUT2 #( .INIT ( 4'hE ))
  out3 (
    .I0(out),
    .I1(out1_14),
    .O(user_out) );
```

Post-synthesis simulation model can be generated using the following command:

```
$ netgen -w -ofmt verilog -sim sim.ngc post_synthesis.v
```

Post-translate simulation model is implemented using X_LUT6 and X_LUT2 primitives, which are parts of Xilinx SIMPRIMS simulation library. SIMPRIMS library is used for gate-level timing simulation.

```verilog
wire out;
wire out1_14;
X_LUT6 #( .INIT ( 64'hFFFFFFFFFFFFFFFE ))
  out1 (
    .ADR0(user_in[3]),
    .ADR1(user_in[2]),
    .ADR2(user_in[5]),
    .ADR3(user_in[4]),
    .ADR4(user_in[7]),
    .ADR5(user_in[6]),
    .O(out) );

X_LUT6 #( .INIT ( 64'hFFFFFFFFFFFFFFFE ))
  out2 (
    .ADR0(user_in[9]),
    .ADR1(user_in[8]),
    .ADR2(user_in[11]),
    .ADR3(user_in[10]),
    .ADR4(user_in[1]),
    .ADR5(user_in[0]),
    .O(out1_14));

X_LUT2 #( .INIT ( 4'hE ))
```

```
  out3 (
    .ADR0(out),
    .ADR1(out1_14),
    .O(user_out) );
```

Post-translate simulation model can be generated using the following command:

```
$ netgen -w -ofmt verilog -dir netgen/synth -sim sim.ngd
  post_translate.v
```

Post-map simulation model is also implemented using X_LUT6 and X_LUT2 primitives. The difference from the post-translate model is that post-map model also includes placement information, and additional timing information in the Standard Delay Format (SDF).

```
initial $sdf_annotate("netgen/map/sim_types_map.sdf");
wire out;
wire out1_82;
X_LUT6 #(
  .LOC ( "SLICE_X4Y2" ),
    .INIT ( 64'hFFFFFFFFFFFFFFFE ))
  out2 (
    .ADR0(user_in_9_IBUF_0),
    .ADR1(user_in_8_IBUF_0),
    .ADR2(user_in_11_IBUF_0),
    .ADR3(user_in_10_IBUF_0),
    .ADR4(user_in_1_IBUF_0),
    .ADR5(user_in_0_IBUF_0),
    .O(out1_82));
X_LUT6 #(
    .LOC ( "SLICE_X4Y2" ),
    .INIT ( 64'hFFFFFFFFFFFF0000 ))
  out3 (
    .ADR0(1'b1),
    .ADR1(1'b1),
    .ADR2(1'b1),
    .ADR3(1'b1),
    .ADR4(out),
    .ADR5(out1_82),
    .O(user_out_OBUF_78));
X_LUT6 #(
    .LOC ( "SLICE_X7Y2" ),
    .INIT ( 64'hFFFFFFFFFFFFFFFE ))
  out1 (
    .ADR0(user_in_3_IBUF_0),
    .ADR1(user_in_2_IBUF_0),
```

```
    .ADR2(user_in_5_IBUF_0),
    .ADR3(user_in_4_IBUF_0),
    .ADR4(user_in_7_IBUF_0),
    .ADR5(user_in_6_IBUF_0),
    .O(out));
```

Post-map simulation model can be generated using the following command:

```
$ netgen -s 3 -pcf sim_types.pcf -sdf_anno true
  -sdf_path "netgen/map" -w -dir netgen/map -ofmt verilog -sim
  sim.ncd post_map.v
```

Post-par simulation model differs from the post-map in that post-par also includes all the routing information.

Post-par simulation model can be generated using the following command:

```
$ netgen -s 3 -pcf sim_types.pcf -sdf_anno true
  -sdf_path "netgen/par" -insert_pp_buffers true -w
  -dir netgen/par -ofmt verilog -sim sim.ncd post_par.v
```

Post-par simulation model includes all the information to perform an accurate timing simulation.

58
IMPROVING SIMULATION PERFORMANCE

FPGA design and verification engineers spend a significant part of their time performing functional simulations. For a large FPGA design, running a system level simulation can easily take several hours. If an engineer performs, on average, ten simulations a day that take thirty minutes each, then a 30% speed improvement will allow the performing of fourteen additional simulations of the same design. More simulation turns allow for the achieving of verification goals faster.

In general, improving simulation performance involves the following types of changes:
- choosing the right simulation type
- performing profiling to identify simulation bottlenecks
- optimizing device under test, testbench, and simulation models
- reducing simulation database size
- reducing the number of simulation events
- enabling optimization options in simulation tools
- reducing verbose and visibility level of a simulated design
- following simulation tool best practices
- selecting the right simulator, simulation flow, and environment

Researching different simulation performance options and implementing them is a long-term effort. It is important to thoroughly document all the findings, establish a set of recommendations, and disseminate and actively enforce them across the design teams.

Simulation type

Choosing the right simulation type can have a dramatic effect on performance. The performance difference between gate level, RTL, and transaction level simulations is in one, or even two, orders of magnitude. Transaction level simulation is the fastest, because it is compiled into the smallest database and contains the least amount of simulation events. On the other side of the spectrum is gate level simulation, which contains timing, placement, and routing information of the final FPGA design. This point is discussed in more detail in Tip #57.

Profiling

Simulation profiling is the process of getting detailed information on how the simulation engine is utilizing the CPU. For the duration of the simulation run, profiling utility collects the information on how much time and how many CPU cycles were spent in different design units, or any HDL statement in the profiled code. Profiling results are used to identify design units or code sections that use the most CPU resources and subsequently optimize those sections to improve simulation performance.

The profiling process is usually non-intrusive and doesn't require modification of the source code. The profiling is controlled with compile and simulation options.

Device under test code optimizations

Designers can use the following methods to optimize device under test (DUT) code. Compiler directives, such as `ifdef SIMULATION or `ifndef SIMULATION, can be used to conditionally enable portions of the code for simulation or synthesis. For example, if the design has several interfaces, such as PCI Express, USB, and Ethernet, and the test case only exercises USB, there is no reason for PCI Express interface and Ethernet MAC code to participate in the simulation. Other candidates for including under conditional compilation are debug modules such as Xilinx Integrated Logic Analyzer (ILA) and Virtual IO (VIO) cores.

The effort of implementing conditional compilation directives and tying off large modules is negligible compared with the time gained by decreased simulation runtime. When using conditional compile, it's important to make sure to exclude files that are not part of the simulation from the filelist. That will also save some compile time.

A simple change that significantly reduces simulation time is to shorten or completely bypass device or IP core initialization cycle during the simulation. For example, it might take several milliseconds of simulation time, which takes a very long time for a large design, to perform PCI Express link training, SerDes calibration, or memory controller initialization. Most of the IP cores provide a parameter to bypass or shorten the initialization. Alternatively, designers can use Verilog `force` statement to force internal signals to certain state.

Another optimization is to reduce the period of timers in the design. Timers are used for different purposes; for example, measuring delays or sending periodic events. The circuit might not require simulating a timer with a long period if it produces equivalent results when the timer is using a much lower period.

Making more complex code changes to a working design in order to improve simulation performance is not desirable. It might decrease code readability, cause the design not to meet timing constraints, or even introduce new bugs.

Testbench optimizations

One approach for testbench optimization is raising the level of abstraction. Transaction-level simulations that focus on cycle-based signals and transactions perform faster than event-based RTL that use transitions in time. SystemVerilog defines the `clocking` block, which is a key element in a cycle-based methodology.

A testbench written in Verilog can take advantage of Programming Language Interface (PLI) and the Verilog Procedural Interface (VPI) routines. The PLI/VPI is an extension mechanism that allows functions written in other programming languages to access low-level design information. Carefully designed PLI/VPI extensions can significantly improve simulation performance.

Simulation model optimizations

The Xilinx CoreGen utility has an option to generate the core as a structural netlist or behavioral model. The behavior core model performs faster than the structural one.

Performance can be improved even further by replacing generated core models with simplified ones. Good candidates are clock management models of Xilinx PLL, DCM, or MMCM primitives. For simple clock configurations, those complex models can be replaced with the equivalent one-line Verilog code.

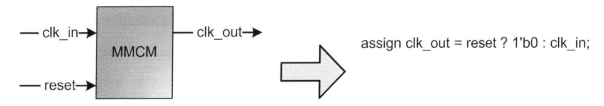

Figure 1: Replacing MMCM model with an equivalent code

Large DDR memory models use a lot of simulation resources. In some designs, the combination of a memory controller with an external DDR memory model can be replaced with the equivalent Block RAM with the interface adaptations.

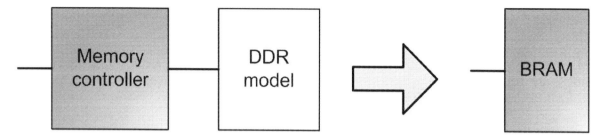

Figure 2: Replacing DDR model with BRAM

Reducing the number of simulation events

Reducing the number of simulation events can have significant effect on performance.

A simple change is decreasing the resolution of the `` `timescale `` compiler directive.

For example, change

```
`timescale 1ns/1ps
```

to

```
`timescale 1ns/100ps
```

Some simulation models do require higher resolution, and decreasing the resolution can affect simulation results.

Another optimization is reducing the clock frequency to the lowest possible.

Also, disable or ignore timing delays on all gates, switches, and continuous assignments, and don't perform timing checks. Simulators have various options that control timing delays and checks. Some of these options in VCS and ModelSim simulators are +delay_mode_path, +delay_mode_zero, +delay_mode_distributed, +delay_mode_unit, and +notimingcheck.

Optimization options

Simulation tools have various optimization options that enable faster simulation. For example, Aldec Riviera and Riviera-PRO simulators have -O<n> global optimization option, where <n> specifies the optimization level 0-3. The -O0 switch lowers the optimization to the minimum. Maximum optimization is enabled with -O3. Mentor ModelSim SE and DE have a `vopt` command that accepts different optimization option parameters.

2-state simulation

Using 2-state versus 4-state simulation might be considered for improving simulation performance. Some simulators provide an option to switch to a 2-state simulation mode, which converts x and z values to logic 1 and 0. VCS provides a `+2state` option to turn on the 2-state simulation mode.

Incremental compilation

All commercial simulators support incremental compilation. When specified, the simulator only re-compiles the modules in the design that have changed since the last time. This is a simple method to reduce compile time but not simulation time, which usually far exceeds the compile time. VCS simulator `-Mupdate` option enables incremental compilation. `-incr` option enables incremental compile in ModelSim simulator.

Reducing verbose level

Each simulator has options that control a generation of debug information, such as different verbose levels, warning, informational, and other diagnostic messages.

Reducing verbose level and the amount of produced messages can have a positive effect on performance

Reduce visibility of a simulated design

Capturing every value change on every signal of a small design is feasible. However, for large designs, the overhead required to record all the events overwhelms available system resources. The simulation quickly fills the available disk space and increases the run time several times. Simulation of a large FPGA design can easily produce gigabytes of dump data. Narrowing the scope of captured data is a simple way to improve simulation speed and reduce the amount of consumed disk space. The tradeoff is reduced visibility of a simulated design. Designers will need to determine which signals are essential for sufficient understanding of a problem in every simulation run. Also, disabling glitch-detection and capturing delta cycle information can significantly decrease the size of a dump file.

Concurrent execution

Concurrent execution is not the optimization method per se, but rather reorganization of the testbench to parallelize some of the simulation tasks.

Using multiple threads that perform different tasks concurrently rather than sequentially can speed up simulation. Verilog and SystemVerilog enable multi-threaded execution using `fork/join` mechanism. Disadvantages of a multi-threaded simulation are the additional overhead required for thread coordination, synchronization, and data-sharing complications.

The following is a simple example of using `fork/join` to send packets on multiple interfaces concurrently.

```
initial begin
  send_n_packets = 1000;
  reset();
  repeat(send_n_packets) begin
    fork
      send_if1();
      send_if2();
      send_if3();
    join
    check();
  end
end
```

Following simulator best practices

Established commercial simulators have a wealth of information, such as user manuals, whitepapers, and answer records that contain useful tips on how to improve simulation performance. An example is the Synopsys SolvNet portal, which is an excellent source of information on the VCS simulator.

Upgrading to a faster simulator

In some situations the way to significantly improve simulation performance is to migrate to a higher-performing simulator. The need for a new simulator may arise for several reasons. The license for an existing simulator is about to expire, or there aren't a sufficient number of licenses for a growing design team. The alternative simulator has higher performance, and it also offers a more cost effective license upgrade path. The existing simulator doesn't meet all the project requirements; for example, it doesn't run on Linux, or doesn't support SystemVerilog. The process of simulator selection is discussed in Tips #60 and 61.

Simulation environment

An upgrade to a more powerful workstation with faster processor speed, more memory, and a hard disk drive with higher RPM speed can easily double simulation performance.

Simulation flow

Using a command-line version of the simulator tool instead of GUI can save several hundred of megabytes of memory.

59
SIMULATION AND SYNTHESIS RESULTS MISMATCH

Many times FPGA designers encounter a situation where a design passes all simulation test cases, synthesizes correctly, and meets timing constraints during physical implementation, but still doesn't function correctly when loaded to an FPGA. This is often called simulation and synthesis results mismatch. The following is a list of some of the common reasons for a simulation and synthesis mismatch.

Incorrect simulation environment

Simulation environment doesn't accurately model actual devices connected to the FPGA. It can be an incorrect functional model of a device. For example, the simulation model of a DDR3 memory is different than what is actually being used on board.

Incorrect device interface simulation

Simulation environment incorrectly models the timing behavior of the interface between an FPGA and a peripheral device.

Insufficient simulation coverage

Simulation test cases are running at speeds orders of magnitude slower than the real device. The testbench stimulus might not cover enough corner cases and logic conditions due to limited simulation time.

Incorrect IO constraints

FPGA IO pins are not properly constrained. That can be an IO location, standard, voltage level, drive strength, or slew rate. Another frequent cause of problems is swapped positive and negative sides of a differential IO or a clock.

Incorrect timing constraints

FPGA logic is either not constrained at all or constrained incorrectly. That will result in random failures: state machines enter invalid states, FIFOs are written and read incorrectly, occasional memory data corruptions, and many other symptoms that occur intermittently and indicate timing problems in the design.

It is recommended to always use the –u option in the TRACE timing analysis tool to report unconstrained timing paths.

Clock domain crossing

There are several types of problems caused by clock domain crossing issues. Incorrect design of the clock synchronization logic may result in simulation and synthesis mismatch.

Compiler directives and Verilog attributes

There are several Verilog attributes and compiler directives that are interpreted differently by the simulation and synthesis tools. Synthesis attributes such as `parallel_case`, `full_case`, `syn_keep`, `syn_preserve`, and several others are ignored by the simulator.

Verilog 2-state vs. 4-state logic

Synthesis tools treat 'x' as "don't care" and make logic optimizations. Internal 'z' values that model tri-stated logic are either converted to the equivalent circuit or ignored. Using casex or casez constructs can produce a mismatch.

Incorrect project settings

The project might be set to use a speed grade lower than the actual FPGA part. For example, a project is set to speed grade -3 (fast) but the FPGA is -1 (slow). The FPGA configuration controller will not detect the mismatch and complete the configuration. However, the symptoms of the functional failure will be the same as if the design had incorrect timing constraints.

Synthesis and physical implementation tool options

Using certain synthesis and physical implementation options that alter the original design can cause synthesis and simulation mismatch. Some examples are enabling optimization options, flattening design hierarchy, and using safe state machine implementation, which adds additional logic to recover from illegal state, enabling retiming.

Asynchronous reset

Using asynchronous reset can cause several types of design problems not seen during simulation. The reset release might not be seen at the same time by all state machine registers due to large delays. This can cause incorrect register initialization and the state machine to enter an invalid state. The reset signal might contain glitches that can be interpreted as a valid reset.

Hardware failure

The design might not work because of the hardware failure. It can be caused by a multitude of reasons: invalid voltage supplied to an FPGA, wrong clock frequency, a faulty or misbehaving peripheral device, or a signal integrity issue. It can even be a damaged FPGA as a result of overvoltage or of very high or low temperature outside of the allowed operating range.

Synthesis or physical implementation tool bug

There is a possibility that a bug in a synthesis or physical implementation tool causes the problem. However, this is rarely the case in practice. Synthesis and physical implementation tools are mature and rigorously tested by vendors before being released to FPGA developers.

60
SIMULATOR SELECTION

FPGA developers spend a significant amount of time performing functional simulation of their designs. Selecting the best simulator that offers the right mix of features, performance and cost is important, and can result in significant improvements in productivity. The need for a simulator selection arises in a newly formed company, or in a new project. Also, there are several reasons why design teams might want to change an existing simulator. The license for an existing simulator is about to expire, or there isn't a sufficient number of licenses for a growing design team, and the competing simulator offers more appealing cost structure and license upgrade path. The existing simulator doesn't meet all the project requirements; for example, it doesn't run on Linux operating system, or doesn't support SystemVerilog. The existing simulator doesn't scale and has inadequate performance to simulate a rapidly growing design.

Simulator selection is an important decision that has a lasting impact of the team productivity. All commercial simulator vendors offer a time- or feature-limited license to perform evaluation. Evaluation is perhaps the best way to determine if the simulator meets feature and performance requirements, and uncover hidden portability and other issues. Design teams should consider all options, including open source simulators and free simulators provided by the FPGA vendor, which might be sufficient for the project.

The following are some of the most important criteria to consider during simulator selection.

Cost

Simulator is an expensive design tool and cost is a very important factor in the simulator selection process. Simulator pricing information is not readily available. However, the pricing, or quote, is usually obtained by contacting a sales representative of the simulation tool vendor. The sales price can be subsequently negotiated, depending on the licensing options and the account size.

Optional simulator features, such as mixed language support, code coverage, assertion library, enabling performance optimizations may have a significant addition to the basic cost of the simulator.

Licensing options

Because of its high cost, all commercial simulators utilize stringent licensing schemes to control the use of the tool. Usually, licenses come in two flavors: (i) a single-use license tied to a specific workstation by using unique Ethernet MAC address or a hard-drive ID, and (ii) multi-use or floating license controlled from a license server. Popular licensing software used by most of the commercial simulators is FLEXlm from Flexera Software.

It is important to find out license upgrade options, for example switching from a single-use to a multi-use license, or adding more licensees to the existing multi-use license.

Performance

Performance is perhaps the second most important consideration after cost during simulator selection. Simulation performance is measured in units of simulation cycles/sec, or Hertz and is discussed in more detail in Tip #64. Performance characteristics of a simulator depend on the design, testbench, and the workstation. Performing simulation of the actual design is the most accurate way to measure performance.

An important criterion is performance scalability. Many commercial simulators don't scale well - simulation performance decreases rapidly as the design or simulation testbench grows in size.

Memory utilization

A simulator utilizes several hundreds of Mbytes of memory even for small to medium-size FPGA design simulation. Large designs or longer simulations can easily require several Gbytes of memory and better memory utilization can become an important requirement for the simulator selection.

Language support

All commercial simulators support Verilog-95 and Verilog-2001 versions. Many simulators already support the latest Verilog-2005 (IEEE 1364-2005 standard) and VHDL (IEEE P1076-2008/D4.2 draft). SystemVerilog is supported by the high-end versions of the commercial simulators such as ModelSim-SE or as an add-on option, which requires a separate license. Mixed Verilog and VHDL language support often require a separate license as well.

Operating system support

All of the commercial simulators targeting FPGA designs provide the best support for Windows operating system. Linux, Solaris, and UNIX is either not supported at all, or only supported by the high-end versions of the simulator. One example is ModelSim-PE, which only supports Windows.

Support for a 64-bit processor version usually doesn't incur an extra cost. It is provided as a separate software installation.

Integration with FPGA simulation libraries

An important consideration is integration with different simulation libraries provided by the FPGA vendor. For example, Xilinx provides a tool called `compxlib`, which compiles simulation libraries for Mentor Graphics ModelSim, Cadence NCSim, and Synopsys VCS simulators. For other simulators the integration process is less straightforward.

PLI and VPI

The Verilog PLI (Programming Language Interface) and VPI (Verilog Procedural Interface) provide a standard mechanism to access and modify data in a simulated Verilog model. The interfaces are implemented as a library of C functions.

PLI and VPI are supported by the high-end versions commercial simulators, such as ModelSim-SE, Riviera-PRO, or VCS.

Lint

Some commercial simulators, for example Riviera-PRO and ModelSim, have integrated lint capability.

Assertions, code, and functional coverage

Code coverage provides a measure of completeness of design testing. There are several types of code coverage: statement, branch, condition, expression, toggle, state machine, among others. Functional coverage provides information about the quality of the design verification process. It's defined by user, and operates at a higher level than HDL code coverage. Assertions are monitor-like processes that continuously track design activities and report if simulation objects have the expected values. Constructs for specifying assertions are incorporated into SystemVerilog.

Assertions, code and functional coverage are supported by the high-end versions commercial simulators, such as ModelSim-SE, or Riviera-PRO.

Advanced GUI features

Advanced GUI features include debugger, memory viewer, dataflow window, cross-probing, waveform comparison, and more. These features are supported by the high-end simulator versions, or as an add-on option.

The dataflow is a GUI feature that allows exploring connectivity and hierarchy of the simulated design, analyzing the dataflow across instances, concurrent statements, signals, nets, and registers, and tracking back the source through the layers of code hierarchy. Waveform comparison enables comparing two or more waveform views and is invaluable during regression to compare current simulation outcome with the reference.

61

OVERVIEW OF COMMERCIAL AND OPEN-SOURCE SIMULATORS

There are several commercial and open source simulators available for FPGA designers. Each one provides a unique feature set that makes it more suitable for a specific project than another: performance, cost, licensing options, language support, integration with other design tools, and many others.

Xilinx automatically generates simulation script examples for ModelSim, NCSim, and VCS simulators for many of its large IP cores, such as memory controller (MIG), PCI Express interface, and Ethernet MAC.

All commercial simulators provide a time-limited or feature-limited evaluation option. FPGA designers should take advantage of it before making the final decision of which simulation tool to choose.

Simulator: ISIM
Company: Xilinx
http://www.xilinx.com/support/documentation/plugin_ism.pdf
License: commercial, part of Xilinx ISE software

Xilinx ISIM is an excellent choice for small- to medium-size FPGA designs. It's integrated with Xilinx ISE tools and doesn't require a separate license. The biggest ISIM disadvantage is that it doesn't scale well for larger designs. Compared with other commercial simulatos, ISIM is much slower and requires more memory. ISIM also offers a co-simulation option, which requires a separate license.

Simulator: ModelSim
Company: Mentor Graphics
http://model.com
License: commercial

ModelSim simulator is by far the most popular choice for the FPGA design simulation. It is the most affordable option among commercial simulators, has an excellent GUI, and has good performance. ModelSim offers three versions - PE, DE, and SE – that differ in price and provided features. Comparison table is available at this URL: http://model.com/content/compare-modelsim-product-line

Simulator: VCS
Company: Synopsys
http://www.synopsys.com/Tools/FunctionalVerification/Pages/VCS.aspx
License: commercial

VCS simulator is at the high end of the performance and feature set spectrum. It is the fastest, but the most expensive simulation tool. It is mainly used for doing functional simulation of ASIC designs but often used in large FPGA designs as well.

Simulator: NCSim
Company: Cadence
http://www.cadence.com/products/ld/design_team_simulator/pages/default.aspx
License: commercial

NCSim is a core simulation engine and part of the Incisive suite of tools. It is intended for design and verification of ASICs and FPGAs.

Simulator: Active-HDL, Riviera
Company: Aldec
http://www.aldec.com/Products/default.aspx
License: commercial

Aldec offers Active-HDL, Riviera, and Riviera-PRO simulation and functional verification tools for FPGA designers. Their feature set and performance are compatible to the ModelSim.

There are several open source HDL simulator engines, waveform viewers, code coverage, and other tools. Icarus Verilog and Verilator are by far the most popular and well maintained.

Simulator: Icarus Verilog
http://bleyer.org/icarus

Icarus Verilog is an open source compiler implementation for Verilog HDL. Icarus is maintained by Stephen Williams, and it is released under the GNU GPL license.

Simulator: Verilator
http://www.veripool.org/wiki/verilator

Verilator is an open source Verilog HDL simulator written and maintained by Wilson Snyder. Verilator is designed to achieve the highest simulation performance. It is a cycle-based simulation engine, which works with a synthesizable subset of the Verilog HDL. It also supports Verilog `initial` statements, blocking/non-blocking assignments, functions, tasks, multi-dimensional arrays, signed numbers, simple forms of SystemVerilog assertions, and coverage analysis.

62

DESIGNING SIMULATION TESTBENCHES

A simulation testbench is defined as the HDL code that provides a repeatable set of stimuli to a Design Under Test (DUT). A testbench can be as simple as a module that generates clock, reset, and data input to a DUT, and as complex as constrained random data stimulus, self-checking of the results, and monitor of different internal signals for errors.

Essential requirements for good testbench architecture are modularity, scalability, automation, and reuse. Modular architecture allows verification of any part of the design, from the top level to all the submodules, without significant changes to the test environment. Scalable architecture lends itself to adding new features without significant decrease in performance and increase in resource utilization. Automation includes generating stimulus data, self-checking test results, and regression mechanisms. Large parts of the testbench can be reused in other projects if it's architected using Object-Oriented Principles, such as abstraction by hiding implementation details.

There are several verification frameworks and methodologies, such as Open Verification Methodology (OVM), Universal Verification Methodology (UVM), and Verification Methodology Manual (VMM), used for ASIC and FPGA design verification.

The following figure shows a testbench architecture that shares components used in the majority of the verification frameworks: DUT, Driver, Monitor, Transactor, and Checker.

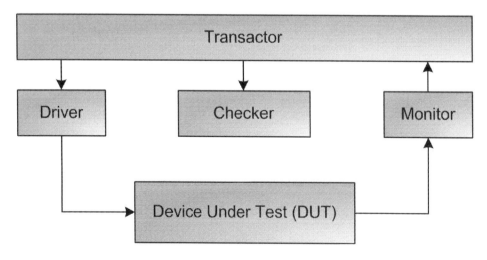

Figure 1: Testbench architecture

Driver is a component that employs various simulation techniques, such as direct and random stimulus, to exercise a DUT.

Monitor is a component that follows a subset of top-level ports and internal signals of the DUT.

Checker is a component that processes test results from the Monitor and performs comparison with the expected values. This is also called self-checking mechanism. The Checker produces a test report that is posted on a scoreboard.

Transactor controls the overall execution of the test, and coordinates the activities of Driver, Monitor, and Checker.

Language selection

SystemVerilog is a language of choice for designing testbenches. It offers all the needed features for designing comprehensive, modular, and scalable simulation environments: more compact code creation, Object-Oriented Programming (OOP), assertions, randomization, and code coverage. Using OOP features of the SystemVerilog raises the level of abstraction by building data structures with self-contained functionality that allow data encapsulation, hiding implementation details, and enhance re-usability of the code. Unfortunately, SystemVerilog is only supported by the high-end versions of the commercial simulators. Small and budget-constrained projects often cannot afford more expensive simulators with SystemVerilog support, and resort to using Verilog as the main language, which hinders the productivity of a design and verification team.

Modeling FPGA-specific primitives and IP cores

FPGA vendors provide simulation models of the FPGA-specific primitives. Xilinx-specific simulation primitives are part of the ISE software installation, and organized into several libraries: UNISIM, UNIMACRO, SIMPRIM, and XilinxCoreLib. The following table summarizes the libraries.

Table 1: Xilinx simulation libraries

Library	Use case	Examples
UNISIM	RTL and post-synthesis simulation	AND, OR, XOR gates Flip-flops and latches IBUF, OBUF MMCM, other clock-related models RAM, ROM
UNIMACRO	RTL simulation	FIFO, Counters, BRAM
SIMPRIM	Gate-level and timing simulation	The same as UNISIM

Library	Use case	Examples
XilinxCoreLib	RTL simulation	Complex FIFOs, Block RAM and distributed memories, shift registers

Encrypted simulation models using SecureIP specification are provided for more complex IP cores and primitives, such as PCI Express interface, Ethernet MAC, and GTX/GTH transceivers.

Modeling devices

Simulation models for relatively simple peripheral devices, such as I2C, UART, DRAM, flash memories, are usually supplied by the device vendor.

Modeling busses

Bus functional models (BFM) are provided for complex devices for which behavioral model would be too expensive to create or too slow to use. BFM attempts to model component interface, rather than component functions. Examples of BFM are processors, PCI Express endpoint or host, and USB device or host.

63

SIMULATION BEST PRACTICES

Communication between simulation threads

Components of a simulation testbench, such as `initial`, `fork-join` and `always` blocks, execute concurrently as separate threads or processes. A typical testbench has multiple threads performing different tasks. The threads need to be spawned, share data among each other, and synchronized. Multiple threads waiting to execute at one simulation time point have to be scheduled in queues, also referred as event queues. A simulator can only execute one thread at a time in a single-core CPU. In a multi-core CPU the simulator may execute multiple threads in parallel without predetermined execution order. If a simulation testbench is not written correctly this can create a race condition, meaning that the simulation results depend on the order of execution of CPU and the simulator.

Concurrent simulation threads require communication to establish control for execution sequence. There are three main methods to implement thread communication in Verilog.

Using events

In this case, one thread is waiting for an event to be triggered by another thread. The following is a simple example of event-based communication.

```
initial begin
  event DONE;
  fork
     my_task1();
     my_task1();
  join
  task my_task1();
     @(DONE);
     $display("event received");
  endtask
  task my_task2();
     ->DONE;
     $display("event sent");
  endtask
```

```
end // initial
```

Resource sharing

Concurrent threads can be synchronized using a shared resource. A thread tries to access a shared resource and waits if it's unavailable. It resumes the execution when another thread releases the resource. SystemVerilog provides support for `semaphore` class to implement resource sharing. The following is an example of using semaphores.

```
semaphore sem1 = new(1);
sem.get(1); // semaphore is taken
fork
  begin: thread1
    sem.get(1); // tries to get the semaphore
  end
join
sem.put(1); // releases semaphore; thread1 is served
```

Data passing

SystemVerilog enables data passing between threads using `mailbox` functionality. A thread sends data by putting messages into a mailbox. Another thread retrieves the data from the mailbox. If the message is unavailable the thread has an option to wait or resume the execution. The following is an example of using mailboxes.

```
mailbox #(bit[15:0]) mbox = new(1);
bit [15:0] data = 16'h1234;
mbox.put(data);
fork
  begin: thread1
    status mbox.try_get(data);
    mbox.get(data);
  end
join
```

Simulation delta delays

In a given simulation time, a simulator executes multiple concurrent statements in `initial`, `fork-join` and `always` blocks and continuous assignments in the testbench. When all the events scheduled for the current simulation time are updated, the simulator advances the simulation time. Each event update in the current simulation cycle is executed at the delta cycle. Updating the `clk3` signal in the following code example takes two delta cycles from the time `clk1` has changed, even if it appears to change in the same simulation time.

```
always @(*) begin
  clk2 <= clk1;
  clk3 <= clk2;
end
```

Many commercial simulators, such as ModelSim and VCS, have an option to display simulation delta cycles.

The mechanics of simulation time, event queues, and the effect of delta cycles on simulation results is often not well understood, even by experienced FPGA designers. Adding #0 (explicit zero delay) is a frequently used technique to fix issues in simulation testbenches related to delta cycles. However, it is not a good design practice. There are books [1], papers, and simulator user guides that discuss simulation time, event queues, and delta cycles. The most reliable and comprehensive source of information on this subject remains the Verilog specification.

The following example illustrates how a delta cycle added to a clock signal can cause incorrect simulation results. The circuit, shown in the following figure, consists of two registers. The Clk3 signal is connected to the right register, and is unintentionally delayed with two zero-delay buffers. There is combinatorial logic between the two registers.

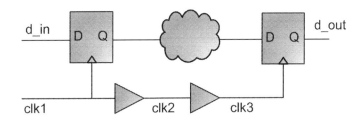

Figure 1: Clock signal is unintentionally delayed with two buffers

The following is a code example of the above circuit. The logic between two registers is implemented using d_delta1, and d_delta2 signals.

```
module tb;
  reg clk1;
  reg clk2,clk3;
  reg data;
  reg d_in, d_out;
  reg d_delta1,d_delta2;
  reg reset;
 initial begin
    reset     = 1;
    data      = 0;
    #15; reset = 0;
```

```verilog
    #15;
    @(posedge clk1);
      data = 1;
    @(posedge clk1);
      data = 0;
    #50;
    $finish(2);
  end
  initial begin
    clk1 = 0;
    forever #5 clk1 = ~clk1;
  end
  always @(*) begin
    clk2 <= clk1;
    clk3 <= clk2;
  end
  always @(*) begin
     d_delta1 <= d_in;
     d_delta2 <= d_delta1;
  end
  always @(posedge clk1)
    if(reset)   d_in <= 1'b0;
    else        d_in <= data;
  always @(posedge clk2)
    if(reset)   d_out <= 1'b0;
    else        d_out <= d_in;
endmodule
```

The value of the d_out output depends on the amount of delay introduced by the combinatorial logic between registers. This creates a race condition between the arrival of clock edge and data to the register on the right.

The following waveform shows incorrect simulation results: a pulse on the d_in input appears on the output in the same clock cycle.

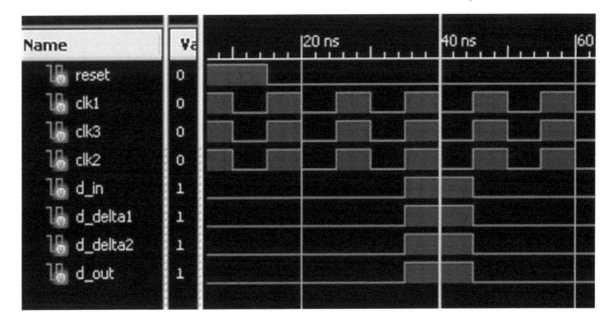

*Figure 2: Incorrect **d_out** due to delta delays on the clock signal*

After reducing the combinatorial logic delay, the simulation is correct.

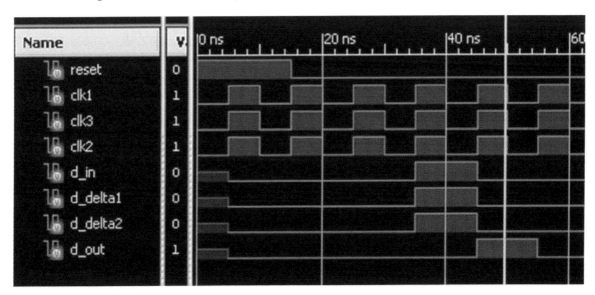

*Figure 3: Correct **d_out** when the combinatorial delay is reduced*

There are several ways to fix this problem. One is to add a non-zero delay:

```
always @(posedge clk1)
   if(reset) d_in <= #1 1'b0;
   else           d_in <= #1 data;
```

However, if the simulator resolution is smaller than that delay, the delay will be rounded down to 0ns and will become a delta delay, as in the original code. Another way is to use blocking assignment in combinational logic:

```
always @(*) begin
  d_delta1 = d_in;
  d_delta2 = d_delta1;
end
```

The third way is to eliminate delta delays on the clock signals and ensure that clock edges line up to the exact delta at the destination registers. Changing `clk2` to `clk1` in the above example achieves that.

```
always @(posedge clk1)
   if(reset)  d_out <= 1'b0;
   else       d_out <= d_in;
```

Using `timescale directive

Verilog `timescale directive specifies the time unit and time precision of the modules that follow it. It has the following syntax:

`timescale <time_unit>/<time_precision>`

The `time_unit` is the unit of measurement for time and delay values. The `time_precision` specifies how delay values are rounded before being used in simulation. The following is a code example that illustrates the `timescale directive operation.

```
// delays are measured in 1ns units with 100ps precision
`timescale 1ns/100ps

module timescale_test;
  reg clk1,clk2;

  localparam HALF_PERIOD1 = 2.5,
             HALF_PERIOD2 = 3.333;
  initial begin
    clk1 = 0;
    forever #HALF_PERIOD1 clk1 = ~clk1;
  end

  // incorrect, will be rounded up to 3.3
  initial begin
    clk2 = 0;
    forever #HALF_PERIOD2 clk2 = ~clk2;
  end
endmodule
```

The following figure is a simulation waveform showing that clk2 period is rounded down to 6.600ns from the originally specified 6.666ns.

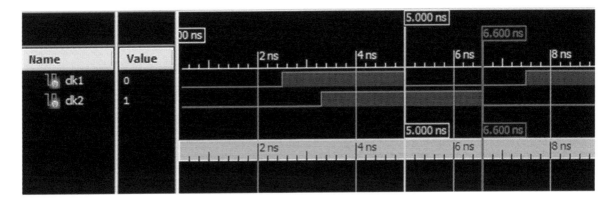

Figure 4: Using `timescale directive

It is important to understand that the `timescale directive is not specific to files and modules. It can be overridden by another `timescale encountered in a different file during the compile process. Therefore, depending on the compile order of the files, simulation results might be different. Also, if the `timescale directive is not present in a Verilog file, the compiler might insert a default value. That situation will cause portability issues between different simulation tools.

To avoid these problems, it is recommended to specify the `timescale directive before each module in both the design and testbench files.

Simulation tools provide global options to control simulation time unit and precision. ModelSim and VCS provides a -timescale option, which specifies the timescale for modules that don't have explicitly defined `timescale directives. VCS provides an a-override_timescale option, which overrides the time unit and precision for all the `timescale directives in the design.

Displaying state variables

Simulation tools provide several options to display state variable: hexadecimal, decimal, binary, symbolic, and ASCII string. Displaying state variable using symbolic representation requires certain configuration, which depends on the simulator. The following Verilog code example shows how to view state variable using an ASCII string.

```
localparam STATE_INIT  = 3'd0,
           STATE_ONE   = 3'd1,
           STATE_TWO   = 3'd2,
           STATE_THREE = 3'd3;
reg [2:0] state_cur, state_next;
```

```verilog
reg [1:11*8] state_str; // current state shown as ASCII
always @(posedge clk) begin
  if(reset) begin
    state_cur        <= STATE_INIT;
    state_outputs    <= 4'b0;
  end
  else begin
    state_cur        <= state_next;
    state_outputs[0] <= state_cur == STATE_INIT;
    state_outputs[1] <= state_cur == STATE_ONE;
    state_outputs[2] <= state_cur == STATE_TWO;
    state_outputs[3] <= state_cur == STATE_THREE;
  end
end
always @(*) begin
  state_next = state_cur;
  case(state_cur)
    STATE_INIT:   if(state_inputs[0])state_next = STATE_ONE;
    STATE_ONE:    if(state_inputs[1]) state_next= STATE_TWO;
    STATE_TWO:    if(state_inputs[2]) state_next = STATE_THREE;
    STATE_THREE:  if(state_inputs[3]) state_next= STATE_INIT;
  endcase
end
// state_str is an ASCII representation of state_cur
always @(*) begin
  state_str = "";
  case(state_cur)
STATE_INIT:    state_str = "STATE_INIT";
    STATE_ONE:     state_str = "STATE_ONE";
    STATE_TWO:     state_str = "STATE_TWO";
    STATE_THREE:   state_str = "STATE_THREE";
  endcase
end
```

Resources

[1] Janick Bergeron, "*Writing Testbenches: Functional Verification of HDL Models*", Springer, 2003. ISBN 9781402074011

64
MEASURING SIMULATION PERFORMANCE

There are several situations when developers need to measure simulation performance. Some of them are:
- Evaluating different simulators
- Comparing the performance of the same simulation tool running on different hardware platforms and operating systems
- Comparing the performance of the same simulation running with different options, for example enabled debug mode, or different amounts of waveform dump.
- Comparing simulation performance of different projects.
- Tracking simulation performance of a project during the product development and verification cycle.

Simulation performance can be measured using the following metrics.

Total System Time

Simulation performance can be measured in the units of system time (sometimes referred to as *wall time*). The problem with this method is it produces different results depending on the CPU load at the time of simulation run.

Normalized Simulation Time

Total simulation time is normalized by the system time. Sometimes this metric is referred as *ticks per second*. The disadvantage of this method is that simulation time can have different meaning depending on the `timescale` resolution settings. That causes the measurement unit to be different across different projects.

```
sim_time_norm = (total simulation time)/(total system time)
```

Simulation Frequency

Simulation frequency is the most widely used metric to describe the simulation performance. Simulation frequency is defined as the number of simulation cycles divided by a cycle time.

Typically, the fastest clock in the system is used to determine a cycle time. Measurement units of a simulation frequency are Hertz, or cycles per second.

There are several other metrics used for the cost comparison of different simulation tools. Examples include: "cost per simulation cycle", "cost per simulation frequency", and "number of simulation cycles a year".

Choosing the right metric for measuring simulation performance that produces meaningful results is not always a simple task. It requires some experimentation and correlation of the results with the expected values for similar designs and simulation tools. For example, it is expected that simulation frequency for software simulation tools is in the range of 10Hz-10kHz. Hardware-assisted simulation tools, such as co-simulators, typically perform in 10kHz to 100kHz range. Emulation platforms perform in the 1MHz range. FPGA-based prototyping platforms are the fastest, and can run at 10MHz or more.

The following is an example of simulation performance results. The example used a counter project from Tip #25, and Xilinx ISIM simulator. The results are provided for illustration purposes only, and might vary on different systems.

Table 1: Simulation performance example

Simulation time	10ms
System time	80s
Clock frequency	100MHz
Number of simulation clocks	10ms*100MHz = 1,000,000 clocks
Simulation frequency	1,000,000 clocks / 80s = 12,500 Hz

Simulation time can be obtained by using $display system function in the testbench. For example:

```
$display("[%0t] starting simulation", $realtime);
$display("[%0t] finishing simulation", $realtime);
```

System time can be measured by using UNIX/Linux `time` or `date` commands:

```
$ time my_sim_script.sh
```

It can also be measured by writing a simple PLI function, as shown in the following example, and integrating it with the simulation environment.

```
int get_systime()
{
    time_t seconds;
    seconds = time (NULL);
    return seconds;
}
```

For long simulations the time can be measured manually, where the accuracy of measurement start and end is less important.

ModelSim simulator provides a `simstat` command that reports various statistics about the current simulation, such as total allocated and used memory, cumulative "wall clock time" and processor time, the number of context swaps, and page faults.

65

OVERVIEW OF FPGA-BASED PROCESSORS

Embedded processing became an important segment of the FPGA application ecosystem. FPGA speed and capacity reached the point where it can accommodate multiple high-performance processor cores running a full-featured embedded operating system such as Linux, a network protocol stack, or a video processing application.

The trend is tighter integration of multi-core embedded processors and peripherals with the FPGA fabric, such as new Xilinx Zynq-7000 system-on-chip (SoC) platform.

Comparing it to the high-end stand alone embedded processors, FPGA-based processors and microcontrollers it falls behind in performance. However, using an FPGA-based processing solution is often advantageous when the highest possible performance is not required by the application or is less important than other factors. Using an FPGA-based processor greatly simplifies board design by requiring less components and a smaller PCB area. Among other advantages are tighter integration with the rest of the FPGA logic, higher level of configurability and customization, wider choice of peripheral devices and IP cores, easier addition of hardware acceleration co-processors and multiple processor cores. Another important consideration is an integrated build flow.

There are several metrics used to describe processor performance metrics. Most frequently used are Million Instructions per Second (MIPS), Dhrystone, Dhrystone MIPS (DMIPS), and DMIPS/MHz. Dhrystone refers to a synthetic computing benchmark program intended to be representative of a general processor performance. Unlike other processor benchmark software, using Dhrystone benchmark is free. Dhrystone provides a more meaningful representation of the CPU performance results compared to MIPS. Another popular representation of the Dhrystone benchmark is the DMIPS (Dhrystone MIPS), obtained when the Dhrystone score is divided by 1757. A normalized DMIPS/MHz metrics is frequently used to compare the performance of different processors.

The following figure illustrates the architecture of a chip that combines a high-performance Intel Atom processor and Altera FPGA fabric. The processor has 512Kbyte cache and running at 1.3GHz. The FPGA is connected to the processor using PCI Express x1 link.

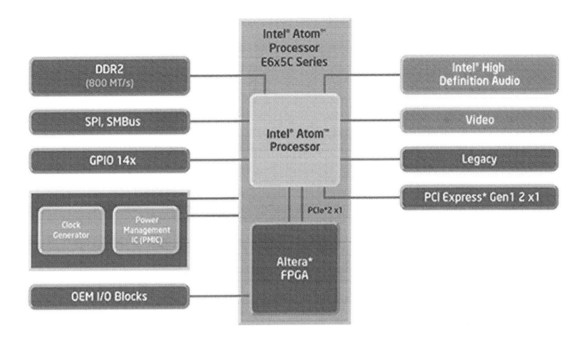

Figure 1: Combined Intel Atom processor and Altera FPGA (source: Intel Atom E6x5C datasheet)

Many applications, such as those that need to perform fast processing of the data, require a high level of parallelization. The following figure shows an example of architecture that utilizes multiple 32-bit Xilinx Microblaze processors running in parallel to read and process data sent over a 256-bit bus. Those types of applications take advantage of the fact that reading data from external memory is several times faster than processing it on a single Microblaze.

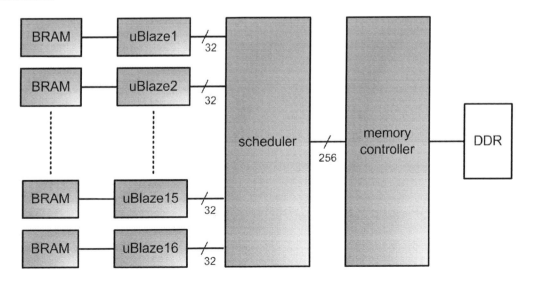

Figure 2: Using parallel Microblaze processors

Each of the sixteen processors is connected to an embedded RAM, which contains the code and data sections. The logic utilization of such architecture can be relatively small. Microblaze processors can have a basic configuration without caches and peripheral devices, and run a single application optimized for code size. The scheduler reads the data from the external memory over a 256-bit bus, and schedules jobs among sixteen processors in a balanced manner to keep them evenly utilized.

Another application example is a single-core Microblaze processor that implements a USB Host Controller for a custom device. The block diagram of that application is shown in the following figure.

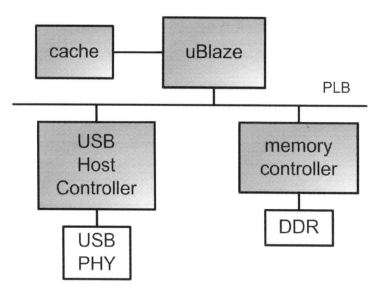

Figure 3: A single Microblaze processor application

This application might be running an embedded operating system and a USB protocol stack, and requires a relatively large amount of FPGA embedded memory. However, having the highest performance is not necessary to utilize the full capacity of the USB.

Processors supported by Xilinx FPGAs

Zynq-7000 Extensible Processing Platform
www.xilinx.com/zynq

Xilinx Zynq-7000 Extensible Processing Platform is a product family that includes a dual-core ARM Cortex-A9 processor, peripheral devices, and programmable FPGA fabric.

Processor: MicroBlaze
http://www.xilinx.com/support/documentation/sw_manuals/mb_ref_guide.pdf
http://www.xilinx.com/products/design_resources/proc_central/microblaze_faq.pdf

MicroBlaze is a soft-core processor IP core that is implemented using FPGA logic resources. It has a 32-bit RISC architecture with an instruction set optimized for embedded applications. MicroBlaze is highly configurable with over 70 configuration options, a wide combination of peripherals, memory and interfaces. It can be configured as a very small footprint microcontroller, up to a high performance processor running Linux. Configuration features include Memory Management Unit (MMU), configurable-size data and instruction caches, and JTAG control for debug. Microblaze logic utilization requirement ranges from between 300 and 2500 Virtex-6 slices.

Microblaze offers several interface choices to connect it to peripheral devices and hardware acceleration co-processors. Starting from version 8.0, MicroBlaze supports a high performance AXI4 interface. AXI4 can be used to connect both caches and peripherals. There is a dedicated Fast Simplex Link (FSL) for connecting low-latency co-processors. Memory can be connected using Local Memory Bus (LMB). Microblaze also supports legacy PLB bus for connecting non-cache peripherals.

Microblaze can have a single precision Floating Point Unit (FPU), optimized for performance and low latency.

Processor: PowerPC
Some Virtex-4 and Virtex-5 FPGA families include an embedded PowerPC processor. The processor is not available in Virtex-6 and Spartan-6 families, because Xilinx transitions to ARM processors in the next generation FPGAs.

Processor: OpenRISC
License: LGPL
http://opencores.org/project,or1k
http://opencores.org/openrisc,or1200

OpenRISC project provides an open source implementation of a 32- and 64-bit RISC processor architecture with DSP features, and a complete set of open source software development tools, libraries, operating systems and applications. Reported logic utilization on Virtex-5 FPGAs ranges between 500 and 1500 slices.

There are several other open source processors in different stages of development available on the OpenCores.org website.

The following table summarizes key performance characteristics of different processors.

Table 1: Processor performance comparison

Processor	Frequency (MHz)	DMIPS	DMIPS/MHz	Number of cores
Zynq-7000	800	n/a	n/a	2
Microblaze	106-235	100-280	0.95-1.30	1-8**
OpenRISC OR1200	60	50	0.83	1
Intel Atom E6xx	600-1600	717-2462	1.2 – 1.55*	1-2

* Not official numbers. The values are reported by third parties.

** Microblaze can have up to eight cores sharing the same bus. The total number of stand-alone cores is limited by the amount of available FPGA logic and memory resources. The Microblaze Debug Module (MDM) can support up to eight processors at a time.

Intel Atom E6xx is provided as an example of a high-end stand alone embedded processor, and shows how it performs against its FPGA-based counterparts.

Resources

[1] Xilinx embedded processing portal
http://www.xilinx.com/technology/embedded.htm

[2] Intel Atom processor E6xx series
http://edc.intel.com/Platforms/Atom-E6xx/

66
ETHERNET CORES

Ethernet is the predominant wired connectivity standard which is used in a wide range of applications. The biggest advantage of using Ethernet in FPGA applications is its universality, wide use, and excellent choice of IP cores. Ethernet has a wide variety of speed, interface, and configuration options to meet most of the system connectivity needs. 10/100 Mbit/sec are low-speed low-cost Ethernet options used in control and industrial applications. 1-Gigabit Ethernet offers better performance, and can be used in applications that require Internet connectivity. 10-Gbit Ethernet is slowly finding acceptance, and has a potential to replace other protocols, such as Fibre Channel and Infiniband operating at a similar speed.

A complete Ethernet MAC (EMAC) subsystem architecture is illustrated in the following figure.

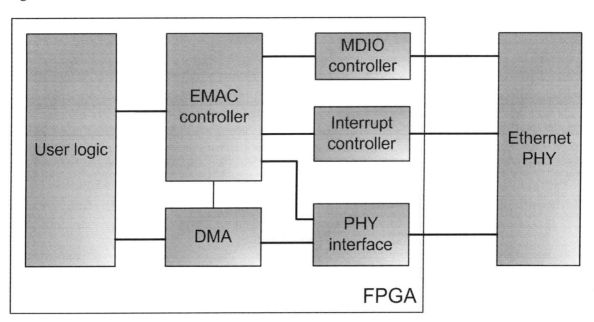

Figure 1: Ethernet MAC subsystem architecture

Ethernet PHY is an external device connected to FPGA using three groups of signals: MDIO, interrupts, and PHY interface. Additional signals are specific to the PHY device, and include clocks, resets, configuration, LED interface, JTAG, and others.

EMAC subsystem consists of six main functional components which are briefly described below.

Physical layer (PHY) interface

The interface between Ethernet MAC and PHY is based on the Media Independent Interface (MII) standard. There are different MII speed and pin count options, which are briefly described in the following table.

Table 1: Ethernet MII interfaces

MII standard	*Frequency, MHz*	*Description*
MII	2.5 or 25	Used for 10/100 Mbit/sec Ethernet
RMII	50	MII with reduced pin count
GMII	125	MII for Gigabit Ethernet
RGMII	125	GMII with reduced pin count
SGMII	1,250	Serial GMII with a very low pin count

MDIO and Interrupt controller

Management data (MDIO) controller implements a shared two-wire serial management interface to access PHY device. User logic, EMAC controller, and Host software use MDIO to configure auto-negotiation and other parameters of the PHY, and retrieve the current status. MDIO is designed for transparent PHY access, which is independent of other modules.

Interrupt controller

Interrupt controller processes different interrupts coming from the PHY, such as Rx frame notification, Tx frame completion, link configuration change, and others.

Direct memory access (DMA) controller

DMA controller incorporates RAM to buffer Rx and Tx Ethernet frames, and provides a simple interface to send and receive frames from the user logic.

EMAC controller

EMAC controller implements Ethernet MAC protocol, and provides user logic a simple interface to MDIO and interrupt controllers.

User logic

User logic uses custom or industry standard interfaces to connect with EMAC and DMA modules. User logic can include embedded processor to implement Internet protocol stack on top of Ethernet MAC. Tip #67 discusses some of the user logic implementation options.

The following figure shows an example Ethernet router application utilizing four Ethernet PHYs.

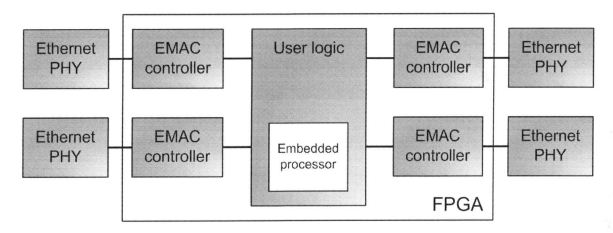

Figure2: Four port router application

Ethernet MAC cores

FPGA developers have several alternatives to add Ethernet connectivity to their designs.

Xilinx Virtex-6 FPGAs already include multiple tri-mode Ethernet MAC (TEMAC) modules. Xilinx CoreGen application can be used to generate a wrapper for those modules with different configuration options: Ethernet speed, PHY interface (MII, RGMII, SGMII), full/half duplex, flow control, receive frame filtering based on MAC address, and many others.

Xilinx also provides an option to generate an Ethernet MAC core for the FPGA families without an embedded Ethernet MAC. A portal that contains all the information about Ethernet support by Xilinx is [1].

There are several open source and commercial Ethernet MAC IP cores. CAST Inc. provides 10/100 Mb/s and Gigabit Ethernet MAC IP cores [2]. Open source Ethernet MAC IP cores are available in [3] and [4].

Resources

[1] Xilinx Ethernet resources
http://www.xilinx.com/ethernet

[2] CAST Gigabit Ethernet MAC
http://www.cast-inc.com/ip-cores/interfaces/mac-1g/index.html

[3] Tri-mode Ethernet MAC
http://opencores.org/project,ethernet_tri_mode

[4] 10/100 Mb/s Ethernet MAC
http://opencores.org/project,ethmac

67
DESIGNING NETWORK APPLICATIONS

Most of the FPGA applications that require network connectivity utilize Ethernet and Internet protocol suite. Those applications have a wide range of requirements, such as high performance, high reliability and availability, low logic utilization, and low design complexity. The requirements are often incompatible, and require different implementation approaches. For example, reliability and availability requirements are more important requirements for embedded web servers than high performance, whereas high performance is the main requirement for applications that require transferring large amounts of data. Applications utilizing small FPGAs are more concerned with low logic utilization.

Internet protocol suite

The set of communication protocols used for Internet connectivity is commonly referred to as an Internet protocol suite. The following figure shows the Internet protocol suite that contains protocols frequently used in FPGA network applications. It is by far incomplete, and doesn't show security, routing, and network management protocols.

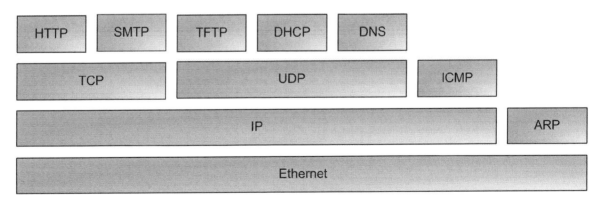

Figure 1: Internet protocol suite

Protocols essential for the network operation are Ethernet, ARP, IP, ICMP, UDP, and DHCP. The rest of the protocols are optional. The following table provides a very brief description of the Internet protocols.

Table 1: Internet protocols

Protocol	Description
ARP	Address Resolution Protocol (ARP) determines device Ethernet MAC address from its IP address.
IP	Internet Protocol (IP) is the primary communication protocol to transfer data packets across the networks.
DHCP	Dynamic Host Configuration Protocol (DHCP) is used for dynamic assignment of IP address to a device. Another way to assign IP address is static.
ICMP	Internet Control Message Protocol (ICMP) is used to send control packets, such as echo requests.
UDP	User Datagram Protocol (UDP) is a simple data transfer protocol between devices.
TCP	Transmission Control Protocol (TCP) is another protocol for transferring data between devices. TCP ensures reliable data transmission between hosts and other protocol features that make it more complex than UDP.
DNS	Domain Name System (DNS) is a system used to perform resolution of domain names in text format (URL) into an IP address.
TFTP	Trivial File Transfer Protocol (TFTP) is a simple file exchange protocol.
SMTP	Simple Mail Transfer Protocol (SMTP) is a standard to send and receive e-mail messages.

Embedded software implementation

A standard approach for implementing network applications in FPGA is using an embedded processor running the Internet protocol suite. System architecture of a typical implementation is shown in the following figure.

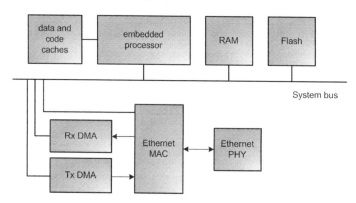

Figure 2: Network application implementation using embedded processor

The main system components are embedded processor, Ethernet MAC, RAM and Flash memories, and system bus.

Embedded processor can be FPGA-based, such as Xilinx Microblaze, or external. Different embedded processor options are discussed in Tip #65. The processor can connect to a variety of memories: flash, code and data caches, RAM that contains the executed and data storage.

Using code and data caches help improve processor performance, but not essential. The processor can use flash memory for initial boot up.

System bus realization depends on the embedded processor. ARM processors use AXI; Microblaze use PLB; PowerPC use LocalBus. In some applications, System bus can be customized to implemented features not available in industry standard busses.

Ethernet MAC and DMA provide the interface to Ethernet PHY device. Ethernet MAC implementation options are discussed in Tip #66.

There are several options to implement software running on an embedded processor, mainly driven by application requirements. Using a commercial or open-source operating system usually provides the best flexibility, but lowest network performance. Lightweight IP (LwIP) [3] is a popular open source networking stack implementation. It can be used in a stand-alone mode that doesn't require an operating system. Another option is Treck [4], a commercial high performance network stack. Treck achieves its high performance by minimizing the number of frame copies between different memory buffers, the approach also known as True Zero Copy.

Custom implementation

Many FPGA network applications transfer large amounts of data, and require the highest possible upload or download performance which approaches the Ethernet wire-speed limit. In cases when the application doesn't require using TCP protocol, security, or web server, it can be implemented without using an embedded processor.

The following figure shows the system architecture of a network application that doesn't require an embedded processor.

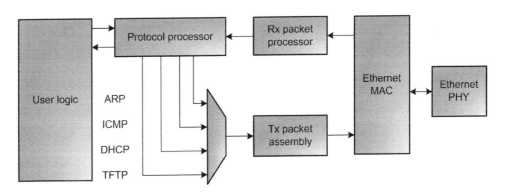

Figure 3: Custom implementation of a network application

The main components of a custom implementation are:

- Ethernet MAC: a module that interfaces with Ethernet PHY device.
- Tx packet assembly: a module that performs assembly of transmit packets.
- Rx packet processor: a module that performs checksum verification and packet filtering based on the IP address and protocol.
- Protocol processor: a module that interfaces with the user logic, receive and transmit packet processors. Protocol processor contains state machines that implement protocols, such as ARP, ICMP, DHCP, and other. Protocol processor is also responsible for local IP address assignment, which can be static or dynamic.
- User logic: a module that implements a simple application-level protocol, such as TFTP.

Implementing more complex application, security, and transport protocols, such as TCP without using an embedded processor is possible, but impractical. There are several published research papers discussing logic-based TCP implementation. However, FPGA logic and embedded memory utilization of a full-featured TCP implementation is prohibitively high. Also, development, verification, and compliance effort is substantial. In many cases UDP is a suitable replacement for TCP. A simple congestion control, flow control, and retransmission algorithms can be pushed up to the higher protocol level, and be implemented as part of the application level protocol, such as TFTP.

Internet protocols were not designed for hardware implementation in general. One example is the checksum field of IP and UDP protocols, which is located in the packet header. The application needs to store the entire packet in memory, calculate the checksum, and only then send the packet, which results in decreased performance and requires more memory. In contrast, PCI Express and USB protocols define the checksum or CRC fields in the end of the packet. The checksum can be calculated while the packet is sent.

The biggest advantages of the custom implementation are higher performance and deterministic processing latency. It can easily achieve Ethernet wire-speed limit. Custom Gigabit Ethernet implementations mentioned in the technical literature use less than two thousand Xilinx Virtex-5 slices. Custom implementation also has simpler FPGA and PCB design. It doesn't require an embedded processor and external memories. An additional advantage is the lack of an embedded software development, which results in a simpler tool flow.

Performance

There are different metrics used to measure network application performance: raw data, transport-level (TCP/UDP) payload, useful payload at the application level, or channel utilization. The following table shows expected application performance of different network implementations over a Gigabit Ethernet link.

Table 2: Network application performance

Application	Performance, MByte/sec
Linux OS, standard network stack	10-15
LwIP network stack	10-25
Treck	Up to 60
Custom implementation	Up to 90

An open-source Wireshark Ethernet analyzer is a tool that enables the most accurate measurement of raw and transport-level performance. Iperf [5] application can be used to measure application-level performance over TCP or UDP protocols.

There are several factors that affect performance: Ethernet connection speed (10/100Mbs, 1Gbs), packet size, full or half duplex, flow control, and traffic mix on the link. Packet size can be controlled by configuring user logic or Ethernet MAC, and has a dramatic effect on performance. FPGA speed has an important impact on performance as well. Some of the performance measurements results on Xilinx Spartan-6 FPGAs are provided in [6].

Resources

[1] Ethernet MAC Embedded Systems for MicroBlaze, Xilinx Application Note XAPP1041
http://www.xilinx.com/support/documentation/application_notes/xapp1041.pdf

[2] Lightweight IP (LwIP) networking stack
[3] LightWeight IP Application Examples, Xilinx Application Note XAPP1026
http://www.xilinx.com/support/documentation/application_notes/xapp1026.pdf

[4] Treck: high performance network stack
http://www.treck.com/

[5] Iperf: performance monitoring application
http://iperf.sourceforge.net

[6] Spartan-6 FPGA Connectivity Targeted Reference Design Performance, Xilinx White Paper WP363
http://www.xilinx.com/support/documentation/white_papers/wp363.pdf

68
IP CORE SELECTION

As FPGA designs grow in complexity, they contain more functional components and Intellectual Property (IP) cores. An IP core is defined as a ready-made functional component that can be instantiated in a design as a black box or a module. Terms IP core and functional component are sometimes used interchangeably.

Large FPGA designs have already became de-facto SoC platforms, which contain multi-core processors, complex interfaces, and a wide variety of peripherals ranging from PCI Express, 10Gig Ethernet, and high-performance memory controllers to simpler UART, I2C, and flash memories. Using IP cores and existing functional components to interface with those peripherals using standard interfaces is a prudent approach for quicker development of complex and highly integrated FPGA designs, which translates into faster product time-to-market and, in many cases, lower development cost.

Engineers spend increasingly more time not designing basic functional components but finding, evaluating, and integrating existing ones. Using IP cores require less specialized and more system knowledge from the design team. The focus shifts to stitching together, configuring, and optimizing the system, rather than having a detailed understanding of each and every device.

This Tip overviews some of the commonly used criteria to perform IP core selection. The criteria are not organized by the order of importance.

Develop in-house vs. use third party IP

Before embarking on a process of selecting the right IP core, the development team has to consider an option of developing the functional component in-house rather that purchasing a third party IP. This is also known as "build vs. buy". Often, the benefit of purchasing an IP core is not clear. The functional component seems simple enough to implement, and within the competence level of the design team. However, it is hard to accurately quantify the in-house development cost and perform meaningful comparison with the third-party solution because of factors such as later time-to-market, lost revenue, and various hidden costs not taken into account.

The advantages of developing in-house are implementing features that aren't available in third-party cores, custom interfaces with the rest of the design, higher performance, and lower logic utilization by not including unnecessary features. A good example is a custom-built DDR3 memory controller, which has limited set of features and works only with specific memory type, but it's smaller and achieves higher memory access efficiency compared to third-party solutions.

The disadvantages are repeating work that has already been done by others, additional design and verification time, which impacts the project schedule, development and tool cost. IP core certification and interoperability is also an important factor.

Sources for third party IP cores

There are three sources of IP cores for FPGAs: (i) cores provided by FPGA vendor, (ii) commercial IP providers, and (iii) open source. The following table lists some of the IP core providers.

Table 1: IP core providers

IP Core Provider	URL
IP Core search portal	http://www.design-reuse.com
Xilinx IP Center	http://www.xilinx.com/ipcenter/index.htm
ASICS.ws	http://asics.ws
Mentor Graphics Precise-IP	http://www.mentor.com/precision/precise-ip
ZIPcores	http://www.zipcores.com
PLDA	http://plda.com
eInfochips	http://www.einfochips.com
OpenCores	http://opencores.org

There are two main types of IP cores: synthesizable for ASIC and FPGA, and verification.

Verification IP cores are intended for testing compliance and compatibility of designs, such as USB, PCI Express, and Ethernet. Some of the features provided by verification IP cores are Bus Functional Models (BFM), coverage of functional layers, assertion libraries, and constrained random traffic generation.

Xilinx provides synthesizable cores under two programs: LogiCORE, and AllianceCORE. IP cores provided under LogiCORE are tested, documented, and supported by Xilinx. IP cores provided under AllianceCORE are distributed by Xilinx core solution partners.

IP core evaluation

Evaluating the IP core is important to ensure that the core meets all the feature, performance, utilization, and quality requirements. Core evaluation helps uncover various hidden issues, such as clocking scheme incompatible with the rest of the design, synthesis and physical implementation problems for a target FPGA, or actual logic utilization much higher than advertized on the data sheet. Core evaluation also provides an opportunity to establish closer relationship with the IP core provider.

It is convenient to maintain an IP core evaluation checklist that contains different criteria. The checklist helps you to perform side-by-side comparison between different IP core solutions and select the best one.

Performance and FPGA resource utilization

One of the IP core evaluation tasks is determining performance and utilization when the IP core is using specific configuration options, and built for a target FPGA. Performance refers to meeting frequency requirements of all clocks in the design. FPGA resource utilization includes not only logic utilization, but also embedded memory, IO, and clocking resources. It is important to use correct core configuration, and not rely on the example numbers advertized in the data sheet.

Deliverables

IP cores are delivered as generic RTL source code or a synthesized netlist in Electronic Design Interchange Format (EDIF). Both RTL and netlist can be encrypted to provide another level of protection. RTL source code can be mangled or obfuscated. This option is often used during IP core evaluation to hide some of the implementation details, and make it more difficult to reverse-engineer the core. Different IP core protection options are discussed in Tip #69.

The netlist is specific to an FPGA family. It is less portable and has fewer customization options but is less expensive than the RTL option. The netlist also provides better IP protection. It is more difficult to tamper or reverse engineer a netlist, although not impossible.

Cost

Most of the FPGA IP cores cost less than $100K, much lower than their ASIC counterparts. However, the cost structure might be complex and include up-front costs, license costs, maintenance and technical support costs, and royalties.

Typically, the up-front cost of the cores provided by FPGA vendor is lower comparing to commercial IP providers. The up-front cost is higher for RTL source code.

IP core usage model has a large impact on the cost. The most restrictive usage model is single use, which allows using the IP core only for a single project. Other usage models are product line use, and company-wide use.

Some of the complex IP cores include royalties as part of their cost structure. Royalty is the agreed portion of the income, usually percentage of product sales, paid to the core vendor. For expensive cores, it may be possible to negotiate the cost. For instance, the IP core vendor may agree to lower the up-front cost at the expense of higher royalties.

Maintenance and technical support fees are typically charged on the annual basis. Maintenance includes updates to the latest core version that supports new features and implemented bug fixes.

Licensing options

Licensing options refer to both intended use of the core, which is briefly discussed above, as well as the way of generating it. IP core generation can be unrestricted, or tied to a specific workstation by the means of license server. Licensing terms of an IP core can be complex and cause a lot of legal problems in the future. It is recommended to get an attorney that specializes in intellectual property to review the licensing agreement before signing it.

It is important to inquire about the license upgrade path, for example from a single-use license to a multi-use product line.

Customization

Most IP cores, even the simplest ones, require customization. IP cores delivered as RTL can be customized by changing parameters and defines in the source code itself. IP cores delivered as a netlist typically include a software utility with a GUI that enables core customizations. Xilinx CoreGen utility is an example. If existing core customization options are not sufficient, many IP core vendors provide customization services.

IP core verification

It is important to make sure that the IP core comes with a well documented design verification process, exhaustive test benches that include both test vectors and expected results, scripts, and simulation flows.

Documentation and code quality

Make sure that the IP core is delivered with sufficient documentation that describes IP core architecture, principles of operations, main internal and external interfaces, register access, clock and reset schemes. Scrutinize the available RTL code and interface description for adherence to the industry-standard coding conventions.

Portability

FPGA vendor IP is typically provided as a configurable netlist for a specific FPGA family, which makes it is less portable than cores from commercial IP providers. Changing the FPGA vendor or family may require different IP core licensing, updating core interfaces and configuration parameters, and resolving integration and performance issues.

Reputation

Reputation and proven track record of the IP core vendor is an important requirement. Before licensing a complex and expensive IP core, it is customary to ask for references from existing customers.

Roadmap

It's often an important requirement to know the roadmap for a specific IP core development. A good example is a core that implements a communication interface standard, such as PCI Express. Since its inception PCI Express specification underwent several major changes, which required IP core modification.

69
IP CORE PROTECTION

IP core protection is becoming more important as the cores become more complex and expensive to develop. The goals of the IP core protection are: preventing things such as unauthorized use of the core, tampering, reverse engineering, theft, and to ensure the core is used according to the license agreement.

There are several IP core protection schemes. Choosing the best one depends on several criteria: IP core delivery method (RTL or netlist), cost structure (upfront fee, royalties), recipients or licensees (individual product, product line, company-wide), and terms of use (IP core evaluation, or commercial use). IP core vendors may choose to protect their cores at several levels in order to handle a variety of misuse scenarios.

Developing new IP core protection methods is an ongoing effort, and attracts a lot of attention from the industry and academic communities. A lot of research articles are published on this subject, and several novel ideas have been proposed. Many of these are patented.

Different ways of adding an invisible IP core digital watermark have been widely discussed in the literature. The idea is to add a digital signature that uniquely identifies both the design and the design recipient. This technique relies on a procedure that spreads a digital signature in FPGA look-up tables of designs at the HDL level, not increasing the area of the system. The technique also includes a procedure for signature extraction that allows detecting the ownership rights without interfering with the normal operation of the system.

The following is a list of different IP core protection options commonly used in the industry.

RTL Licensing

Unmodified RTL is the most flexible, albeit the most expensive, commercial IP core delivery option. One way to protect the unmodified IP core RTL is to include proper license terms, copyright, and terms of use description in the header of each file. That approach is frequently used by cores with one of the open source licenses. Adding the header to a file doesn't restrict the access to the RTL, but serves as a warning or deterrence against the misuse of the core.

The following is an example of a file header in one of Xilinx IP cores.

```
//////////////////////////////////////////////////////////////////
// Copyright (c) 1995-2010 Xilinx, Inc.  All rights reserved.
//////////////////////////////////////////////////////////////////
////
//
//      ____  ____
//     /   /\/   /
//    /___/  \  /     Vendor: Xilinx
//    \   \   \/      Version: M.53d
//     \   \          Application:
//     /   /          Filename:
//    /___/   /\      Timestamp: Sat Jan 29 18:20:00 2010
//    \   \  /  \
//     \___\/\___\
//
//
// Description :
//     Xilinx Functional Simulation Library Component
//
// Purpose:
//     This verilog netlist is a verification model and uses
//     simulation primitives which may not represent the true
//     implementation of the device, however the netlist is
//     functionally correct and should not be modified. This
//     file cannot be synthesized and should only be used
//     with supported simulation tools.
//////////////////////////////////////////////////////////////////
```

Tamper proofing schemes are implemented in software to ensure that the original RTL code has not been changed. A simple tamper-proofing technique is to compare the RTL with the expected checksum or cryptographic hash. However, it's difficult to conceal the nature of the checks; once they are detected, they can be removed or bypassed.

Code obfuscation

Code obfuscation, or mangling, is defined as changing the original code for the purpose of making it difficult for human understanding, without changing its functionality. The goals are to conceal the code purpose (security through obscurity), hide the implementation details, or deter reverse engineering. Code obfuscation doesn't prevent IP core reverse engineering, but rather makes this process more difficult.

There are several existing commercial and open source tools that perform HDL code obfuscation, as shown in the following list.

Tool: Verilog Source Code Obfuscator
http://www.semdesigns.com/products/obfuscators/VerilogObfuscator.html

Tool: VO – Verilog Obfuscator
http://www.eda-utilities.com/vo.htm
Synopsys VCS simulator provides an `-Xmangle` option to produce a mangled version of the HDL file.

Code obfuscation option is frequently used during IP core evaluation to enable full access to the core, but still hide implementation details, and prevent customization.

Encrypted RTL

Some vendors deliver their IP cores as an encrypted RTL. This option is more flexible than the netlist, because it allows synthesizing the core for different FPGA families.

Synopsys VCS simulator provides several options to encrypt source files: `+autoprotect`, `+protect [file suffix]`, and `+object_protect <source file>`.

Netlist

IP cores can be delivered as a synthesized netlist. This delivery option is usually cheaper than the RTL, but less flexible. It also provides better protection: it's more difficult to tamper with or reverse engineer a netlist, although not impossible. There are several commercial and open source netlist viewing and exploration tools.

There are tools that can obfuscate the netlist. Xilinx provides a utility called `obngc`, which obfuscates .ngc files.

Restricted functionality

Another approach to protect IP cores against unauthorized use is limiting core functionality based on the license. There are few ways to achieve that.

- Restricting the core feature set. For example, only allowing the use of 100Mbs speed in an Ethernet MAC core.
- Limiting the operation time. For example, disabling the core after one hour of continuous operation.
- Artificially reduce performance. For example, limiting the DMA speed of a PCI Express core.

Restricting the core functionality is typically used for the IP core evaluation.

70
IP CORE INTERFACES

LocalLink

LocalLink is a high performance Xilinx-specific protocol, designed to provide user interface to IP cores and functional blocks. LocalLink is used in several Xilinx and third party IP cores, such as Ethernet MAC, PCI Express, Aurora, memory controller, and many others. LocalLink interface defines a set of signals that allow for the transfer of generic, protocol-independent packets. LocalLink is a synchronous and point-to-point protocol, and provides receive and transmit flow control. The figures below show LocalLink timing diagrams of transmit and receive data transfer.

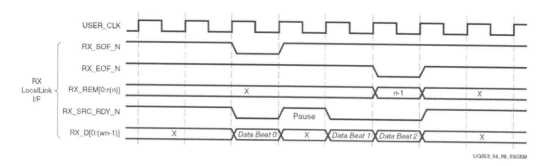

Figure 1: LocalLink data transmit (source: Xilinx Aurora User Guide)

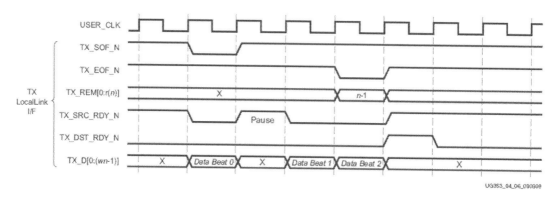

Figure 2: LocalLink data receive (source: Xilinx Aurora User Guide)

PLB

Processor Local Bus (PLB) is part of the CoreConnect processor bus architecture for SoC designs. The specification is designed by IBM, and available as a no-fee, no-royalty architecture to EDA tool vendors, core IP and chip-development companies. PLB is licensed by over 1500 companies. The following table outlines main PLB characteristics.

Table 1: PLB Characteristics

Bus Feature	Description
Topology	Multi-master, programmable-priority, arbitrated bus
Bus width	32,64,128 bit
Address space	64 bit
Bandwidth	Up to 2.9 GB/s
Other features	Separate read and write data buses Supports concurrent reads and writes, fixed and variable-length bursts, and bus locking

URL: http://www.xilinx.com/products/ipcenter/dr_pcentral_coreconnect.htm

AMBA AXI4

Advanced Microcontroller Bus Architecture (AMBA) is the on-chip bus architecture from ARM. EXtensible Interface 4 (AXI4) is the fourth generation of the AMBA AXI protocol, which defines an interconnect standard optimized for use in FPGAs.

The following figure shows an example of a MicroBlaze processor design using AXI interconnect to peripheral devices.

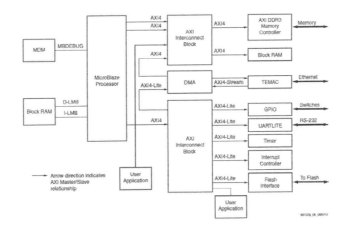

Figure 3: Design architecture using AXI interconnect (source: Xilinx AXI4 IP)

The following table outlines main AMBA AXI4 characteristics.

Table 2: AMBA AXI4 Characteristics

Bus Feature	Description
Topology	Point to point master/slave, arbitrated crossbar switch
Bus width	Up to 256-bit
Address space	64-bit
Bandwidth	5.8 GByte/sec *
Other features	Burst transactions, up to 256 data beats per burst. Unidirectional high-speed data streaming.

* Measured throughput on Xilinx ML605 development board
URL: http://www.xilinx.com/ipcenter/axi4.htm
　　　http://www.xilinx.com/ipcenter/axi4_ip.htm

Wishbone

The Wishbone Bus is a popular open source architecture for System on Chip (SoC) IP core interconnect. A large number of open source designs with Wishbone interconnect are available on the OpenCores.org. The following figure depicts Wishbone interface between Master and Slave.

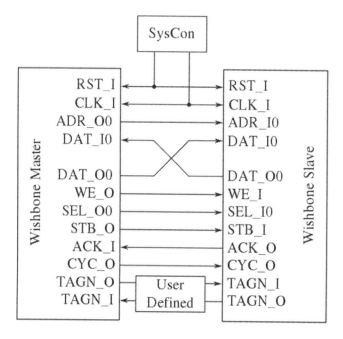

Figure 4: Wishbone interface

The following table outlines main Wishbone characteristics.

Table 3: Wishbone Characteristics

Bus Feature	*Description*
Topology	Wishbone supports several common bus topologies: point-to-point, shared, hierarchical and switched. It supports -bit bus size
Bus width	8, 16, 32, and 64 bit
Address space	32 bit

For the detailed description of Wishbone signals, refer to the datasheet at http://cdn.opencores.org/downloads/wbspec_b4.pdf

There are several open source Wishbone controller implementations available on OpenCores.org.

URL: http://opencores.org/project,wb_conmax
http://opencores.org/project,wb_dma

71

SERIAL AND PARALLEL CRC

Cyclic Redundancy Check (CRC) is one of the most popular error detection codes. CRC is used in communication protocols, storage devices, and other applications that require detecting bit errors in the raw data. CRC is implemented as a Linear Feedback Shift Register (LFSR) using registers and XOR gates, and is a remainder of the modulo-2 long division operation.

This Tip presents a practical method of generating Verilog or VHDL code for the parallel CRC. This method allows fast generation of a parallel CRC code for an arbitrary polynomial and data width. There are several existing tools that can generate the code, and a lot of examples for popular CRC polynomials. However, oftentimes it is beneficial to understand the underlying principles in order to implement a customized circuit or optimize an existing one.

CRC Overview

CRC properties are defined by the generator polynomial length and coefficients. The protocol specification usually defines CRC in hexadecimal or polynomial notation. For example, CRC5 used in USB protocol is represented as 0×5 in hex notation or as $G(x)=x^5+x^2+1$ in the polynomial notation:

Hex notation 0x5 ↔ Polynomial notation $G(x) = x^5+x^2+1$

This CRC is typically implemented in hardware as an LFSR with a serial data input, as shown in the following figure.

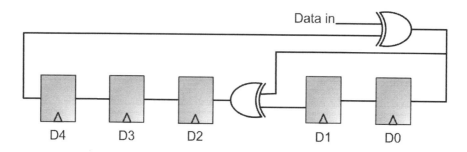

Figure 1: USB CRC5 implementation as LFSR using generator polynomial $G(x)=x5+x2+1$

In many cases serial LFSR implementation of the CRC is suboptimal for a given design. Because of the serial data input, it only allows the CRC calculation of one data bit for every clock. If a design has an N-bit datapath, meaning that every clock CRC module has to calculate CRC on N bits of data, serial CRC will not work.

One example of this is USB 2.0, which transmits data at 480 MHz on the physical level. A typical USB PHY chip has a 8 or 16-bit data interface to the chip that does the protocol processing. A circuit that checks or generates CRC has to work at that same speed.

Another more esoteric use case is the calculation of a 64-bit CRC on data written and read from a 288-bit wide memory controller (two 64-bit DDR DIMMs with ECC bits).

To achieve a higher throughput, serial LFSR implementation of the CRC has to be converted into a parallel N-bit wide circuit, where N is the design datapath width, so that every clock N bits are processed. This is a parallel CRC implementation.

A simplified block diagram of the parallel CRC is shown in the following figure. The next state CRC output is a function of the current state CRC and the data.

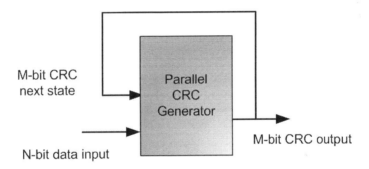

Figure 2: Parallel CRC block diagram

Even though CRC was invented almost half a century ago and has gained widespread use, it still sparks a lot of interest in the research community. There is a constant stream of research papers and patents that offer different parallel CRC implementations with speed and logic area improvements.

There are several research papers that describe different methods of parallel CRC calculation for hardware description languages (HDL). The most notable ones are mentioned at the end of this Tip. However, most proposed methods are academic and focus on the theoretical aspect of the parallel CRC generation. They are too impractical to implement in software or hardware for a quick HDL code generation of CRC with arbitrary data and polynomial widths.

An additional requirement on the parallel CRC generation method is that it has to accept any data width, not only power-of-2, to be useful. Going back to the USB 2.0 CRC5 example, a convenient data width to use for parallel CRC of polynomial width of 5 is 11, since USB packets using CRC5 are 16 bit. Another example is 16-lane PCI Express with a 128-bit datapath (16 8-bit symbols). Because the beginning of a packet is a K-code symbol and doesn't participate in the CRC calculation, the parallel CRC data is 120-bits wide.

The following is a brief overview of a modulo-2 polynomial arithmetic.

A polynomial is a value expressed in a form:

$$P(x) = \sum_{i=0}^{N} p(i)x^i = p(0) + p(1)x + \cdots + p(N)x^N$$

where p(i)={0,1}

Polynomial addition and subtraction operations use bitwise XOR, as shown in the following example:

```
P(x)     = x³+x²+1
Q(x)     = x²+x+1
P(x)+Q(x)= x³+(x²+x²)+x+(1+1) = x³+x
```

Polynomial multiplication by 2 is a left shift, and unsigned division by 2 is the right shift. Modulo-2 polynomial division is realized the same way as long division over integers. Cyclic left and right shifts are multiplication and division by $(2 \bmod 2^n-1)$.

Parallel CRC Generation

The following is a Verilog example of a module that generates parallel USB CRC5 with 4-bit data.

```verilog
module crc5_parallel(
    input [3:0] data_in,
    output reg[4:0] crc5,
    input rst,
    input clk);
 // LFSR for USB CRC5
 function [4:0] crc5_serial;
    input [4:0] crc;
    input data;
   begin
      crc5_serial[0] = crc[4] ^ data;
      crc5_serial[1] = crc[0];
      crc5_serial[2] = crc[1] ^ crc[4] ^ data;
      crc5_serial[3] = crc[2];
      crc5_serial[4] = crc[3];
   end
 endfunction
 // 4 iterations of USB CRC5 LFSR
```

```verilog
    function [4:0] crc_iteration;
        input [4:0] crc;
        input [3:0] data;
        integer i;
    begin
        crc_iteration = crc;
        for(i=0; i<4; i=i+1)
            crc_iteration =
            crc5_serial(crc_iteration, data[3-i]);
    end
    endfunction
    always @(posedge clk, posedge rst) begin
        if(rst) begin
            crc5 <= 5'h1F;
        end
        else begin
            crc5 <= crc_iteration(crc5,data_in);
        end
    end
endmodule
```

A synthesis tool will perform loop unrolling to synthesize parallel CRC from a serial representation. However, the resulting implementation might be suboptimal, and the low level implementation using a XOR tree for each CRC output bit will produce a more efficient circuit. The following is a description of a practical method of generating a parallel CRC. It works on any polynomial and data size, and is independent of the target technology. The method description is shown step-by-step and is accompanied by an example of parallel CRC generation for the USB CRC5 polynomial $G(x) = x^5 + x^2 + 1$ with 4-bit data width.

The method takes advantage of the theory published in [1] and [2], and leverages a simple serial CRC generator and linear properties of the CRC to build a parallel CRC circuit.

Step 1: Let's denote N=data width, M=CRC polynomial width. For parallel USB CRC5 with 4-bit datapath, N=4 and M=5.

Step 2: Implement a serial CRC generator routine for a given polynomial. It can be done using different programming language or scripts, for instance C, Java, Verilog or Perl. A Verilog function *crc5_serial* shown below could be used for the serial USB CRC5.

```verilog
// A Verilog function that implements serial USB CRC5
function [4:0] crc5_serial;
    input [4:0] crc;
    input data;
    begin
```

```
      crc5_serial[0] = crc[4] ^ data;
      crc5_serial[1] = crc[0];
      crc5_serial[2] = crc[1] ^ crc[4] ^ data;
      crc5_serial[3] = crc[2];
      crc5_serial[4] = crc[3];
   end
endfunction
```

Denote this routine as CRC_{serial}.

Let's also build a routine $CRC_{parallel}(N_{in}, M_{in})$, which calls CRC_{serial} N times, the same as the number of data bits, and returns M_{out}. The following pseudo-code is an example of $CRC_{parallel}$:

```
routine CRC_parallel(N_in, M_in)
    M_out = M_in
    for(i=0;i<N;i++)
        M_out = CRC_serial(N_in , M_out)
return M_out
```

Step 3: Parallel CRC implementation is a function of N-bit data input and M-bit current CRC state, as shown in the previous figure. This method is going to take advantage of the following two matrices:

Matrix H1. It describes M_{out} (next CRC state) as a function of N_{in} (input data) when $M_{in}=0$:

$M_{out} = CRC_{parallel}(N_{in}, M_{in}=0)$
H1 matrix is of size [NxM]

Matrix H2. It describes M_{out} (next CRC state) as a function of M_{in} (current CRC state) when $N_{in}=0$:

$M_{out} = CRC_{parallel}(N_{in}=0, M_{in})$
H2 matrix is of size [MxM]

Step 4: Build the matrix H1. Using $CRC_{parallel}$ routine from **step 2** calculate CRC for the N values of N_{in} when $M_{in}=0$. The values are one-hot encoded. That is, each of the N_{in} values has only one bit set. For N=4 the values are 0×1, 0×2, 0×4, 0×8 in hex representation.

The following table shows matrix H1 values for USB CRC5 with N=4 and $M_{in}=0$.

Table 1: Matrix H1 for USB CRC5 with N=4

	Mout[4]	Mout[3]	Mout[2]	Mout[1]	Mout[0]
Nin[0]	0	0	1	0	1

Nin[1]	0	1	0	1	0
Nin[2]	1	0	1	0	0
Nin[3]	0	1	1	0	1

Step 5: Build the matrix H2. Using CRC$_{parallel}$ routine from **step 2** calculate CRC for the M values of M$_{in}$ when N$_{in}$= 0. The values are one-hot encoded. For M=5 M$_{in}$ values are 0x1,0x2,0x4,0x8,0x10 in hex representation.

The following table shows the matrix H2 values for USB CRC5 with N=4 and N$_{in}$= 0.

Table 2: Matrix H2 for USB CRC5 with N=4

	Mout[4]	Mout[3]	Mout[2]	Mout[1]	Mout[0]
Min[0]	1	0	0	0	0
Min[1]	0	0	1	0	1
Min[2]	0	1	0	1	0
Min[3]	1	0	1	0	0
Min[4]	0	1	1	0	1

Step 6: Use the data from matrices H1 and H2 shown in the previous two tables to construct the parallel CRC equations. Each set bit j in column i of the matrix H1, and that's the critical part of the method, participates in the parallel CRC equation of the bit M$_{out}$[i] as N$_{in}$[j]. Likewise, each set bit j in column i of the matrix H2 participates in the parallel CRC equation of the bit M$_{out}$[i] as M$_{in}$[j].

All participating inputs M$_{in}$[j] and N$_{in}$[j] that form M$_{out}$[i] are XOR-ed together.

For USB CRC5 with N=4 the parallel CRC equations are as follows:

```
Mout[0] = Min[1] ^ Min[4] ^ Nin[0] ^ Nin[3]
Mout[1] = Min[2] ^ Nin[1]
Mout[2] = Min[1] ^ Min[3] ^ Min[4] ^ Nin[0] ^ Nin[2] ^ Nin[3]
Mout[3] = Min[2] ^ Min[4] ^ Nin[1] ^ Nin[3]
Mout[4] = Min[0] ^ Min[3] ^ Nin[2]
```

M$_{out}$ is the parallel CRC implementation.

The underlying principles of this method are the way the matrices H1 and H2 are constructed, in which the rows are linearly independent, and the fact that CRC is a linear operation:

```
CRC(A+B) = CRC(A) + CRC(B)
```

The resulting Verilog module that generates parallel USB CRC5 with 4-bit data is as follows:

```verilog
module crc5_4bit(
   input [3:0] data_in,
   output [4:0] crc_out,
   input rst,
   input clk);

   reg [4:0] lfsr_q,lfsr_c;
   assign crc_out = lfsr_q;

   always @(*) begin
     lfsr_c[0] = lfsr_q[1] ^ lfsr_q[4] ^ data_in[0] ^ data_in[3];
     lfsr_c[1] = lfsr_q[2] ^ data_in[1];
     lfsr_c[2] = lfsr_q[1] ^ lfsr_q[3] ^ lfsr_q[4] ^ data_in[0] ^ data_in[2] ^ data_in[3];
     lfsr_c[3] = lfsr_q[2] ^ lfsr_q[4] ^ data_in[1] ^ data_in[3];
     lfsr_c[4] = lfsr_q[0] ^ lfsr_q[3] ^ data_in[2];
   end // always

   always @(posedge clk, posedge rst) begin
     if(rst) begin
        lfsr_q <= 5'h1F;
     end
     else begin
        lfsr_q <= lfsr_c;
     end
   end // always
endmodule // crc5_4
```

Other Parallel CRC Generation Methods

There are several other methods for parallel CRC generation. Each method offers unique advantages, but has drawbacks as well. Some are more suitable for high-speed designs where the logic area is less of an issue. Others offer the most compact designs, but have a resulting lower speed. The following are the most notable methods.

The method described in [1] derives a recursive formula for parallel CRC directly from a serial implementation. The idea is to represent an LFSR for serial CRC as a discrete-time linear system:

```
X(i+1) = FX(i)+U(i)    [eq1]
```

Where vector $X(i)$ is the current LFSR output, $X(i+1)$ is the output in the next clock, vector $U(i)$ is the i-th of the input sequence, F is a matrix chosen according to the equations of serial LFSR.

For example, USB CRC5 $G(x) = x^5 + x^2 + 1$ will produce the following matrix:

$$F = \begin{bmatrix} p(4) & 1 & 0 & 0 & 0 \\ p(3) & 0 & 1 & 0 & 0 \\ p(2) & 0 & 0 & 1 & 0 \\ p(1) & 0 & 0 & 0 & 1 \\ p(0) & 0 & 0 & 0 & 0 \end{bmatrix} = \begin{bmatrix} 0 & 1 & 0 & 0 & 0 \\ 0 & 0 & 1 & 0 & 0 \\ 1 & 0 & 0 & 1 & 0 \\ 0 & 0 & 0 & 0 & 1 \\ 1 & 0 & 0 & 0 & 0 \end{bmatrix}$$

Where $p(i)$ are polynomial coefficients.

Addition and multiplication operations are bitwise logic XOR and AND respectively.

After m clocks the state is $X(i+m)$, and the solution can be obtained recursively from [eq1]

$$X(i+m) = F^m X(i) + F^{m-1} U(i) + \ldots + F X(i+m) + U(i+m) \qquad [eq2]$$

where m is the desired data width.

Each row k of $X(i+m)$ solution is a parallel CRC equation of bit k.

An important result of this method is that it establishes a formal proof of solution existence. It's not immediately obvious that it's possible to derive parallel CRC circuit from a serial one.

The method described in [5] uses 2-stage CRC calculation. The idea is that checking and generating CRC is done not with generator polynomial G(x), but with another polynomial M(x) = G(x) * P(x). M(x) is chosen such as it has fewer terms than G(x) to simplify the complexity of the circuit that realizes the division. The result of the division by M(x), which has a fixed length, is divided again by G(x) to get the CRC.

The method described in [4] allows calculating CRC with byte enable. In many cases it's important. For example, if the data width is 16-bit but a packet ends on an 8-bit boundary it'd require having two separate CRC modules: for 8 and 16-bit. The byte enable method allows reusing the 16-bit CRC circuit to calculate 8-bit CRC.

The method described in [2] uses DSP unfolding technique to build a parallel CRC. The idea is to model an LFSR as a digital filter and use graph-based unfolding to unroll loops and obtain the parallel processing.

Other methods include using Lookup Tables (LUTs) with pre-computed CRC values [3].

Performance Results

Logic utilization and timing performance of a parallel CRC circuit largely depends on the underlying target technology, data width, and the polynomial width. For instance, Verilog or VHDL code will be synthesized differently for Xilinx Virtex-6 and Virtex-4 FPGA families, because of the difference in underlying LUT input size. Virtex-6 has 6-bit LUTs as opposed to 4-bit LUTs in Virtex-4.

In general, logic utilization of a parallel CRC circuit will grow linearly with the data width. Using the big-O notation, logic size complexity is $O(n)$, where n is the data width. For example, each of the CRC5 5 output bits is a function of 4 data input bits:

```
CRCout[i] = Function(CRCin[4:0], Data[3:0]).
```

Doubling the data width to 8 bits will double the number of participating data bits in each CRC5 bit equation. That will make the total CRC circuit size up to 5x2=10 times bigger. Of course, not all bits will double – that depends on the polynomial. But the overall circuit growth is linear.

Logic utilization will grow as a second power of the polynomial width, or $O(n^2)$. Doubling the polynomial width in CRC5 from 5 to 10 (let's call it CRC10, which has different properties), will double the size of each CRC10 output bit. Since the number of CRC outputs is also doubled, the total size increase is up to $2^2=4$ times.

Timing performance of the circuit will decrease because it will require more combinational logic levels to synthesize CRC output logic given the wider data and polynomial inputs.

The following table summarizes the logic utilization of parallel CRC circuits for USB CRC5 and popular Ethernet CRC32. The target FPGA is Xilinx Virtex-6 LX75.

Table 3: Logic utilization results

	Registers	*LUTs*	*Slices*
USB CRC5 with 4-bit data using "for loop"	5	5	2
USB CRC5 with 4-bit data using "XOR"	5	5	2
CRC32 with 32-bit data using "for loop"	32	198	81
CRC32 with 32-bit data using "XOR"	32	131	61

As expected, the number of registers is 5 and 32 for CRC5 and CRC32. For small CRC5 circuit there is no difference in the overall logic utilization. However, for larger CRC32 the code using "XOR" method produces more compact logic than the "for loop" approach. Note that the results are specific to the targeted technology and synthesis tool settings.

Summary

To summarize, the parallel CRC generation method described in this Tip leverages a serial CRC generator and linear properties of the CRC codes to build $H1_{NxM}$ and $H2_{MxM}$ matrices.

Row [i] of the H1 matrix is the CRC value of N_{in} with a single bit [i] set, while $M_{in}=0$.

Row [i] of the H2 matrix is the CRC value of M_{in} with a single bit [i] set, while $N_{in}=0$.

Column [j] of H1 and H2 matrices contains the polynomial coefficients of the CRC output bit [j].

There is an online Parallel CRC Generator tool at available at OutputLogic.com that takes advantage of this method to produce Verilog or VHDL code given an arbitrary data and polynomial width.

References

[1] G. Campobello, G Patane, M Russo, "Parallel CRC Realization" http://ai.unime.it/~gp/publications/full/tccrc.pdf

[2] G.Albertango and R. Sisto, "Parallel CRC Generation", IEEE Micro, Vol. 10, No. 5, October 1990, pp. 63-71.

[3] A. Perez, "Byte-wise CRC Calculations", IEEE Micro, Vol. 3, No. 3, June 1983, pp. 40-50

[4] Adrian Simionescu, Nobug Consulting http://space.ednchina.com/upload/2008/8/27/5300b83c-43ea-459b-ad5c-4dc377310024.pdf

[5] R. J. Glaise, "A two-step computation of cyclic redundancy code CRC-32 for ATM networks", IBM Journal of Research and Development Volume 41, Issue 6 (November 1997) pp 705 - 710

72

SCRAMBLERS, PRBS, AND MISR

Although Scramblers, MISR, and PRBS are used in very different applications, they belong to the class of functional blocks, whose implementation is based on a linear feedback shift register (LFSR).

Scramblers

Scramblers are used in many communication protocols such as PCI Express, SAS/SATA, USB, and Bluetooth to randomize the transmitted data in order to remove long sequences of logic zeros and ones. The operation of the descrambler on the receive side is identical to the scrambler and, in most cases, the same implementation can be shared between the two. The theory behind serial and parallel scramblers is very similar to the CRC and is discussed in more detail in Tip #71.

The following figure shows a block diagram of a data scrambler.

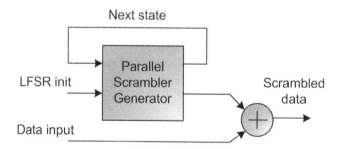

Figure 1: Scrambler block diagram

A scrambler generator is usually implemented as an LFSR. The LFSR is initialized for every new packet, and then advanced for every valid data. The LFSR outputs are XOR-ed with the input data, which results in a scrambled data.

A parallel scrambler generator can operate on input data wider than one bit, which results in higher throughput. Essentially, a serial scrambler is a special case of a parallel scrambler when the input data width is 1 bit.

Scramblers can be defined using Fibonacci and Galois notation. Both notations are equivalent and there is a conversion process, which involves reversing the LFSR taps and finding the new initialization value. Also, there are two main methods to generate scrambled data: frame-synchronous and self-synchronous. The next LFSR state of a frame-synchronous scrambler depends only on the current LFSR state, as shown in the above figure. However, self-synchronous scramblers use both the current LFSR state and the input data to derive the next LFSR state.

The following is a parallel scrambler implementation example for 8-bit data and the polynomial used in PCI Express protocol.

```
//-----------------------------------------------
// scrambler for lfsr[15:0]=1+x^3+x^4+x^5+x^16;
//-----------------------------------------------
module scrambler(input [7:0] data_in,
     input scram_en, scram_rst, rst, clk,
     output reg [7:0] data_out);
  reg [15:0] lfsr_q,lfsr_c;
  reg [7:0] data_c;
  always @(*) begin
 lfsr_c[0]  = lfsr_q[8];
 lfsr_c[1]  = lfsr_q[9];
 lfsr_c[2]  = lfsr_q[10];
 lfsr_c[3]  = lfsr_q[8]  ^ lfsr_q[11];
 lfsr_c[4]  = lfsr_q[8]  ^ lfsr_q[9]  ^ lfsr_q[12];
 lfsr_c[5]  = lfsr_q[8]  ^ lfsr_q[9]  ^ lfsr_q[10] ^ lfsr_q[13];
 lfsr_c[6]  = lfsr_q[9]  ^ lfsr_q[10] ^ lfsr_q[11] ^ fsr_q[14];
 lfsr_c[7]  = lfsr_q[10] ^ lfsr_q[11] ^ lfsr_q[12]^fsr_q[15];
 lfsr_c[8]  = lfsr_q[0]  ^ lfsr_q[11] ^ lfsr_q[12]^lfsr_q[13];
 lfsr_c[9]  = lfsr_q[1]  ^ lfsr_q[12] ^ lfsr_q[13] ^lfsr_q[14];
 lfsr_c[10] = lfsr_q[2]  ^ lfsr_q[13] ^ lfsr_q[14]^lfsr_q[15];
 lfsr_c[11] = lfsr_q[3]  ^ lfsr_q[14] ^ lfsr_q[15];
 lfsr_c[12] = lfsr_q[4]  ^ lfsr_q[15];
 lfsr_c[13] = lfsr_q[5];
 lfsr_c[14] = lfsr_q[6];
 lfsr_c[15] = lfsr_q[7];

 data_c[0] = data_in[0] ^ lfsr_q[15];
 data_c[1] = data_in[1] ^ lfsr_q[14];
 data_c[2] = data_in[2] ^ lfsr_q[13];
 data_c[3] = data_in[3] ^ lfsr_q[12];
 data_c[4] = data_in[4] ^ lfsr_q[11];
 data_c[5] = data_in[5] ^ lfsr_q[10];
 data_c[6] = data_in[6] ^ lfsr_q[9];
 data_c[7] = data_in[7] ^ lfsr_q[8];
 end // always
always @(posedge clk, posedge rst) begin
```

```
  if(rst) begin
    lfsr_q   <= {16{1'b1}};
    data_out <= {8{1'b0}};
  end
  else begin
    lfsr_q <= scram_rst ? {16{1'b1}} : scram_en ? lfsr_c :
    lfsr_q;data_out <= scram_en ? data_c : data_out;
  end
end // always
endmodule // scrambler
```

Serial and parallel scrambler codes for different data widths and polynomials can be generated by the online tool offered on OutputLogic.com website.

PRBS

Pseudorandom Binary Sequence (PRBS) patterns are used to test the robustness of communication links in many applications. The most important PRBS property is the white spectrum of its pattern in the frequency domain. PRBS checker and generator circuits are implemented using LFSR. PRBS sequence is defined by one of the polynomials specified in the ITU-T O.150 standard to achieve certain characteristics, such as jitter, eye symmetry, and other spectral properties. Specific PRBS sequences are also referred as PRBS7, PRBS15, PRBS23, and PRBS29. PRBS7 and PRBS15 are pseudorandom data sequences with a maximum run length of seven and fifteen consecutive zeroes or ones respectively. The longer the maximum run length, the greater the spectral contents of that sequence and the more strenuous the test that the PRBS sequence provides. PRBS29 has a longest maximum run length and is the most strenuous PRBS sequence to be used for the test. A sequence that toggles every clock can be considered as PRBS1 because the maximum run length is one.

PRBS checker or generator circuit can be implemented using example code described in [1].

MISR

Multiple Input Shift Register (MISR) circuits are used in applications that require Automatic Test Pattern Generation (ATPG), such as Built-In Self Test (BIST). The MISR circuit is based on LFSR. However, the main difference from other LFSR-based circuits is that MISR utilizes multiple data bits to determine its next state, as shown in the following figure.

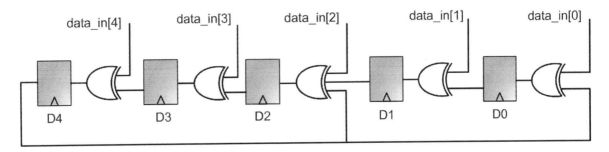

Figure 2: MISR implementation

MISR circuits allow for the generating and storing of signatures from the test responses. Because of this property, MISR circuits are often referred to as compressors or compactors.

Resources

[1] An Attribute-Programmable PRBS Generator and Checker, Xilinx Application Note XAPP884
http://www.xilinx.com/support/documentation/application_notes/xapp884_PRBS_Generator Checker.pdf

73
SECURITY CORES

Encryption, authentication, cryptographic hash functions, public key cryptography, and other security-related algorithms are computationally intensive, and implementing them in FPGA allows significant performance acceleration compared with the traditional implementation using an embedded processor. There are several available security cores targeting FPGA—both open source and commercial—which offer different architectural features and are optimized for area or speed.

Advanced Encryption Standard (AES)

Advanced Encryption Standard (AES) is an encryption standard that uses block cipher and symmetric keys. The standard defines three cipher variants: AES-128, AES-192, and AES-256. The number refers to a key size of 128, 192, and 256, respectively. AES is used extensively in communication protocols such as Bluetooth and 802.11 (Wi-Fi), data storage devices, and many other applications. Xilinx FPGAs are using AES for bitstream encryption/decryption.

AES was designed using a principle of a substitution-permutation network. It uses 10, 12, or 14 encryption rounds for a key size of 128, 196, or 256 bits, for encrypting or decrypting 128-bit data blocks. In a single round, AES operates on all 128 input bits. Each round consists of several processing steps that involve both intermediate results and the encryption key.

AES standard has been designed for efficient implementation in both hardware and software. FPGA designers typically implement it as a deep pipeline, and it combines look-up tables and XOR operations

There are several open source and commercial AES implementations targeting FPGAs. The following is a short list of AES cores.

Vendor: ASICS.ws
License: modified BSD
Language: Verilog
http://opencores.org/project,aes_core

Vendor: Helion Technology Limited
License: commercial
Language: Verilog, VHDL

http://www.heliontech.com/aes.htm

Source: Saar Drimer, "Security for volatile FPGAs", Cambridge University
License: Open source
Language: Verilog
http://www.cl.cam.ac.uk/~sd410/aes2/

Most AES cores are implemented using generic FPGA logic, such as look-up tables and registers. The above source offers three different high-throughput AES implementations that take advantage of BRAM and DSP48 embedded modules in Xilinx FPGAs instead.

Data Encryption Standard (DES)

Data Encryption Standard (DES) is another encryption standard that uses block cipher. It uses symmetric 56-bit encryption key. It is considered less secure than AES because of its short key length. The following is an open source DES implementation.

Vendor: ASICS.ws
License: modified BSD
Language: Verilog
http://opencores.org/project,des

Secure Hash Algorithm (SHA)

A cryptographic hash function is a method of creating a short message digest. Hash functions are used for digital signatures, random number generators, and other applications. Secure Hash Algorithm (SHA) is one of the cryptographic hash functions. SHA include SHA-0, SHA-1, SHA-2, and SHA-3 standards. SHA-3 is still in development. SHA-0 is the original version, which was withdrawn due to a flaw, and subsequently replaced with SHA-1. SHA algorithms were designed for efficient implementation in both software and hardware.

SHA-1 operates on 32-bit words and produces a 160-bit digest.

SHA-2 is a family of two similar hash functions with 256- and 512-bit digest sizes. They're also known as SHA-256 and SHA-512.

The following is an open source SHA implementation.

Source: OpenCores.org
License: LGPL
Language: Verilog
http://opencores.org/project,sha1
http://opencores.org/project,sha_core

MD5

Message-Digest algorithm 5 (MD5) is another popular hash function that produces 128-bit digest. The following is a commercial MD5 implementation.

Vendor: Posedge Silicon
License: commercial
Language: Verilog
http://www.posedge.com/html/products-ipsec.html

Posedge Silicon offers AES, DES, SHA, and MD5 cores as part of the IP Security (IPSEC) engine.

RSA

RSA is an algorithm for public key cryptography that uses asymmetric keys. RSA stands for Rivest, Shamir, and Adleman—researchers who first publicly described the algorithm.

Public-key cryptography refers to a set of methods for transforming a data message into a form that can be read only by the intended recipient. Public key cryptography is a technology employed by many cryptographic algorithms and cryptosystems such as Transport Layer Security (TLS) internet standard, Secure Sockets Layer (SSL), PGP, GPG, and many others.

The following is an open source implementation of the 512-bit RSA algorithm.

Source: OpenCores.org
License: LGPL
Language: VHDL
http://opencores.org/project,rsa_512

74

MEMORY CONTROLLERS

Memory controllers are required for different memory types: Flash, PROM, SRAM, and DRAM. This Tip discusses memory controllers for DRAM because their complexity far exceeds controllers for other memory types.

A generic design architecture using memory controller is shown in the following figure.

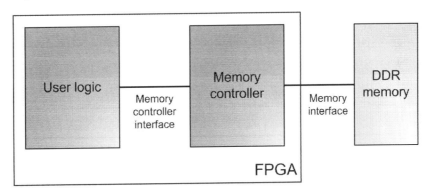

Figure 1: Design architecture using memory controller

It consists of the memory controller module connected to external DDR DRAM memory using standard memory interface. The interface is slightly different for DDR2, DDR3, QDR, and other memory types and is defined by JEDEC [1].

The interface between memory controller and the user logic can be an industry standard, such as AHB, AXI, PLB, and Avalon, or customized. In many cases, a custom interface allows easier integration with the user logic, or lower logic utilization of the memory controller.

A high performance DDR memory controller is a complex functional module that translates read and write requests into a complex series of commands required by DRAM. Its main blocks are:

- IO logic that interfaces with the DDR memory and responsible for correct data capturing on both rising and falling clock edges. It bridges and synchronizes the high data rate DRAM IO with the memory controller logic.

- Read and write logic responsible for efficient scheduling and arbitration of read and write bursts of data.

- Control logic, which periodic memory refreshes and other commands.

- Memory initialization logic, which carries out initialization sequence, calibration, and self-test.

The majority of FPGA designers take advantage of several available memory controller IP cores. Existing memory controller IP cores support a wide range of memory types and speeds, good memory efficiency for random read/write access, and provide one or more standard interfaces for integrating with the user logic.

However, some designs only work with a specific memory type and speed or require custom features that are not available in existing memory controllers. A good application example that benefits from a custom-designed memory controller is a protocol analyzer. A protocol analyzer for high speed protocols, such as 16-lane PCI Express Gen2, requires a very wide - 256-bit or more - custom interface to the user logic. It also does not need a random read/write access. The protocol analyzer performs contiguous write during capture mode and contiguous read during data upload.

DRAM selection

FPGA designers have an option to use an individual DRAM module, or more integrated DIMM or SODIMM, which offer larger memory size.

The following figure illustrates a dual in-line memory module (DIMM). A DIMM comprises of a multiple DRAM modules mounted on a PCB.

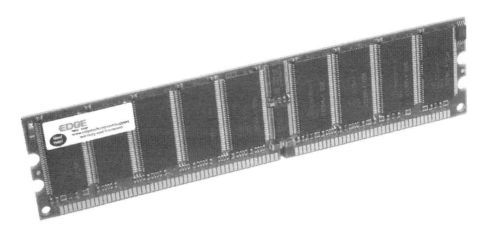

Figure 2: DIMM (source: EDGE Tech)

Another option is a small outline dual in-line memory module (SODIMM), which has smaller form factor than DIMM.

Figure 3: SODIMM (source: OCZ Technology)

The following is the overview of the most important DRAM characteristics.

Performance

FPGA IO performance can be a limiting factor to utilize the maximum speed supported by a DIMM. The following table provides the IO performance characteristics of Xilinx Virtex-6 FPGAs.

Table 1: IO performance (source: Xilinx Virtex-6 Switching Characteristics)

Description	Speed Grade			
	-3	-2	-1	-1L
Networking Applications				
SDR LVDS transmitter (using OSERDES; DATA_WIDTH = 4 to 8)	710 Mb/s	710 Mb/s	650 Mb/s	585 Mb/s
DDR LVDS transmitter (using OSERDES; DATA_WIDTH = 4 to 10)	1.4 Gb/s	1.3 Gb/s	1.25 Gb/s	1.1 Gb/s
SDR LVDS receiver (SFI-4.1)[1]	710 Mb/s	710 Mb/s	650 Mb/s	585 Mb/s
DDR LVDS receiver (SPI-4.2)[1]	1.4 Gb/s	1.3 Gb/s	1.0 Gb/s	0.9 Gb/s
Maximum Physical Interface (PHY) Rate for Memory Interfaces[2][3]				
DDR2	800 Mb/s	800 Mb/s	800 Mb/s	606 Mb/s
DDR3	1066 Mb/s	1066 Mb/s	800 Mb/s	800 Mb/s
QDR II + SRAM	400 MHz	350 MHz	300 MHz	–
RLDRAM II	500 MHz	400 MHz	350 MHz	–

The higher IO speed achieved by Virtex-6 FPGA is 1066 Mb/s. The fastest DDR3 DRAM at the time of writing this book is 1866 Mb/s.

There is a minimum DRAM operating frequency requirement specified by JEDEC [1], which is often ignored by designers. For example, DDR2 memories are allowed to operate at a frequency higher than 125MHz.

FPGA fabric performance might be limiting performance factor as well. Designers can choose higher FPGA speed grade to achieve better performance.

Capacity

The capacity of an individual DRAM module is limited and ranges between 1Gbit and 8Gbit. The growth of the memory capacity is achieved by increasing the number of DRAM modules on a DIMM. A technology known as memory ranks is used to increase memory capacity, while keeping the same form factor. A memory rank is a unique, independently-addressable data area of a memory module. Depending on how a DIMM is manufactured and which DRAM chips it is made of, a single memory module can comprise 1, 2 or 4 ranks making it a single, dual or quad rank module. Using multi-ranking memory requires memory controller support.

DRAM stacking is the latest development in a quest to increase memory capacity. DRAM stacking consists of using two standard DRAM modules, where one DRAM is placed on top of another, as shown in the following diagram.

Figure 4: DRAM stacking

Buffering is an implementation feature of DIMMs, which includes extra logic to improve the timing characteristics of memory address and control busses. Buffered DIMMs allow for placing more memory modules on a DIMM PCB to increase the overall memory capacity. Buffered DIMMs require memory controller support.

Another method to increase capacity is to utilize an Error Correction Code (ECC) bit. Many DRAM modules have an ECC bit for each byte. Using an ECC bit as a data can increase capacity by 12.5%. For a 16GByte memory that amounts to additional 2GBytes. The main disadvantage of using an ECC bit as data is misaligned memory accesses. However, this might be acceptable for custom-designed applications. Accessing an ECC bit requires memory controller support.

Voltage levels

Not all DRAM voltage levels can be supported by FPGAs. For example, an increasing number of DRAM memories operate at 1.35V, which is not supported by Virtex-6.

Memory controller efficiency

Efficiency is an important characteristic of a memory controller. There are several definitions of the memory controller efficiency (η) used in the technical literature. One definition is the ratio of the user data to all accesses that occur on the memory interface, i.e.:

```
η = user data/all memory accesses
```

Memory controller efficiency is lower than 100% due to the overhead, which includes memory controller housekeeping activities, such as periodic DRAM refresh and scheduling of read and write transfers. The efficiency varies for different memory access types, such as read-only, write-only, contiguous or random access. Usually an efficiency above 90% is considered good.

Most of the memory controller IP core vendors publish memory efficiency numbers. However, these numbers may not be accurate for a particular user application. The simplest and the most accurate way to determine the maximum memory controller efficiency is to perform a functional simulation that mimics memory accesses done by the user application.

Memory controller cores

Xilinx provides the memory controller core [3] as part of the ISE installation. The Xilinx Memory Interface Generator (MIG) can be used to generate the memory controller code for different memory types and clock speeds. The MIG can also be used to generate a wrapper for the embedded memory controller block (MCB) in Spartan-6 FPGAs.

The following figure shows the interface of Xilinx memory controller for Virtex-6 FPGA.

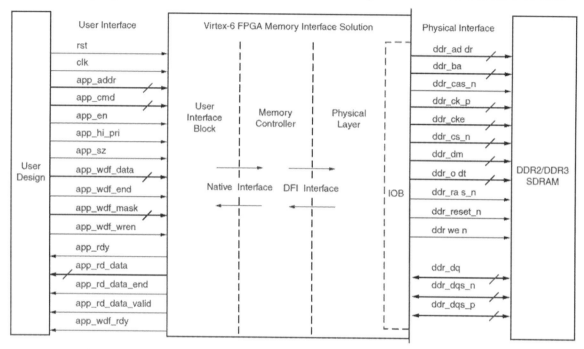

Figure 5: Xilinx memory controller interface (source: Xilinx User Guide UG406)

Xilinx also provides a multi-channel memory controller core (MPMC) as part of the EDK tool. MPMC is built on top of MIG, and is designed to interface with embedded processors via AHB, AXI, or PLB bus. MPMC also provides a configurable interface for performing DMA.

The alternative to Xilinx MIG is the memory controller IP core by Northwest logic [4]. The memory controller core supports a wide variety of DRAMs, including DDR3, LPDDR2, Mobile DDR, and RLDRAM. The core supports AHB, AXI, PLB, and Avalon busses for interfacing with the user logic. Other key features of this core are high memory efficiency, high clock rate, low latency, and integrated memory test core with pseudo-random address and data patterns.

Integration and bring-up challenges

FPGA designers are facing numerous challenges during the integration and bring-up of memory controller cores including IO assignment, designing a clocking scheme, floorplanning, and timing closure.

Interfacing with a DRAM requires using over a hundred of FPGA IO pins. Many of the IOs are clock-capable that are used to strobe the data. Control signals are clocked at double the data rate. In order to reduce the possibility of encountering a problem during FPGA physical implementation, it is recommended to use default IOs provided by the memory controller generation tools instead of self-assigning the IOs.

Meeting the timing requirements of a high-speed memory controller is challenging and, in most cases, requires floorplanning. Because of its relatively large size and the many IO pins it uses, floorplanning of the memory controller is not localized to a specific FPGA die area.

Memory controller bring-up includes successfully calibrating IOs and passing memory tests.

A more detailed discussion of these challenges cannot be provided in the limited scope of this book. However, an excellent source of additional information is the Xilinx Virtex-6 memory interface solution user guide [5].

Resources

[1] JEDEC DDR3 standards
http://www.jedec.org/category/technology-focus-area/main-memory-ddr3-sdram

[2] Xilinx memory solutions
http://www.xilinx.com/memory

[3] Xilinx memory controller
http://www.xilinx.com/support/documentation/ip_documentation/ug406.pdf

[4] Northwest logic memory controller
http://www.nwlogic.com/docs/Memory_Interface_Solution_Overview.pdf

[5] Xilinx Virtex-6 Memory Interface Solution User Guide UG406
http://www.xilinx.com/support/documentation/ip_documentation/ug406.pdf

75
USB CORES

Universal Serial Bus (USB) is a popular standard that provides robust plug-and-play connectivity. It was initially developed to connect personal computers to peripheral devices. Over time USB has been adopted by a wide range of FPGA applications. Since its inception in 1994, USB specification has undergone three major revisions: USB 1.1 in 1995, 2.0 in April 2000, and 3.0 in November 2008.

USB specification defines three types of devices: host controllers, hubs, and functions. USB physical interconnect has a tiered-star topology with the host controller at the center, which initiates all inbound and outbound transactions. Each wire segment between host controller, hub, and a function is a point-to-point connection.

USB uses an addressing scheme that allows for the connection of up to 127 hubs and functions to a single host controller.

USB 3.0 delivers ten times faster data transfer speed than USB 2.0. USB 3.0 uses very different signaling scheme than previous USB versions but maintains backwards compatibility by keeping the same USB two-wire interface. The following table shows performance of different USB versions.

Table 1: Performance of different USB versions

USB version	*Speed*	*Data rate*
USB 1.1	Low speed	1.5Mbit/sec
USB 1.1	Full speed	12Mbit/sec
USB 2.0	High speed	480Mbit/sec
USB 3.0	Super speed	5Gbit/sec

One of the characteristics of a USB device is its device class. USB devices that have similar attributes and services belong to the same device class, which allows for the sharing of device driver design and other functional components. Examples of USB device classes are mass storage, audio, video, human interface device (HID), and vendor specific. A full list of USB device classes is maintained by the USB IF [1].

USB Implementers Forum (IF) [2] is a non-profit organization that provides support for advancement and development of and ensures quality of USB devices. All USB devices should pass compliance and certification process by USB IF.

The following figure shows the architecture of a USB subsystem.

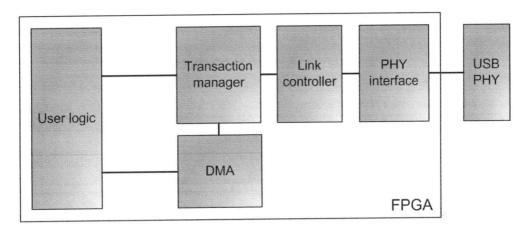

Figure 1: USB subsystem architecture

Physical layer (PHY) interface

USB defines UTMI, ULPI, and PIPE standards to interface between PHY and the rest of the device. The following table briefly describes the standards.

Table 2: USB PHY interfaces

PHY IF	*USB version*	*Description*
UTMI	2.0/1.1	USB Transceiver Macrocell Interface (UTMI) facilitates integration between different USB PHYs and host/device IP cores.
ULPI	2.0/1.1	UTMI Low Pin Interface (ULPI) defines a lower pin count PHY interface option compared with UTMI. Lower pin count is achieved by providing a bi-directional data bus and by eliminating static interface signals by moving their functionality into internal PHY registers.
PIPE	3.0	16-bit PIPE interface specification [4] is intended to facilitate the development of functionally equivalent USB 3.0 and PCI Express PHYs, and interfacing with the protocol link layer.

Link controller

Link controller implements USB link layer protocol, including link commands, flow control, and power management.

Transaction manager

Transaction manager implements USB protocol and transport layers and provides user logic a simple interface to access internal configuration, control, and status registers.

Direct memory access (DMA) controller

DMA controller incorporates RAM to buffer Rx and Tx USB packets and provides a simple interface to send and receive data from the user logic.

User logic

User logic uses custom or industry standard interfaces to connect with Transaction Manager and DMA modules. User logic can include an embedded processor.

USB cores

There are several available commercial and open-source cores for USB hosts and devices and USB 2.0/1.1 and USB 3.0 versions. The following is the partial list of USB IP cores targeting FPGAs.

USB2.0 device IP cores

Vendor: ASICS.ws
License: GPL
http://opencores.org/project,usb
Vendor: Xilinx
License: commercial
http://www.xilinx.com/products/ipcenter/xps_usb2_device.htm

USB3.0 device IP cores

Vendor: ASICS.ws
License: commercial
http://www.asics.ws/doc/usb3_dev_brief.pdf
Vendor: PLDA
License: commercial
http http://www.plda.com/prodetail.php?pid=136
Vendor: PLDA
License: commercial

http://www.cast-inc.com/ip-cores/interfaces/usbss-dev/index.html

USB3.0 host IP cores

Vendor: PLDA
License: commercial
http http://www.plda.com/prodetail.php?pid=142

Resources

[1] USB device classes
http://www.usb.org/developers/defined_class

[2] USB Implementers Forum
http://www.usb.org

[3] The list of certified USB products
http://www.usb.org/kcompliance/view

[4] PIPE interface specification
http://download.intel.com/technology/usb/USB_30_PIPE_10_Final_042309.pdf

76
PCI EXPRESS CORES

PCI Express is a packet-based, point-to-point serial interface technology that provides interconnect solutions for chip-to-chip and backplane switching fabric applications. Since its inception, PCI Express has become a de facto standard, gradually replacing its predecessors – PCI and PCI-X. To facilitate its adoption, PCI Express was designed to be fully software compatible with PCI.

There are three types of PCI Express devices: Endpoint, Root Port, and Switch. To scale bandwidth, the specification allows multiple serial lanes to be joined to form a higher bandwidth link between PCI Express devices. The specification defines x1, x2, x4, x8, and x16 lane configurations.

The three main PCI Express revisions – 1.1, 2.0, and 3.0 – were made available in 2005, 2007, and 2010, respectively. They are also known as Gen1, Gen2, and Gen3, reflecting on successive generations.

The following table shows performance of different PCI Express versions.

Table 1: Performance of different PCI Express versions

PCI Express version	*Data rate per lane*	*Maximum payload rate for 16 lane configuration.*
PCI Express 1.1	2.5Gbit/sec	4GByte/sec (*)
PCI Express 2.0	5Gbit/sec	8GByte/sec
PCI Express 3.0	8Gbit/sec	16GByte/sec

* PCI Express 1.1 and 2.0 links are 8b/10b encoded, which lowers payload rate by 20%. The numbers don't include transaction level packet overhead.

PCI Special Interest Group (SIG) [1] is a non-profit organization that delivers PCI Express standard and organizes developer conferences and compliance workshops to advance PCI Express technology and ensure quality of PCI Express devices.

The following figure shows PCI Express subsystem architecture.

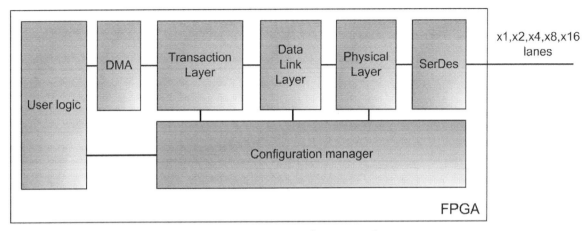

Figure 1: PCI Express subsystem architecture

Mechanical

In addition to a standard edge connector, a lesser known PCI Express connectivity option is using an external Host Cable and ExpressCard adapters. An ExpressCard slot is included in many laptop computers. The following figure shows the adapters manufactured by One Stop Systems [3].

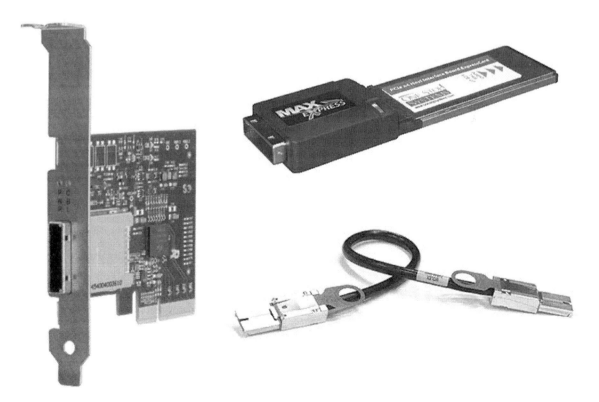

Figure 2: PCI Express cable and Express Card adapters (source: One Stop Systems)

Standard PCI Express slots are shown in the following figure.

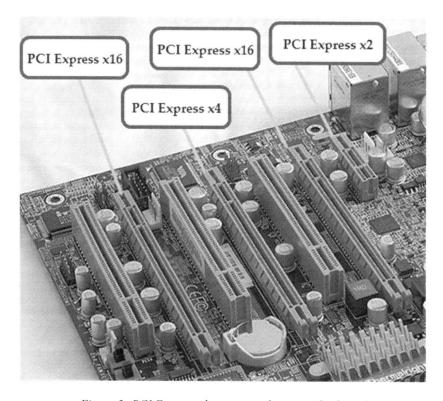

Figure 3: PCI Express slots mounted on a motherboard

Physical Layer (PHY) interface

Serializer/deserializer (SerDes) is a commonly used option in FPGA applications to interface to the PCI Express physical layer. Xilinx Virtex-6 GTX/GTH transceivers can also be used for that purpose. Other physical layer functions are alignment of data across lanes, scrambling/descrambling, and Link Training and Status State Machine (LTSSM).

Data Link Layer

Data Link layer implements packet acknowledgement and retransmission, CRC calculation and checking, flow control, and power management.

Transaction Layer

Transaction Layer implements end-to-end CRC, interrupts, device configuration, and assembly of transaction level packets. Transaction level interfaces with the DMA controller to provide a simple interface to send and receive data from the user logic.

Configuration manager

Configuration manager is responsible for supporting device configuration space. Configuration space is accessible by user logic to determine device address, PCI Express capabilities, current status, and other information.

PCI Express cores

There are several available commercial and open-source cores for PCI Express hosts and devices. The following is the partial list of the PCI Express IP cores targeting FPGAs.

Vendor: Xilinx
http://www.xilinx.com/support/documentation/ip_documentation/v6_pcie_ds715.pdf
All Xilinx Virtex-6 LXT and SXT FPGAs include integrated PCI Express interface blocks that can be configured to support 1.1 and 2.0 specifications running at 2.5 and 5.0 GHz, Endpoint or Root Port, and x1, x2, x4, or x8 lane configurations. The Xilinx CoreGen application can be used to generate a wrapper for those blocks. Xilinx also provides an option to generate a PCI Express interface core for the FPGA families without an embedded PCI Express block. A portal that contains all the information about PCI Express support by Xilinx is [1].

Vendor: PLDA
http://www.plda.com/prodetail.php?pid=177
PLDA provides a soft IP core for PCI Express endpoint compliant with 1.1, 2.0, and 3.0 specifications.

Vendor: Northwest Logic Inc.
http://www.nwlogic.com/products/pci_express_solution.html
Northwest Logic provides a soft IP core for PCI Express endpoint compliant with 1.1, 2.0, and 3.0 specifications.

Custom PCI Express cores

Designing a custom PCI Express core is necessary when an FPGA application requires features and configuration options not supported by any of the existing IP cores. For example, PCI Express protocol analyzers and traffic generators require x16 lane configuration and support for port bifurcation (multiple links over the same PCI Express port).

Resources

[1] PCI Special Interest Group
http://www.pcisig.com

[2] Xilinx PCI Express portal
http://www.xilinx.com/pcie

[3] One Stop Systems
http://www.onestopsystems.com/

77

MISCELLANEOUS IP CORES AND FUNCTIONAL BLOCKS

This Tip provides an overview of miscellaneous IP cores and functional blocks that are widely used in FPGA designs, and don't fall into any of the previous categories.

I2C

I2C is a popular two-wire, bidirectional serial protocol that provides a simple and efficient method of data exchange between devices. There are several open source and commercial implementations of the I2C controller.

Vendor: ASICS.ws
License: modified BSD
http://opencores.org/project,i2c
Vendor: CAST, Inc.
License: commercial
http://www.cast-inc.com/ip-cores/interfaces/i2c/index.html

UART

A universal asynchronous receiver/transmitter (UART) is an asynchronous receiver and transmitter that translates data between parallel and serial forms. UARTs are commonly used in conjunction with communication standards such as RS-422 or RS-485. The data format and transmission speeds are configurable, and electric signaling levels and methods, such as differential signaling, are typically handled by an external driver circuit. There are several open source and commercial implementations of the UART controller.

Vendor: OpenCores
License: GPL
http://opencores.org/project,mmuart

SPI, SPI Flash

Serial Peripheral Interface (SPI) is a full-duplex, synchronous channel that supports a four-wire interface (receive, transmit, clock and slave select) between one master and one or more slaves. SPI controllers are implemented as a stand-alone hardware module, or as an embedded software driver.

There is a class of Flash memories that use SPI. Xilinx uses SPI Flash as one of the FPGA configuration methods. After the configuration, the SPI Flash device can be accessed by the FPGA user logic. Xilinx provides a `xilflash` driver as part of the Embedded Development Kit (EDK) to access SPI Flash devices.

Vendor: OpenCores
License: GPL
http://opencores.org/project,spiflashcontroller

NOR Flash

There is no an available open source or commercial implementation of a NOR flash controller at the time of book writing. Xilinx `xilflash` driver can be used to access NOR flash devices.

NAND Flash

NAND Flash is a complex device, and there aren't many stand-alone hardware controllers that support it. Typically, a NAND Flash access is implemented as an embedded software driver.

Vendor: CAST Inc.
License: commercial
http://www.cast-inc.com/ip-cores/memories/nandflash-ctrl/index.html

CORDIC

The CORDIC (stands for COordinate Rotation DIgital Computer) is a popular algorithm used to evaluate many mathematical functions, such as trigonometric, hyperbolic, planar rotation, square root, logarithms, and others. There are several open source and commercial implementations of the CORDIC algorithm.

Vendor: Xilinx
License: commercial
http://www.xilinx.com/products/ipcenter/CORDIC.htm
Vendor: ASICS.ws
License: GPL
http://opencores.org/project,cordic

Floating Point Unit (FPU)

A hardware implementation of the Floating Point Unit (FPU) can significantly accelerate floating point arithmetic operations performed by an embedded processor. There are several open source and commercial FPU implementations. Xilinx provides an FPU core as part of the EDK.

Vendor: ASICS.ws
License: GPL
http://opencores.org/project,fpu

78
IMPROVING FPGA BUILD TIME

FPGA build is a multi-stage process of creating a bitstream from the RTL description and design constraints. Performing FPGA builds is a time and resource consuming process. Building a large FPGA design with high logic utilization and fast clocks can take several hours, or even a day. Building an FPGA design is also an ongoing activity that engineers spend a lot of time on during the design cycle. Reducing FPGA build time will increase the number of design turns and will allow faster debug and timing closure.

One approach to improve design build time is to profile steps comprising the build and focus on optimizing the ones that take most of the time. FPGA place and route is usually the longest build step. Design synthesis can also take up to several hours to complete for large designs, but it is typically faster than the place and route.

Build time optimization techniques include floorplanning the design, reducing routing congestion and logic utilization, adding timing constraints, using appropriate tool options and design methodology, changing coding style, upgrading build machine, and improving the build flow.

Floorplanning

Floorplanning FPGA designs generally improve build runtime and make it more consistent. It is recommended to floorplan not only large and complex designs, but also the ones with low logic utilization. It might seem counterintuitive, but in some cases it takes a very long time to build small designs targeting large FPGAs. Physical implementation tools might have too many degrees of freedom at their disposal, which results in a long time to converge on the best placement and routing.

After the design meets timing requirements, it is recommended to lock down all used BRAMs and DSPs. Locked BRAMs and DSPs will act as a seed to guide physical implementation tools to place and route the rest of the logic resources. Exporting area constraints of all BRAM and DSP instances used in the designs can be easily performed by Xilinx PlanAhead tool. However, it is not desirable to lock down individual registers and LUTs, since that can lead to over-constraining the design and worse runtime results. Different floorplanning techniques are discussed in Tips #95 and 96.

High design congestion and logic utilization

Designs with high logic utilization and routing congestion exhibit increasingly long place and route times. Virtex-6 Routing Optimization white paper [1] offers several recommendations on how to detect and reduce high routing congestion. It is possible to build a design with logic utilization levels approaching 100%. However, highly utilized designs don't leave enough room for place and route tools to perform optimizations in order to meet performance goals. The tools are forced to use less efficient logic placement and routing, which results in excessive runtime. It is recommended to keep the overall logic utilization of a design that uses high frequency clocks under 75%.

False path and multicycle path constraints

Constraining false and multicycle paths reduce the number of nets and relax performance requirements that place-and-route tools have to meet. It is important not to over-constrain the design by adding too many false and multicycle paths constraints, which can have an opposite effect and increase the runtime.

Tool options

Reducing place-and-route and optimization effort levels can have a significant effect on the runtime. Another important Xilinx MAP and PAR tool option to use is Multi-threading (-mt), which takes advantage of multiple CPUs to perform the place-and-route.

Reset scheme

Changing synchronous reset of the registers to asynchronous relaxes performance requirements and may lead to a noticeable place-and-route runtime improvement. Tip #29 discusses several tradeoffs of using different reset schemes.

Synthesis tools

Design synthesis can be a significant contributor to the overall build runtime. It might take from less than a minute up to several hours for large FPGA designs to complete the synthesis. Third party synthesis tools offer various optimization options that affect synthesis runtime. The netlist produced by a synthesis tool might also have a positive effect on the runtime of a subsequent place-and-route.

Although improving build runtime is usually not the main reason for changing a synthesis tool, that criteria might have some weight in the process of selecting a new synthesis tool.

Upgrading to a more powerful build server

An effective way to improve build runtime is by using a dedicated build server with a more powerful multi-core CPU, larger amount of memory, and faster hard drive.

The following tables contain technical characteristics of a notebook and a build server, and runtime and memory utilization results of Xilinx memory controller core (MIG) built on those machines.

Table 1: Build machine characteristics

	Notebook	*Build server*
OS	32-bit Win XP	64-bit Ubuntu Linux
CPU	2-core Intel Pentium, 2GHz	12-core Intel i7 @ 3.33GHz
Memory	3GByte	16GByte
Hard drive	7200 RPM SATA	15K RPM SAS

Table 2: Build runtime and memory usage of a memory controller design

Design	*Xilinx memory controller, 250MHz, 978 slices, Virtex-6 LX75T-2*			
Build machine	64-bit Linux server		32-bit Win XP notebook	
Tool (ISE 12.4)	Time	Memory	Time	Memory
XST	31sec	790MB	1min 13sec	420MB
MAP	26sec	664MB	1min 54sec	371MB
PAR	52sec	768MB	1min 12sec	353MB

Another example is a design that contains eight instances of Ethernet CRC32 checker with 256-bit data width. That design has different characteristics than the memory controller. It is dominated by LUTs that implement XOR trees with longer combinatorial paths.

Table 3: Build runtime and memory use of a CRC32 design

Design	*Eight instances of CRC32 with 256-bit data width, 333MHz, 1918 slices, Virtex-6 LX130T-2*			
Build machine	64-bit Linux server		32-bit Win XP notebook	
Tool (ISE 12.4)	Time	Memory	Time	Memory
XST	25sec	439MB	52sec	180MB
MAP	2min 24sec	841MB	4min 44sec	410MB

| PAR | 7min 20sec | 822MB | 14min 52sec | 441MB |

Although both designs are relatively small, the difference in build times between the machines is significant for synthesis and physical implementation tools. Also, the tools have higher memory utilization on a build server compared to a notebook.

The above results are project- and tool-specific, and are intended only for illustrating the effect of build machine technical characteristics on the build runtime.

Independent benchmarks report that using Linux operating system results in 5-10% build runtime improvement using Xilinx tools compared to Windows running on the same machine.

Design methodology

Taking advantage of incremental design methodologies can reduce the build runtime. Xilinx PlanAhead supports hierarchical design partitioning [2]. Module instances with high logic utilization and timing critical paths can be assigned to a partition. Partition instructs synthesis and implementation tools to use previous implementation results of that module if it has not been modified. The runtime improvement is proportional to the amount logic preserved by partitions. PlanAhead GUI provides an interface to manage partitions.

Synopsys Synplify supports Compile Point synthesis flow, which is based on the traditional bottom-up design methodology with several improvements. The design is decomposed into smaller parts, or points, that are synthesized, constrained and optimized independently. Compile Point synthesis flow automates the process of maintenance and dependency tracking of those parts.

Improving build flow

Some build time improvement can be achieved by automating pre- and post-build tasks using a script: getting the latest code from the repository, incrementing build number, processing tool reports, sending email notifications to the build stakeholders, and archiving build results.

Processing tool reports is important to determine if the build is successful or not. An accompanied website contains a Perl script, named report_xplorer.pl, that performs analysis of the tool reports by searching for certain keywords such as "combinatorial loops", "unassigned IO", "timing score", "overmapped region", and others.

Resources

[1] Virtex-6 FPGA Routing Optimization Design Techniques
http://www.xilinx.com/support/documentation/white_papers/wp381_V6_Routing_Optimization.pdf

[2] Hierarchical Design Methodology Guide
http://www.xilinx.com/support/documentation/sw_manuals/xilinx12_1/Hierarchical_Design_Methodology_Guide.pdf

79
DESIGN AREA OPTIMIZATIONS: TOOL OPTIONS

This Tip discusses different synthesis and physical implementation tool options that can be used to reduce area utilization of a design. The tools make a lot of optimizations to achieve the best results by default. The effectiveness of different synthesis and physical implementation area optimization options to a large extent depends on the design and FPGA family. Engineers can experiment with tool options that are more applicable to a specific design to further improve area utilization.

It is important to analyze design utilization results using the default tool options first, and based on that information devise an optimization strategy and set realistic goals. Performing design area optimizations usually comes at a cost of increased delays and decreased performance. Therefore, the very first questions to answer are: what is the purpose of optimizing the area, and is it is worth the effort and lower design performance.

The following table lists some of the Xilinx XST synthesis and physical implementation tool options that can be used for design area optimization.

Table 1: Tool options used during area optimization

Option	Flag	Tool
Optimization goal	-opt_mode	XST
Keep hierarchy	-keep_hierarchy	XST
Maximum fanout	-max_fanout	XST
Register duplication	-register_duplication	XST,MAP
Resource sharing	-resource_sharing	XST
Slice utilization ratio	-slice_utilization_ratio	XST
BRAM utilization ratio	-bram_utilization_ratio	XST
DSP utilization ratio	-dsp_utilization_ratio	XST
Use DSP block	-use_dsp48	XST
Reduce control sets	-reduce_control_set	XST
Optimize primitives	-optimize_primitives	XST

Equivalent register removal	-equivalent_register_removal	XST, MAP
Register balancing	-register_balancing	XST
LUT combining	-lc	XST
FSM encoding	-fsm_encoding	XST
Global optimization	-global_opt	MAP
Slice packing	-c	MAP
Combinatorial logic optimization	-logic_opt	MAP

Information on the effectiveness of using different optimization options is provided in a Physical Synthesis Report (PSR). The following figure shows a summary section of the PSR report.

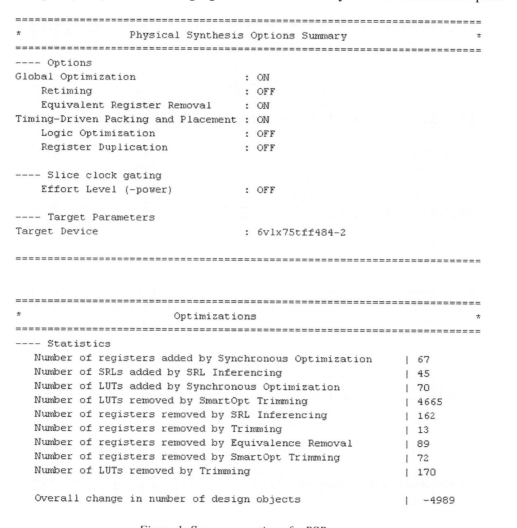

Figure 1: Summary section of a PSR report

Optimization options

Both synthesis and physical implementation tools perform optimizations that affect logic utilization. XST provides the Optimization Goal option (-opt_mode area) that gives priority to the synthesis strategy to reduce the total amount of logic. Xilinx MAP performs several pre- and post-mapping optimizations: equivalent register removal, combinatorial logic optimization, and global optimization.

Resource sharing

Resource sharing allows the use of the same arithmetic operations by independent functions. Resource sharing achieves the opposite effect to the logic replication option. To achieve the best area optimization results, it is recommended to use this option for designs with a lot of mathematical functions.

Setting maximum fanout

Maximum fanout is a synthesis option that limits the fanout of nets or signals. Lowering the fanout limit will cause replication of source registers, and can improve design performance. However, it will have the opposite effect on the logic utilization.

Flattening design hierarchy

Flattening design hierarchy is a synthesis option. It allows the tool to perform optimizations across module boundaries, which can result in more efficient combining of logic operations, and overall area reduction.

FSM encoding

Finite State Machine (FSM) encoding can be controlled by a synthesis option. Changing FSM encoding can either improve or adversely affect logic utilization. Large state machines can be implemented as an LUT using BRAM. Different FSM encoding options are discussed in Tip #27.

Slice packing

Slice packing ratio is a MAP option (-c) that reduces the total number of slices that MAP can target. For example, setting that option to 80% will instruct the placement tool to use no more than 80% of available slices.

Synthesis tools

FPGA synthesis tools employ different area optimization techniques to produce a more compact netlist. That can have a significant impact on the final design utilization. The quality of results might be important criteria in the process of selecting a new synthesis tool.

Example

Xilinx memory controller (MIG) design was used to illustrate the effect of different synthesis and implementation options on the design area. The design was built for Virtex-6 LX75 FPGA with -2 speed grade.

The following tables show the logic utilization results of seven experiments conducted with the various options.

Table 2: Experiment description

Experiment	Description
1	Default synthesis and physical implementation options
2	Changed XST -keep_hierarchy option to YES
3	Changed XST -opt_mode option to AREA Using this option results in synthesis error.
4	Changed XST -register_duplication option to NO
5	Changed XST -equivalent_register_removal option to NO
6	Changed MAP -global_optimization option to ON
7	Changed MAP –c option to 50

The following table shows post-synthesis logic utilization estimates for the design. Note that the number of slices is not available at this stage.

Table 3: Post-synthesis logic utilization estimates

Experiment	Number of LUTs	Number of registers	Number of control sets
1	2856	2354	198
2	3073	2354	292
3	Not available: using this option results in synthesis error		
4	2864	2284	190
5	2883	2386	324
6	2856	2354	198
7	2856	2354	198

The following table shows the area utilization of the design after place-and-route.

Table 4: Post-place-and-route logic utilization results

Experiment	Number of slices	Number of LUTs	Number of registers	Number of control sets
1	978	2579	2343	201
2	1269	2783	2347	218
3	Not available: using this option results in synthesis error			
4	1043	2634	2273	193
5	1075	2684	2350	326
6	1018	2772	2180	119
7	978	2579	2343	201

Even after experimenting with a limited number of XST and MAP options, the results allow several interesting observations.

In this particular design, using -opt_mode=area option resulted in synthesis failure. Experiments with other designs that have different characteristics show that synthesis or physical implementation might fail when a certain combination of options is used.

The difference between post-synthesis and post- place-and-route results of LUT and register utilization indicates the effectiveness of the MAP optimization. For example, enabling -global_optimization MAP option in experiment 6 reduced the number of LUTs from 2856 to 2772.

There is a significant difference in LUT, register, and slice utilization when using different options. Slice utilization ranges between 978 and 1269. The variation is 26%.

Changing MAP slice packing -c ratio from 100 to 50 in experiment 7 didn't have any effect on logic utilization. The reason is that the utilization of this particular design is too low for this option to take any effect.

All projects, code, and reports for the above examples are available on the accompanying website.

80
DESIGN AREA OPTIMIZATIONS: CODING STYLE

Priority encoders

It is generally recommended to use `case` statements instead of nested `if-else` constructs and conditional "?" operators, which are synthesized as priority structures. Synthesis tools usually create priority-independent logic when using `case` statements, which have lower combinatorial delays and better performance. However, using `case` statements can increase logic utilization. The following are three examples that implement the same logic function using nested conditional operators, and `case` statements.

```verilog
module example1( input [5:0] sel,
   input [3:0] a,b,
   output reg [3:0] result);
  always @(*) begin
    result =  sel[0] ? a + b : sel[1] ? a - b :
              sel[2] ? a & b : sel[3] ? a ^ b :
              sel[4] ? ~a : ~ b;
    if(~|sel)
        result = 4'b0;
    end // always
endmodule // example1

module example2( input [5:0] sel,
   input [3:0] a,b,
   output reg [3:0] result);
  always @(*) begin
    casex(sel)
      6'bxxxxx1: result = a + b;
      6'bxxxx10: result = a - b;
      6'bxxx100: result = a & b;
      6'bxx1000: result = a ^+ b;
      6'bx10000: result = ~a;
      6'b100000: result = ~b;
      default:   result = 4'b0;
```

```verilog
      endcase
    end // always
endmodule // example2
module example3 (input [5:0] sel,
    input [3:0] a,b,
    output reg [3:0] result);
  always @(*) begin
    result = 4'b0;
    casex(1'b1)
      sel[0]: result = a + b;
      sel[1]: result = a - b;
      sel[2]: result = a & b;
      sel[3]: result = a ^+ b;
      sel[4]: result = ~a;
      sel[5]: result = ~b;
    endcase
  end // always
endmodule // example3
```

The following table shows the logic utilization of three examples after physical implementation.

Table 1: Logic utilization of priority encoder examples

Module	Partition	Slices*	Slice Reg	LUTs
priority_encoder/		4/26	0/0	1/46
+example1		8/8	0/0	13/13
+example2		6/6	0/0	16/16
+example3		8/8	0/0	16/16
+priority_encoder		0/0	0/0	0/0

The first example uses the least LUTs, but it's packed less efficiently into slices compared to the two other examples.

Reset scheme

The choice of the reset scheme can have a significant effect on a design area. Registers in Xilinx FPGAs can be configured to have either asynchronous or synchronous reset, but not both. Trying to implement both types of resets will result in a less efficient logic, as illustrated in the following example.

```verilog
module reg_set_reset(input clk, reset,set,
```

```verilog
                   input clk_en,
                   input [3:0] data_in,
                   output reg data_out);
  always @(posedge clk , posedge reset)
    if(reset)
       data_out <= 1'b0;
    else if(set)
       data_out <= 1'b1;
    else if(clk_en)
       data_out <= &data_in;
    else
       data_out <= data_out;
endmodule // reg_set_reset
```

Synthesis tool will add an extra LUT to implement a synchronous reset. That will result in the total logic utilization of 2 LUTs.

Unnecessary use of resets can prevent the inference of SRL primitives and prevent synthesis tools from performing different area optimizations. It is recommended not to reset registers when it is not required, such as for power-up initialization.

Tip #29 discusses other tradeoffs of using different reset schemes.

Control sets

A control set is defined as a unique group of clock, clock enable, and reset signals connected to a register. All registers in a Xilinx Virtex-6 slice share the same control set: there is only one clock, clock enable, and reset signal that can enter a slice. That restriction has a major implication on slice packing and the overall logic utilization. Registers with different clock, clock enable, or reset cannot be packed into the same slice. The following example illustrates how mixing synchronous and asynchronous resets affects slice packing because of the control set restriction.

```verilog
module control_sets1(input clk, areset, sreset,
                     input clk_en,
                     input [5:0] data_in1,data_in2,
                     output reg data_out1,data_out2);
  always @(posedge clk, posedge areset)
    if(areset)
          data_out1 <= 1'b0;
    else
          data_out1 <= clk_en ? &data_in1 : data_out1;
  always @(posedge clk)
    if(sreset)
          data_out2 <= 1'b0;
```

```
      else
            data_out2 <= clk_en ? &data_in2 : data_out2;
endmodule // control_sets1
# both registers are constrained into a single slice
INST "data_out1" LOC = SLICE_X28Y2;
INST "data_out2" LOC = SLICE_X28Y2;
INST "data_out1" IOB = FALSE;
INST "data_out2" IOB = FALSE;
```

Attempting to place both `data_out1` and `data_out2` registers into the same slice will result in the following placement error.

```
Section 1 - Errors
------------------
ERROR:Pack:2811 - Directed packing was unable to obey the user design
   constraints (LOC=SLICE_X28Y2) which requires the combination of the symbols
   listed below to be packed into a single SLICEL component.

   The directed pack was not possible because: A flop using synchronous
   set/reset cannot be combined with one that uses asynchronous set/reset.

   The symbols involved are:
         FLOP symbol "data_out1" (Output Signal = data_out1_OBUF)
         FLOP symbol "data_out2" (Output Signal = data_out2_OBUF)
```

Figure 1: Control set restriction error produced during MAP

Using either synchronous or asynchronous reset for both registers will fix the problem.

MAP report includes the information of how many slices are lost due to control set restrictions. This is illustrated in the following figure.

```
Slice Logic Distribution:
   Number of occupied Slices:                        1 out of    6,822    1%
   Number of LUT Flip Flop pairs used:               2
      Number with an unused Flip Flop:               0 out of    2        0%
      Number with an unused LUT:                     0 out of    2        0%
      Number of fully used LUT-FF pairs:             2 out of    2      100%
   Number of unique control sets:                    1
   Number of slice register sites lost
      to control set restrictions:                   6 out of   54,576    1%
```

Figure 2: Lost slices due to control set restrictions

XST provides a Reduce Control Set (-reduce_control_set) option that attempts to reduce the number of control sets in the design by performing logic conversion.

Using CFGLUT5 primitive

CFGLUT5 is a dynamically reconfigurable 5-input loop-up table primitive available in Xilinx FPGAs. It enables changing LUT configuration during circuit operation. Using CFGLUT5 primitive can save a lot of logic resources. The following example shows how a CFGLUT5 can be used to implement an 80-bit pattern matcher.

```
module pattern_match1(input clk,clk_en,cfg_in,
                      input [79:0] pattern_in,
                      input [79:0] pattern_mask,
                      input [79:0] pattern_match,
                      output [31:0] match_cfglut);
  wire [16:0] cfg_local;
  assign cfg_local[0] = cfg_in;
  // 80-bit pattern matcher using CFGLUT5 primitive
  genvar ll;
  generate
    for (ll = 0; ll < 16; ll = ll + 1) begin: gen_cfglut
         CFGLUT5 cfglut(
             .I4 (pattern_in[ll*5+4]),
             .I3 (pattern_in[ll*5+3]),
             .I2 (pattern_in[ll*5+2]),
             .I1 (pattern_in[ll*5+1]),
             .I0 (pattern_in[ll*5]),
             .O5 (match_cfglut[ll*2+1]),
             .O6 (match_cfglut[ll*2]),
             .CE (clk_en),
             .CLK(clk),
             .CDI(cfg_local[ll]),
             .CDO(cfg_local[ll+1]));
    end
  endgenerate // gen_cfglut
endmodule // pattern_match1
```

This example requires 16 cascaded CFGLUT5 primitives to perform an 80-bit pattern match. LUT configuration is changed using CDI and CDO ports. An alternative way to implement an equivalent pattern matcher is shown below. It directly compares 80-bit input data with a mask and match values.

```
module pattern_match2(input clk, reset,
                      input [79:0] pattern_in,
```

```
                      input [79:0] pattern_mask,
                      input [79:0] pattern_match,
                      output reg   match);
   always @(posedge clk)
      if(reset)
         match <= 1'b0;
      else
         match <=
               (pattern_in & pattern_mask) == pattern_match;
endmodule // pattern_match2
```

Although both implementations are functionally the same, the logic utilization is not. Both examples were built for Xilinx Spartan-6 LX25 FPGA. Using CFGLUT5 requires 16 LUTs, which are packed into 5 slices during physical implementation. The second example utilizes 53 LUTs, one register, and is packed into 30 slices. In addition, it would also require 180 registers to store the input data, mask, and match values.

Balanced use of FPGA resources

Although Xilinx FPGAs have different resources – registers, LUTs, BRAMs, and DSPs – registers and LUTs are usually utilized the most. A good area optimization strategy is to try to convert some of the logic that uses registers and LUTs to BRAMs, DSP, and Shift Register LUT (SRL) primitives. BRAMs can be used to implement state machines, look-up tables, or even shift registers and counters. DSP can replace logic that implements arithmetic and logic operations. SRL can replace multiple registers that implement shift registers and delays.

Designs that require a lot of embedded memory, such as processors with large caches, will have highly utilized BRAM resources. Some of the BRAMs can be converted into Distributed RAMs that are implemented using LUTs.

ASIC designs ported to FPGA are usually LUT-dominated: the ratio of registers to LUTs is heavily biased towards the LUTs. That leaves a lot of unused registers, and results in inefficient packing into slices. Finding ways to convert some of the registers into slices, for example by performing combinatorial logic optimization, will result in the overall area reduction.

81

DESIGN POWER OPTIMIZATIONS

With the demand for better energy efficiency, lowering FPGA power consumption is often at the top of the list of design criteria, along with cost, logic capacity, and performance. High FPGA power consumption can lead to lower device reliability due to high junction temperature, higher system cost due to large power supplies, and more complex PCB design. Optimizing FPGA power consumption is a system-level effort that encompasses system architecture, careful component selection, PCB and logic design, and smart use of low-power features of synthesis and physical implementation tools.

Total FPGA power consumption consists of static and dynamic components. Dynamic power consumption is the result of charging and discharging of the CMOS gate capacitance during switching between logic zero and one states. A simple model of dynamic power consumption is given in the following equation:

$$P = C \cdot V^2 \cdot F \cdot A$$

C is the total CMOS gate load capacitance that needs to be charged or discharged with every transition. V is the supply voltage to the gate. F is the operating frequency. A is the activity factor, which corresponds to the overall toggle rate.

Static power is consumed due to the leakage of currents across gates and from drain to source in CMOS transistors. As transistor dimensions shrink and threshold voltages decrease, leakage becomes a more dominant portion of the total power consumption. Leakage is also sensitive to temperature variations, and therefore, not uniform across the die. Static power depends on the device family, size, and junction temperature.

FPGA power consumption varies significantly in configured and non-configured states. When the FPGA transitions from a non-configured to a configured state, it draws excessive power, which can shut down power supplies if the PCB power distribution scheme is not properly designed. Designers should also consult FPGA datasheet to determine the power consumed during FPGA configuration.

The methodology to decrease FPGA power consumption is to reduce factors that contribute to dynamic and static power components.

Static power consumption increases with the temperature. As FPGA heats up, it causes increased transistor leakage currents. Reducing junction temperature by using fans, heat sinks, or design modifications helps reduce static power. Another option is reducing voltage levels of the IOs. FPGA IOs are organized into groups called banks. Each bank requires a separate power supply. An effective way to reduce static power is maximizing the number of unused and unpowered banks.

Decreasing dynamic power can be achieved by:
- Minimizing gate load capacitance C by reducing the amount of logic and minimizing interconnect between the logic gates.
- Reducing FPGA operating voltages.
- Reducing operating frequencies.
- Reducing the overall toggle rate of the design.

FPGA selection

FPGA selection has a significant impact on design power consumption. Xilinx Virtex-6 and Spartan-6 FPGA families have a special -1L speed grade option for low-power applications, which requires lower core voltage. FPGAs with smaller die size and lower pin count consume less power. Spartan FPGAs support a special low-power suspend mode.

PCB design

Factors that significantly affect power consumption are the number of FPGA IOs and their characteristics: IO voltage levels, drive strength, slew rate, single-ended or differential type, and terminations. As an example, a 64-bit bus with external 100Ω terminations and powered by 2.5V will dissipate $64 \times 2.5^2/100 = 4W$ of power. Using internal FPGA terminations, such as Xilinx DCI (digitally controlled impedance) can simplify board design by not requiring external terminations, but significantly increase power consumption.

Other good PCB design practices to reduce the overall power consumption include avoiding resistive loads, grounding unused FPGA pins, and taking advantage of the on-die decoupling capacitors.

XST synthesis options

XST provides -power option, which enables synthesis techniques to reduce dynamic power consumption

MAP and PAR options

MAP and PAR have -power option, which enables placement and routing optimizations to reduce dynamic power consumption. The main disadvantage of enabling this option is increased runtime and decreased design performance. -activityfile option allows providing an optional switching activity data file to guide power optimizations.

Physical Synthesis Report (PSR) contains optimization details performed by the tools.

Clock gating

FPGA designers can take advantage of clock gating techniques to reduce the average toggle rate, which contributes to the dynamic power consumption. Clocks that drive logic, embedded memory, SerDes, and other FPGA primitives can be disabled when their operation is not required.

Disabling unused functional blocks

A substantial power reduction can be achieved by deasserting enable inputs to modules that use Xilinx BRAMs, such as RAMs, ROMs, and FIFOs, when they're not accessed. Other functional blocks that can be disabled are SerDes transceivers, and large IP cores such as Ethernet MAC and PCI Express interface.

Embedded software optimizations

Many FPGA designs include software running on embedded processor. An often overlooked method to reduce FPGA power is by implementing a few embedded software optimizations. One method is to enter sleep or idle mode where the processor doesn't execute the instructions. During sleep mode the processor doesn't perform accesses to external memory or using peripheral devices, such as Ethernet controller, which consumes power. An external interrupt or an expired watchdog timer can wake up the processor when required. More sophisticated power optimization methods include slowing down the processor clock based on the utilization. Power optimization in embedded designs is an active research area, and there are several more methods that can be borrowed to FPGA designs.

Resources

[1] Using Digitally Controlled Impedance, Xilinx Application Note XAPP863
http://www.xilinx.com/support/documentation/application_notes/xapp863.pdf

[2] H. Hassan and M. Anis, *"Low-Power Design of Nanometer FPGAs: Architecture and EDA"*, Morgan Kaufmann, 2009

[3] Virtex-5 FPGA System Power Design Considerations, Xilinx White Paper WP285
http://www.xilinx.com/support/documentation/white_papers/wp285.pdf

82

BRINGING-UP AN FPGA DESIGN

The main requirement during FPGA design bring up is being systematic. It requires following a set of checks, and meticulously testing each and every functionality module in the design before concluding that everything is working and moving to the production phase.

The following figure shows an example of FPGA design bring up sequence. The details can vary between projects, but the general flow is similar: develop board bring up procedure, checks before and after board power up, configuring FPGAs, unit-level tests, system-level tests, migration to the production phase.

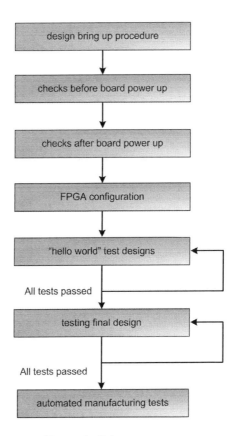

Figure 1: Bring-up sequence

Developing a design bring up procedure

Developing a detailed design bring up procedure is important in order to ensure that the design bring up work is systematic, and the range of tests is comprehensive. The procedure documentation can be reused later on to document the manufacturing tests.

Typically, the procedure is developed by both PCB and FPGA design teams.

Checks before board power up

There are two types of checks to perform before board power up: visual inspection, and shorts.

Visual inspection of the board is focusing on the mechanical aspects: all the electronic components are soldered; there are no solder bridges and no visible bad solder joints; all ground, power pins are connected.

Shorted circuits: check for shorted circuits on all power rails coming in and out of all voltage regulators. It's not enough to only check for shorted main power.

Checks after board power up

Checks to perform after the board power up are categorized as follows: voltage levels, power sequencing, power consumption, clocks, resets, heat levels, mechanical failures.

Voltage levels: check that voltages on all power supply rails are within the acceptable range.

Monitor for voltage changes – sudden spikes or drops – when operating condition change. For example, FPGA is configured, or an external Ethernet device is plugged in.

Power supply sequencing: check that power is supplied to all power rails in the expected sequence.

Check that power consumption on all power supply rails is within the expected range. Different ways to instrument the board to measure power consumption is described in Tip #83.

Use an oscilloscope to observe the quality of clocks. Noisy clocks can cause a lot of intermittent design problems that are difficult to troubleshoot.

Check for the correct reset sequence. Releasing the reset in incorrect order can cause different race conditions that are difficult to troubleshoot.

Signal integrity checks: there is a wide range of checks related to signal integrity. Use an oscilloscope to observe the quality of differential signals, and signals that require terminations, such as memory interfaces.

Check the temperatures of electronic components that consume a lot of power: FPGAs, processors, voltage regulators. Don't use your hands. There are cheap and accurate remote temperature sensors.

Mechanical failures: check that board remains functional after applying mild mechanical pressure. It is difficult to quantify the amount of pressure you should use. That depends on the project. Boards that are in harsh environments, such as military aircrafts, are subjected to different levels of mechanical stress than boards for test and measurement equipment. However, if simply moving the board, or touching an electronic component to check the temperature causes the board to fail, that indicates a mechanical problem.

FPGA Configuration

At this point in the design bring up, the sequence of the FPGAs are ready to be configured. The configuration can be performed using JTAG or using one of the SelectMAP modes implemented on board. JTAG method provides more visibility into the configuration process. There are two outcomes of the FPGA configuration: either it successfully completed, or it failed during one of the steps. Debugging FPGA configuration issues presents unique challenges. Tip #85 provides more detailed discussion on troubleshooting FPGA configuration issues.

"Hello World" tests

In the software world there is a famous "Hello World" program. All it does is print a "Hello World" diagnostic message. The importance of working a "Hello World" program is that it proves that the many parts of the system work. One of the FPGA equivalents of "Hello World" is a simple design that toggles a pin to blink an LED. Being able to blink an LED means that an FPGA can be configured, that the clock is coming into the design, and the FPGA is up and running.

"Hello World" can be a metaphor for various unit-level tests. A unit-level test focuses on comprehensively testing specific functional module. Some examples are:

Ethernet tests: MDIO, PHY interface (RGMII, SGMII, or other), 10Mbs/100Mbs/1Gbs configurations, performance tests

I2C, UART

Memory tests: DDR memories, asynchronous RAMs

Flashes and other non-volatile memories: SPI, parallel flash, EERPOM

GPIO tests

Each unit test can be implemented as a separate FPGA design. That has several advantages, such as faster build time, and easy isolation of a problem.

Testing the final design

After all "hello world" tests pass, it is time to test the final FPGA design. This is a system-level test that focuses on proper integration of all functional modules in the design. It can uncover new problems which are different from the unit-level tests.

Automated manufacturing tests

After all tests have passed, the next step is to develop a set of manufacturing tests that can be run automatically on each production board. Manufacturing tests can be largely based on the tests performed during the design bring up. Manufacturing tests have to run reasonably fast, be mostly non-interactive, and not require a lot of product knowledge. Most likely they're performed by a person unfamiliar with the product and in a remote facility. The procedures to run manufacturing tests have to be well documented.

83
PCB INSTRUMENTATION

Designers use different printed circuit board (PCB) instrumentation to debug boards with FPGAs. System Monitor is a Xilinx specific instrumentation. Test points, JTAG connectors, MICTOR, and voltage and current monitors are generic.

System Monitor board instrumentation

The following figure shows System Monitor dedicated pins and a board connection diagram using internal and on-chip voltage reference.

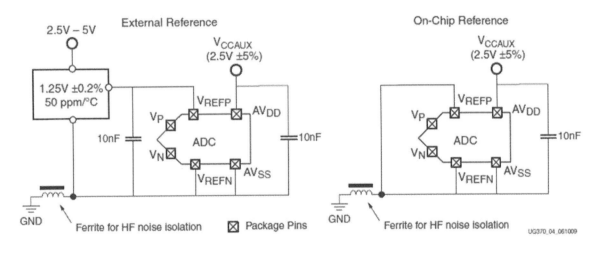

Figure 1: SystemMonitor board connection diagram (source: Xilinx SystemMonitor User Guide)

System Monitor has six dedicated pins. V_p and V_n provide a dedicated differential analog input channel. V_{refp} and V_{refn} pins are used to access external reference voltage. AV_{dd} and AV_{ss} pins are used to decouple power supplies for the System Monitor analog to digital (ADC) circuits. Auxiliary analog inputs, $V_{auxp}[15:0]$ and $V_{auxn}[15:0]$, are additional analog inputs shared with regular IO pins and have lower input bandwidth than dedicated V_p and V_n.

V_p / V_n and $V_{auxp}[15:0]$ / $V_{auxn}[15:0]$ can be driven by any unipolar or bipolar measurement source, as shown in the following figure.

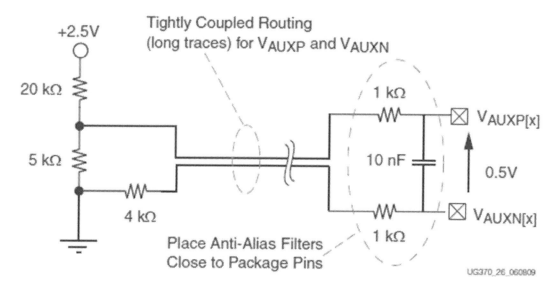

Figure 2: Connecting Vaux pins to a measurement source (source: Xilinx SystemMonitor User Guide)

System Monitor operation is covered in more detail in Tip #88.

Test points

A test point is a hole or via in the PCB used to attach a multimeter or oscilloscope probe to measure a signal at that point.

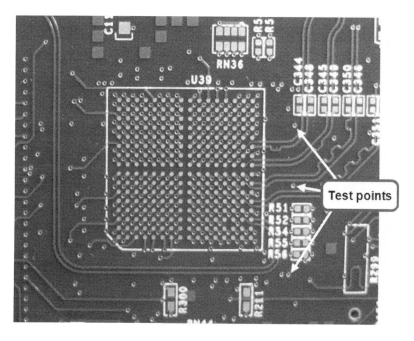

Figure 3: PCB test points

JTAG connector

JTAG connector is used by Xilinx ChipScope or iMPACT software for FPGA configuration, for accessing System Monitor, and for using integrated logic analyzer (ILA).

Chipscope operation is covered in more detail in Tip #86.

Matched Impedance Connectors (MICTOR)

As the name suggests, MICTOR is a special connector that provides impedance matching. Probing a high-speed signal without matched impedance can cause reflections and distort the measurement results and the signal itself. MICTOR is typically used to connect external logic analyzer equipment.

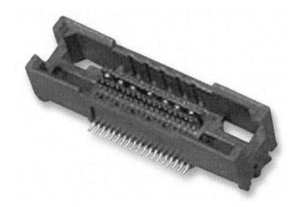

Figure 4: MICTOR connector (source: Tyco Electronics)

Monitoring DDR memory interfaces presents a special challenge. DDR memories are high speed and high pinout devices, and they are often placed very close to FPGA. In many cases, there is no easy way to access DDR interface signals. An invaluable tool is a DDR DIMM bus probe that allows passive probing of the signals.

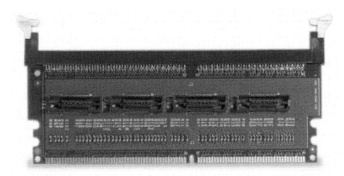

Figure 5: DDR DIMM Mictor bus probe (Source: ByteTools)

Voltage monitors

System Monitor provides V_{ccint} and V_{ccaux} voltage measurements on Xilinx FPGAs. To measure other on-board voltages, dedicated ADC chips can be used. The ADC output can be connected to one of the System Monitor V_p/V_n or $V_{auxp}[15:0]/V_{auxn}[15:0]$ pins. Some voltage regulators, such as LTC3562 from Linear Technology, have an integrated voltage controller that can be accessed from the I^2C interface.

Current monitors

Unlike voltage, current cannot be measured directly. There are dedicated current monitoring IC (for example, the Maxim MAX4374) that provide overcurrent or undercurrent monitors and overcurrent protection.

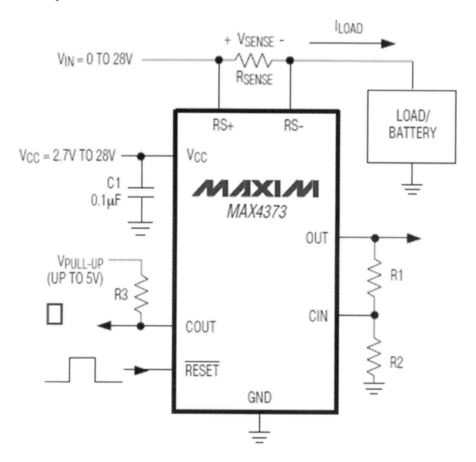

Figure 6: MAX4374 operating circuit (Source: Maxim Corporation)

A simpler method is adding a very small, typically 0.02Ω resistor in series to each of the power supply rails. Measuring the voltage across that resistor will also provide a current according to the Ohm's law: `I=V/R=V/0.02`

84
PROTOCOL ANALYZERS AND EXERCISERS

Almost any non-trivial FPGA design utilizes one or more communication protocols to interface with the peripheral devices. As the name suggests, Protocol Analyzers is a class of test equipment that helps troubleshoot protocols problems. For simpler protocols like I2C, developers can get around by using an oscilloscope, or a logic analyzer. That is not feasible for more complex, multi-layer protocols, such as USB or PCI Express.

Although protocols vary in speed and complexity, protocol analyzers share some of the common features: capture memory, triggering, filtering, and packet-based traffic display.

Protocol exerciser is a supporting tool which maximizes the benefit of passive capturing and analysis of the traffic. Protocol exerciser can force system under test to operate in varying conditions by generating greatest variety of protocol data. The exerciser allows users to reliably recreate an error condition by replicating the traffic between system under test and a real device.

An integrated protocol analyzer/exerciser system can be used in many situations: stress tests, device response to protocol error injections, compliance tests, and system characterization.

The following table lists popular protocol analyzers and exercisers for some of the commonly used protocols.

Table 1: protocol analyzers

Protocol / version, speed	*Vendor*	*URL*
Ethernet 10Mbs, 100Mbs, 1Gbs	Wireshark	http://www.wireshark.org
USB 1.1, 2.0, 3.0	SerialTek LeCroy Ellisys	http://serialtek.com http://lecroy.com http://www.ellisys.com
PCI Express gen1, gen2	LeCroy Agilent	http://www.home.agilent.com
SAS/SATA 1.5, 3, 6Gbs	SerialTek LeCroy JDS Uniphase	http://www.jdsu.com

Protocol / version, speed	Vendor	URL
I2C	Corelis	http://www.corelis.com
SPI	Beagle	http://www.totalphase.com
Bluetooth	LeCroy Ellisys Frontline	http://www.fte.com

85

TROUBLESHOOTING FPGA CONFIGURATION

FPGA configuration is a complex, multi-stage process, and often requires a significant effort to ensure its reliable operation in the lab and in the field under different conditions. There is a number of arcane and hard to debug problems that can cause FPGA configuration to fail, starting with poor signal integrity on a PCB to an incorrectly programmed bitstream. A good methodology for troubleshooting issues encountered during FPGA configuration is employing a systematic approach and divide-and-conquer strategy. The idea is to identify different stages performed during the configuration process, and troubleshoot them one by one, starting from the beginning, instead of going in a backward direction. Those stages are specific to FPGA configuration mode and design implementation.

This Tip discusses several problems commonly encountered during the configuration, and offers a few recommendations on how to solve them. The FPGA configuration process is discussed in more detail in Tips #36 and 37.

The flow to troubleshoot FPGA configuration consists of three main steps:

- Troubleshooting PCB-related issues
- Using JTAG to configure FPGA
- Configuring FPGA using SelectMAP

PCB-related issues

Most FPGA configuration problems related to PCB can be debugged using standard lab equipment, such as an oscilloscope and logic analyzer that can operate at configuration interface frequencies. Xilinx Virtex-6 PCB Design Guide [2] is an excellent source on this information.

Operating conditions

Meeting FPGA operating conditions, such as correct supply voltages and temperature, is required not only for configuration, but also for correct FPGA operation in general. Designers should check correct V_{ccint} (core), V_{ccaux}, V_{cco}, and voltage levels on the rails powering FPGA banks.

Power sequencing

Incorrect power sequencing is another source of FPGA configuration problems. Configuration start has to be delayed until all FPGA power rails are stable and have reached correct operating voltages.

Power consumption profile

A PCB power scheme has to be designed to support a FPGA power consumption profile. The profile is uneven. FPGA consumes little power in unconfigured state. The power consumption increases during configuration. Finally, there is a jump in power consumption when FPGA enters the configured state. That requires an accurate power estimate, which is discussed in Tip #40.

Signal integrity

There are strict requirements on signal integrity of the configuration interface signals, such as PCB routing and terminations. For example, configuration clock (CCLK) in Virtex-6 FPGAs has to use LVCMOS IO standard with fast slew rate and 12mA current. CCLK trace should not have branching (directly routed between two points), and have 50Ω impedance. Proper attention should be paid to the signal integrity of configuration pins that are shared between the configuration and user logic.

Damaged FPGA

Damaged FPGA can be the reason behind failing configuration. It is not uncommon to damage an FPGA IO or fabric due to overvoltage during bringing up of a new design. Tip #89 discusses options to deal with damaged FPGAs.

Configuration clock

In master configuration modes FPGA is driving the CCLK. In Virtex-6 FPGAs CCLK has a maximum frequency of 100MHz and a tolerance level of 60%. Such a high tolerance can exceed the maximum frequency of an external non-volatile memory, and this should be taken into consideration during the memory selection and when choosing the configuration frequency.

Using JTAG

Using JTAG to perform FPGA configuration helps isolate a broad range of problems related to PCB-related issues, correct programming of the external non-volatile memory, and communicating with FPGA over SelectMAP interface. The bitstream can be programmed from either iMPACT or ChipScope tool. A subsequent reading of configuration status registers can provide valuable clues that help troubleshoot the problem. The following is the log produced by ChipScope that shows the status bits in configured and unconfigured FPGA states.

```
COMMAND: open_cable
INFO: Started ChipScope host (localhost:50001)
INFO: Successfully opened connection to server:
localhost:50001
INFO: Successfully opened Xilinx Platform USB Cable
INFO: Cable: Platform Cable USB, Port: USB21, Speed: 12 MHz
INFO: DEV:1 MyDevice1 (XC6VLX240T) is not configured
COMMAND: show_config_status 1
INFO:
```

Table 1: FPGA configuration status bits

Unconfigured FPGA state			Configured FPGA state		
Bit 31:	0	EFUSE_BUSY	Bit 31:	0	EFUSE_BUSY
Bit 30:	0		Bit 30:	0	
Bit 29:	0	BAD_PACKET	Bit 29:	0	BAD_PACKET
Bit 28:	0	HSWAP_EN	Bit 28:	0	HSWAP_EN
Bit 27:	0		Bit 27:	0	
Bit 26:	**1**	**BUS_WIDTH**	**Bit 26:**	**0**	**BUS_WIDTH**
Bit 25:	**0**	**BUS_WIDTH**	**Bit 25:**	**1**	**BUS_WIDTH**
Bit 24:	1	FS	Bit 24:	1	FS
Bit 23:	1	FS	Bit 23:	1	FS
Bit 22:	1	FS	Bit 22:	1	FS
Bit 21:	0		Bit 21:	0	
Bit 20:	**0**	**STARTUP_STATE**	**Bit 20:**	**1**	**STARTUP_STATE**
Bit 19:	0	STARTUP_STATE	Bit 19:	0	STARTUP_STATE
Bit 18:	0	STARTUP_STATE	Bit 18:	0	STARTUP_STATE
Bit 17:	0	MON_OT_ALARM	Bit 17:	0	MON_OT_ALARM
Bit 16:	0	SEC_VIOLATION	Bit 16:	0	SEC_VIOLATION
Bit 15:	0	ID_ERROR	Bit 15:	0	ID_ERROR
Bit 14:	**0**	**DONE**	**Bit 14:**	**1**	**DONE**
Bit 13:	**0**	**RELEASE_DONE**	**Bit 13:**	**1**	**RELEASE_DONE**
Bit 12:	1	INIT_B	Bit 12:	1	INIT_B
Bit 11:	1	INIT_COMPLETE	Bit 11:	1	INIT_COMPLETE
Bit 10:	0	MODE M2	Bit 10:	0	MODE M2
Bit 9:	1	MODE M1	Bit 9:	1	MODE M1
Bit 8:	0	MODE M0	Bit 8:	0	MODE M0
Bit 7:	**0**	**GHIGH_B**	**Bit 7:**	**1**	**GHIGH_B**
Bit 6:	**0**	**GWE**	**Bit 6:**	**1**	**GWE**
Bit 5:	**0**	**GTS_CFG_B**	**Bit 5:**	**1**	**GTS_CFG_B**
Bit 4:	**0**	**EOS**	**Bit 4:**	**1**	**EOS**
Bit 3:	1	DCI_MATCH	Bit 3:	1	DCI_MATCH
Bit 2:	1	DCM_LOCK	Bit 2:	1	DCM_LOCK

Unconfigured FPGA state				Configured FPGA state			
Bit 1:	0	PART_SECURED		Bit 1:	0	PART_SECURED
Bit 0:	0	CRC_ERROR		Bit 0:	0	CRC_ERROR

The differences between configured and unconfigured states are in BUS_WIDTH, which is undetermined before the configuration, STARTUP_STATE, DONE, EOS, and several other bits. The bit that indicates the configuration completion is End Of Sequence (EOS). A bit that can be set during failed configuration is CRC_ERROR, indicating bitstream corruption.

Configuring FPGA using SelectMAP

The following figure shows and example of SelectMAP interface timing.

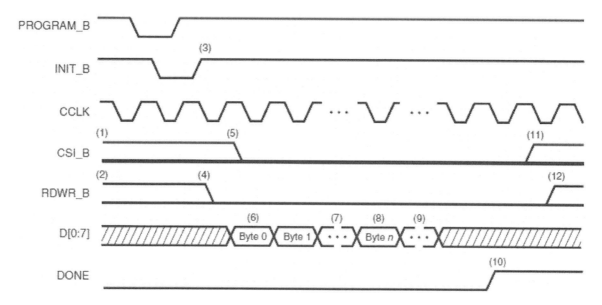

Figure 1: SelectMAP timing (source: Xilinx Virtex-6 Configuration User Guide)

Upon successful completion of the configuration, Xilinx FPGA asserts DONE output, and sets EOS bit in configuration status register. Some of the configuration problems during this stage are the incorrect use of SelectMAP signals, a corrupted bitstream, swapped bits or bytes, and incorrectly set options in the bitstream header. Another common problem is an incorrect bitstream format programmed into the configuration memory. Xilinx `bitgen`, the tool that produces the bitstream, supports three output formats: RBT in ASCII format, BIT, which includes the header, and BIN. Only BIN should be used for programming the FPGA over SelectMAP interface.

Fallback

Fallback is an optional configuration recovery mechanism invoked by FPGA when the configuration attempt fails. During fallback, FPGA attempts to use an alternative bitstream programmed at a known address in external configuration memory.

Configuration readback

Configuration readback is a feature that allows users to read FPGA configuration memory through SelectMAP, JTAG, or ICAP interfaces. Readback is another tool to troubleshoot and verify FPGA configuration.

Functional simulation

Designers can use JTAG_SIM_VIRTEX6 and SIM_CONFIG_V6 primitives, which provides simulation models of configuration controller. This allows performing functional simulation of configuration interfaces and components, which can help uncover some of the configuration issues.

Resources:

[1] Xilinx Virtex-6 FPGA Configuration
http://www.xilinx.com/products/design_resources/config_sol/v6/config_v6.htm

[2] Xilinx Virtex-6 PCB Design Guide
http://www.xilinx.com/support/documentation/user_guides/ug373.pdf

86
USING CHIPSCOPE

Xilinx ChipScope is a system of IP cores and software that can be used in place of test equipment, such as a logic analyzer and oscilloscope, to debug an FPGA design. ChipScope provides a variety of debug capabilities: integrated logic analyzer (ILA) to capture the data, Virtual IO (VIO) to inject short signal sequences into the design and monitor slowly changing signals in real time, and software to display and analyze the sample data. Compared with other test equipment, ChipScope is a cost-effective tool, and doesn't require an external header. It utilizes the same JTAG connector that is already present in most of the designs for FPGA configuration. ChipScope software is simple to use, and the addition of ILA and VIO cores into the design can be integrated into Xilinx design flow. ChipScope enables very fast iterative design debug and verification. However, it is not intended to replace functional simulation.

ChipScope primitives

There are three main cores used in a ChipScope system:

ILA

Integrated Logic Analyzer (ILA) consists of embedded FPGA memory to store captured samples and control logic to enable triggering, sample filtering, sequencers, and other features.

VIO

Virtual IO (VIO) provides virtual inputs and outputs. Virtual inputs connect to the user design and can change its logic state or inject a short signal sequence from the software. Virtual outputs are used to monitor slowly changing signals in real time.

ICON

Integrated Controller (ICON) is a wrapper around Xilinx BSCAN primitive that provides access to a JTAG port. It is used as an interface between JTAG and VIO/ILA cores.

The Xilinx CoreGen tool can be used to configure and generate a wrapper for ICON, ILA, and VIO primitives. The primitives can also be instantiated directly in the code. The following figure illustrates a ChipScope system block diagram, where two ILA and a VIO cores are connected to an ICON.

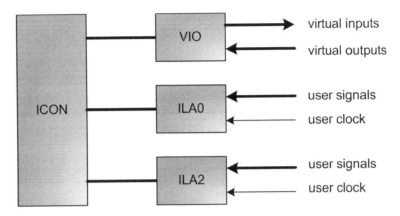

Figure 1: ChipScope system block diagram

In addition, ChipScope cores can be inserted into the synthesized design netlist from PlanAhead. This method saves synthesis time and leaves the original code unchanged. The FPGA Editor can be used to change clock, data, and trigger signals connected to ILA cores in the design after place-and-route.

Example

The following is a simple code example of using ChipScope ILA, VIO, and ICON cores. The example is built for a Xilinx ML605 development board with a Virtex-6 LX240T FPGA. There are two inputs connected to corresponding buttons that drive two LEDs. The LEDs are also connected to the outputs from a VIO core.

```
module chipscope(input btn0,btn1,
            output led0,led1,
            input sys_clk_in_p, sys_clk_in_n);
    wire clkin;
    wire [35:0] CONTROL0, CONTROL1;
    wire [1:0]  vio_sync_out;
    wire [7:0]  ILA_DATA;
    wire [3:0]  ILA_TRIG;

    // data and triggers to ILA
    assign ILA_DATA = {btn0,btn1,led0,led1};
    assign ILA_TRIG = {btn0,btn1,led0,led1};

    // LEDs are turned on by pushing a button or toggling VIO
    assign led0 = btn0 | vio_sync_out[0];
    assign led1 = btn1 | vio_sync_out[1];

    IBUFGDS clkin_buf (.I  (sys_clk_in_p),
```

```verilog
                        .IB (sys_clk_in_n),
                        .O  (clkin));

    // ICON core instantiation connected to ILA and VIO
    chipscope_icon icon (
            .CONTROL0(CONTROL0),
            .CONTROL1(CONTROL1));

    // VIO core instantiation
    chipscope_vio vio (
            .CONTROL(CONTROL0),
            .CLK(clkin),
            .ASYNC_IN({btn0,btn1}),
            .SYNC_OUT(vio_sync_out));

    // ILA core instantiation
    chipscope_ila
      ila (
            .CONTROL(CONTROL1),
            .CLK(clkin),
            .DATA(ILA_DATA),
            .TRIG0(ILA_TRIG[0]),
            .TRIG1(ILA_TRIG[1]),
            .TRIG2(ILA_TRIG[2]),
            .TRIG3(ILA_TRIG[3]));
endmodule // chipscope
```

```
# design constraints: pin locations and clock period
NET "btn0"    LOC = "A18"  ;
NET "btn1"    LOC = "H17"  ;
NET "led1"    LOC = "AD21" ;
NET "led0"    LOC = "AH28" ;

NET "sys_clk_in_p" DIFF_TERM = "TRUE";
NET "sys_clk_in_p" IOSTANDARD = LVDS_25;
NET "sys_clk_in_n" DIFF_TERM = "TRUE";
NET "sys_clk_in_n" IOSTANDARD = LVDS_25;
NET "sys_clk_in_p" LOC = J9;
NET "sys_clk_in_n" LOC = H9;

NET "sys_clk_in_p" TNM_NET = "sys_clk_in_p";
TIMESPEC TS_sys_clk_in_p = PERIOD "sys_clk_in_p" 5 ns;

NET "sys_clk_in_n" TNM_NET = "sys_clk_in_n";
TIMESPEC TS_sys_clk_in_n = PERIOD "sys_clk_in_n" 5 ns;
```

The following figure shows ChipScope software view of the ILA waveforms at the top, and the VIO inputs and outputs at the bottom.

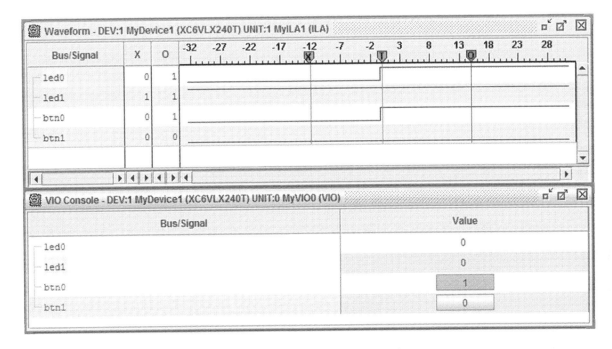

Figure 2: ChipScope VIO and ILA console views

The top view shows that `led0` and `btn0` signals change their state from zero to one at the trigger position. The bottom view depicts the state of `btn0` and `btn1` virtual inputs, and the status of `led0` and `led1` virtual outputs.

Remote Access

ChipScope software is designed as a client-server system. The client, which provides a user interface, can remotely access the server. Remote access offers convenience: The board can be located in the lab or another place, and be accessed from a client over the network. ChipScope server can be launched by calling `cse_server` command from Xilinx ISE installation. The server can communicate with the board using Xilinx or a third party JTAG cable adapter. Xilinx offers a USB-to-JTAG adapter. Catapult EJ-1 from ByteTools [2] is an Ethernet-to-JTAG adapter that allows ChipScope software to communicate with the board using a standard Ethernet cable.

ChipScope features

The following is the list of main ChipScope features.
- Configurable width and depth of captured data.

- Configurable number of trigger ports.
- Trigger condition sequencer, up to 16 levels deep.
- Triggering on rising, falling, or any edge of a signal.
- Triggering based on comparison result with a multi-bit value.
- Triggering based on event count.
- Triggering and data capture are synchronous to user clock.
- Support for multiple ILA cores.

There are several powerful ChipScope features that are well documented but nevertheless used less frequently.

- Storage qualification, which enables filtering of irrelevant samples.
- Trigger input from external equipment.
- Trigger output port, which can be used to trigger external test equipment or another ILA core.
- Accessing ChipScope using Tool Command Language (TCL) scripts. Scripting is convenient for automating the initialization, configuration, and monitoring of multiple boards

ChipScope restrictions and limitations

ChipScope ILA and VIO cores are implemented using regular FPGA logic, embedded memory, and routing resources, and therefore subject to the same limitations as the rest of the user design. Adding a probe from an IO, a LUT, or a register will require changing the routing of an existing design. That can have an adverse effect on timing. ChipScope ILA uses a substantial amount of FPGA embedded memory resources, which are shared with the rest of the design. That requires careful estimate of the ILA memory requirements. Large ILA cores might require floorplanning to lessen the impact on the build time in designs with high logic utilization. ILA cores using a high frequency clock need to meet timing constraints in order to provide valid results. Not meeting timing constraints by the ILA will have the same consequences as with any other synchronous logic: The data sampled by the clock will be unreliable.

It is a good design practice to always register sampled signals at the input to the ILA. That effectively decouples the probes from the rest of the design and also makes the timing closure easier. It avoids metastability problems when sampling asynchronous signals from an IO or an unrelated clock domain.

Developers should not expect to find the same signals in the post place-and-route design as in the original code. The original logic can undergo a number of transformations during synthesis and physical implementation: design hierarchy can be flattened and optimized across module boundaries, state machine encoding can be changed to improve performance, enabling retiming might move around registers and combinatorial logic, enabling global optimization might trim large functional blocks, registers can be replicated to reduce fanout, and the list can go on.

Another recommendation is not to directly connect state machine registers to the ILA inputs. Doing that prevents state machine encoding optimization by the synthesis tool. The following coding style can be used instead.

```
wire [1:0] ila_probe;
assign ila_probe[0] = (my_state_q == STATE_1);
assign ila_probe[1] = (my_state_q == STATE_2);
```

Estimating ChipScope ILA size

ChipScope ILA core consumes a lot of FPGA embedded memory resources, and therefore it is important to accurately estimate its storage requirements. The amount of used memory is a function of the number of samples and the data width. For example, capturing 1024 samples of 36-bit data requires a single 36 Kbit BRAM. If the clock frequency is 200MHz, or a 5ns period, 1024 samples are captured in 5.12us.

CoreGen also provides memory utilization when the ILA core is generated.

Resources

[1] Xilinx ChipScope portal
http://www.xilinx.com/tools/cspro.htm

[2] ByteTools Catapult Ethernet to JTAG cable
http://www.byte-tools.com/

87
USING FPGA EDITOR

Xilinx FPGA Editor is an invaluable tool to view, analyze, and make small changes to the implemented design at the lowest level of FPGA fabric. FPGA Editor can be used to quickly create small patches, such as adding pull-up resistor to an IO, changing memory contents, or modifying LUT equation. After making those changes, it is only required to execute `bitgen` to create a new bitstream, instead of running full build. That saves a lot of valuable development time. The following is a list of common tasks that can be performed by the FPGA Editor:

- Manually place and route critical components.
- Cross-probe design components with the Timing Analyzer.
- Design analysis
- Create a script that can be played back later on.
- Add or change an IO
- Change BRAM contents.
- Change LUT equations.
- Change IO properties
- Add design probes to examine signal states. Probes can be added to a ChipScope Integrated Logic Analyzer (ILA) and Virtual IO (VIO) cores or an external IO.

FPGA Editor can read post-MAP or post-PAR Native Circuit Description (NCD) file and Physical Constraints File (PCF).

Adding Probes to ChipScope ILA and VIO Cores

FPGA Editor allows easy addition, change, or removal of ChipScope ILA probes, triggers, and clock signals. The probes can be saved in a Probe Script File (.scr), and executed later using subsequent versions of the design.

Changing BRAM Content

FPGA Editor allows changing Block RAM (BRAM) contents. This is illustrated in the following figure.

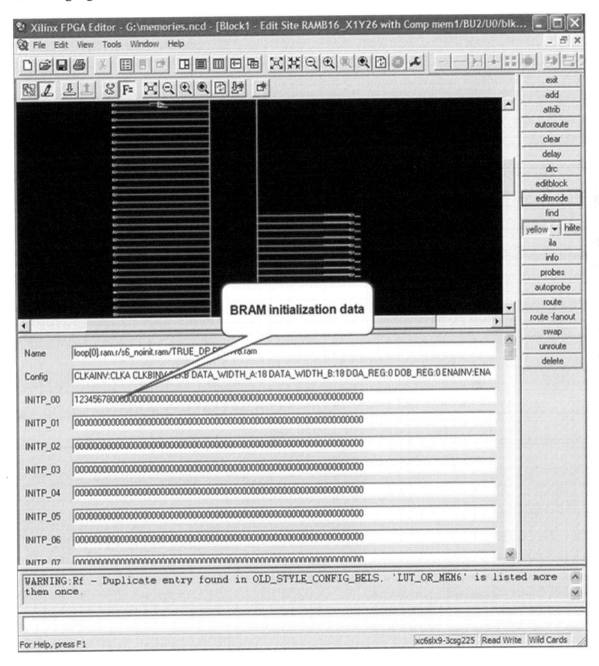

Figure 1: Changing BRAM contents in FPGA Editor

This method allows making small modifications to individual BRAMs. A more suitable method to change large portions of the BRAM is from a file in the "Block RAM Data" box of the File->Open dialog.

Modifying LUT equations

FPGA Editor allows modifications of LUT equations. That operation can be performed by selecting a LUT component in FPGA Editor and executing `editblock` command. The following figure illustrates different options to modify LUT equations: assigning a constant logic zero or one, adding a route-thru, and defining a generic logic equation.

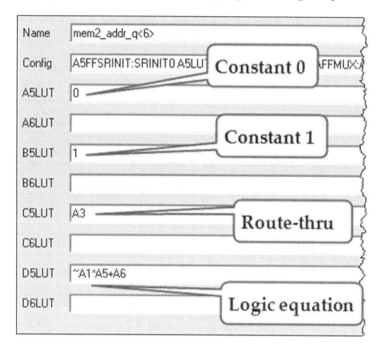

Figure 2: Modifying LUT equations

The valid operators are:
* : Logical AND
+ : Logical OR:
@ : Logical XOR
~ : Unary NOT
A, B, C, and D are the LUT outputs.

Using TIEOFF components

TIEOFF components provide access to power nets. Connecting a TIEOFF to a LUT or another component is a convenient way of assigning it to a logic zero or one. The following figure shows an FPGA Editor view of a Configurable Logic Block (CLB) that consists of two Slices, and its corresponding TIEOFF.

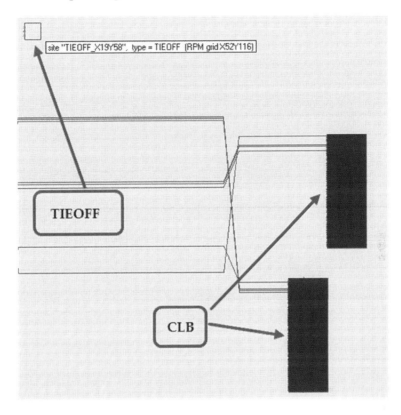

Figure 3: A TIEOFF component

Selecting a TIEOFF in FPGA Editor will display information containing the TIOFF site coordinates, which can be referenced later on:
site "TIEOFF_X19Y58", type = TIEOFF (RPM grid X52Y116)

A TIEOFF has three outputs: a week KEEP1, a HARD1, which represents logic one, and HARD0, which represents logic 0. The following figure shows a close-up view of a TIEOFF component.

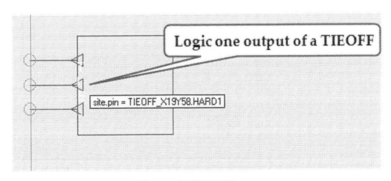

Figure 4: TIEOFF ports

Manual and Directed Routing

FPGA Editor allows manual routing of a net. Directed Routing (DIRT) can be used to preserve routing of existing nets and is often used as a routing constraint of time critical nets in the design. That operation is performed from the Tools->Directed Routing Constraints dialog of the FPGA Editor. The following is a DIRT constraint example of "mem2_wen_q<1>" net:

```
# DIRT constraint example
NET "mem2_wen_q<1>"
INST "mem2_wen_q<1>" LOC=ILOGIC_X12Y21;
INST "out12" LOC=SLICE_X12Y16;
INST "mem2_dinb<1>" LOC=SLICE_X14Y29;

ROUTE="{3;1;6slx9csg225;bc1a6e0!-1;41757;-37374;S!0;-162;-
830!1;-524;4!2;"
"-9747;1487!3;-12477;5681!3;-15908;-6300!4;-3415;12195!5;-
4464;-2830!6;"
"-4633;4881!7;-1625;-3757!8;89;4385!9;-778;-
824!10;1811;1891!11;683;-712;L"
"!12;685;-680;L!}";
```

Design analysis

FPGA Editor provides a number of commands to perform design analysis. The following is an example of calling a `delay` command when `mem2_wen_q<13>` net is selected.

```
delay
Net "mem2_wen_q<13>": driver - comp.pin "mem2_wen_q<13>.Q4",
site.pin "ILOGIC_X0Y6.Q4"
  2.392ns - comp.pin "out12.B2", site.pin "SLICE_X12Y16.B1"
  3.062ns - comp.pin "mem2_dinb<13>.D4", site.pin
 "SLICE_X16Y29.D6"
```

FPGA Editor will display detailed information about the net delay. That can be useful to calculate skew of high-fanout signals.

Changing IO properties

FPGA Editor allows changing all the available properties of an IO: slew rate, terminations, enabling a pull-up or pull-down resistor, selecting drive strength, and others. The following figure shows FPGA Editor IO properties view of a Spartan-6 FPGA.

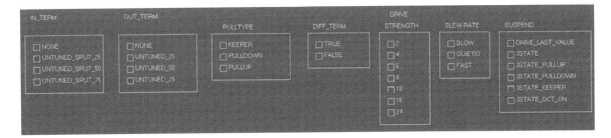

Figure 5: Spartan-6 IO properties view

Using FPGA Editor in command line mode

`fpga_edline` is a command-line version of the FPGA Editor. It can be used to automate design modifications, for example, as part of a build process, by running a script with the sequence of FPGA Editor commands.

Resources

[1] FPGA Editor Guide
http://www.xilinx.com/itp/3_1i/pdf/docs/fpg/fpg.pdf

88
USING XILINX SYSTEMMONITOR

Xilinx Virtex-6 FPGAs have built-in SystemMonitor module that can provide on- and off-chip thermal and supply voltage information. Using SystemMonitor is instrumental for both initial design bring-up and subsequent monitoring of FPGA and board-level operating conditions. SystemMonitor can detect FPGA overheat and out of range supply voltages, and trigger an alarm to notify the user design.

The following figure shows SystemMonitor block diagram.

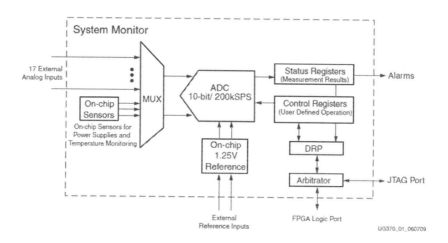

Figure 1: SystemMonitor block diagram (source: Xilinx Virtex-6 System Monitor User Guide)

At the heart of the SystemMonitor is Analog-to-Digital Converter (ADC). ADC is constantly digitizing on-chip temperature and voltage sensors, external analog inputs, and storing the most recent measurements in the registers. The registers can be accessed from the user design through the Dynamic Reconfiguration Port (DRP) or JTAG. SystemMonitor provides several alarm signals that can be individually configured with temperature and voltage thresholds. Alarm signals allow a simpler interface to the SystemMonitor from the user design comparing to the DRP.

SYSMON primitive can be directly instantiated in the design. However, it is recommended to use SystemMonitor wizard in Xilinx CoreGen utility to generate a wrapper to ensure correct attributes and configuration parameters.

The following figure shows block diagram of a SystemMonitor sample design.

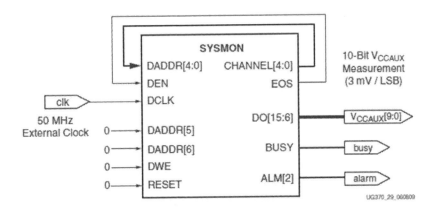

Figure 2: SystemMonitor sample design (source: Xilinx Virtex-6 System Monitor User Guide)

The SystemMonitor can be accessed from the JTAG test access port (TAP) even when the FPGA is not configured. Xilinx ChipScope application has SystemMonitor console view that can read and plot current, minimum, and maximum temperatures of the FPGA die, V_{ccint} (core) and V_{ccaux} voltages. The following figure depicts ChipScope SystemMonitor console view of a Virtex-6 LX240T device.

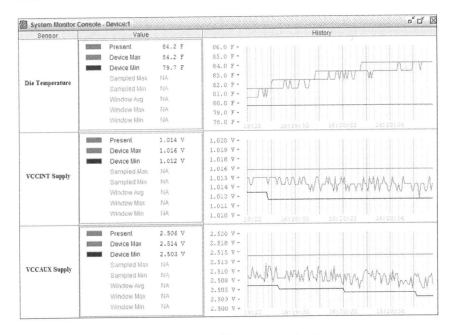

Figure 3: SystemMonitor console view

Resources

[1] Xilinx Virtex-6 FPGA System Monitor User Guide UG370
http://www.xilinx.com/support/documentation/user_guides/ug370.pdf

89
FPGA FAILURE ANALYSIS

An FPGA is a complex electronic device connected to multiple peripherals and powered by several power sources with different voltages. A large FPGA has over a thousand pins and can be connected to ten or more voltage regulators. Therefore, it is not uncommon that during the initial board bring-up FPGA gets damaged. That can happen for several reasons. It can be a simple mistake in the design that can be easily found by using an oscilloscope. It can also be a mistake during board manufacturing and component assembly process that can be found through visual inspection.

However, that is not always the case. The damage can be caused by a strong electrostatic discharge (ESD) or a weak electrical overstress (EOS). The problem might not be reproducible and may occur only on some boards. The cost of an FPGA and a prototype board can easily reach thousands of dollars, and designers might be reluctant to use other boards before determining the root cause of the failure. Design teams, especially in small companies, might not have the necessary lab equipment to perform necessary tests.

The character of the FPGA damage varies. It can be as simple as one damaged IO pin, which is relatively easy to detect and in some cases to find a work around. In other cases the damage can occur to internal logic in FPGA fabric. This problem is more difficult to find, because the exact same design might work on one board and not on another. The damage can be so extensive that it renders the entire FPGA unusable. For example, any damage to FPGA configuration controller circuits will prevent the bitstream to configure an FPGA.

Xilinx offers a service to perform failure analysis on a damaged FPGA chip to help determine the root cause. Surprisingly, not many FPGA and PCB designers are aware of that service. In many cases it is indispensable and the only way to find the cause of the failure.

A failure analysis service [1] performs visual, mechanical, and electrical failure checks. Visual inspection checks soldering problems, such as missing solder balls. Mechanical inspection performs acoustic microscopy to check for die cracks and other mechanical defects. Electrical checks include X-ray inspection, Time Domain Reflectometry (TDR), and Quantum Focus Infrascope (QFI) to determine pin and fabric damage on the die. At the end it provides a comprehensive report that includes photos made at high magnification, findings, conclusions, and recommendations.

The following is a die photo made at 200x magnification. It shows damage to one of the FPGA IOs caused by the electrical overstress. The arrow points to the fused metallization on the device die.

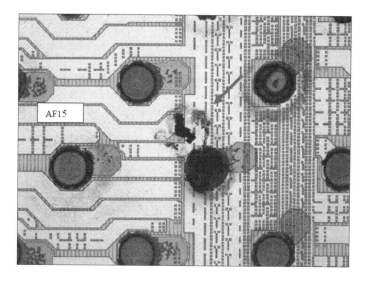

Figure 1: FPGA die photo showing IO damage

The following is a die photo showing the damaged region of the FPGA fabric.

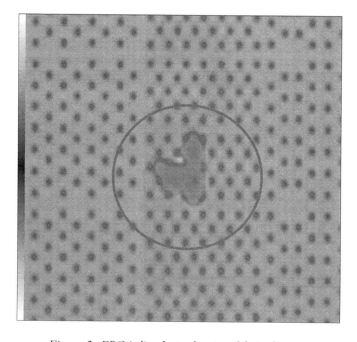

Figure 2: FPGA die photo showing fabric damage

Resources

[1] Xilinx FPGA failure analysis service
http://www.xilinx.com/products/quality/rma.htm

90
TIMING CONSTRAINTS

Design timing constraints can be provided as an input to synthesis or physical implementation tools. Xilinx physical implementation tools use proprietary User Constraints File (UCF) format [1]. Synopsys Synplify works with timing constraints in Synopsys Design Constraints (SDC) format. Xilinx XST uses XST Constraint File (XCF) syntax, which is very similar to the UCF. This Tip provides an overview of the most frequently used timing constraints in Xilinx UCF format. It uses a simple example to show the constraints syntax.

```verilog
// constraints.v: implements a data_in signal synchronizer
module constraints( input clk1,clk2,reset,
                    input data_in,
                    output reg data_out);
  reg data_in_q, data_out_q;

  always @(posedge clk1, posedge reset)
    if(reset)
      data_in_q <= 1'b0;
    else
      data_in_q <= data_in;

  always @(posedge clk2, posedge reset)
    if(reset) begin
      data_out_q <= 1'b0;
      data_out   <= 1'b0;
    end
    else begin
      data_out_q <= data_in_q;
      data_out   <= data_out_q;
end
endmodule // constraints
```

```
# constraints.ucf
NET "clk1" TNM_NET = clk1;
TIMESPEC TS_clk1 = PERIOD "clk1" 5 ns HIGH 50%;
NET "clk2" TNM_NET = clk2;
TIMESPEC TS_clk2 = PERIOD "clk2" 4.1 ns HIGH 50%;

# either of the following constraints can be used for
```

```
# clock domain crossing paths
# TIMESPEC "TS_CDC_1" = FROM "clk1"   TO "clk2"    TIG;
TIMESPEC "TS_CDC_1"  = FROM "clk1"   TO "clk2"    5ns;
NET "data_in_q" TIG;

NET "data_in"  OFFSET = IN 5 ns VALID 5 ns BEFORE "clk1" RISING;
NET "data_out" OFFSET = OUT 4.1 ns AFTER "clk2";

NET "reset" MAXDELAY = 1 ns;
NET "reset" MAXSKEW  = 2 ns;

INST "data_out_q" IOB = TRUE;
```

PERIOD constraint

PERIOD constraint applies to a design clock, and defines its period. PERIOD covers all synchronous paths within the clock domain, and may also contain paths that cross related clock domains. The following is an example of a PERIOD constraint that applies to `clk1`, and defines its period to be 5ns.

```
NET "clk1" TNM_NET = clk1;
TIMESPEC TS_clk1 = PERIOD "clk1" 5 ns HIGH 50%;
```

OFFSET IN/OUT constraint

OFFSET IN and OFFSET OUT constraints specify the timing relationship between the external clock input and the associated data input or output. The following is an example of an OFFSET constraint applicable to `data_in` and `data_out` with relationship to the `clk1` input.

```
NET "data_in"  OFFSET = IN 5 ns VALID 5 ns BEFORE "clk1" RISING;
NET "data_out" OFFSET = OUT 4.1 ns AFTER "clk2";
```

The first constraint specifies that `data_in` will be valid at the input at most 5ns before the rising edge of `clk1`. The second constraint specifies that `data_out` output is valid at most 4.1ns after the transition of `clk1`.

The OFFSET constraint can be applied to specific IO net, a group of nets covering multiple IOs, and globally.

OFFSET constraint specifies a valid timing range on the FPGA inputs and outputs with regard to the clock. It doesn't guarantee fixed and predictable timing, which will vary between builds. For that reason it is recommended to place input and output registers in the IO block (IOB) to ensure consistent timing delays.

MAXDELAY and MAXSKEW

MAXDELAY (Maximum Delay) constraint defines the maximum allowable delay on a net. MAXSKEW (Maximum Skew) is a constraint that specifies the maximum amount of skew on a net. MAXSKEW can be used to control the skew of local clocks, resets, or high-fanout control signals. The following is an example of using MAXDELAY and MAXSKEW constraints.

```
NET "reset" MAXDELAY = 1 ns;
NET "reset" MAXSKEW  = 2 ns;
```

FROM:TO constraint

FROM:TO is used to constraint paths between time groups. The following are examples of using the FROM:TO constraint.

```
TIMESPEC "TS_CDC_1" = FROM "clk1"   TO "clk2"   5ns;
TIMESPEC "TS_CDC_1" = FROM "clk1"   TO "clk2"   TIG;
```

The first constraint specifies that all paths from `clk1` to `clk2` groups will not exceed 5ns. The second one excludes all paths between `clk1` to `clk2` groups from the timing analysis.

TIG constraint

TIG (Timing Ignore) is a constraint that causes all paths going through a specific net to be excluded from the timing analysis. The following is an example of a TIG constraint that excludes `data_in_q` path from the timing analysis.

```
NET "data_in_q" TIG;
```

Constraints priority

In case more than one timing constraint applies to a specific path, they are resolved according to their priority. The general rule is: the more generic the timing constraint the lower its priority. The following list is the constraint priority, from lowest to highest:

PERIOD, OFFSET IN/OUT, FROM:TO, MAXDELAY, and TIG. Constraint Interaction report (TSI) provides detailed information on how physical implementation tools resolved the overlapping timing constraints.

Resources

[1] Xilinx Constraints User Guide
http://www.xilinx.com/support/documentation/sw_manuals/xilinx11/cgd.pdf

91
PERFORMING TIMING ANALYSIS

Xilinx provides a tool called TRACE (The Timing Reporter and Circuit Evaluator), to perform static timing analysis of the design and to verify that the design meets all the specified timing constraints. To effectively use TRACE, FPGA designers need to become familiar with the options that the tool provides and understand timing reports to analyze the results.

Using Xilinx Timing Analyzer

Some of the frequently used TRACE options are described in the following table. The complete description of the tool can be found in the Xilinx Command Line Tools User Guide.

Table 1: TRACE options

TRACE option	Description
-e <limit>	Generate an error report. The optional <limit> is an integer limit on the number of items reported for each timing constraint.
-v <limit>	Generate a verbose report. The optional <limit> is an integer limit on the number of items reported for each timing constraint.
-n <limit>	Report paths per endpoint instead of per timing constraint.
-tsi <tsifile.tsi>	Generate a Timing Specification Interaction (TSI) report.
-l <limit>	Limit the number of items reported for each timing constraint in the report. This option becomes important for large designs to limit the size of the generated report and reduce TRACE runtime.
-u <limit>	Report paths not covered by any timing constraints. Many design problems are caused by a failure to constrain all paths. It is recommended to always enable this option when performing timing analysis.

Examples of using TRACE

The following are some examples of using TRACE in command line mode.

```
# synopsys:
# trce [-e|-v [<limit>]] [-l <limit>] [-n <limit>]
# [-u <limit>]
# [-a] [-s <speed>]
# [-o <report[.twr]>]
# [-stamp <stampfile>]
# [-tsi <tsifile[.tsi]>]
# [-xml <report[.twx]>]
# [-nodatasheet]
# [-timegroups]
# [-fastpaths]
# [-intstyle ise|xflow|silent] [-ise <projectfile>]
# <design[.ncd]> [<constraint[.pcf]>]
$ trce -e 100 -l 500 -u 100 -o my_project.twr my_project.ncd
my_project.pcf
$ trce -v 100 -l 500 -u 100 -tsi -timegroups -o
my_project.twr my_project.ncd my_project.pcf
```

The required input to TRACE is the Native Circuit Description (NCD) file, which is produced by MAP or PAR tools. The Physical Constraints File (PCF) contains all the design constraints and can be provided as an option. The output of the TRACE is an ASCII timing report file that has a .twr extension. There is an option to generate an output in XML format that has a .twx extension.

Understanding Xilinx Timing Reports

TRACE timing analysis reports contain detailed timing information organized by timing constraints, nets, endpoints, clocks, timing group, unconstrained paths, timing errors, and several other criteria.

The following is an example design that contains a Mixed Mode Clock Manager (MMCM), a dual port RAM, two clock domains, and a clock domain crossing signal. The simple design is used to showcase different parts of a timing analysis report.

```
// Verilog implementation
module dual_port_ram( input clka,clkb,reset,
                     input wea,web,
                     input [15:0] dina,dinb,
                     input [9:0] addra,addrb,
                     output reg [15:0] douta_qo,doutb_qo,
                     output reg wea_qo);
wire [15:0] douta,doutb;
wire clka_mmcm;

always @(posedge clka_mmcm)
```

```verilog
    if(reset)
       douta_qo   <= 'b0;
    else
       douta_qo <= douta;
  always @(posedge clkb)
    if(reset) begin
       doutb_qo   <= 'b0;
       wea_qo     <= 1'b0;
    end
    else begin
       doutb_qo <= doutb;
       wea_qo     <= wea;   // clock domain crossing
    end
  blk_mem mem (
     .clka(clka_mmcm),
     .wea(wea),
     .addra(addra),
     .dina(dina),
     .douta(douta),
     .clkb(clkb),
     .web(web),
     .addrb(addrb),
     .dinb(dinb),
     .doutb(doutb));

  clka_mmcm mmcm (
     .CLK_IN1      (clka),
     .CLK_OUT1     (clka_mmcm),
     .RESET        (reset));
endmodule
// UCF timing constraints
NET "clka" TNM_NET = clka;
TIMESPEC TS_clka = PERIOD "clka" 8 ns HIGH 50%;

NET "clkb" TNM_NET = clkb;
TIMESPEC TS_clkb = PERIOD "clkb" 4.4 ns HIGH 50%;

NET "wea" OFFSET = IN 6 ns VALID 6 ns BEFORE "clka" RISING;
NET "web" OFFSET = IN 1.7 ns VALID 1.7 ns BEFORE "clkb"
RISING;

INST "douta_qo<*>" TNM = douta;
TIMEGRP "douta" OFFSET = OUT 7 ns AFTER "clka";

NET "reset" MAXDELAY = 3.5 ns;
NET "reset" MAXSKEW = 3 ns;
```

The following part of the timing report indicates that the MAXDELAY constraint failed by 0.484ns.

```
==================================================
Timing constraint: NET "reset_IBUF" MAXDELAY = 3.5 ns;
  1 net analyzed, 1 failing net detected.
  1 timing error detected.
   Maximum net delay is   3.984ns.
--------------------------------------------------
 Slack:    -0.484ns reset_IBUF
 Error:    3.984ns delay exceeds   3.500ns timing constraint
 by 0.484ns
 From                To                        Delay(ns)
 N15.I               OLOGIC_X0Y28.SR           3.548
 N15.I               OLOGIC_X12Y30.SR          3.121
 N15.I               OLOGIC_X0Y24.SR           3.540
 N15.I               OLOGIC_X12Y38.SR          3.037
--------------------------------------------------
```

The MAXSKEW constraint is met:

```
==================================================
Timing constraint: NET "reset_IBUF" MAXSKEW = 3 ns;
  1 net analyzed, 0 failing nets detected.
  0 timing errors detected.
   Maximum net skew is   2.927ns.
--------------------------------------------------
```

Several paths miss the 4.4ns PERIOD timing constraint on `clkb`. The following is a section of the timing report that shows that a path from BRAM to doutb_qo misses timing by 0.386ns.

```
==================================================
Timing constraint: TS_clkb = PERIOD TIMEGRP "clkb" 4.4 ns
HIGH 50%;

  16 paths analyzed, 16 endpoints analyzed, 8 failing
  endpoints
  8 timing errors detected. (8 setup errors, 0 hold errors, 0
  component switching limit errors)
   Minimum period is   4.786ns.
--------------------------------------------------
Slack: -0.386ns (requirement - (data path - clock path skew +
uncertainty))
Source:mem/BU2/U0/blk_mem_generator/valid.cstr/ramloop[0].ram
.r/s6_noinit.ram/TRUE_DP.PRIM18.ram (RAM)
Destination:            doutb_qo_8 (FF)
```

```
   Requirement:              4.400ns
   Data Path Delay:          5.134ns (Levels of Logic = 0)
   Clock Path Skew:          0.383ns (0.841 - 0.458)
   Source Clock:             clkb_BUFGP rising at 0.000ns
   Destination Clock:        clkb_BUFGP rising at 4.400ns
   Clock Uncertainty:        0.035ns
   Clock Uncertainty:        0.035ns ((TSJ^2 + TIJ^2)^1/2 + DJ) / 2 +
PE
      Total System Jitter (TSJ):    0.070ns
      Total Input Jitter (TIJ):     0.000ns
      Discrete Jitter (DJ):         0.000ns
      Phase Error (PE):             0.000ns
Maximum Data Path at Slow Process Corner:
mem/BU2/U0/blk_mem_generator/valid.cstr/ramloop[0].ram.r/s6_n
oinit.ram/TRUE_DP.PRIM18.ram to doutb_qo_8
```

The following part of the timing report indicates that one of the OFFSET constraints failed by 0.445ns.

```
================================================
Timing constraint: COMP "web" OFFSET = IN 1.7 ns VALID 1.7 ns
BEFORE COMP
"clkb" "RISING";
 4 paths analyzed, 4 endpoints analyzed, 4 failing endpoints
 4 timing errors detected. (4 setup errors, 0 hold errors)
 Minimum allowable offset is   2.145ns.
--------------------------------------------------
Slack: -0.445ns (requirement - (data path - clock path -
clock arrival + uncertainty))
Source: web (PAD)
Destination:mem/BU2/U0/blk_mem_generator/valid.cstr/ramloop[0
].ram.r/s6_noinit.ram/TRUE_DP.PRIM18.ram (RAM)
   Destination Clock:     clkb_BUFGP rising at 0.000ns
   Requirement:           1.700ns
   Data Path Delay:       4.655ns (Levels of Logic = 1)
   Clock Path Delay:      2.535ns (Levels of Logic = 2)
   Clock Uncertainty:     0.025ns
   Clock Uncertainty:     0.025ns  ((TSJ^2 + TIJ^2)^1/2 + DJ) / 2 +
PE
      Total System Jitter (TSJ):    0.050ns
      Total Input Jitter (TIJ):     0.000ns
      Discrete Jitter (DJ):         0.000ns
      Phase Error (PE):             0.000ns
```

Several paths are unconstrained:

```
=============================================
Timing constraint: Unconstrained OFFSET OUT AFTER analysis
for clock "clkb_BUFGP"
 17 paths analyzed, 17 endpoints analyzed, 0 failing endpoints
 0 timing errors detected.
 Maximum allowable offset is   6.658ns.
=============================================
Timing constraint: Unconstrained OFFSET IN BEFORE analysis
for clock "clka_mmcm"
 42 paths analyzed, 42 endpoints analyzed, 0 failing endpoints
 0 timing errors detected.
 Minimum allowable offset is   6.983ns.
=============================================
Timing constraint: Unconstrained path analysis
 35 paths analyzed, 35 endpoints analyzed, 0 failing endpoints
 0 timing errors detected. (0 setup errors, 0 hold errors)
 Maximum delay is   3.339ns.
=============================================
```

The report contains several other sections with useful information—timegroups, derived constraint report, data sheet report, timing constraint interactions—that, for brevity, were not included here. The complete timing report is available on the accompanying website.

92

TIMING CLOSURE FLOWS

Timing closure is the process of meeting timing constraints during the physical implementation of an FPGA design. Timing closure is perhaps the most unpredictable among FPGA design tasks in terms of the amount of time and effort it takes to complete. Even the most experienced FPGA designers often find it difficult to accurately estimate the scope of work, which can adversely affect project schedules.

Timing closure is an iterative process involving incremental changes of the code, area and timing constraints, and tool options until the performance goals of the design are met. It can take several hours, or even a day, for a large FPGA design utilizing high frequency clocks to build. It is not uncommon to have 50-100 design builds to achieve the timing closure. If each build takes six hours, or four builds a day, the timing closure task can be completed in two to four weeks. Reducing that time requires a good knowledge of design tools, FPGA architecture, and the design itself.

The following figure provides an example of a timing closure flow.

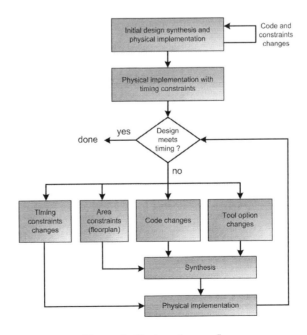

Figure 1: Timing closure flow

Initial design synthesis and physical implementation

Initial design synthesis and physical implementation is performed using default tool options and without any timing and area constraints. IO constraints should be specified. The goal of this step is to ensure that it is feasible to synthesize, place, and route the design. The quality of results should also be realistic, i.e.the FPGA resource utilization should be within the expected range and place and route tools don't produce errors and all constraints except timing and area are met. Xilinx MAP and PAR tools provide a "Non Timing Driven" option (-ntd) that ignores timing constraints during place and route. Another option is to set the XIL_TIMING_ALLOW_IMPOSSIBLE environment variable to 1 to allow the tools to bypass any timing constraint that is impossible to meet.

It can take several iterations of code and constraints changes to successfully complete this step. Place and route tools will provide the estimate of the maximum attainable frequency. Analyzing those results will help devise the most appropriate strategy to achieve timing closure.

Synthesis and physical implementation with applied timing constraints

The next step is to build the design after applying timing constraints. Based on the analysis of timing the results after physical implementation, a designer has the following options: add or change area constraints (floorplan), change the timing constraints, change the code, or change the tool options. The decision regarding which change to make mainly depends on the severity of the timing violation. This sequence of steps is an iterative process, which will result in design timing closure upon its successful completion. Designers should focus on resolving the worst performing paths in each build iteration. Another approach is to start with a more relaxed set of timing constraints, such as a lower frequency clock period, and gradually tighten them in every build iteration until they reach the target.

The subject of the timing closure is broad enough to be comprehensively covered in this book. There are a number of research papers and design guides written by FPGA vendors that propose different methodologies and tool flows to reduce the effort it takes to achieve timing closure. FPGA design tool vendors constantly add new features, such as more user-friendly floorplan editors, hierarchy-based floorplanning, partition-based flows, and top-down and bottom-up design methodologies that help improve productivity. Unfortunately, timing the closure of large and complex designs remains a mostly manual task that demands a lot of effort from FPGA designers to perform report analysis and make code, constraints and tool option changes based on that.

Understanding timing score

The timing closure is achieved when all timing constraints are met and the timing score reported by the PAR tool is zero. Not meeting timing constraints can result in intermittent design failures under different operating conditions or on different devices.

However, static timing analysis is performed for the worst possible temperature and voltage operating conditions by default. The following figure shows the timing analysis of a path that fails timing by 391ps.

```
================================================================================
Timing constraint: TS_clk1 = PERIOD TIMEGRP "clk1" 3.33 ns HIGH 50%;
 559 paths analyzed, 305 endpoints analyzed, 16 failing endpoints
 16 timing errors detected. (16 setup errors, 0 hold errors, 0 component switching limit errors)
 Minimum period is   3.721ns.
--------------------------------------------------------------------------------
Slack (setup path):     -0.391ns (requirement - (data path - clock path skew + uncertainty))
  Source:               crc1/data_in_10 (FF)
  Destination:          crc1/lfsr_q_13 (FF)
  Requirement:          3.330ns
  Data Path Delay:      3.664ns (Levels of Logic = 2)
  Clock Path Skew:      -0.022ns (0.310 - 0.332)
  Source Clock:         clk1_BUFGP rising at 0.000ns
  Destination Clock:    clk1_BUFGP rising at 3.330ns
  Clock Uncertainty:    0.035ns

  Clock Uncertainty:          0.035ns  ((TSJ^2 + TIJ^2)^1/2 + DJ) / 2 + PE
    Total System Jitter (TSJ):  0.070ns
    Total Input Jitter (TIJ):   0.000ns
    Discrete Jitter (DJ):       0.000ns
    Phase Error (PE):           0.000ns
```

Figure 2: Timing analysis of a path

The timing analysis model assumes 35ps of clock uncertainty, which provides certain safety margin. In addition, it uses default temperature and voltage settings as shown in the following figure.

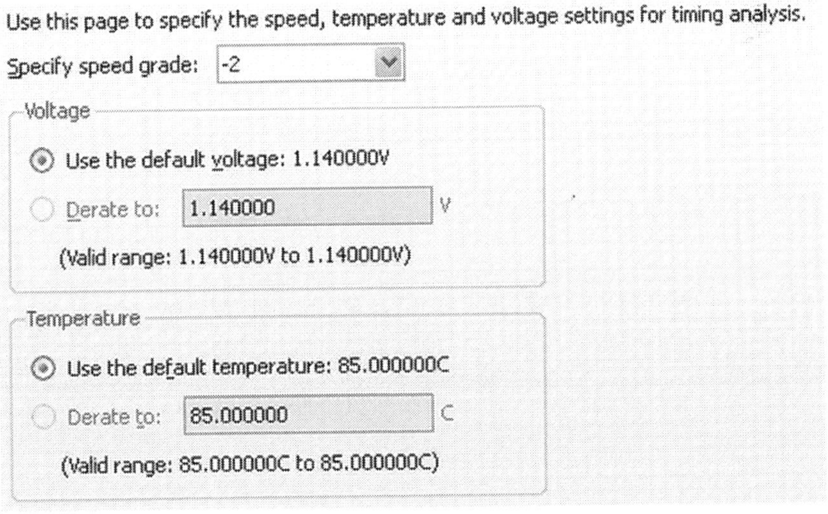

Figure 3: Default temperature and voltage settings

Changing the settings to lower temperature and higher voltage that reflect realistic operating conditions of the device will result in easier-to-achieve timing closure.

93

TIMING CLOSURE: TOOL OPTIONS

This Tip discusses different synthesis and physical implementation tool options that can be used during timing closure to improve design performance. Tool options are very design specific. The same tool option settings will usually achieve incomparable performance results for different designs. It is recommended to start the timing closure process using default tool options.

The following table lists some of the Xilinx XST synthesis and physical implementation tool options that can be used during the timing closure.

Table 1: Tool options used during timing closure

Option	*Flag*	*Tool*
Optimization goal	-opt_mode	XST
Keep hierarchy	-keep_hierarchy	XST
Maximum fanout	-max_fanout	XST
Register duplication	-register_duplication	XST
Resource sharing	-resource_sharing	XST
Equivalent register removal	-equivalent_register_removal	XST, MAP
Register balancing	-register_balancing	XST
Pack registers into IOB	-iob	XST
LUT combining	-lc	XST
FSM encoding	-fsm_encoding	XST
Effort level	-ol	MAP,PAR
Cost table	-t	MAP,PAR
Retiming	-retiming	MAP
SmartGuide	-smartguide	MAP,PAR
Timing-driven placement	-timing	MAP
Combinatorial logic optimization	-logic_opt	MAP
Timing mode	-ntd	MAP,PAR

Using Cost Tables

Cost table is a MAP and PAR option that initializes the place and route process with a seed value ranging between 1 and 100. Each cost table value results in a slightly different placement. Both MAP and PAR use the same cost table; if they're different, PAR will issue a warning and will use the cost table from MAP. Xilinx documentation doesn't provide detailed information on the cost table implementation, and what effect it achieves. A general recommendation is to try different cost table values and select the one that achieves the best performance results. However, it is impractical to try all 100 cost table values on a large design.

In order to understand the effect of the cost table option on the design performance, Xilinx memory controller (MIG) core was build for Virtex-6 LX75 FPGA using all possible cost table values. The target frequency was 250MHz. The following chart shows the results. Horizontal axis is a cost table value from 1 to 100. The vertical axis is the maximum frequency.

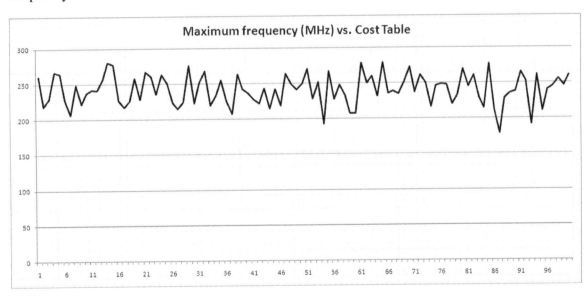

Figure 1: Maximum frequency vs. Cost Table

The next chart depicts a histogram view of the same results that shows the distribution of maximum achievable frequencies. Horizontal axis is divided into maximum frequency range bins. Vertical axis is the number of cost table values that fall into corresponding maximum frequency range. For example, there are 10 cost tables out of 100 that achieved the maximum frequency between 220 and 230MHz.

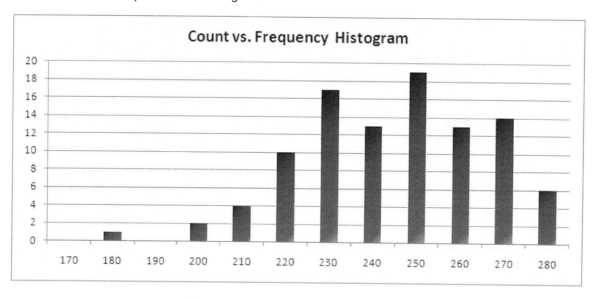

Figure 2: Count vs. frequency histogram

One observation is that adjacent cost table values can produce very different performance results. For example, cost table 1 and 2 result in maximum frequency of 260 and 219MHz respectively. The minimum frequency across all cost tables is 178.6 MHz, and the maximum is 280 MHz. The variation is 101.4MHz, which is 44% of the average maximum frequency.

Another observation is that maximum frequencies as a function of the cost table form a curve with seemingly independent and randomly distributed values. The histogram view also does not resemble a bell-shaped curve.

Based on the above results, using any 10-15 adjacent cost table values will provide a good confidence level that one of the values will contain the maximum frequency.

Retiming

Retiming is the process of moving register stages in attempt to balance combinatorial delay one each side of the registers. Retiming does affect the functionality of the design by adding additional latency, because it does not change the number of registers in a path from a primary input to a primary output of the pipeline. Retiming can be performed during synthesis by using `-register_balancing` XST option, or during MAP global optimization by using `-retiming`. Retiming results are design dependent, and might not provide any benefit in highly pipelined designs.

Effort level

Better performance results can be achieved using higher place and route effort level. The disadvantage of using a higher effort level is a longer build time. It is recommended to avoid using the highest effort level early in the timing closure process.

Placing registers in IOB

Placing registers in the IO Blocks (IOB) provides the fastest clock-to-output and input-to-clock delays. XST `-iob` option controls the use of IOB registers for inputs, outputs, or both.

FSM encoding

Changing FSM encoding to one-hot can improve the state machine logic performance.

Flattening design hierarchy

Flattening design hierarchy allows tools to perform optimizations across module boundaries, which may result in improved performance. In the process of design flattening, a synthesis tool will rename nets, move around registers and combinatorial logic, and change the hierarchical structure of the design. That will make it more difficult to locate the signals during design debug while using FPGA Editor, ChipScope, or adding area and timing constraints. It is recommended to preserve hierarchy in the beginning of the timing closure process, and flatten the design across as few boundaries as possible as the last effort to improve performance.

Resource sharing

Resource sharing allows logic that implements arithmetic operators to be shared with other functions. Resource sharing achieves the opposite effect than logic replication option. It is recommended that resource sharing be disabled in order to improve performance.

Using SmartXplorer

SmartXplorer is a tool that iterates through the synthesis and physical implementation, trying different combination of properties called design strategies. SmartXplorer will stop when the timing closure is achieved, or when it reached the maximum number of iterations. When complete, SmartXplorer identifies the best implementation and saves its results.

94

TIMING CLOSURE: CONSTRAINTS AND CODING STYLE

This Tip provides an overview of coding style options and different timing constraints that can be used during timing closure. Changing the code is a preferred method to improve design performance compared to using tool optimization options. Usually, changing the code achieves better and more consistent performance results. Another advantage is better code portability, because the algorithms behind the tool options can change between different tool versions.

Using synthesis constraints

It is recommended to use timing constraints during both synthesis and physical implementation. Synthesis tools are timing driven, and will attempt to generate a netlist that meets all the constraints. Without timing constraints, the synthesis tool will use arbitrary assumptions to generate the netlist, which might be suboptimal for a particular design.

Multicycle paths

A multicycle path is best described as a path between registers that is not updated on consecutive clock cycles. The following figure shows an example of a circuit that contains a multicycle path.

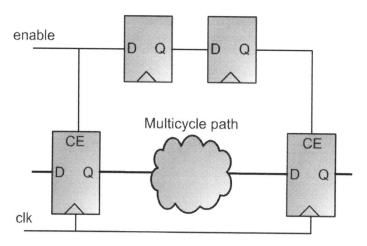

Figure 1: A circuit with a multicycle path

The combinatorial path from the left to the right register forms a 3-clock multicycle path, as long as enable signal is asserted for one clock with at least two periods between assertions.

Multicycle paths are usually associated with the clock enable control signals, but this not always the case. The multicycle path constraint applies to a path between two registers. It can be defined relative to an existing clock period constraint multiplied by a multi-cycle factor. If the clock in the above example is 100MHz, the multicycle path between the registers can be constrained to a lower 10ns x 3=30ns value instead of the original 10ns.

False paths

Paths in a design that are not required to be constrained are defined as false paths. False paths can be excluded from static timing analysis by using TIG constraint.

Correctly identifying multicycle and false paths required a good knowledge of the design. Cobalt Timing Constraint Generation tool [1] can perform design analysis, and automatically identifies and generates constraints for false and multicycle paths.

Although multicycle and false path constrains can improve design performance, over-constraining, or adding too many constraints to the design can adverse effect on the place and route time.

Reducing fanout

A high fanout contributes to long routing delays. The fanout can be reduced using either manual duplication of a source register or specifying a `-max_fanout` XST synthesis option. Using manual register duplication allows better control, and more portable code. The disadvantage of reducing fanout by register duplication is increased logic utilization.

Using dedicated routing resources

Designers can use dedicated low-delay routing resources to implement long control signals.

Reset scheme

The choice of design reset scheme can have a profound effect on performance. The tradeoffs of using different reset schemes are discussed in Tip #29.

Pipelining

Pipelining combinatorial logic can result in significant performance improvement. It is not always possible to add pipeline stages, because the design might not allow the increase in latency. Pipelining is discussed in Tip #33.

Reducing the number of logic levels

It is recommended that the number of combinatorial logic levels is kept in a ballpark of 5-7 for designs targeting Virtex-6 FPGAs and running at 200-250MHz frequencies.

Priority encoders

It is recommended to use `case` statements instead of nested `if-else` constructs. Using `case` usually creates logic with lower combinatorial delays. The same recommendation applies to nested conditional operators "?". In case of mixed use of `case` and `if-else` constructs it's recommended to combine them into a larger `case`.

Registering all inputs and outputs in a module

It is recommended to register all input and output ports of a module. That helps achieve predictable timing within a module when its placement changes. Registering all module ports may neither be possible nor desirable in all cases. That also may lead to increased logic utilization.

Using dedicated IP cores

Using performance-optimized IP cores to implement wide counters and arithmetic functions instead of generic code can result in some performance improvement.

Using DSP48 and SRL

An effective way to improve performance is by using DSP48 blocks to implement complex arithmetic functions.

Replacing multiple pipelined registers with an SRL can improve performance because SRL eliminates potentially long routing delays between the registers. One caveat is that an SRL has high clock-to-output delay. It is beneficial to place a register stage on the SRL output.

Lowering clock frequency

Often, design clock frequency can be lowered without affecting the functionality. Some designs, such as protocol processors, may allow lowering the clock frequency by half, while doubling the datapath width.

Faster FPGA speed grade

If none of the performance improvement options achieves satisfactory results, designers might need to resort to using a faster FPGA speed grade. The main disadvantage of this option is higher cost.

Resources

[1] Blue Pearl Software
http://www.bluepearlsoftware.com

95
THE ART OF FPGA FLOORPLANNING

Floorplanning is the process of adding placement and routing constraints to the design. Floorplanning a large, high speed design is the key to achieving timing closure. Good floorplanning can dramatically improve the design performance, and ensure consistent quality of the build results. Poor floorplanning can have an opposite effect, namely, making it impossible to meet timing constraints and cause inconsistent build results.

Effective FPGA floorplanning is a skill that is acquired with experience. It requires an excellent knowledge of the design and its performance goals, tool options, a deep understanding of the target FPGA architecture and capabilities, and the ability to make the necessary code and design constraints changes based on the timing results analysis. Floorplanning is a process that requires visualizing how parts of the synthesized design will fit into different areas of the FPGA device.

In ASIC world floorplanning is an engineering specialization. One or more engineers can be working full time on floorplanning a large chip. FPGA floorplanning is much simpler, and it's usually done by the same engineer who does the design.

Floorplanning is recommended not only for large, highly utilized, and high speed designs, but also for the small ones. Floorplanning a small design can be as simple as assigning a single placement constraint. Even if the design has low frequency clocks and meets timing, it's often desirable to add placement constraints to improve the build runtime and consistency of the results.

Floorplanning is a task tightly intertwined with the timing closure and, to some extent, logic design. It is recommended to start the the preparations early in the design cycle. For example, floorplanning considerations may have some weight in the process of partitioning the design into modules.

Xilinx PlanAhead is a main tool used for the design floorplan. Advanced users can floorplan the design manually by adding placement constraints directly into the constraints file. PlanAhead also supports automated floorplan. However, experience shows that the manual floorplan of large designs produces better results.

FPGA floorplanning flow

Floorplanning an FPGA design generally consists of steps shown in the following figure.

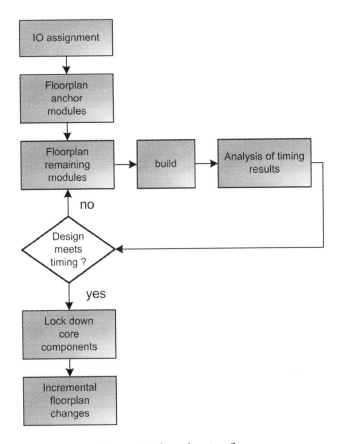

Figure 1: Floorplanning flow

IO assignment

Most of the FPGA designs require specific IO assignment. Locking down all design IOs is the very first task to complete before specifying any other placement and routing constraints. Not doing so may result in suboptimal results. It can also lead to a wasted time, as subsequent IO changes may require floorplan changes as well.

Floorplanning anchor modules

After all IOs are assigned, the next step is to floorplan all anchor modules. Those are the modules whose placement is unlikely to change. Some examples are modules that are connected to IOs, user logic modules interfacing to embedded FPGA primitives such as PCI Express interface, Ethernet MAC, or transceivers. At this point, modules that have a lot of

Floorplanning remaining modules

Floorplanning the rest of the design is an iterative process of adding placement and routing constraints, building the design, analyzing the timing report, and making the necessary adjustments. It continues until the timing closure is achieved. This is the longest step, and that can take several weeks for large, high speed designs. During the process, designers might need to make changes to the existing floorplan: move floorplanned regions, increase or decrease their size, or floorplanning modules at the lower level of hierarchy to improve granularity.

Lock down core components

To preserve the results, it is recommended that one locks down all BRAM, DSP, and clock manager modules after the design meets timing, and no major design changes are anticipated. This measure is intended to improve consistency and runtime in subsequent builds.

Incremental floorplan changes

Some minor floorplan changes might be required later in the design cycle due to changed timing constraints, addition of new features that increases or decreases logic utilization, or bug fixes.

Placement and routing constraints

Placement and routing constraints are provided as an input to physical implementation tools. Xilinx physical implementation tools use proprietary User Constraints File (UCF) format [1]. The syntax of the most frequently used placement and routing constraints is shown in the following example.

```
// pr_constraints.v: two toggling registers
module pr_constraints(input clk, reset,
                     output reg data_out_0,data_out_1);
  always @(posedge clk) begin
    if (reset) begin
      data_out_0 <= 1'b0;
      data_out_1 <= 1'b0;
    end
    else begin
      data_out_0 <= ~data_out_0;
      data_out_1 <= ~data_out_1;
    end
```

```
end // always
endmodule // pr_constraints
# pr_constraints.ucf: placement and routing constraints
NET "data_out_0" LOC = P16;
NET "data_out_1" LOC = D6;
INST "data_out_0" AREA_GROUP = " ag_data_out_0";
AREA_GROUP "ag_data_out_0" RANGE=SLICE_X44Y40:SLICE_X45Y42;
AREA_GROUP "ag_data_out_0" GROUP=CLOSED;
AREA_GROUP "ag_data_out_0" PLACE=CLOSED;
CONFIG PROHIBIT=SLICE_X06Y0:X14Y20;
CONFIG PROHIBIT=P15;
NET "data_out_1_OBUF"
ROUTE="{3;1;6slx25csg324;477afbc1!-1;8040;6064;S!0;-845;-
504!1;0;344!1;" "-9743;1431!2;845;144;L!3;-16261;1!5;-22484;-
4!6;-17991;3!7;-12477;5681!8;"
"0;12800!9;0;12800!10;0;12800!11;0;13872!12;0;12800!13;0;1280
0!14;0;12800!"
"15;0;13872!16;305;7589!17;0;3200!18;1855;1675!19;686;18!20;8
0;20!21;" "-1490;2207!22;-1311;251;L!}";
NET "data_out_1" LOC=D6;
INST "data_out_1_OBUF" LOC=SLICE_X29Y41;
INST "data_out_1" LOC=SLICE_X29Y41;
```

AREA_GROUP constraint

AREA_GROUP is a placement constraint that applies to a group of FPGA resources, such as slices, BRAMs, DSP, MMCM, and others. It allows constraining placement of that group to a specific range inside the FPGA. The basic syntax of the AREA_GROUP is shown in the following example.

```
INST "data_out_0" AREA_GROUP = "ag_data_out_0";
AREA_GROUP "ag_data_out_0" RANGE=SLICE_X44Y40:SLICE_X45Y42;
AREA_GROUP "ag_data_out_0" GROUP=CLOSED;
AREA_GROUP "ag_data_out_0" PLACE=CLOSED;
```

The example defines a group "ag_data_out_0" that constrains register data_out_0 to a range of slices SLICE_X44Y40:SLICE_X45Y42. GROUP and PLACE properties of the group specify if the logic inside the group can be combined with the logic not belonging to that group. Using GROUP and PLACE properties may improve consistency of the build, but will result in higher logic utilization, because some of the logic resources remain unused.

Directed routing constraint

ROUTE constraint enables the ability to lock down specific routes. It should only be used for a small number of high speed routes that are unlikely to change. One example of using directed routing is in a memory controller to lock down routes interfacing with the IO pins to control the delay. The detailed syntax of the ROUTE constraint is not documented. FPGA Editor can be used to generate the constraint by selecting a net and selecting an appropriate option in Tools->Directed Routing Constraints dialog.

PROHIBIT constraint

PROHIBIT constraint disallows place and route tools to use specific FPGA resources, such as slices, BRAMs, DSP, IOs, and others. The following is example of prohibiting the use of specific IO pin and a range of slices.

```
CONFIG PROHIBIT=SLICE_X06Y0:X14Y20;
CONFIG PROHIBIT=P15;
```

PROHIBIT constraint is useful for reserving specific logic area for future use. It can also be used as an opposite of an AREA_GROUP constraint for simple designs.

Save net flag

Save net flag (S) is a constraint attached to a net or signal, and prevents its removal. It can be used during the initial design phase to prevent removal of unconnected module inputs and loadless outputs. Its syntax is given in the following example.

```
NET "data_out_1" S;
```

Location constraint

LOC is a location constraint where a specific component is placed within an FPGA. An example is an IO location, which is used in almost every design.

```
NET "data_out_0" LOC = P16;
```

Understanding routing delays

An integral part of effective floorplanning is understanding routing delays. Routing delays are specific to FPGA family and speed grade. They also depend on how different resources are laid out on the FPGA die. Xilinx Virtex-6 and Spartan-6 FPGAs have columnar structure: IOs, BRAMs, and DSP blocks are organized in columns. Logic resources are structured in tiles. Tiles are replicated horizontally and vertically, and form a grid. FPGAs might have areas that don't contain any logic resources, or are occupied by a large embedded block, such as a PCI Express interface core. All of that affects routing delays of the signals.

The following example illustrates some of the worst case routing scenarios, and examines the delays.

```
module routing(input data_in_0,data_in_1,data_in_2,data_in_3,
         output data_out_0,data_out_1,data_out_2,data_out_3 );
   assign data_out_0 = data_in_0;   // horizontal route
   assign data_out_1 = data_in_1;   // vertical route
   assign data_out_2 = data_in_2;   // diagonal route
   assign data_out_3 = data_in_3;   // routing around
endmodule // routing
# IO placement
NET "data_in_0"  LOC = N3;
NET "data_out_0" LOC = P16;

NET "data_in_1"  LOC = P6;
NET "data_out_1" LOC = D6;

NET "data_in_2"  LOC = V3;
NET "data_out_2" LOC = B16;

NET "data_in_3"  LOC = C7;
NET "data_out_3" LOC = A8;
```

The design was built for Spartan-6 LX25 FPGA. This device has an area that doesn't contain logic resources. One of the nets is routed around that area. The figure below shows the routes as seen in FPGA Editor.

434   *100 Power Tips for FPGA designers*

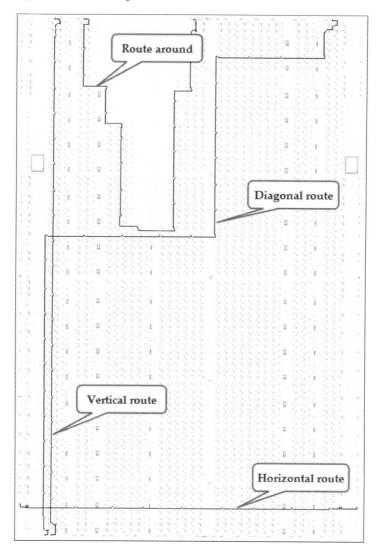

Figure 2: Routing example on Spartan-6 LX25

FPGA Editor reports the following route delays:

```
# Horizontal route
net "data_out_0_OBUF":
    7.267ns - comp.pin "data_out_0.O", site.pin "P16.O"
    driver - comp.pin "data_in_0.I", site.pin "N3.I"
net "data_out_1_OBUF"
net "data_out_2_OBUF"

# Vertical route
net "data_out_1_OBUF":
    9.957ns - comp.pin "data_out_1.O", site.pin "D6.O"
    driver - comp.pin "data_in_1.I", site.pin "P6.I"
```

```
net "data_out_3_OBUF"
# Diagonal route
net "data_out_2_OBUF":
    13.725ns - comp.pin "data_out_2.O", site.pin "B16.O"
       driver - comp.pin "data_in_2.I", site.pin "V3.I"
# routing around
net "data_out_3_OBUF":
    9.968ns - comp.pin "data_out_3.O", site.pin "A8.O"
       driver - comp.pin "data_in_3.I", site.pin "C7.I"
net "data_out_0_OBUF"
```

Routing delays in the above example range from 7.267ns to 13.724ns. If, for example, a design uses a 200MHz clock, a delay on one of those routes exceeds the clock's period. If such a design has two connected modules that are floorplanned in different corners of this FPGA, it'd be infeasible to meet timing constraints. A reset controller running at 200MHz and distributes a synchronous reset signal to the rest of the design might have a problem meeting timing even if it's floorplanned in the middle of the FPGA die.

Crossing FPGA tiles

The following example illustrates how crossing FPGA tiles reduces performance due to increased routing delays of signals that cross a tile. The example contains four instances of CRC32 checker module with 16-bit data. All instances are completely independent from each other. They have separate data, enable, and clock inputs and outputs. The instances are floorplanned in such a way that each region has exactly the same area but different placement. The size of the regions is chosen such that logic utilization of each is around 70%. Also, all regions are closed: they only contain logic that belongs to the corresponding instance.

The following is the code for the top-level module of the example.

```
module crossing_tile_example(input clk1,clk2,clk3,clk4,
   input crc_en1,crc_en2,crc_en3,crc_en4,
   input rst,
   input [15:0] data_in1,data_in2,data_in3,data_in4,
   output reg [31:0] crc_out1, crc_out2, crc_out3, crc_out4);

   crc crc1 (  .data_in_i(data_in1),
              .crc_en_i(crc_en1),
              .crc_out(crc_out1),
              .rst(rst), .clk(clk1));
   crc crc2 (  .data_in_i(data_in2),
              .crc_en_i(crc_en2),
              .crc_out(crc_out2),
```

```
                      .rst(rst), .clk(clk2));
   crc crc3 (  .data_in_i(data_in3),
               .crc_en_i(crc_en3),
               .crc_out(crc_out3),
               .rst(rst), .clk(clk3));
   crc crc4 (  .data_in_i(data_in4),
               .crc_en_i(crc_en4),
               .crc_out(crc_out4),
               .rst(rst), .clk(clk4));
endmodule // crossing_tile_example
# area and period constraints
NET "clk?" TNM_NET = "clk_crc";
TIMESPEC TS_clk_crc = PERIOD "clk_crc" 3.33 ns HIGH 50 %;
INST "crc1*" AREA_GROUP = "crc1";
AREA_GROUP "crc1" RANGE=SLICE_X0Y47:SLICE_X3Y55;
AREA_GROUP "crc1" GROUP=CLOSED;
AREA_GROUP "crc1" PLACE=CLOSED;
INST "crc2*" AREA_GROUP = "crc2";
AREA_GROUP "crc2" RANGE=SLICE_X0Y2:SLICE_X17Y3;
AREA_GROUP "crc2" GROUP=CLOSED;
AREA_GROUP "crc2" PLACE=CLOSED;
INST "crc3*" AREA_GROUP = "crc3";
AREA_GROUP "crc3" RANGE=SLICE_X22Y3:SLICE_X23Y21;
AREA_GROUP "crc3" GROUP=CLOSED;
AREA_GROUP "crc3" PLACE=CLOSED;
INST "crc4*" AREA_GROUP = "crc4";
AREA_GROUP "crc4" RANGE=SLICE_X2Y23:SLICE_X21Y24;
AREA_GROUP "crc4" GROUP=CLOSED;
AREA_GROUP "crc4" PLACE=CLOSED;
```

The figure below shows how the four instances are floorplanned on Spartan-6 LX9 FPGA.

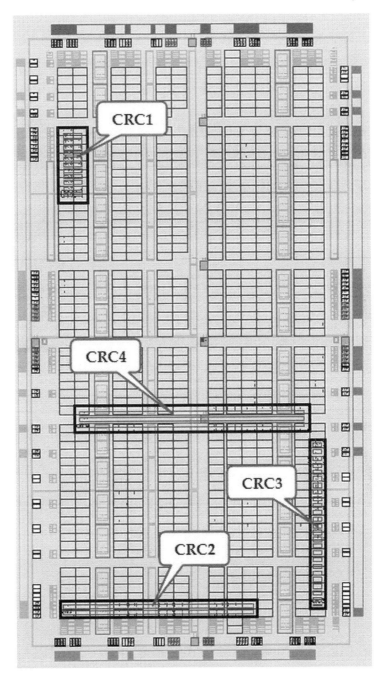

Figure 3: PlanAhead view of Spartan-6 LX9 FPGA

crc1 instance is floorplanned to fit into a single tile.
crc2 instance is floorplanned as an elongated rectangle that crosses several horizontal tiles.
crc3 instance is floorplanned as an elongated rectangle that crosses several vertical tiles.
crc4 instance is floorplanned to cross both horizontal and vertical tiles.
The following table shows performance results of the four instances.

Table 1: Performance results of the example

```
-------------------------------------------------------------------------------
Constraint                            |   Check  | Worst Case | Best Case  | Timing | Timing
                                      |          |   Slack    | Achievable | Errors | Score
-------------------------------------------------------------------------------
TS_clk4 = PERIOD TIMEGRP "clk4" 3.33 ns H | SETUP  |  -0.988ns |   4.318ns  |    57  | 12867
IGH 50%                               | HOLD     |   0.501ns  |            |     0  |     0
-------------------------------------------------------------------------------
TS_clk3 = PERIOD TIMEGRP "clk3" 3.33 ns H | SETUP  |  -0.690ns |   4.020ns  |    51  |  7952
IGH 50%                               | HOLD     |   0.456ns  |            |     0  |     0
-------------------------------------------------------------------------------
TS_clk2 = PERIOD TIMEGRP "clk2" 3.33 ns H | SETUP  |  -0.649ns |   3.979ns  |    78  | 21291
IGH 50%                               | HOLD     |   0.470ns  |            |     0  |     0
-------------------------------------------------------------------------------
TS_clk1 = PERIOD TIMEGRP "clk1" 3.33 ns H | SETUP  |  -0.391ns |   3.721ns  |    16  |  1970
IGH 50%                               | HOLD     |   0.481ns  |            |     0  |     0
-------------------------------------------------------------------------------
```

`Crc1` has the best performance, `crc2` and `crc3` have a very similar performance, and `crc4` is the worst one.

This example is provided for illustration purposes only. The design and placement constraints were carefully selected to show the effect of crossing tiles on performance. Most of the real world designs contain modules that are large enough to fit into a tile. However, it is recommended in general to floorplan a module in as few tiles as possible.

Miscellaneous floorplanning tips

- Avoid overlapping floorplanned regions.

- Use `GROUP` and `PLACE` properties of the `AREA_GROUP` constraint to prevent the outside logic being placed in the floorplanned region.

- Limit the logic utilization of a floorplanned region under 75%.

- Floorplan pipelined data such that it flows horizontally.

- Floorplan long carry chains such that they flow vertically.

- Register all inputs and outputs of the modules on the boundary of a floorplanned region.

Resources

[1] Xilinx Constraints User Guide
http://www.xilinx.com/support/documentation/sw_manuals/xilinx11/cgd.pdf

96

FLOORPLANNING MEMORIES AND FIFOS

Floorplanning FIFOs

There are three options to floorplan a FIFO: close to the read-side logic, close to the write-side logic, or in the middle between the two.

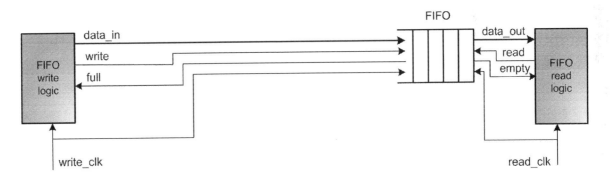

Figure 1: FIFO is placed close to the read-side logic

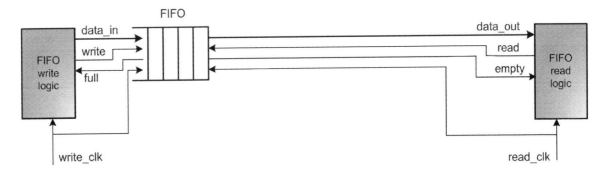

Figure 2: FIFO is placed close to the write-side logic

It is difficult to choose the option that will result in the best performance based on the design analysis. To do so requires considering several factors: read and write clock frequencies, FIFO clock to data output delay, routing, and logic delays on the read and write sides. It is recommended to integrate a FIFO into the design in a way that allows easy change of the FIFO placement, and experimenting with different options.

A simple design that consists of a FIFO, write, and read logic has been used to analyze the timing budget of the read- and write-side logic. The following figure shows the floorplanned design.

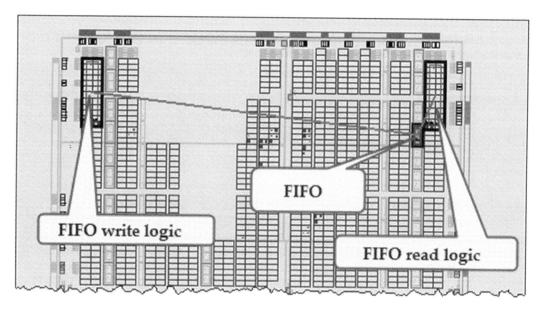

Figure 3: FIFO is placed close to the read-side logic: PlanAhead view

The figures below show critical paths with the worst timing on the FIFO read and write sides. Both read and write clocks are constrained to 100MHz.

```
=================================================================
Timing constraint: Default period analysis for net "wr_clk_BUFGP"
 440 paths analyzed, 291 endpoints analyzed, 0 failing endpoints
 0 timing errors detected. (0 setup errors, 0 hold errors)
 Minimum period is   8.357ns.
-----------------------------------------------------------------

Paths for end point fifo/BU2/U0/grf.rf/mem/gbm.gbmg.gbmga.ngecc.bmg/blk_mem_generator/valid.cstr/ramloop[(
-----------------------------------------------------------------
Delay (setup path):     8.357ns (data path - clock path skew + uncertainty)
  Source:               fifo/BU2/U0/grf.rf/gl0.wr/qwas.wsts/ram_full_i (FF)
  Destination:          fifo/BU2/U0/grf.rf/mem/gbm.gbmg.gbmga.ngecc.bmg/blk_mem_generator/valid.cstr/raml
  Data Path Delay:      8.296ns (Levels of Logic = 2)
  Clock Path Skew:      -0.026ns (0.374 - 0.400)
  Source Clock:         wr_clk_BUFGP rising
  Destination Clock:    wr_clk_BUFGP rising
  Clock Uncertainty:    0.035ns

  Clock Uncertainty:         0.035ns  ((TSJ^2 + TIJ^2)^1/2 + DJ) / 2 + PE
    Total System Jitter (TSJ):   0.070ns
    Total Input Jitter (TIJ):    0.000ns
    Discrete Jitter (DJ):        0.000ns
    Phase Error (PE):            0.000ns

  Maximum Data Path at Slow Process Corner: fifo/BU2/U0/grf.rf/gl0.wr/qwas.wsts/ram_full_i to fifo/BU2/U0,
    Location              Delay type         Delay(ns)  Physical Resource
                                                        Logical Resource(s)
    -------------------------------------------------   -------------------
    SLICE_X4Y66.AQ        Tcko                 0.476    fifo_full
                                                        fifo/BU2/U0/grf.rf/gl0.wr/qwas.wsts/ram_full_i
    SLICE_X3Y67.A5        net (fanout=1)       0.842    fifo_full
    SLICE_X3Y67.A         Tilo                 0.259    fifo_data_in<6>
                                                        data_src/fifo_write1_INV_0
    SLICE_X39Y65.A6       net (fanout=2)       4.760    fifo_write
    SLICE_X39Y65.A        Tilo                 0.259    fifo/BU2/U0/grf.rf/ram_wr_en
                                                        fifo/BU2/U0/grf.rf/gl0.wr/ram_wr_en_il
    RAMB16_X2Y32.WEA1     net (fanout=12)      1.370    fifo/BU2/U0/grf.rf/ram_wr_en
    RAMB16_X2Y32.CLKA     Trcck_WEA            0.330    fifo/BU2/U0/grf.rf/mem/gbm.gbmg.gbmga.ngecc.bmg/bl
                                                        fifo/BU2/U0/grf.rf/mem/gbm.gbmg.gbmga.ngecc.bmg/bl
                                               -------
    Total                                      8.296ns (1.324ns logic, 6.972ns route)
                                                       (16.0% logic, 84.0% route)
```

Figure 4: Timing analysis of a FIFO full to data in path

```
Paths for end point fifo/BU2/U0/grf.rf/gl0.rd/rpntr/gc0.count_6 (SLICE_X42Y34.CE), 2 paths
-----------------------------------------------------------------------------------------
Delay (setup path):     6.661ns (data path - clock path skew + uncertainty)
  Source:               fifo/BU2/U0/grf.rf/gl0.rd/gras.rsts/ram_empty_i (FF)
  Destination:          fifo/BU2/U0/grf.rf/gl0.rd/rpntr/gc0.count_6 (FF)
  Data Path Delay:      6.626ns (Levels of Logic = 2)
  Clock Path Skew:      0.000ns
  Source Clock:         rd_clk_BUFGP rising
  Destination Clock:    rd_clk_BUFGP rising
  Clock Uncertainty:    0.035ns

  Clock Uncertainty:        0.035ns   ((TSJ^2 + TIJ^2)^1/2 + DJ) / 2 + PE
    Total System Jitter (TSJ):  0.070ns
    Total Input Jitter (TIJ):   0.000ns
    Discrete Jitter (DJ):       0.000ns
    Phase Error (PE):           0.000ns

Maximum Data Path at Slow Process Corner: fifo/BU2/U0/grf.rf/gl0.rd/gras.rsts/ram_empty_i to fifo/BU2/U0
  Location         Delay type        Delay(ns)   Physical Resource
                                                 Logical Resource(s)
  ---------------------------------------------------------------------
  SLICE_X46Y48.AQ   Tcko              0.525      fifo/BU2/U0/grf.rf/gl0.rd/gras.rsts/ram_empty_fb_i
                                                 fifo/BU2/U0/grf.rf/gl0.rd/gras.rsts/ram_empty_i
  SLICE_X50Y67.B6   net (fanout=1)    1.731      fifo_empty
  SLICE_X50Y67.B    Tilo              0.254      data_sink/fifo_read_q
                                                 data_sink/fifo_read1_INV_0
  SLICE_X46Y48.A5   net (fanout=1)    1.778      fifo_read
  SLICE_X46Y48.AMUX Tilo              0.326      fifo/BU2/U0/grf.rf/gl0.rd/gras.rsts/ram_empty_fb_i
                                                 fifo/BU2/U0/grf.rf/mem/gbm.tmp_ram_rd_en1
  SLICE_X42Y34.CE   net (fanout=6)    1.699      fifo/BU2/U0/grf.rf/mem/gbm.tmp_ram_rd_en
  SLICE_X42Y34.CLK  Tceck             0.313      fifo/BU2/U0/grf.rf/gl0.rd/rpntr/gc0.count<8>
                                                 fifo/BU2/U0/grf.rf/gl0.rd/rpntr/gc0.count_6
  ---------------------------------------------------------------------
  Total                               6.626ns (1.418ns logic, 5.208ns route)
                                             (21.4% logic, 78.6% route)
```

Figure 5: Timing analysis of a FIFO empty to data read path

The critical timing path on the FIFO write side is `fifo_full` to `data_in`. The biggest contributors are routing delays from `fifo_full` to the write logic, and `data_in` back to the FIFO. There are three long routes on the FIFO read side: `fifo_empty` to data read logic, `read_enable` to FIFO, and `data_out` from the FIFO back to the read logic.

In both cases, the total timing budget is dominated by the routing delays. Both read and write critical paths have only two logic levels and low fanout. In this particular example, the best method to achieve significant performance improvement is to move read and write logic closer to the FIFO.

Floorplanning memories

RAM and ROM modules that are implemented using distributed memories become part of general purpose logic. However, using Block RAM (BRAM) primitives presents some floorplanning challenges. BRAMs are located at specific places on FPGA die, which leads to significant routing delays between logic and BRAM. Also, BRAMs have a very large clock to data output delay. The same applies to all modules, such as FIFOs and ChipScope ILA cores, which use BRAMs internally.

The following simple design illustrates those challenges. It consists of a ROM implemented using a BRAM primitive. Its data output is connected to a register.

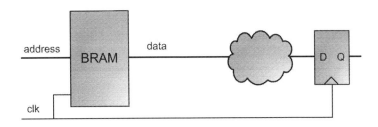

Figure 6: Long delay on a BRAM data output

```
module bram_floorplanning(input   clk,reset,
                          input   [9:0] rom_addr,
                          output  [31:0] data_out);
  wire [31:0] rom_dout;
  // The ROM is implemented using a BRAM
  rom rom (.clka(clk),
           .addra(rom_addr),
           .douta(rom_dout));

  // Data sink contains a register connected to the ROM output
  data_sink data_sink (
          .clk(clk),
          .reset(reset),
          .data_in(rom_dout),
          .data_out(data_out));
endmodule // bram_floorplanning
```

```
# timing and area constraintsNET "clk"
TNM_NET = "clk";
TIMESPEC TS_clk = PERIOD "clk" 200 MHz HIGH 50 %;

INST "data_sink" AREA_GROUP = "data_sink";
AREA_GROUP "data_sink" RANGE=SLICE_X41Y40:SLICE_X48Y49;
INST "rom" AREA_GROUP = "rom";
AREA_GROUP "rom" RANGE=RAMB16_X1Y20:RAMB16_X1Y22;
```

The design is built for Spartan-6 LX25 FPGA. The figure below shows how the design is floorplanned. It also points to three BRAM columns available on that FPGA.

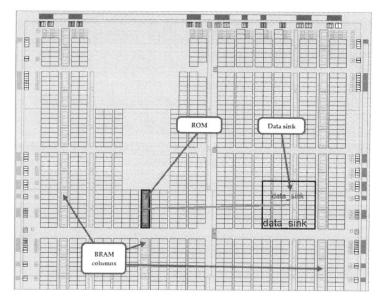

Figure 7: Spartan-6 LX25 device view showing ROM and data sink placement and BRAM columns

Although the register could have been placed closer to the ROM, doing that is often not possible in highly utilized designs. The example design was constrained to run at 200MHz, but failed to meet timing with the critical path missing 0.903ns, as shown on the timing report.

```
====================================================================================
Timing constraint: TS_clk = PERIOD TIMEGRP "clk" 200 MHz HIGH 50%;
 64 paths analyzed, 64 endpoints analyzed, 62 failing endpoints
 62 timing errors detected. (62 setup errors, 0 hold errors, 0 component switching limit errors)
 Minimum period is   5.903ns.
------------------------------------------------------------------------------------
Slack (setup path):     -0.903ns (requirement - (data path - clock path skew + uncertainty))
  Source:               rom/BU2/U0/blk_mem_generator/valid.cstr/ramloop[1].ram.r/s6_noinit.ram/SP
  Destination:          data_sink/data_in_q_23 (FF)
  Requirement:          5.000ns
  Data Path Delay:      5.825ns (Levels of Logic = 1)
  Clock Path Skew:      -0.043ns (0.435 - 0.478)
  Source Clock:         clk_BUFGP rising at 0.000ns
  Destination Clock:    clk_BUFGP rising at 5.000ns
  Clock Uncertainty:    0.035ns

  Clock Uncertainty:          0.035ns   ((TSJ^2 + TIJ^2)^1/2 + DJ) / 2 + PE
    Total System Jitter (TSJ):  0.070ns
    Total Input Jitter  (TIJ):  0.000ns
    Discrete Jitter     (DJ):   0.000ns
    Phase Error         (PE):   0.000ns

  Maximum Data Path at Slow Process Corner: rom/BU2/U0/blk_mem_generator/valid.cstr/ramloop[1].ra
    Location             Delay type         Delay(ns)  Physical Resource
                                                       Logical Resource(s)
    -------------------------------------------------  -------------------
    RAMB16_X1Y22.DOA5    Tcko_DOA              2.900   rom/BU2/U0/blk_mem_generator/valid.cstr/ra
                                                       rom/BU2/U0/blk_mem_generator/valid.cstr/ra
    SLICE_X42Y40.D5      net (fanout=1)        2.560   rom_dout<23>
    SLICE_X42Y40.CLK     Tas                   0.365   data_sink/data_in_q<22>
                                                       rom_dout<23>_rt
                                                       data_sink/data_in_q_23
                                            ---------  -------------------
    Total                                      5.825ns (3.265ns logic, 2.560ns route)
                                                       (56.1% logic, 43.9% route)
```

Figure 8: Critical path is the BRAM data out

Two main components of the failing path are 2.9ns clock to data output delay of the BRAM, and 2.56ns routing delay between the BRAM and the register. One solution to improve performance is to register the output of a BRAM. This is a BRAM option that doesn't require additional logic resources, but adds one clock latency. After making that change, the design meets timing.

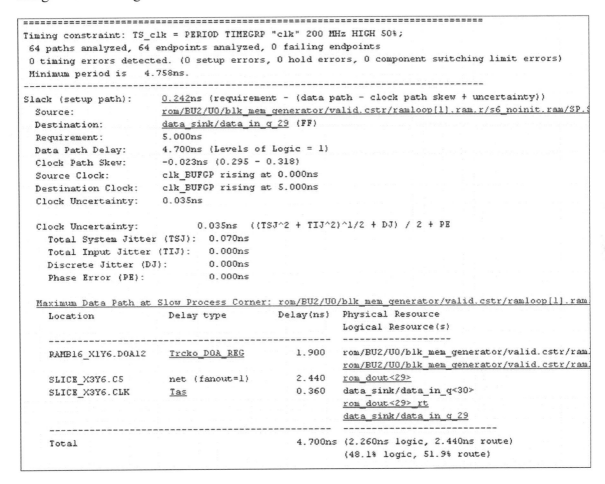

Figure 9: Registering BRAM output improves performance

Now, the design has positive slack of 0.242ns, and the new clock to data output delay went down from 2.9 to 1.9ns.

Different BRAM timing and performance information can be found in Xilinx Switching Characteristics documents for a corresponding FPGA family [1], [2]. The data on Spartan-6 BRAM performance is shown in the figure below.

Symbol	Description	Speed Grade				Units
		-4	-3	-2	-1L	
Block RAM Clock to Out Delays						
T_{RCKO_DO}	Clock CLK to DOUT output (without output register)[1]	1.85	2.10	2.90	3.50	ns, Max
$T_{RCKO\_DO\_REG}$	Clock CLK to DOUT output (with output register)[2]	1.60	1.75	1.90	2.30	ns, Max
Setup and Hold Times Before/After Clock CLK						
$T_{RCCK\_ADDR}/T_{RCKC\_ADDR}$	ADDR inputs[3]	0.35 / 0.10	0.40 / 0.12	0.40 / 0.15	0.50 / 0.15	ns, Min
T_{RDCK_DI}/T_{RCKD_DI}	DIN inputs [4]	0.30 / 0.10	0.30 / 0.10	0.30 / 0.12	0.40 / 0.15	ns, Min
T_{RCCK_EN}/T_{RCKC_EN}	Block RAM Enable (EN) input	0.21 / 0.05	0.22 / 0.06	0.28 / 0.10	0.26 / 0.10	ns, Min
$T_{RCCK\_REGCE}/T_{RCKC\_REGCE}$	CE input of output register	0.20 / 0.10	0.20 / 0.10	0.25 / 0.12	0.28 / 0.15	ns, Min
T_{RCCK_WE}/T_{RCKC_WE}	Write Enable (WE) input	0.25 / 0.10	0.33 / 0.10	0.46 / 0.12	0.28 / 0.15	ns, Min
Maximum Frequency						
F_{MAX}	Block RAM in all modes	320	280	260	150	MHz

Figure 10: BRAM switching characteristics (source: Xilinx Spartan-6 DC and Switching Characteristics)

Analyzing that data before implementing and floorplanning the design can save valuable time spent on unnecessary iterations of code changes, floorplan modifications, and builds.

Another recommendation is not to generate large RAM, ROM, FIFO and other cores that contain many BRAMs. Splitting them into smaller size modules will make it easier to do floorplanning because of lower granularity. For example, instead of generating a large 256-bit 1024-entry FIFOs, split it into eight smaller ones, 32-bit each. The disadvantage of doing that is a slight increase in logic utilization because of the duplicated control logic in each FIFO.

Resources

[1] Spartan-6 FPGA Data Sheet: DC and Switching Characteristics

http://www.xilinx.com/support/documentation/data_sheets/ds162.pdf

[2] Virtex-6 FPGA Data Sheet: DC and Switching Characteristics

http://www.xilinx.com/support/documentation/data_sheets/ds152.pdf

BUILD MANAGEMENT AND CONTINUOUS INTEGRATION

Existing FPGA design tools are inadequate to perform the build management and continuous integration tasks required for complex FPGA projects and large design teams.

Continuous Integration (CI) refers to the process of applying quality control during FPGA development and involves performing frequent integration for small code changes. CI is used ubiquitously in software development teams.

Build management tasks include running builds on distributed systems, build scheduling and automation, load balancing across multiple systems and processors, interfacing with source code repositories, pre-processing project filelists, and post-processing and managing build results.

Many design teams resort to developing ad hoc applications and scripts to automate build management and CI. However, those solutions are not scalable, don't provide sufficient flexibility and control over the build process, and don't allow easy integration with other tools.

There are several available commercial and open source build management and CI solutions. The most popular ones are TeamCity, Hudson CI, and CruiseControl.

TeamCity

URL: http://www.jetbrains.com/teamcity

TeamCity is commercial Distributed Build Management and Continuous Integration software. It is free for certain configurations. It features a computing grid to run parallel builds on multiple Build Agents, integration with Amazon EC2 cloud, on-the-fly reporting of results, user notifications, customizable statistics, and many other features.

Hudson CI

URL: http://hudson-ci.org/

Hudson CI is an extensible continuous integration server. It is an open source solution and boasts a large group of contributors. Its main feature is plug-in architecture, which makes it very configurable and allows easy development of custom extensions, or plug-ins.

CruiseControl

URL: http://cruisecontrol.sourceforge.net/

CruiseControl is another popular open source CI framework. It is written in Java and includes many plug-ins, which make it very extensible.

98
VERILOG PROCESSING AND BUILD FLOW SCRIPTS

Different scripting languages, such as Perl, TCL, bash, and csh, are used extensively during FPGA design flow. Scripts are used to run design tools in command line mode, to check the results, and to process the reports to automate FPGA builds.

Using scripts is convenient for pre-build tasks, including processing the RTL to set the correct build revision and performing macro substitution. Scripts can be used to analyze RTL code; for example, in building module hierarchy or in extracting signal names.

Xilinx ISE and PlanAhead installation directories have numerous Perl, TCL, and shell scripts that can be useful for automating build flow. Tip #8 provides several script examples of using Xilinx tools in command line mode.

Below is a list of some Verilog language and build report processing scripts.

Name: report_xplorer.pl
http://outputlogic.com/100_fpga_power_tips
The script parses Xilinx build reports to check for design errors and other potential problems.

Name: xilinx_bitstream_parser.pl
http://outputlogic.com/100_fpga_power_tips
The script parses Xilinx FPGA bitstreams in RBT format

Name: v2html
http://www.burbleland.com/v2html/v2html.html
V2html script converts Verilog designs into HTML files. Once converted, the files can be opened in a web browser. The HTML files contain color-coded Verilog keywords, comments, and signals. Modules, functions, and tasks are hyperlinked, which allows for navigation through the design hierarchy.

Name: Verilog-Perl
http://www.veripool.org/wiki/verilog-perl
The Verilog-Perl library is a building point for Verilog support in the Perl language. It includes support for processing Verilog keywords and numbers, extracting a netlist out of Verilog files, and building module hierarchy.

99

REPORT AND DESIGN ANALYSIS TOOLS

FPGA synthesis and physical implementation tools produce a great number of reports that contain various information on errors and warnings, logic utilization, design frequency, timing, clocking, and many other factors. Xilinx and other FPGA design tools provide basic GUI view of some of the most important and frequently used information in the reports, but that is not always sufficient. There are several third-party commercial and free tools that perform more comprehensive report analysis and do more user-friendly presentation.

The following is a list of the three most popular report and design analysis tools for Xilinx FPGAs: TimingDesigner, ADEPT, and ReportXplorer.

Name: TimingDesigner
Company: EMA Design Automation, Inc
License: commercial
URL: http://www.timingdesigner.com

TimingDesigner is an interactive static timing analysis and diagramming tool. The tool allows users to model different timing specifications and a range of conditions using spreadsheets, to analyze timing reports from third party tools, such as Xilinx TRCE, and to organize different timing diagrams within a single project tree.

TimingDesigner Kits is another product, which provides a library of timing protocols associated with commonly used design components such as SDRAM and DDR memory, as well as several common processors and FPGA libraries. Each Design Kit Component is parameterized to accurately represent configuration options that affect timing relationships.

Name: Advanced Debugging/Editing/Planning Tool (ADEPT)
License: free
URL: http://mysite.verizon.net/jimwu88/adept/

Advanced Debugging/Editing/Planning Tool (ADEPT) has been developed and is actively maintained by Jim Wu, a Xilinx applications engineer. ADEPT augments the capabilities of Xilinx ISE software by providing a more user-friendly view of clocking resources, the locations and attributes of different FPGA functional blocks, an analysis of logic utilization by hierarchy, and many other features.

Name: ReportXplorer
Provider: OutputLogic.com
License: free
URL: http://outputlogic.com

ReportXplorer is a web-based viewing and analysis tool for Xilinx FPGA build reports. It can be used in several cases and situations:

- To provide more comprehensive report viewing and analysis capabilities compared to existing tools.

- To enable report viewing in a system that doesn't have FPGA design tools installed, such as on a Mac computer or a mobile device.

- To enable report viewing of a design build that doesn't have an associated Xilinx ISE project, such as script-based builds.

- Side-by-side comparison of multiple reports opened in the same or different applications.

Because it's a web-based application, ReportXplorer doesn't require installation. ReportXplorer is also inherently secure because it is an entirely client-based application. No confidential design information contained in the build reports is sent to the server. All the report processing is done locally on a client inside a web browser sandbox.

100

RESOURCES

The last Tip in this book lists miscellaneous resources related to the FPGA and logic design that haven't been mentioned before.

Most of the code examples, scripts, and projects are available online at
http://outputlogic.com/100_fpga_power_tips/

Xilinx datasheets, application notes, white papers, and user guides

Datasheets offer definitive introduction to the silicon capabilities, including functional, switching, and performance characteristics. User guides introduce the features and functions of the FPGA devices.

http://www.xilinx.com/support/documentation/data_sheets.htm
http://www.xilinx.com/support/documentation/user_guides.htm
Xilinx provides over a thousand application notes and white papers that address specific issues and design considerations. Many application notes include source code.

http://www.xilinx.com/support/documentation/application_notes.htm
http://www.xilinx.com/support/documentation/white_papers.htm

Periodic publications: magazines, journals, newsletters

Xcell Journal: an official Xilinx quarterly magazine
http://www.xilinx.com/publications/xcellonline
EEtimes: Electronic Industry magazine. It aggregates a lot of product, design, training, and news information.
http://www.eetimes.com
Programmable Logic Design newsletter
http://www.eetimes.com/design/programmable-logic

User forums

Xilinx user forum boasts over ten thousand registered users. FPGA designers can try finding an answer there before opening a WebCase with Xilinx technical support.
http://forums.xilinx.com

Altera forum
http://www.alteraforum.com
EDA board
http://www.edaboard.com

User groups

FPGA
http://groups.google.com/group/comp.arch.fpga
Verilog
http://groups.google.com/group/comp.lang.verilog
SNUG: Synopsys User Group
http://www.synopsys.com/Community/snug/Pages/default.aspx

Resource aggregators

Verilog.net is the most popular resource aggregation site that includes links to free design tools, books, papers, and magazines.
http://verilog.net

Papers

Sunburst Design, Inc. A wealth of high-quality papers on different aspects of logic design, simulation, and using Verilog and SystemVerilog languages.
http://www.sunburst-design.com/papers/

Intel atom processor core made FPGA-synthesizable. Perry H. Wang, Jamison D. Collins, Christopher T. Weaver, Blliappa Kuttanna, Shahram Salamian, Gautham N. Chinya, Ethan Schuchman, Oliver Schilling, Thorsten Doil, Sebastian Steibl, Hong Wang. s.l. : FPGA 2009 209-218, 2009.

Conferences

Yearly ACM/SIGDA International Symposium on Field-Programmable Gate Arrays
http://www.isfpga.org

ACRONYMS

ASIC	Application Specific Integrated Circuit
ASSP	Application Specific Standard Product
DRC	Design Rule Check
DUT	Device Under Test
EDIF	Electronic Design Interchange Format
EDA	Electronic Design Automation
EDIF	Electronic Design Interchange Format
EDK	Embedded Development Kit
FPGA	Field Programmable Gate Array
GPGPU	General Purpose Graphics Processor Unit
HDL	Hardware Description Language
IC	Integrated Circuit
ISE	Integrated Software Environment
LRM	Language Reference Manual
LUT	Look Up Table
NVM	Non-volatile memory
PCB	Printed Circuit Board
PVT	Process, voltage, temperature
RTL	Register Transfer Level
SDC	Synopsys Design Constraints
SOC	System On Chip
SSN	Simultaneously Switching Noise
STA	Static Timing Analysis
UCF	User Constraints File
XST	Xilinx Synthesis Technology. XST is a Xilinx synthesis tool

INDEX

Advanced Encryption Standard (AES), 157, 350
analysis
    reports, 40
    timing, 411
    thermal, 204
ASIC (Application Specific Integrated Circuit)
    emulation, 221
    vs. FPGA, 218
    partitioning, 228
    prototyping, 221
asynchronous reset, 137
black box, 310
Block RAM (BRAM), 162
build flow, 24
Chipscope, 390
clocking scheme, 87, 94
clock
    domain crossing, 99
    gating, 235
    skew, 87
    synchronization, 104
coding style, 51
combinatorial circuits, 241
configuration
    FPGA, 175
constraints
    placement, 428
    routing, 428
    timing, 408

control set, 368
CORDIC, 355
CRC (Cyclic Redundancy Check), 322
critical path
    floorplanning, 439
JTAG, 379
DSP (Digital Signal Processing)
    DSP48, 131
    multipliers, 131
DLL (Delay Locked Loop)
    DCM, 87
    MMCM, 89
    PLL, 87
encryption
    AES, 336
embedded memories, 162
estimate
    area, 185
    cost, 209
    power, 195
    speed, 192
    resources, 185
Ethernet, 301
FIFO, 112
floorplanning, 428
FPGA
    configuration, 175
    vendors, 3
hierarchy
    flattening, 361
IO (Input/Output)

inferring IOB registers, 71
IP Core
- Ethernet, 301
- evaluation, 310
- PCI Express, 350
- USB, 346

latches, 238
LFSR (Linear Feedback Shift Register), 322
logic
- levels, 121
- replication, 191

LUT (look-up table), 10
mapping, 22
memory
- controller, 339
- embedded, 162
- Inference, 68

metastability, 100
optimizations
- area, 361
- logic, 366
- power, 372

PCI Express
- IP cores, 350

packing
- slices, 187

partitioning
- algorithms, 228
- ASIC, 229
- flow, 232

pipeline

latency, 156
throughput, 157
place and route, 26
PCB (Printed Circuit Board)
instrumentation, 379
polynomial
CRC, 322
LFSR, 323
power
dynamic, 195
estimate, 195
optimization, 372
static, 195
priority encoders, 62, 366
processor, 296
protocol
I2C, 354
PCI Express, 350
USB, 346
register
balancing, 161
duplication, 361
pipelining, 425
shift (SRL), 70
transfer level (RTL), 17
reset
asynchronous, 137
global, 140
synchronous, 141
hybrid, 144
routing

    delay, 428
    estimating, 188
    resources, 12
security
    IP cores, 336
shift register, 70, 131
simulation
    code coverage, 258
    performance, 267
    speed, 267,
    testbench, 282
    toggle coverage, 258
    tools, 276
    types, 262
skew
    clock, 87
state machines, 126
synchronization, 104
synthesis
    directives, 217
    optimizations, 40
    tools, 21
testbench, 282
timing
    analysis, 411
    constraints, 408
    closure, 417
USB
    IP cores, 346
validation, 217
verification, 258

Made in the USA
Lexington, KY
28 August 2013